THE ORIGINS
OF MODERN TREATMENT
AND
EDUCATION
OF PHYSICALLY HANDICAPPED
CHILDREN

THE ORIGINS
OF MODERN TREATMENT
AND
EDUCATION
OF PHYSICALLY HANDICAPPED
CHILDREN

Edited by
William R.F. Phillips
and
Janet Rosenberg

ARNO PRESS

A New York Times Company
New York • 1980

Editorial Supervision: Doris Krone

First Publication 1980 by Arno Press Inc.

Copyright © 1980 by Arno Press Inc.

THE PHYSICALLY HANDICAPPED IN SOCIETY
ISBN for complete set: 0-405-13100-3
See last pages of this volume for titles.
Publisher's Note: This volume has been reprinted from the best available copy.

Manufactured in the United States of America

Library of Congress Cataloging in Publication Data
Main entry under title:

The Origins of modern treatment and education of
    physically handicapped children.

    (Physically handicapped in society)
    1. Physically handicapped children--Rehabilitation
--History. 2. Physically handicapped children--Care
and treatment--History. 3. Physically handicapped
children--Education--History. I. Phillips, William
R. F. II. Rosenberg, Janet. III. Series. [DNLM:
1. Education, Special--History--Collected works.
2. Handicapped--History--Collected works. 3. Reha-
bilitation--History--Collected works. 4. Rehabilitation centers--History--Collected works. LC4219 069]
HV903.074   362.4'3'088054   79-6010
ISBN 0-405-13102-X

CONTENTS

McMurtrie, Douglas C.
A STUDY OF THE CHARACTER AND PRESENT STATUS OF
PROVISIONS FOR CRIPPLED CHILDREN IN THE UNITED
STATES. (Reprinted from *American Journal of Care for Cripples,*
Vol. 2, No. 1) New York, 1916

Bartine, Oliver H.
HISTORY OF THE NEW YORK SOCIETY FOR THE RELIEF OF THE
RUPTURED AND CRIPPLED. (Reprinted from *American Journal of
Care for Cripples,* Vol. 3, No. 2) New York, 1916

Harper, Grace S.
TWO CASES CRIPPLED BY INDUSTRIAL ACCIDENTS: A
COMPARISON OF METHODS OF AFTER-CARE. (Reprinted from
American Journal of Care for Cripples, Vol. 2, No. 4) New York, 1915

Shrady, Katherine W. Ambrose
THE HISTORY OF THE FEDERATION OF ASSOCIATIONS FOR
CRIPPLES. (Reprinted from *American Journal of Care for Cripples,*
Vol. 1, No. 1) New York, 1914

Newman, George
EDUCATION AND CARE OF THE CRIPPLED CHILD. (Reprinted
from *American Journal of Care for Cripples,* Vol. 3, No. 2) New
York, 1916

McMurtrie, Douglas C.
TRAINING FOR CRIPPLED BOYS AND CRIPPLED SOLDIERS.
(Reprinted from *American Journal of Care for Cripples,* Vol. 3, No. 4)
New York, 1916

Schulthess, Wilhelm
THE HISTORICAL DEVELOPMENT AND PRESENT STATUS OF
CARE FOR CRIPPLES IN SWITZERLAND. (Reprinted from
American Journal of Care for Cripples, Vol. 2, No. 1) New York,
1915

Rummelkoff, I.
THE CARE OF THE CRIPPLED IN NORWAY. (Reprinted from *The
Cripple's Journal,* Vol. 3, No. 10) London, 1926

Turner, Henry
CRIPPLEDOM IN SOVIET RUSSIA. (Reprinted from *The Cripple's
Journal,* Vol. 3, No. 12) London, 1927

Ferenczi, Emerich
STATE PROVISION FOR CRIPPLES IN HUNGARY. (Reprinted from
American Journal of Care for Cripples, Vol. 6, No. 1) New York,
1918

THE LITTLE CRIPPLES AT MUNICH. (Reprinted from *American Journal of Care for Cripples,* Vol. 4, No. 2) New York, 1917

Muskat, Gustav
THE COPENHAGEN INSTITUTION FOR CRIPPLES. (Reprinted from *American Journal of Care for Cripples,* Vol. 1, No. 3) New York, 1914

Biesalski, Konrad
MODERN METHODS OF CARE FOR CRIPPLES IN GERMANY. (Reprinted from *American Journal of Care for Cripples,* Vol. 1, No. 4) New York, 1914

McMurtrie, Douglas C.
COMPILATION OF STATE LAWS RELATING TO PROVISIONS FOR CRIPPLED CHILDREN. (Reprinted from *American Journal of Care for Cripples,* Vol. 5, No. 2) New York, 1917

GENEVA SUPPLEMENT: THE FIRST INTERNATIONAL CONFERENCE: PROCEEDINGS AND RESULTS. (Reprinted from *The Cripple,* Vol. 5, No. 22) London, 1929

Licht, Sidney
NOTES ON PHYSICAL MEDICINE IN EUROPE IN 1951. (Reprinted from *American Journal of Physical Medicine, Occupational Therapy and Rehabilitation,* Vol. 30) Baltimore, 1951

ON THE CARE OF CRIPPLED AND DEFORMED CHILDREN

Newton M. Shaffer

Original Communications.

ON THE CARE OF
CRIPPLED AND DEFORMED CHILDREN.*

By NEWTON M. SHAFFER, M. D.,

PROFESSOR OF ORTHOPÆDIC SURGERY,
CORNELL UNIVERSITY COLLEGE OF MEDICINE.

So far as I can learn, the first effort to afford organized relief to the deformed and crippled among the poor of New York city was made in May, 1863, by the New York Society for the Relief of the Ruptured and Crippled. Under the leadership of its founder, Dr. James Knight, who gathered about him such men as James Lenox, Robert B. Minturn, Robert M. Hartley, John C. Green, Stewart Brown, A. R. Wetmore, Jonathan Sturges, James W. Beckman, John David Wolfe, Henry S. Terbell, and George W. Abbe, the work very rapidly took a prominent place among the great charities of our city. As I had the honor to be connected with the institution when it opened its doors for the reception of patients, in the very minor capacity of a medical student, and as I graduated in medicine under its auspices and filled the position of its first assistant surgeon, I can recall very distinctly the different stages of the development of this great work, and have watched, with much gratification, its progress and success.

Dr. Knight was a true philanthropist, a genuine friend of the crippled child, of more than ordinary versatility in adapting mechanical means to pathological ends in the treatment of the deforming diseases of childhood, and an almost unrecognized and neglected pioneer in the early work of what is now known as modern orthopædic surgery. In many respects he was a great man, and his self-sacrificing devotion to the work he founded has never met the recognition it deserves. I desire to place on record my humble appreciation of his unselfish efforts to relieve human suffering, and to emphasize the fact that it was owing to his energy and devotion that New York city first recognized the necessity of extending the hand of relief to the poor cripple.

Early in his work, and before the institution moved into its present ample hospital building, Dr. Knight recognized the importance of both mental and physical training as an important adjunct to the medical part of the work. He instituted a class in light gymnastics and calisthenics, and instruction, both religious and secular, was made part of the daily life of the patient. This work has been maintained since Dr. Knight's death.

The next important movement in the direction of the care of crippled and deformed children occurred in 1866, under the auspices of the New York Orthopædic Dispensary and Hospital. Its founders were Theodore Roosevelt and Howard Potter, who, with the assistance

of Dr. John T. Metcalfe and Dr. Cornelius R. Agnew, secured the cooperation of Dr. Charles Fayette Taylor in forming this organization. . Commencing simply as a dispensary, and with a board of trustees which comprised, among others, and including the founders, James Brown, William E. Dodge, James Boorman Johnston, Robert Lenox Kennedy, John L. Aspinwall, David Dows, Allen Campbell, Roswell D. Hitchcock, Robert Winthrop, and Charles Fayette Taylor, it soon became a factor in the charitable world, and rapidly assumed an enviable position both as regards its methods and its work.

The genius of Dr. Taylor in designing apparatus for the relief and cure of deformity made him a benefactor of his race, and his early retirement from active practice, through ill health, was a loss to the medical profession.

Mental training has always been a feature of the work in the wards of the Orthopædic Hospital. At present two teachers are employed: one in kindergarten work for the younger patients, the other in giving regular lessons to the older children.

As the writer stepped, so to speak, from a position in the Ruptured and Crippled Hospital to an almost similar one in the Orthopædic Hospital, and as his connection with the latter covers more than a quarter of a century, it is with peculiar satisfaction that he has watched the great growth of both of these institutions, which have done more than any other institutions in the country to afford relief to the crippled poor.

The next important step in this work of caring for deformed children occurred in 1872, when St. Luke's Hospital, attracted by the work of the Orthopædic Hospital, invited one of the surgeons of the latter institution to become an active member of its medical staff, creating for him the office of "orthopædic surgeon." The orthopædic service of St. Luke's Hospital has since been one of its distinctive features, and it was the first large general hospital to recognize orthopædic surgery as a specialty.

Soon after this event there was a pretty general recognition of the necessities of the crippled and deformed on the part of many medical institutions. The New York Hospital, the Roosevelt Hospital, the Vanderbilt Clinic, the Postgraduate Hospital, the Polyclinic Hospital, St. Mary's Hospital, and other institutions opened their doors to crippled children, and organized either an outdoor or an indoor service, or both, for the treatment of the deformed.

In other large cities, and in some smaller ones, the growth of the movement to afford relief to the crippled and deformed has been very gratifying. In Boston, Dr. Buckminster Brown was placed in charge of a ward in the Samaritan Hospital, exclusively devoted to the relief of cripples, in 1861. This was two years before New York recognized Dr. Knight's effort, and the Children's Hospital of Boston is now a model in its

---

* Read before the National Conference of Charities and Correction, New York, May 23, 1898.

orthopædic work. In Philadelphia the University of Pennsylvania has an elaborate and well-equipped orthopædic dispensary and hospital, founded largely by Dr. A. Sydney Roberts, and it also has other well-known institutions where the crippled and deformed are cared for. In Chicago, Baltimore, Rochester, Buffalo, St. Paul, Minneapolis, and elsewhere, the crippled and deformed are provided for, and all, or nearly all, this advance in the use of modern methods of caring for the deformed poor may be traced to New York, and to the personal influence of four great men—viz., Dr. James Knight, the philanthropist and organizer; Dr. Charles Fayette Taylor, the mechanical genius and enthusiastic leader; Dr. Lewis A. Sayre, the impressive teacher and eminent author, and Dr. Henry G. Davis, who revolutionized the treatment of joint and spinal diseases, and whose originality and genius made him the father of American orthopædic surgery.

It may, I think, be taken for granted, from a medical and surgical aspect, that the importance of caring for the crippled and deformed has been very generally recognized during the past quarter of a century the world over; though, strange as it may seem, the medical profession is still in many important medical centres, and especially abroad, unwilling to grant to orthopædic surgery the status it deserves. There still clings to the mechanical treatment of deformities in some minds the feeling that it is *infra dignitatem;* that to manipulate apparatus or to undertake to perform the necessary mechanical operations for treating deformity is, in some obscure way, outside of, strictly speaking, surgical lines. And, while this foolish prejudice is becoming modified, and especially so in New York, there are to-day in some sections of the country prominent surgeons who habitually refer patients with deformity to some commercial instrument maker, whose knowledge is limited to the shop in which he works, and whose education is far from equipping him to give the patient the relief which he has a right to demand. The day is coming when the instrument maker will occupy the same relation to the surgeon that the pharmacist does to the physician, when a " brace " for deformity will be à written " prescription " of the surgeon, and when the surgeon will know in detail what is needed for the relief or cure of deformity, and when he will rely upon his own experience and knowledge rather than upon the ignorant assistance and cooperation of a purely mercantile class.

Hence, in speaking of the care of crippled children, I desire to emphasize the statement that we need better educational facilities in our colleges for teaching orthopædic surgery—just as good, indeed, as are now given for other departments. Every medical college should have an orthopædic laboratory, just as there are laboratories for other necessary medical and surgical instruction. The student, under the direction of his teacher, should be taught, not that Smith's brace for clubfoot or Jones's splint for hip disease is used in the treatment of these

conditions, with perhaps a perfunctory demonstration of their application, but he should be educated in the principles underlying their utility, and should also be made proficient in their practical application. We all know how extensive and prolonged is the technical education demanded of those who, for example, are educated in the construction of a railroad bridge. The mechanical principles involved in the construction of a brace for spinal disease or clubfoot are certainly not less important, and yet there is no, strictly speaking, technical education upon these points in any of our medical schools. The next progressive step in the surgical care of deformities will be to establish a mechanical laboratory where the practical use of apparatus in the treatment of deformities may be intelligently taught in all our medical colleges.

It is my intention, with the approval of the proper authorities, to establish such a laboratory in connection with the Cornell University Medical College.

Still, we all recognize how much has been accomplished since the pioneer institutions, especially the New York Orthopædic Dispensary and Hospital, have pointed out the way. The condition of the crippled and deformed has advanced in many important respects during the past thirty-five years. It rests with an organized body like that which I now have the honor to address, to study the problems and advance the interests of those who, if unrelieved, must become a burden upon the state, or, at least, be hopelessly relegated to the nonproducing class.

We must all recognize the fact that the average cripple needs much time for treatment, and that the period at which the most good can be done is at an early age, certainly before adolescence. There are some conditions, like knock-knee, bowleg, and clubfoot, which may sometimes demand the direct (operative) surgical method, and which may not therefore require a long detention in a hospital; but many of the deforming diseases of childhood—for instance, Pott's disease of the spine (hunchback), hip disease, infantile paralysis, etc.—those which are the most disabling and the most chronic, are dependent upon causes which the knife can not always reach. They demand, many times—especially those dependent upon tuberculosis—years of active mechanical treatment, not, however, in bed, but in portative apparatus, which permits of gentle outdoor exercise. The question of education, or indeed of suitable mental occupation, during this period of enforced mechanical treatment and prolonged convalescence is a most important one. Some orthopædic hospitals have made systematic education a feature of their work, but much more remains to be done.

The medical and surgical treatment of the physical ills of the body should always be supplemented by a similar effort to educate the mind of the cripple, so that when he is cured he may meet his more fortunate fellows on an equal educational ground. But there are some deformities which are practically incurable, just as there are congenital deficiencies of the human frame which art may minimize, but science can never restore. This class has not received the attention it deserves in this country. As Dr. Augustus Thorndike, of Boston, in a most excellent essay on The Compensatory Education of Cripples, read before the New England Branch of the American Association for the Advancement of Physical Culture, and about to be published in *The Quarterly Journal of Physical Culture*, says:

" There should be three sides to all education—mental, physical, and industrial—yet many of the homes and schools for cripples to-day confine their attention to only one side. There is no class of children more likely to be benefited by careful physical training than children left with a weak or shriveled leg or arm as the result of infantile paralysis or chronic joint disease."

In Boston, under the auspices of a board of trustees comprising Augustus Hemenway, Arthur A. Carey, E. Pierson Beebe, Miss Judith D. Beal, Joseph S. Bigelow, F. J. Cotting, E. H. Clement, Dr. Edward H. Bradford, Dr. Augustus Thorndike, and others, an Industrial School for Crippled and Deformed Children has been organized and has been in successful operation for three or more years. Dr. Bradford, in his report for the trustees, says:

" It should be the work of an industrial institution for cripples to train the pupils for an occupation suitable to each individual case, and to furnish aid in finding work for those who may be capable of doing excellent work, but who, by their infirmity, are unable to solicit work."

It is not within the limits of this short sketch to detail all the admirable work done in this institution, whose patients, many of them, are still under careful orthopædic supervision, while being taught on the plan as outlined above. In many instances a congenital defect makes ordinary treatment useless. Among the inmates of this excellent institution is one, for example, who, having no arms, has learned to do typewriting with his toes.

I visited this school a few days ago with Dr. Thorndike, and found there much of interest and value. Forty children with various deformities were under careful mental and industrial training.

In Copenhagen there is a " Society for Cripples and Invalids" which has both hospital and dispensary departments. During 1895 there were treated by this society, paralytics, 177; those lacking one hand or a portion thereof, 117; other cripples, 119—total, 373. The following trades are taught: For men and boys, cabinet making, basket making, wood carving, turning in wood, shoemaking, and brush making; for women and girls, hand weaving, plain needlework, and dressmaking.

In Sweden and Norway there are four schools. Very much the same work is done in these schools as in the Copenhagen school. Special mechanical devices

are used to enable paralytics to hold and work with various tools, and some pupils are even taught to work with their teeth, etc.

In various parts of Europe institutions of this kind exist, and their usefulness, especially in Italy, where deforming and disabling diseases are frequent, must be apparent; and among the many I might cite as having come under my own observation in this country, and as reported in Dr. Thorndike's exhaustive paper, is the Daisy Field Hospital and Home, located in Englewood, N. J., where children are taught to wash and iron their doll's clothes, to sew, to embroider, to make candy, canned fruit, etc., as well as to read and write; while at Philadelphia, at the Home of St. Giles the Cripple, basket making and carpentering are regularly taught.

This necessarily hasty and imperfect review shows America to be much behind Europe in the matter of industrial schools for cripples. It should not be so. In connection with every home and hospital where cripples are treated, the physical, mental, and industrial training should accompany the medical and surgical treatment whenever the combination is practicable; just as the moral and an adjusted religious training should enter into the school life of such societies.

Early in the history of the New York Orthopædic Dispensary and Hospital, in 1871, a system of outdoor visitation was inaugurated, it being recognized that much could be done if the interest of the patients was kept alive by periodical and friendly visits. This work was at first undertaken by a corps of lady visitors. Many patients not eligible for hospital care, and yet demanding minor but essential attention at home, rather than the skilled professional attendance provided at a hospital, were reached in this way, and much good was accomplished.

This system of visitation became such an important feature of the outdoor work that, when it outgrew the ability of the ladies to meet the demand, one and later on two surgeons have been employed to do this service, which supplements greatly that of the hospital; and some patients who might otherwise have relapsed after their discharge have been kept on the way to ultimate recovery.

Mr. C. Loring Brace, the secretary of the Children's Aid Society, writes me as follows regarding the Henrietta Industrial School at No. 224 West Sixty-third Street, under the direction of the Children's Aid Society:

" Our attention was called to the number of crippled children living in tenement houses who, because of the poverty and shiftlessness of their parents, were growing up almost entirely neglected. We determined to establish a class of these children in one of our schools as an experiment, and I think when you see it that you will agree that it is very successful. We purchased a wagonette and the children are brought to school in the morning and taken home in the afternoon by our teacher, receiving a lunch at the school. As we expected, we found children of all ages absolutely ignorant, and we have undertaken to teach them according to their needs, and it is possible that later on we may also teach them trades, so that they may be self-supporting. Different heights of tables, chairs, and all descriptions of reclining chairs, etc., are necessary in such a class. It is the duty of the teacher also to wash the children and rearrange their braces, etc., and advise with the parents regarding the children, and to be helpful in whatever way is possible. Especially it is the duty of the teacher to induce the parents to take the children to clinics and dispensaries for medical help.

"Our industrial schools are partly supported by public funds through the board of education and partly by contributions of charitable people, and the schools are under our oversight, but subject to the supervision of the superintendent of the board of education. This arrangement allows of much more individual care and much better acquaintance with the needs of the neglected little ones than if such a school were entirely under the charge of public authorities. The effort has been so successful that we propose to establish other classes like this one in other tenement districts as means permit."

I visited this school with Mr. Brace and found twenty-eight children with various deformities, under the treatment of various medical institutions, all of whom were receiving instruction, and all were happy in their work.

They belong to a class which can not, at present, be reached except by some organized body like the Children's Aid Society. Neglected at home, rejected by the public schools, incapacitated by physical deformity, and unable to care for themselves, this work, like the Boston home, supplies a very urgent need in the intelligent care of the crippled and deformed, and it must commend itself to all who are interested in this class of relief. As an aid to the outdoor departments of the various medical institutions designed to relieve the poor cripple, it is a necessity. I trust this school may be duplicated many times in different parts of the city and in different sections of the country at large.

Turning from this interesting and instructive side of the dispensary work, we may now consider a most important phase of hospital labor.

In a hospital devoted to the care of chronic deformities in childhood, the wards, after a time, become almost hopelessly encumbered with convalescent patients, who need only a minimum amount of attention, but who exclude the more acutely suffering from receiving the benefit of skilled professional care. In my own work I have often been confronted with a problem like this: A child with, say, hip disease or spinal disease is nearly well; perhaps the patient has been an inmate of the hospital for three or four years. He has no suitable home to go to, or perhaps, in effect, no home at all. If the patient is discharged, he is certain to lack even the slight attention which is necessary to keep the apparatus applied, and which is demanded in order to secure the best

attainable result. If the patient be retained, a bed is occupied which is urgently demanded by an acutely suffering child with perhaps the same disease. What shall we do? On the one hand, we can not make a "home" of the hospital, and, on the other hand, if the patient is discharged, he is almost certain to relapse. Too frequently the patient is discharged to make room for another with the hope that a relapse, after all, may not occur. But this is all wrong.

The solution of this problem, it seems to me, is to have a country home, not too far removed from the city dispensary and hospital, under the care of a resident surgeon, where, with stated professional visits from the attending surgeon, and with specially trained nurses, the necessary medical supervision can be maintained, the mental, physical, and industrial training can be pursued, and the climatic treatment can be made to supplement the efforts of the surgeon.

I know that the question of such a country home has been seriously considered by both the Orthopædic and the Ruptured and Crippled Hospitals, and it is certain that if such an adjunct could be added to these institutions much permanent good could be acomplished.

And why should not the State aid in such an effort? A strictly dependent and even to-day a much-neglected class is being only half cared for by the excellent medical institutions established for its relief. The educational and charitable systems of the State should be adapted to meet the demands of this class of crippled and deformed as fully as are those for the deaf, the dumb, the blind, or the insane. And this is true from a medical standpoint also. A child with a curable deformity demanding prolonged treatment should be treated as well as taught until he is fully recovered, and not, when convalescence is fairly established and he is sure with proper care to recover, be sent out of the hospital to relapse, after a few weeks or months, and to become ultimately a more than useless member of society, perhaps a permanent burden upon the State.

The problems involving the care of crippled and deformed children can only be touched upon in a paper of this brief character. It is a subject well worthy the attention of this conference, and I regret that the time at our disposal is so brief that it can not receive more consideration at your hands.

28 East Thirty-eighth Street.

NOTES ON THE EARLY HISTORY
OF CARE FOR CRIPPLES

Douglas C. McMurtrie

NOTES ON THE EARLY HISTORY OF CARE FOR CRIPPLES *

Douglas C. McMurtrie
New York

The cripple has long been considered, at least in literary fields, as the prototype of the handicapped and miserable creature. We may, therefore, expect a study of the history of the attitude of society toward the deformed to throw considerable light on the growth of a sense of community responsibility for the welfare of unfortunate members. The subject thus touches intimately the general history of medicine.

From the earliest times the lot of the cripple has been a hard one. The first mention of physical deformity carries with it stigma in other respects as well. With primitive peoples the cripple was very commonly exposed or abandoned to perish of neglect.[1] Among Indian peoples the Chiriguana are reported as addicted to this practice.[2] Waitz reports that the Salivas, like many others, are accustomed to destroy deformed children, since they attribute the deformity to the influence of evil spirits.[3] The same practice existed among the Carib tribes of the Antilles.[4] Among the Aztecs [5] deformed persons could be

---

* Reprinted by permission from the *Johns Hopkins Hospital Bulletin*, Baltimore, 1914, xxv, 57–62. Article in that publication entitled "Early History of the Care and Treatment of Cripples."

[1] Albert Hermann Post, *Grundriss der ethnologischen Jurisprudenz.* Oldenburg and Leipzig, 1894. Vol. 2, p. 10–12.

[2] Thouar, *Deutsche geogr. Blätter*, vii, 66.

[3] Theodor Waitz, *Anthropologie der Naturvölker.* Leipzig, 1892, Vol. 3, p. 394. *Also see* A. O. Humboldt and Bonpland, *Reise in die Aequinoctialgegenden des Neuen Continentes in den Jahren 1799–1804.* Stuttgart and Tübingen, 1845.

[4] Albert Hermann Post, *Bausteine für eine allgemeine Rechtswissenschaft auf vergleichend-ethnologischer Basis.* Oldenburg, 1880–1881, Vol. 2, p. 119.

[5] Joseph Kohler, *Recht der Azteken*, p. 46.

sacrificed in time of famine and need. They could also be sacrificed at the death of kings and great men. Deformed infants were abandoned or killed by various tribes living on the islands of the Pacific; Australia,[6] Hawaii,[7] and others,[8] as they were by some negro-peoples as well.[9] In the kingdom of Assinie on the Gold Coast, children with six fingers on either or both hands were buried alive.[10] Among the Indo-Germanic peoples exposure of deformed infants [11] was a custom of frequent occurrence. In the early law of Northern Germany the right to kill monsters and deformed persons is often mentioned.[12]

Isolated cases of the practice of the exposure of infants occur in Japan,[13] as in other countries, but it has never approached recognition as a general custom. From the myth of the god Hiruko (leech-child) it may be inferred that the abandonment of deformed infants was not uncommon in the earliest times. The *Nihongi* tells us that the god had completed his third year and was still unable to walk. His parents, therefore, placed him in the rock-camphor-boat of heaven and set him adrift.

Data concerning the exposure of infants in Persia [14] are scanty. According to the Avesta,[15] all deformities were regarded as the work of the Evil One. It is not impossible, therefore, that deformed children were exposed with more or less frequency.

[6] Albert Hermann Post, *Bausteine für eine allgemeine Rechtswissenschaft auf vergleichend-ethnologischer Basis*, Oldenburg, 1880–1881. Vol. 2, p. 119. *Also* Joseph Kohler, in *Zeitschrift für vgl. Rechtswissenschaft*, vii, 355. *Also* Waitz-Gerland, *Anthropologie*, Vol. 6, p. 779.

[7] Waitz-Gerland, *Anthropologie*, Vol. 6, pp. 139–140.

[8] Albert Hermann Post, *Bausteine für eine allgemeine Rechtswissenschaft au vergleichend-ethnologischer Basis*. Oldenburg, 1880–1881, Vol. 2, p. 119.

[9] Albert Hermann Post, *Afrikanische Jurisprudenz*, Oldenburg. 1887, Vol. 1, p. 285.

[10] *Globus*, 1891, No. 11, p. 176, after Reichenbach, *Étude sur le Royaume d'Assinie. Bull. Soc. Géogr.*, 1890, p. 316.

[11] Grim, *Rechtsaltert*, p. 456.

[12] Maurer, *Wasserweihe des germ. Heidentums*, 1880, p. 44 ff.

[13] James Hastings, *Encyclopædia of Religion and Ethics*, Edinburgh, 1908. Vol. I, p. 7. Article by W. G. Aston.

[14] *Ibid.*, Vol. I, p. 7, Article by Louis H. Gray.

[15] Vendîdâd, ii, 29.

Among the Pima Indians, a North American tribe, with the consent of the parents, deformed infants were taken by the mid-wife, who watched them until they died of exposure and want of nourishment.[16]   So strong was the feeling of the Pimas against the abnormal that they tried in recent years to kill a grown man who had six toes.

In this connection, James Mooney of the Bureau of American Ethnology, in a communication to me, notes as follows:

Among the Kiowa I knew personally a twelve-year-old girl, of receding forehead and halfwitted, who had been buried alive immediately after birth and rescued and brought to the Catholic mission by a captive woman who knew what was about to be done.   The missionary priest, from his experience waiting on their sick in camp, believed that they had killed other defective infants at birth.   I know also of instances of abandonment of the helpless aged in the same tribe.

Travelers have asserted the existence of the practice of killing defective infants, in various tribes, and I am inclined to think that it was quite general.   Some tribes, especially in Oregon, kill one of a pair of twins.   The reason in both cases seems to have been partly economic, to be rid of a future burden, and partly from a superstitious fear of the abnormal.

With the dawn of our present civilization the condition of the cripple did not improve to as great an extent as we should ordinarily expect.   Oriental peoples turned forth their cripples to wander in the wilderness.   The inhabitants of Ancient India cast them into the Ganges; the Spartans [17] hurled them from a precipice into an abyss, *Apothetos*.   The Jews in the earliest times banished their cripples so that they had, perforce, to beg by the roadsides.   The general attitude was to regard physical deformity as a blight sent by God or as a punishment for sin.

The Hebrew scriptures reflect the attitude that the deformed

[16] Frank Russell, *The Pima Indians*.   In *26th Annual Report, Bureau of American Ethnology*.   Washington, 1908, p. 185.

[17] Douglas C. McMurtrie, *The Primary Education of Crippled Children*, New York, 1910, p. 5.

person must be spiritually and mentally unfit as well. In
Leviticus [18] we encounter a passage illustrative of this:

And the Lord spake unto Moses, saying: speak unto Aaron, saying, whosoever he be of thy seed in their generations that hath
any blemish, let him not approach to offer the bread of his God.

For whatsoever man he be that hath a blemish, he shall not
approach; a blind man or a lame, or he that hath a flat nose or
anything superfluous.

Or a man that is brokenfooted, or brokenhanded,

Or a crooktbackt, or a dwarf, or that hath a blemish in his eye,
or be scurvy, or scabbed, or hath his stones broken;

No man that hath a blemish of the seed of Aaron the priest shall
come nigh to offer the offerings of the Lord made by fire; he hath
a blemish; he shall not come nigh to offer the bread of his God.

Later on in the same passage it is stated that the reason for
this is that the sanctuaries be not profaned.

There are references to the cripple in the Old Testament in
the form of similes showing that physical deformity was familiar
to the people.[19]   The first reference to a deformity caused by
accident occurs in the Second Book of Samuel.

And Jonathan, Saul's son, had a son that was lame of his feet.
He was five years old when the tidings came of Saul and Jonathan
out of Jezreel, and his nurse took him up, and fled; and it came to
pass, as she made haste to flee, that he fell and became lame.   And
his name was Mephibosheth.[20]

This accident was probably the forerunner of many subsequent
accidents to children in charge of nurses.

Kindly references to the cripple in early times are scarce.
In Job's recital [21] of his circumstances when God was with him,
recounting his various benevolences, he says, "I was eyes to the
blind and feet was I to the lame."

[18] *Leviticus*, xxi, 16–21.
[19] See *Proverbs*, xxvi, 7.
[20] *II Samuel*, iv, 4.
[21] *Job*, xxix, 15.

In referring to inheritance, the Dâdistân-î-Dînîk,[22] one of the Sacred Books of the East, [23] says " . . . and the share of one of the sons, or even the wife of a son who is blind in both eyes, or crippled in both feet, or maimed in both his hands, is twice as much as that of one who is sound."

The Greeks, worshipping as they did the perfection of bodily form, regarded a cripple as the incarnation of everything unlovely,[24] not only physically, but also mentally and morally. Homer describes Thersites as possessed of every ugly attribute and equally deformed in body and mind.[25] Such was the propensity of this crippled soldier of the army before Troy for indulging in vituperative language that he did not abstain from directing it even against Agamemnon himself. It is related that he ultimately perished at the hand of Achilles, while he was ridiculing the sorrow of that hero for the slain Penthesilia.

The advent of Christianity struck a new note in the attitude toward the crippled and deformed. Even in Isaiah's prophecy [26] of the coming of the Messianic kingdom, he foretells that "then shall the lame man leap as a hart." Christ, referring to His ministry,[27] says: "the blind receive their sight, and the lame walk. . . . " It is also related [28] that "the blind and the lame came to Him in the temple and He healed them."

Many cures of cripples are also attributed to the Apostles. "A certain man lame from his mother's womb" was healed by Peter.[29] It is related that "immediately his feet and ankle bones received strength." During the ministry of Philip [30] "many taken with palsies and that were lame, were healed."

[22] Chapter lxii, paragraph 3.

[23] *Sacred Books of the East*, edited by F. Max Müller, Oxford, 1882. *Pahlavi Texts*, translated by E. W. West.

[24] Douglas C. McMurtrie, *The Primary Education of Crippled Children*, New York, 1910, pp. 5–6.

[25] Homer, *Iliad*, ii, 212 ff.

[26] *Isaiah*, xxxv, 6.

[27] *Matthew*, xi, 5. Also referred to in *Luke*, vii, 22.

[28] *Matthew*, xxi, 14.

[29] *Acts of the Apostles*, iii, 2.

During the mission of the Apostle Paul in Lycaonia, he healed[31] a cripple described as follows: "And there sat a certain man at Lystra, impotent in his feet, being a cripple from his mother's womb, who never had walked." It is interesting to note that this is the first use in the Scriptures of the generic term, cripple. The Greek word Χωλός is used in the original.

The influence of the Christian attitude had some influence upon the lot of the cripple. I recall one illustrative quotation.[32]

Also cripples and the sick who remained alive were left to themselves[33] in Iran as in Armenia and they led a wretched existence. In Armenia it was one of the great services of Christianity that it ameliorated the fate of these unfortunates.[34]

But the new influence was not profound and it did not even permeate the Church in its later development. During the Middle Ages, those burdened with physical deformity were considered as targets for contempt and ridicule, and contumely was continually heaped upon them.[35]

The early Romans had the right to destroy a deformed child provided the child were shown to five neighbors and their assent secured. In the Twelve Tables the decemvirs extended the authority of the father so that he, individually, could destroy or remove crippled children immediately after birth. In many instances they were cast into the street or drowned in the lake into which emptied the sewers of the Eternal City. They were exposed in deserts, in the woods on the banks of the Tiber, in the vegetable market, at a certain pillar in the eleventh district of the city, and, ironically enough, in the very vicinity of the Temple of Mercy. Some few of these unhappy children did not die of exposure or hunger and escaped being torn to pieces by

[30] *Acts of the Apostles*, viii, 7.

[31] *Acts of the Apostles*, xiv, 8.

[32] Fr. Spiegel, *Eranische Alterthumskunde*, Leipzig, 1878. Vol. 3, p. 682.

[33] *i. e.*, abandoned.

[34] See also *Faustus of Byzantium*, iv, Chapter 4, and *Moses of Khorene*, iii, 20.

[35] Douglas C. McMurtrie, *The Primary Education of Crippled Children*, New York, 1910, pp. 6–7.

dogs or being eaten by swine.   But in spite of their lives being
saved, their existence became a wretched and miserable one.
They became the slaves of the person who took them up and
succored them, and they were intentionally crippled to a greater
extent if their deformities when they grew older were not conspicuous enough to render them successful in begging alms for
their master's profit.   Seneca relates how these unfortunates
wandered about exhibiting their mutilated members.   He goes
on to state that they were intentionally deformed by cutting
off their arms, by twisting their shoulders so that they became
humpbacked.   If the master counts over the daily collection of
the beggars and the sum is not enough, he rebukes the wretches,
saying: "You have brought in too little, bring hither the whip;
you can weep and lament now.   If you had appealed this way
to the passer-by you would have had more alms and could have
given me more."   It may be remarked that this system of
peonage in mendicancy is in use even to-day in some communities, notably in Italy and Russia.   In the former country many
children are mutilated so that they may solicit alms in the streets.
In Russia a similar practice is indulged in, the cripples being
exhibited particularly at ceremonies and processions.

Among the Romans the trade in slave dwarfs became so
extensive and profitable that merchants took children and put
them in artificial bandages.[36]   This method, instead of making
them well-proportioned dwarfs, made them misshapen and miserable men.   This gruesome torture and unnatural art of making
dwarfs is also mentioned by Cardanus.[37]   *Nascuntur ex parvo
patre et matre, fasciis arcte colligantur non affatim nutriuntur,
sed teniuntur,* which might be translated: born of small parents,
they are laced with bandages and fed, not heartily, but sparely.
Dwarfs were utilized by the emperor Domitian to engage in
sham battles with women.[38]

[36] Sigaud de la Fond.   *Wunder der Natur.*   Part 2, p. 495, *also* K. F. Flögel, *Geschichte der Hofnarren,* Leignitz and Leipzig, 1789, pp. 507–508.

[37] Cardanus, *De Subtilit.*   Book XI, p. 460.

[38] Xiphilinus, *In Domitiano.*

Blaise de Vigenere in the notes to his *Images et Tableaux de platte peinture de Philostrate Lemnien* remarks that when in Rome in 1566 he was invited to a dinner by Cardinal Vitelli, where the table was served "by at least thirty-four dwarfs, almost all hideous and badly deformed."

With the opening of the Middle Ages the chief occupation of the crippled came to be that of court fool or jester. These personages almost universally found a place in the retinues of princes, and often in the households of noblemen.[39]

These court fools can be divided under two classifications. In the first would come those creatures who by reason of deformity in body or mind were calculated to excite laughter and ridicule. In the second would be placed those chosen for a certain superficial quickness of wit and power of repartee. It is the first class with which we are especially concerned in our study of the attitude of the community toward the crippled and deformed; and they were to be found, unfortunately, in large numbers. The attire [40] of these jesters was distinctive, though varying slightly during different periods.

To judge from the prints and illuminations which are the sources of our knowledge on this matter, it seems to have changed considerably from time to time. The head was shaved, the coat was motley, and the breeches tight, with generally one leg different in color from the other. The head was covered with a garment resembling a monk's cowl, which fell over the breast and shoulders, and often bore asses' ears, and was crested with a cockscomb, while bells hung from various parts of the attire. The fool's bauble was a short staff bearing a ridiculous head, to which sometimes was attached an inflated bladder, by means of which sham castigations were affected.

The impressing of cripples into service as court fools continued and the institution was firmly entrenched for many

[39] K. F. Flögel, *Geschichte der Hofnarren*, Leipzig, 1789. Nick, *Die Hof- und Volksnarren*. Stuttgart, 1861, 2 vols. Ebeling, *Die Kahlenberger, Geschichte der Hofnarren*, Berlin, 1890.

[40] Walter Hepworth, *Encyclopædia Britannica*, Eleventh Edition, New York, 1910, x, 614–615.

years, despite many tendencies operating to improve the situation. Even a number of decrees passed by the Reichstag during the sixteenth century failed to obviate the practice. Not until the time of the Enlightenment was the final stage reached and the custom abolished.

Even after this time the court fool was still in vogue at the Russian court, Peter the Great having so many jesters of this type that it was necessary to divide them into classes.

When the Spaniards under Fernando Cortez accomplished the conquest of Mexico, court fools and deformed human creatures of all kinds were found at the Court of Montezuma.

It will be observed that the most significant fact developed by the history of the court fool is that during the period covered the victims of human deformity were regarded with ridicule and contempt. In the existence of such an attitude on the part of the general public, a sympathetic or merciful consideration can hardly be conceived.

During the latter part of the Middle Ages cripples came to be regarded superstitiously, this attitude being responsible for a miserable existence for those deviating in any way from the normal.[41]

Ignorant people and scholars alike were influenced by such prejudice, and it is easily seen how cripples and deformed people were regarded as devilish monsters. Several circumstances gave rise to the general superstition. One of the most instrumental was the frequent confession on the rack by unmarried pregnant women that they had been seduced by the devil. This led indirectly to the belief that humpbacked and deformed children might have been of diabolical paternity.

Others regarded the deformed as victims of the wrath of God, and put them to death. King Francis I had burned to death at Avignon a woman who had given birth to a mal-

[41] T. D. Herholdt, *Betrachtungen über den medizinischen Aberglauben und über Missgeburten im Allgemeinen*. Appendix to *Beschreibung sechs menschlicher Missgeburten*, Copenhagen, 1830, pp. 83–162.

formed child. Often, on the birth of a cripple or of a child with superfluous members, the attack of a hostile army was feared. There is a similar legend of Babylonian origin.

Martin Luther shared the belief, current at his time, in the theory of changelings. At the birth of an undesirable child it was believed that some diabolical mother had stolen away the right child and substituted her own offspring instead. Thus the child was known as a changeling. Cripples, rachitics and cretins were regarded as changelings. The idea was that if such children were maltreated sufficiently their mothers would come again to get them and leave the rightful children in their stead. It is easy to conceive the attitude which such a concept would engender. Luther [42] also regarded malformed children as mere masses of flesh and considered that killing them was a work well pleasing to God.

Another phase of superstition affected the cripple—the belief that offspring could be harmed by "somebody" or "casting the evil eye" upon the pregnant mother. Parents were inclined to bring the deformity of their child into causal relation to a terrifying pre-natal experience on the part of the mother. In 1673 it is related that a citizen's wife was so frightened at the sight of a one-eyed, lame beggar that when she soon after bore a son, the infant lacked a hand and had a crooked leg. Many other similar instances can be found in literature.

One cripple, Thomas Schweicker (died 1602) of Schwäbisch-Hall, came to be highly regarded [43] on account of his learning and culture.

The first glimmer of hope for the welfare of the cripple began to appear in the eighteenth century, though the progress in this direction was very slow. The first measures did not in a

[42] Martin Luther. *Table-Talk.* (*Table-talk of the devil and his work—Changelings from the devil—History of a changeling at Dessau—Another history of a changeling.*) Theo. Kirchoff. *Grundriss einer Geschichte der deutschen Irrenpflege*, Berlin, 1890, pp. 65–76.

[43] Martin Ulbrich. *Th. Schweicker*, Eisleben, 1909.

strict sense mark the beginnings of care for cripples, but they operated to the ultimate advantages of those who, by reason of their infirmity, were cast upon the pity of their fellow-men. The actuating motive of provision in many cases, however, was utilitarian in character. One object was that all cripples might be confined so that they should not annoy the community by their deformed appearance.

Some of the many monasteries which had not been utilized since the time of the Reformation were thrown open and converted into orphan asylums, mad-houses, or penitentiaries. In the establishment of the various institutions the cripple was frequently considered.

Those handicapped by deformity were best provided for at a hospital for wretched and pauper invalids established at Pforgheim [44] in 1722 by Count Luitgard of Baden. This was later transformed by Count Charles Frederic of Baden into an orphan asylum, but made especial provision for young and old cripples. Kirmsse [45] quotes parts of the official ordinance on this matter as follows:

Cripples, by Margrave Charles Frederic of Baden. The princely ordinance of May 11, 1758, says on this:

"Since we now assume the place of a father to those who are orphaned in our territory or who are otherwise afflicted with grave misfortune, we cannot but desire special experience of our most gracious care to those who, in addition to such afflictions, are at the same time stripped of temporal wealth, and who are, therefore, stricken with double affliction."

"And the third class is composed of those who have such physical defects that they are an especial abomination and disgust to other men whenever they come into their sight. There are utterly misformed cripples and more of the sort."

[44] *Zeitschrift für Krüppelfürsorge*, Hamburg and Leipzig, 1911, iv, 10 ff.
[45] *Ibid.*

IV. Work.

"As many of these inmates as can be employed in any work shall be obliged to perform it, yet with reference to distinction of age, sex, and their physical infirmities. Here it is necessary to see in the first place—unless their deformities are slight—that there shall be sought out for them such tasks as may be performed in their rooms.

X. Punishment.

"Since the other inmates consist of crippled persons, no punishment but a few stripes will be allowed, although they may be chastened either with withdrawal of food or of drink or of both, but in every case after careful consideration of their circumstances.

Duty of Physician.

"In the same (orphan asylum) are found the most utterly wretched of the entire country, including those sick persons who, in consequence of the cross of God laid upon them, are indeed a horror to other men, but all the more a true object of their pity. And, although, according to the measure of our human understanding they are counted among the incurable, nevertheless God has created many means to make their cross endurable. In their case, therefore, the physician must employ all his best science."

Of those capable of instruction it is noted merely that they should be sent to the school of the orphan asylum "when they could stand it." The cripple department was abolished in 1808, probably because the room was needed for the insane.[46]

Such provision for cripples, however, gave them asylum only and did nothing in a constructive way to better their condition, but the rise of the science of orthopedics was responsible for the ensuing improvement. It is true that one of the earliest Hippocratic treatises was orthopedic in character, but the attention which had been given to human deformity by the medical profession had, up to the time of which we are speaking, been inconsequential. One of the first to give extensive consideration to such work was Andry of Paris, who pub-

---

[46] Kelp.   Irrenstatistik im Herzogtum Altenburg, *Allgemeine Zeitschrift für Psychiatrie* 1847, iv, 587 ff.

lished [47] a two-volume work on orthopedics, illustrated. He encountered much skepticism. For example, Siebold, in his *Chirurgisches Taschenbuch* [48] claimed that the cure of club feet was impossible.

Another advance was made in 1780 when J. A. Venel, who was versed in both mechanics and medicine,[49] founded an institution for the deformed, at Orbe, Switzerland. Several other surgeons also did valuable work. The most complete books on the subject were by Jörg.[50]

The theories of the various orthopedists were best put into practice in an institution and a large number of these were founded in the first decades of the nineteenth century; as, for example, those located at Paris, London, Leipzig, Lübeck, Berlin, and Vienna. One at Würzburg, established by Dr. Heine, gained especial fame, being the first of its kind in Germany.

The first institution for the deformed in Prussia was established at Berlin in 1823 by Dr. J. G. Blömer. This was designed for pay patients from among the upper classes, but indigent crippled children were also admitted. Between the years 1823 and 1827 he treated no less than 1179 cases of deformity, of which he claimed to cure 651. In a passage quoted by Kirmsse [51] he thus describes the purpose and management of his institution:

An institution such as to be described has long been needed in our monarchy; all the more so because the forms of disability and sickness in question yield but indifferently to treatment outside of such

---

[47] Berlin, 1744.

[48] Nuremburg, 1792.

[49] *Description de plusieurs nouveaux moyens méchaniques propres à prévenir, borner, et même corriger dans certains cas, les courbes latérales et la torsion de l'épine du dos.* Orbe, 1788.

[50] Ch. G. Jörg. *Ueber die Verkrümmungen des menschlichen Körpers*, Leipzig. *Die Kunst die Verkrümmungen der Kinder zu verhüten und die entstandenen sicher und leicht zu heben.* Leipzig, 1816.

[51] *Zeitschrift für Krüppelfürsorge*, iv, 13 ff.

a sanitarium. The difficulties in private practice are extensive and the curative methods can seldom be applied to as full an extent as is often necessary. Here belongs, among other things, the proper combination and joint application of medical and mechanical treatment, together with the requisite arrangement of suitable occupations for the sick, and the obviation of all factors tending to induce or further increase the physical deformities in question. Upon the persistent and accurate co-ordination of these conditions the possibility of a cure depends; that the elements are usually disparate is responsible for failure in many cases.

Since a large number of the sick who visit the institution are still young, special attention must be devoted to their education. That the invalids may not be impeded in their intellectual development by residence—which is often of long duration—at the institution, my endeavors were naturally directed toward providing for them training adapted to their ages and individual capacities—especially in view of the fact that the intellect is usually very acute and active in sufferers of this type. For still another reason I have been led to devote special attention to the subject of education. In ordinary life a certain obstinacy of character is usually attributed to those who suffer from bodily deformity—unfortunately not always without cause. A very natural cause is the mockery to which these unfortunates are often exposed by their frivolous playmates. They are shunned because their infirmity does not permit them to engage in many games of childhood and youth; they are retsricted to their own company, and, imprisoned in their isolation, become not infrequently malicious. These faults, however, can be more easily removed during youth by continuous moral and intellectual training in an institution; more especially since the similarity of infirmity makes for much in common and demands mutual co-operation. The training is entrusted to a special teacher, who watches in a parental spirit over their morals and instructs them in varied school subjects. Naturally it must be my chief care that such an important position as that of teacher should always be filled by persons of intelligence and integrity.

Not desire of gain; but only the warmest interest in the matter itself, and a deep-seated longing to advance so far as possible the common weal, could lead me to establish an institution for the deformed in which even those of the most slender means can find the fountain of their healing and so look forward to as happy a future as possible.

The number of those seeking assistance, however, soon demanded a large institution. This at the same time placed me in a position further to extend my observations. Nevertheless, there were many difficulties to be contended with in connection with such an institution; the exactions demanded of the man who becomes its head are so considerable that long preliminary work and the greatest exertions were required before the institution could enter upon full activity. Considering the end in view, the earthly reward to be hoped for is extremely scanty in return for the manifold and ceaseless efforts expended; the sweetest recompense here is the consciousness of having laid a small gift on the altar of humanity, and of having opened to the poor no less than to the rich the fountain from which they may hope to draw, without expensive outlay, the healing of their infirmities.

Blömer had a workroom for making apparatus, bandages and artificial limbs. It is not known how long his institution lasted.

A similar institute was founded in Stockholm, Sweden, in 1827 by Dr. Ackermann.[52] There was much difficulty encountered in overcoming public suspicion and distrust. Dr. Günther maintained an institution in Hamburg [53] during the years 1832–1837. While visiting Hamburg, Dr. Zinc of Vienna became acquainted with this establishment and upon his return to Vienna founded a similar one,[54] May 1, 1838. This latter much resembled the institute of Blömer at Berlin.

In the meantime, however, there had been founded in Munich in 1832 the first comprehensive institution for the care and education of cripples. The Königliche Bayerische Zentralanstalt für Erziehung und Bildung krüppelhafter Kinder was brought into being by an eminent philanthropist Johan Nepomuk

[52] C. J. Eckström. *Ars-Berättelse om Svenska Lakäre-Sallskapetts Arbeten*, Stockholm, 1829.

[53] H. Gleiss. *Lebenserinnerungen von Elise Averdieck*, Hamburg, 1908, pp. 48–50.

[54] Erster Bericht, 1853; Jahresbericht . . . für 1853, Vienna, 1854; *Correspondenz-Blatt der deutschen Gesellschaft für Psychiatrie*, 1854, p. 16; *Die angeborener Verrenkungen*, Vienna, 1845,

and the principles then exemplified have, in general, been followed by most of the modern institutions which have since been established. A description of subsequent work, however, is outside the scope of the present article. In Denmark,[55] England,[56] Italy,[57] as well as in Germany [58] and the United States,[59] extensive systems of care have been built up, and in almost every civilized country of the world there is made some provision for the welfare of the cripple.

The community has now realized to a very considerable extent its responsibility toward the cripple and the early vicissitudes to which the deformed were subjected are indeed a matter of history.

[55] Douglas C. McMurtrie. The Copenhagen nstitution for Cripples, *Boston Medical and Surgical Journal*, Boston, 1911, clxv, 794–798.

[56] Douglas C. McMurtrie. Crippled Children in the English Public Schools, *New York Medical Journal*, New York, 1913, xcvii, 188–199.

[57] Douglas C. McMurtrie. The Care of the Crippled and Rachitic in Italy, *Medical Record*, New York, 1911, lxxx, 1218–1222.

[58] Konrad Biesalski, *Umfang und Art des jugendlichen Krüppeltums in Deutschland.* Hamburg and Leipzig, 1910. Also the files of the *Zeitschrift für Krüppelfürsorge.*

[59] Douglas C. McMurtrie. The Care of Crippled Children in the United States. *American Journal of Orthopedic Surgery*, Philadelphia, 1912, ix, 527–556.

THE EDUCATION OF CRIPPLED CHILDREN

Gwilym G. Davis

THE EDUCATION OF CRIPPLED CHILDREN

GWILYM G. DAVIS, M.D.

Philadelphia

When it was suggested that I address you[1] on the subject of
the education of the crippled my first inclination was to decline
because I felt that I had not given sufficient attention to it.   It
is a subject, however, that appeals to me so strongly and seems
to be in such an unsettled, early and primitive stage that I
thought it best to do what little I could to aid in its discussion
and further its progress.

Educators and the general community have not succeeded in
establishing any standard for the education of the normal child,
and yet we, have not only the problems of general education to
deal with, but, in addition, those arising from the crippled condition of the scholars.   It is evident that the methods employed
in the two classes of cases must be different.   It is perhaps
recognized that to keep normal people well, exercise and hard
work are desirable agents to employ.   They can not only endure
being driven but they actually flourish under it, but when a
person is sick and diseased then rest and soothing and supporting
measures are needed.   Crippled children seem to me to constitute a sort of middle class, we should not drive them as we would
the totally well children nor nurse them as we would the sick
ones.   In other words, they should have a distinct, separate,
special method of treatment of their own adapted to their
peculiar needs.

The education of crippled children is intimately associated
with their bodily care.   The two cannot be separated but must

[1] Read before the Orthopedic Section of the New York Academy of Medicine,
December 4, 1913.

be considered together. We therefore find that we are confronted with the following problems—(1). Their maintenance, (2) the care and treatment of their disabilities, (3) their general education, (4) their character formation or moral education, (5) their vocational training and, finally, (6) their later supervision. While some of these can be isolated and treated more or less alone, as a rule, several of them will have to be dealt with at the same time; this of course adds to the difficulties. To conquer a difficult subject it is well to analyze or dissect it and attack it in sections. To let us begin with the subject of maintenance.

1. Maintenance. Maintenance has to do with the method of living and support of the child. It is influenced by its financial position. The children of the well-to-do usually have those interested in them that have both the ability and desire to see that they are well taken care of in all respects. They do not become public charges and do not frequent our charitable institutions; therefore, for the present at least, we can leave them and confine ourselves to those less favored. It is the poor child that is to be considered. These constitute by far the greater number of the crippled. How shall they be taken care of? We know that their home conditions are such that in many cases it is absolutely essential that they be removed elsewhere. It is generally recognized that it is best for the child to live in its own home provided it is a good home but many of these children are orphans, with no home at all, others have dissolute parents. These and many other reasons necessitate that the child be maintained elsewhere if it is to be made a fairly useful member of the community and not become a burden and public charge. The number of cripples is so great and their education and maintenance so expensive that in the present state of society it has been found necessary to establish institutions for them. While the substitution of an institution for a home is admitted by all as an undesirable thing from many points of view, still in some cases it seems to be the only solution that we have at present.

In the dim future I believe cripples will be provided with true home life, but in the meantime it is our duty to see that our institutions resemble the home as much as it is possible to have them. Bodily health has considerable to do with mental development. The inmates of our institutions are usually sufficiently well fed but it is different with those living in their own home. For these some sort of Social Service is necessary so that the food and home surroundings of the child may be improved. When the child attends a day school it has now become the custom in some schools to provide it with suitable nourishment, lunches, etc., which tend to improve and conserve its bodily health. I am convinced that the question of maintenance should be better looked after than was formerly the case. We owe more to the child than simply to furnish it with a brace, and I look for a great field of usefulness in our modern Social Service to enable us to meet this need.

2. Disabilities. If a child can walk to school the problem of its education becomes simplified. If a deformed hand is bettered it may be able to work, therefore orthopedic treatment is of the first importance. The more successful it is the broader is the child's sphere of capabilities. For this reason it is essential that institutions for crippled children should be so equipped as to provide the constant orthopedic treatment that these cases require. Even in the day schools there should be some one capable to do the more simple dressings and adjustment of apparatus that may be needed. The orthodox orthopedic hospitals may relieve the educational institutions of a certain portion of this work but never of all of it. It is, however, just as bad for a school for crippled children to be exploited by ambitious operators as a hospital as it is for a hospital to be allowed through incompetence and neglect to degenerate into a low grade home.

3. General Education. The crippled child has a greater need of a good elementary education than has a normal one. A normal child, owing to the possession of all of its faculties, has a

greater opportunity of acquiring knowledge; a normal child can run around and almost insensibly imbibe knowledge that a crippled child has to have brought to it. For education to be successful one should not forget that it should be sufficiently thorough for the child eventually to become, to at least some degree, self-supporting. The wider the education the greater will be the choice of vocations in later years. For a cripple to be a bookkeeper it is necessary that he should previously have learned to read and write. In these days when professional educators are at variance as to methods we need not take time to discuss them, but we can all agree that what has been called a "common school" education is just as essential to the cripple as it is to the well child. If the state pays for the instruction of the latter it should also contribute for the former. Parents especially are apt to be neglectful and allow a cripple to grow up ignorant. It is our duty to teach them the error of their ways. Family teaching is of the greatest value. There used to be a lot of time lost by the child being in the hospital but we are now remedying that by having teachers come daily into our wards and instruct the patients. To care for the out-patients we have our social workers and our day schools to which the children are brought and from which they are taken back to their homes. Only recently in our city has the public school system provided special facilities for the education of crippled children but it is making good progress. It is not possible to teach cripples in the same manner as well children. They are so few in number, comparatively, and their disabilities so various that it is necessary to devote a large amount of individual attention to each child. Therefore, there should be a larger number of teachers than is necessary in our ordinary public schools. The classes should not be so large.

The question of age here demands consideration. The objection of attempting to instruct a very young child is that it is apt to be so conducted as to prejudice its general health and physical development. We must decide as to when it is best for an individual child to sacrifice a certain portion of its outdoor life for indoor instruction.   How are we to look upon the kindergarten with its pupils, some of whom have not been long out of the diaper stage?   Also the Montessori and Fröbelian methods? To my mind all these various educational methods have their special good points but we must exercise care in imposing them on the individual cripple.   Even in a normal child it is frequently difficult enough to have it develop a normal body, and a cripple burdened with his infirmity demands still greater care and is not fit physically to be given instruction at so early an age as is the well child.   A well-fed child living out of doors is my ideal.   If you want a puppy to grow up to be a big, strong, healthy dog feed it liberally on table scraps and allow it to run at large.   Mental pabulum will not make an emaciated tuberculous child strong.   A word to the wise, however, is I think, sufficient.

4. Character Formation or Moral Education.   While intellectual development is of importance it is insignificant as compared with good character.   A cripple, like others more favored, may be well educated and intelligent but if his knowledge is not used rightly it is a detriment rather than a benefit to society. The problem is how to rear them so that they shall develop into industrious, unselfish, honest and reliable citizens.   How can they ever be made to be self-supporting if they are lazy and unwilling to work?   How can ambition be infused into them so that they will endeavor to help themselves instead of being content to be parasites on the body politic?   How can they be made to view life in a broad, humanitarian way and not devote all their energies to satisfying their own selfish desires?   A failure in the moral training of a cripple means the evolution of an individual, detestable in character, a menace and burden to the community, who is only too apt to graduate into the mendicant and criminal classes.

There are, of course, many things which influence the formation of character.   1 think it is generally recognized that precept or example is the most powerful. If we can surround the cripple with good associations we have the best possible guarantee that he will develop correctly. The greatest influence is exerted by good home life. Children are imitative and are impressed by the people with whom they come in constant contact. In a good home they are shielded from evil associates and influences therefore it is our duty, when possible, to see that the crippled child is not deprived of the benign influence of one or both loving parents. There are some misguided people who think that the best thing for the child is to take it away from its home and parents and rear it in some asylum or so-called "home." This is certainly a mistaken policy. To my mind public charities appear to be possibly necessary evils but evils nevertheless. It is my firm belief that no child should be placed in them that can with justice be kept out. It is far better if we must dole out charity to dispense it in the home. Aid the parents to take care of the child and aid them to educate it and not tempt them to desert it by offering to care for it in a public institution.

Unfortunately it is impossible to provide homes for all the crippled children which exist in our community. Perhaps this is a field of charity which has not been sufficiently tilled. Is not our age both thoughtless and selfish? Is not the public generally too much inclined to hand their charitable duties over to some organized body instead of performing them themselves? Is it not too much the habit for a person to donate a certain sum to charity and then feel that they have done all their duty? The poor do it just as do the rich. A poor person will give to another poorer one a few pennies and concern himself not at all as to whether or not that is the way the unfortunate one ought to be helped; and the rich one does the very same thing, only on a larger scale. While it is best to care for cripples at home, provided it is not vicious, still the number of cripples who lack proper homes either on account of the death of the parents or their deplorable environment and the difficulty of training them is so great that at the present time it seems almost a necessity for us to utilize as far as we can the many institutions which have been established for their care.   In these institutions it seems to me that the main object should be character development and that the educational aim should be secondary.   It is apt, however, to be just the opposite.   It is too liable to occur that while great attention is paid to their schooling too little is paid to what might be called home influences.   If an institution is going to stand *in locus parentis* then the greatest care should be taken to see that all the officials and teachers and employees,— everybody who comes in contact with the children,—be of the best possible character so that as the child grows up he insensibly acquires the views and habits of thought which will best fit him for a future career.   The children should not, so to speak, be handled in masses, but should be brought as far as possible into direct personal and intimate contact with their caretakers and teachers.   These take the place of the lacking parents and form the best possible substitutes.   It is obvious that this requires that the caretaker, of whatever grade, be a person possessing those peculiar qualities especially suitable for the purpose, and such people are not easy to find.   The results, however, will be directly proportionate to the extent to which the teacher or care-taker fulfils these requirements, and surely the selection of such is worthy of most serious attention.   If the necessity of character formation is borne in mind many ways will present themselves by which it may be furthered.

5. Vocational Training.   Manual training is not necessarily vocational.   Its primary object is developmental.   It is to teach children to do things for themselves, to think and reason and accomplish something by their own unaided efforts; in other words, it promotes self-reliance and it has its place as an elementary training, whereas the vocational training ends the school period.   Cripples, from the very nature of their disabilities, are debarred from many avenues of work; but if the desire to work is present the possible field of employment is so large and varied

that something that is suitable to his capabilities can be found for almost every individual. I think it a mistake to restrict vocational training to a few stereotyped forms and confining all to a narrow choice. The probabilities of success are directly proportional to the liking of the cripple for the work that he has been taught to do. For this reason the greatest care should be taken to first find out what is most desired by the child and what he is best fitted for and then an effort should be made to fit him in that line. The resources of many institutions are limited and the choice may not be as wide as desired, but I am convinced that more can be done if greater attention is paid to this aspect of the subject. Why should we insist on making a bookkeeper of a boy who is especially gifted as a wood carver! Why make a bad stenographer out of a naturally good milliner or dressmaker? Where the institution cannot itself furnish the needed facilities they can often be found outside its walls. In private offices and workshops opportunities may be found if there is only someone who will interest themselves to do it. Here is a field for social service. Recently one of my worst paralytics so learned the trade of a jeweler and watchmaker. Another, eighteen years of age, is earning eight dollars a week by designing stamps for hosiery. And the field is limitless. I am convinced that suitable work, which is practically self-supporting, can be found for every cripple who is possessed of the proper character and desires to aid himself. Of course it is unreasonable to expect a tuberculous cripple to earn as much as a healthy individual, but I have seen so many cripples doing so much for themselves that I have great hopes for the future in this direction.

6. Subsequent Supervision. So many cripples as they approach maturity have lost their home ties that, if they are left to fight their way alone, they are apt to retrograde or fail entirely. They should be made to feel that there *is* someone who is interested in them and who is watching their progress. They should be encouraged to keep in touch with their alma mater until they have definitely established themselves and formed a

circle of friends elsewhere. The adult cripple has been too generally treated as a pauper but, if through state aid or private beneficence, a crippled child has been reared and educated and fitted for the duties of life it is certainly our duty to give him that moral support that every beginner in the struggle for existence needs to enable him to safely pass over the bridge which connects the productive and the non-productive periods of life.

These are some of the problems we have to face in caring for crippled children. Time does not permit me to mention all, nor to go into details, but the subject is young. It is but recently that orthopedic surgery itself has become established; our methods of dispensing so-called charity are crude and often misdirected and social service with its great possibilities has just been born. In various localities the conditions are different and the methods vary, but we all have the same ultimate aim. In the institution with which I am connected, the Widener Memorial Industrial School for Crippled Children, it is endeavored to care for, educate and fit for the struggle of life one hundred children—and we are doing what we can. As time passes on its field will no doubt widen and with added experience we are, I feel sure, justified in looking forward to a fruitful future.

THE CARE OF INVALID AND CRIPPLED CHILDREN IN SCHOOL

R.C. Elmslie

Preface.

THE first of the following lectures was delivered in the course of Advanced School Hygiene at University College, London. It aims at defining "Physical Defect" as applied to school children, and specially as used in the Elementary Education (Defective and Epileptic) Act of 1899. In it I have endeavoured to show the importance of educating invalid and crippled children, to define the classes of such children for which we have to make provision, and to show what school provision has been made for them and in what ways this may be usefully extended.

The other four lectures were delivered to the school nurses attached to the London County Council Invalid Schools. In these schools there are collected a very large number of children suffering from a variety of chronic illnesses. Every child in them is more or less diseased or deformed, and his chance in life depends upon the care spent upon him during his childhood. Although medical visits to these schools are frequent and the children are examined as often as possible, a very considerable responsibility must fall upon the school nurses, teachers, and managers. If they are to do their best they must have some small knowledge of the diseases from which the children suffer, of the indications that the disease is progressing satisfactorily or otherwise, of the principles of

3

treatment, and of the special care which the children require in the school, the playground, the ambulance, and the home. It was with a view to supplying this knowledge that these lectures were delivered, and it is hoped that as now printed they will be of use to all those concerned in the management of invalid and crippled children either at school or at home. They have been modified in detail to suit a rather wider public than that for which they were originally written, and they have been condensed to as small a compass as possible. At the same time a small amount of additional matter has been introduced to make the treatment of the subject more complete.

THE
CARE OF INVALID AND CRIPPLED CHILDREN IN SCHOOL.

I.

SCHOOL PROVISION FOR PHYSICALLY DEFECTIVE CHILDREN.

IN the medical supervision of schools it is advisable to adopt a very wide definition of the term "Physical Defect." It should be made to include not only all deformities and diseases of the bones, joints, and spine which obviously cripple the child, but also all general defects of physique and chronic illnesses, anything which continuously interferes either with attendance at school or with the ability of the scholar to follow in full the ordinary school routine. The duties of the medical officer to these physically defective children will then be fourfold :—

1. The separation of children who are physically unfitted to attend the ordinary schools.

2. The supervision of children who show some defect of physique, whether they are in ordinary schools or are in special schools, to see that they are in no way harmed by the school routine of work or of play.

3. To advise the parents of such children when medical or surgical treatment is necessary.

5

4. The supervision of the instruction given to these children, which should be such as will fit them for an occupation suited to their physical defect.

In addition, the statistics compiled in the future as the result of school inspection will be of great importance. For this reason it is essential that accurate recognition of all physical peculiarities and malformations should be arrived at, a matter which is by no means easy. Yet such work, if it is to be carried out at all, is worth doing well. The recognition of the nature of rare defects depends most of all upon the observer knowing of their occasional occurrence. To have never heard of a condition is the best way of failing to find it when it presents itself. To have some knowledge of the pathological anatomy of a rare condition is, in most cases, sufficient to ensure its recognition. For the proper consideration then of physical defect in school children a very wide practical knowledge of medicine and surgery is necessary, in addition to a knowledge of the educational side of the problem.

The Elementary Education (Defective and Epileptic) Act of 1899 gave permission for the establishment of special schools for the education of "children who, by reason of physical defect, are incapable of receiving proper benefit from the instruction in an ordinary public elementary school." The question which at once presents itself is: To what children should this be taken to refer?

The social status of the child must, of course, be considered in coming to any decision upon the point, but it is of less importance than would at first sight appear. It is just as urgently necessary to exclude the crippled or invalid children from a public or secondary school as it is from an elementary school. But whereas in the first case they will presumably be educated at home, in the last they will almost certainly be neglected, unless the education authority makes some special provision for them. It was the recognition of this fact, that very large numbers of children thus remain uneducated, that led to the establishment of special schools for physically defective children, first by private charity, later by the education authorities. The principle thus recognised has now been extended, so that teaching is carried on in some of the

6

children's hospitals in which chronic cases are treated. By these means it is hoped that a large number of children who would otherwise remain in complete ignorance will be enabled to earn their livelihood.

Thus the segregation of physically defective children is necessary only amongst the poorer classes, amongst those children who are educated by the public education authority, and whose parents, if the child remained at home, have neither the leisure to teach him themselves nor the means to provide a governess or master for that purpose. The same groups of children will, amongst the well-to-do, remain at home and be taught privately.

The classes of children found in the schools for whom such special arrangements have to be made are : —

    I. Cripples with active disease.

   II. Cripples with fixed deformity.

  III. Phthisical children with active disease.

  IV. Phthisical children in the convalescent or quiet stage.

   V. Chronic invalids from such conditions as heart disease and recurrent chorea.

  VI. Delicate nervous children.

 VII. Severe cases of malnutrition.

VIII. Children with combined defects (*e.g.*, crippled and mentally defective).

I propose to take these classes *seriatim* to consider briefly the frequence of the conditions found, their educational importance, and the school accommodation required to provide properly for them.

First in importance amongst the crippled children come those with tuberculous disease of the spine, joints, and bones. These diseases account for about half the crippled children in the London schools. The age at which these diseases arise is of importance. I have worked out my own statistics on this point and they agree closely with those published, notably with the extensive statistics of Whitman in New York. Disease of the spine arises in the majority of instances in the first five years, and that of the hip in the first six years. Disease of the knee has its chief incidence more evenly spread over the first ten years. This early incidence explains one great difficulty met with in dealing with these conditions in schools. The disease originates before school life starts, and has often progressed so as to produce a severe deformity before advice is sought. This unfortunate delay in the recognition of tuberculous disease is due to the peculiarly insidious nature of the initial symptoms. It is commonly believed that pain and deformity occur early in disease of the bones and joints. They do not. In nearly all cases the onset is marked only by some slight alteration of gait, by a limp, by peculiar attitudes of standing, by stiffness in ordinary movements. The child becomes disinclined to play, or plays awkwardly, or refuses to stoop to pick up toys. All these symptoms perhaps appear to the parents to be trivial; their significance is realised only by one who is constantly on the look-out for tuberculous disease in childhood. And the actual recognition of the disease depends upon the accurate application of the tests for muscular rigidity applicable to the region indicated. Yet unfortunately it is to treatment in this early stage that we must look for eventual good results. In spinal caries deformity once allowed to occur is practically incapable of correction; in hip disease the supervention of an abscess before treatment has commenced is of most serious import; in knee disease at this early stage there is often a local tuberculous focus in the bone, capable of ready removal, but which, left to itself, extends into the joint and may also cause extensive necrosis of the bone.

With the tendency to admit children to school early, at any rate in towns, and with careful inspection of infant schools, it is to be hoped that the early diagnosis and treatment of tuberculous disease of the bones and joints will improve.

It would be out of place here for me to dwell further upon the actual methods of early diagnosis, but considering that these diseases are responsible for the crippling of very large numbers of children, the great importance of a thorough

8

knowledge of their diagnosis by the school inspector is evident.

The prognosis of these diseases is difficult to ascertain with accuracy on account of their chronic nature. Probably the real death-rate from spinal caries in children is about 30 per cent., that from tuberculous disease of the hip rather lower, and from disease of the knee joint much lower. Death usually occurs from secondary pyogenic infection of an abscess or from phthisis, or general tuberculosis. A more important matter from the point of view of the community is the prognosis as regards deformity. At present it may be said that nearly all cases of spinal caries result in a more or less severe deformity. Indeed the alternative name angular curvature shows in itself that to most the idea of a deformity is an essential part of the disease. This should not be so. Spinal caries should be diagnosed before any deformity exists and by proper treatment should be cured with little or no deformity remaining. And the treatment required is fixation in the recumbent position, continued until all evidence of active disease has disappeared. Recumbency alone is useless, fixation alone is as bad, and proper treatment necessitates secure fixation upon a splint or frame with the spine in the hyper-extended position. Thus only can good eventual results be attained. I do not propose to enter more fully into the details of diagnosis and treatment of spinal caries, but the necessity for early diagnosis and for treatment by prolonged recumbency upon a frame have an important bearing upon the education of those children.

In tuberculous disease of the hip the requirements are the same, but as the early diagnosis is easier and as special hospitals for hip disease in which long periods of recumbency can be kept up, have been established, the results of treatment of hip diseases are rather better than are those of spinal caries.

In disease of the knee joint fixation and rest can be secured upon a Thomas's knee splint, so that absolute recumbency is not necessary, but the treatment has to be just as prolonged.

As to the length of treatment required in these cases, the average will probably be twelve months, and in individual

9

cases several years may be necessary. One other point of prognosis requires to be mentioned, the frequence of recurrence of the disease. Dr. Gee used to say that phthisis is often arrested, seldom cured, and this dictum applies also to tuberculous disease of the bones and joints. Over and over again I see cases of arrested spinal caries or hip disease, in which a slight accident has brought on a recrudescence, after the disease has been quiet for several years.

Three points then concerning tuberculous bone disease have a bearing upon the educational methods to be employed —the early onset of the disease, the prolonged rest required, and the liability to recurrence. In addition the failure of our present methods of treatment result in the occurrence of a severe deformity in a large proportion of the children treated by the methods in vogue in our hospitals. I have alluded to this more fully in the report of the Medical Officer (Education) of the London County Council for 1907, and need not enlarge upon it here. It is probably a matter of common observation to you that these deformities are the usual result of tuberculous bone disease.

So much for this the commonest cause of crippling. The second group of children to whom I shall allude are those with all sorts of deformities, congenital and acquired, unaccompanied as a rule by any active disease necessitating prolonged rest—a very miscellaneous group. Here I include the results of infantile and spastic paralysis, and of the less common varieties of paralysis; severe rickets and all sorts of congenital and acquired deformities. These children, much as they differ physically, have much in common in their educational requirements. In the first place many of them are unfit on account of lameness to get to and from school and to mix with healthy children in their work and in their play. Some special educational provision is necessary for them. In the second place medical supervision is necessary in order that the greatest possible improvement of their physical disability may be brought about. My work in London has shown me how much is necessary and how much may be done in this respect. Deformities are constantly to be found which are capable of correction, but which have been neglected. The commonest examples perhaps of this are the severe deformities of rickets. In the present days of surgery no rickety deformity of the legs should be left without surgical treatment. The parents do not know that correction is possible, or they are careless, or it is too much trouble, or they do not believe in operation. It is, then, our duty to overcome these difficulties by perᵤasion, argument, and gentle force if necessary. So with the cases of infantile paralysis and other conditions capable of improvement. We must secure the greatest possible amelioration. It is the parents' duty to have these things done, but we must help them by advice, and if they are obdurate, must help the children in spite of them. When neglect to secure treatment is evidently affecting the child's health, physique or ultimate prospects, the Children's Act gives considerable power of compulsion. Such compulsion is not to be lightly used, and we should avail ourselves of it only in extreme cases, but the mere threat of its use has had a most salutary effect upon the neglectful parent.

There remains a third educational requirement of all these crippled children. They will in after-life have to compete with the healthy and well-formed, and will have to earn their livelihood in some other way. Technical education is even more necessary for them than for healthy children. For this reason we keep these children in school until they are 16, and for this reason we have recently started trade classes for them in London.

I shall only allude very briefly to the phthisical children. A heated controversy still rages around the frequency of phthisis in children. In one camp are those who diagnose the disease on very slight physical signs and who believe 15 to 30 per cent. of the children in our elementary schools to suffer from phthisis. In the opposite camp are those who require very definite signs for diagnosis and who find the disease in less than $\frac{1}{2}$ per cent. of the children. The pathological evidence is undoubtedly in favour of the second view; for the discovery of chronic pulmonary tuberculosis, either active, or healed, in children in the *post-mortem* room is rare. The question is, however, from the school point of view, not of first-rate importance, for the holders of the second opinion will acknowledge that these alleged phthisical children are delicate, require special care, and perhaps are specially liable to

11

the disease. So that we have to deal with children who are definitely consumptive, few in number, and with children who are delicate and possibly consumptive, very much more numerous.

With regard to the first group, whilst the disease is active the children should not be in school at all, they should be in sanatoria, on this point there will be no difference of opinion. Children with chronic pulmonary tuberculosis in a cured or quiet stage, and delicate, possible phthisical, children are able in many cases to attend ordinary elementary schools. But if they can be treated as physically defective and given special provision in an open-air school their chances of ultimately becoming strong and healthy will be greatly improved.

The next group of children with such chronic illnesses as heart disease, recurrent chorea, asthma, etc., are unable to attend elementary schools, or if they attend are so irregular that they cannot keep pace with the other children. They require special provision for several reasons.

In the first place, the actual physical strain of school may make them break down, this applies particularly to children with severe heart lesions. In the second place, the school routine may cause a recrudescence of their disease, as in the case of chorea. Finally, their frequent absences through illness necessitates special individual teaching if progress is to be made.

The last class consists of children who are physically defective and present some other abnormality. The most important group here is that of the children who are both physically and mentally defective. A very considerable proportion of the children suffering from cerebral, *i.e.*, spastic paralysis, from diplegia, paraplegia, and hemiplegia must be included here. These children present a very difficult social problem. A small proportion can be enabled to earn their living, many of them as soon as their parents cease to support them must drift into the infirmaries and workhouses.

It is perhaps doubtful if children suffering from malnutrition only are properly certifiable as physically defective. It is certain, however, that in addition to a great improvement to their health, they also make better educational progress in special schools conducted on open-air lines.

12

I have now detailed briefly the children who are, in my opinion, physically defective within the meaning of the Act of 1899. The table gives you the proportional importance of the different classes in London, except that the number of cases of phthisis and of children suffering from malnutrition is too low, for the London special schools do not pretend to take in these two classes of children.

LONDON PHYSICALLY DEFECTIVE CHILDREN.

I. Tuberculous Disease—

Spine	323
Hip	376
Knee	137
Various	27

II. Infantile Paralysis 252

III. Spastic Paralysis (Hemiplegia, Paraplegia, Diplegia) 131

IV. Progressive Paralysis 15

V. Various Deformities (including Amputations) 335

VI. Heart Disease 268

VII. Various Chronic Diseases (including Chorea 41, and Phthisis 18) 142

VIII. Various Slight Defects (delicate and nervous children) 135

2,141

Let us now consider what accommodation has been, or should be provided for these children. In the first place, it will be evident from what I have already said, that for the proper treatment of tuberculous bone and joint disease resident institutions, which are both hospitals and schools, are necessary. Their primary importance is, however, as hospitals, and the school work must be subordinated to the surgical treatment. They must provide accommodation for children of all ages, even for infants, and must be prepared to keep the children in until they are well, even if several years' treatment

13

are necessary. They require an expert medical staff, and should best be placed in the country and be conducted upon open-air lines. A practically ideal instance of a hospital organised on these lines is that started by Sir William Treloar at Alton, and in this teaching is also provided. The Alexandra Hospital for Hip Disease only falls below the ideal in one respect, that it is situated in London. Other similar institutions exist, but the provision for these children is not nearly adequate. When the hospital system of this country is properly organised all cases of tuberculous bone and joint diseases requiring hospital treatment will be collected into special institutions of this nature instead of remaining scattered throughout the general hospitals and infirmaries where they get only very inefficient treatment, and usually no education at all.

There is another variety of hospital school in existence which serves a very useful purpose. The treatment of many conditions in children necessitates a very prolonged stay in hospital, and it is not advisable that their education should be at a standstill for all this time. In the Royal National Orthopœdic Hospital in London a school has now been carried on for several years, and I can vouch from personal experience for the fact that great benefit is derived from the work and that the teaching and hospital work need not clash or interfere with each other in any way.

A third variety of resident school is evidently required for the phthisical children, so that sanatorium treatment can be combined with such educational work as the children are fit for.

A fourth variety of resident school is in operation in Manchester. It is practically a combination of convalescent home and school. To it children are, I believe, chiefly drafted from the Pendlebury Hospital for prolonged convalescent treatment. There is very little doubt, I think, that our children's convalescent homes fail signally in the complete absence of any sort of teaching that prevails in most of them. They also in many cases fail to secure a permanent improvement in the health of the children because they take them for too short a period. A re-organisation of most of them upon the lines of the Manchester school would undoubtedly improve their

14

efficiency. The best name to give to this type of school is the " country recovery school."

The non-resident schools for physically defective children were originally instituted in London by charity, and subsequently taken over by the Education Authority; their organisation has been copied in many other localities, but it undoubtedly leaves much to be desired. The schools are scattered over London so that each collects from 60 to 120 children from an area extending perhaps two miles from the school. Some of the children walk; most are collected in ambulances. The school hours are 10 to 12 and 1.30 to 3, but as the ambulances have to do double journeys, some of the children arrive at the school at 9.30, and some do not leave until 3.30, so that each child gets about four hours' instruction in the day. At 12 a dinner is served, for which each child pays twopence. This meal is arranged by a Dinners Committee, which is prepared to grant dinners free or at half-price in cases of poverty. During the last year the amount received in payments has completely covered the cost of the food. The cooking and serving is undertaken at the expense of the London County Council. After the dinner the children play under the supervision of the school nurse and her helpers. The children are seen as nearly as possible at intervals of six months by myself or one of the other medical officers, and if any advice as regards medical treatment, food, etc., is given this is passed on by the school nurse or by one of the managers to the parents. Much of the results upon the health of these children naturally depends upon the voluntary assistance given by the nurse, headmistress, school managers, and representatives of such charitable societies as the Invalid Children's Aid Association and Ragged School Union. These really constitute themselves an informal but highly efficient Care Committee. The principal point in which these schools fail is that, owing to the lack of suitable hospital accommodation, many children remain at these schools attending the general hospitals as out-patients, when they ought to be in-patients of such a country hospital school as I have already suggested. Many also I see going downhill owing to their home surroundings, when I know that a stay in a country recovery school would

15

do them permanent benefit. There is another defect—although perhaps here I am craving for an impossible ideal—the school buildings are good, but are often provided with insufficient ground space. I think that these schools should have been organised from the first on the lines of open-air schools with plenty of fresh air, out-of-door classes, and with longer hours, interrupted by two hours' complete rest in the middle of the day.

Of the next class of school, the non-resident open-air school, I will say little. The organisation of these schools has been so much discussed lately that it is no doubt familiar to you all. The principles adopted are the open-air classes, long day with mid-day rest, three meals in school, and school bathing. These schools have been shown to be of the utmost benefit to the delicate and nervous children, to many of the chronic invalids and to those suffering from malnutrition.

Finally, there are trade schools for these children. Two classes of such schools have been organised—resident schools and day schools. I have already alluded to the necessity for giving an efficient technical training to these crippled and invalid children. All our London schools have After-Care Committees designed to watch the children when they leave, and to endeavour to place them in suitable occupations, either by apprenticeship or otherwise. But this is insufficient; apprenticeship is expensive, and by a proper technical training its period can be shortened; moreover, the earlier manual instruction is carried out the more easily is dexterity attained. For this reason technical training is essential in the senior classes in schools for crippled children. In London two special trade schools for crippled girls have been started and manual centres for boys. Even in London, however, the organisation of these non-resident schools is very difficult owing to the very large area from which the children have to be collected. In smaller towns and country districts the organisation of such schools would undoubtedly be impossible. Resident schools are more easily organised and more efficient; those at present established are all charitable institutions. Wright's Lane Home for boys, the Heritage School of Arts and Crafts at Chailey, and the College for older boys at Alton are excellent examples of institutions of this sort.

INSTITUTIONS FOR PHYSICALLY DEFECTIVE CHILDREN.

1. Resident Hospital Schools.
2. Resident Sanatorium Schools.
3. Country Recovery Schools.
4. Non-resident Invalid Day Schools.
5. Non-resident Open-air Schools.
6. Resident Trade Schools.
7. Non-resident Trade Schools.

I have now enumerated the various defects and diseases occurring in children, which are usually considered to be sufficient to enable us to certify them as physically defective under the Act of 1899. I have briefly described to you what I believe to be their requirements as regards education and medical treatment, and I have detailed the varieties of schools which have been provided for them. I am afraid that the obvious criticism with which you will go away is this, that all this elaboration is possible and useful in an enormous city such as London, but is out of the question in the smaller towns or country districts in which no doubt some of you work. Let me consider this point. Four of these classes of schools are resident schools. These are possible and indeed necessary in every sort of district. Two, the hospital school for the tuberculous children and the sanatorium school, are essentials in the proper re-organisation of our hospital system. If we had a central health department responsible for the organisation of our hospitals and infirmaries, I venture to predict that the first provision for children that it would make would be the establishment of a sufficiency of these two types of hospital. The country recovery school is simply a re-organised and re-constituted convalescent home. There remains only, then, the resident trade school to originate.

The non-resident cripple school is a school for large towns; it is not economically possible in smaller areas. But it is not really necessary in them, for with the removal of the tuberculous children to resident schools there remain only the permanently crippled, who in small areas and with small schools can be accommodated as a rule in the ordinary schools.

Finally, there are the open-air schools : in small towns these should be comparatively inexpensive institutions; they are suitable to a class of children that are always numerous, so that it is possible to organise them even in small towns. In strictly country districts they should be unnecessary.

There are very many questions relating to the physically defective children to which I have been unable to allude in the time at my disposal. I must, however, briefly refer to one further point—the economic question. The expenditure of money upon the education of these crippled and invalid children is constantly criticised upon this point. It is said that they are of no value to the community, and that by helping and educating them we are enabling them to survive and to perpetuate their defects in their children. This criticism is based upon two fallacies. In the first place the majority of these children do survive whether we help them or not, by educating them we are at least helping them to support themselves to save them from being a mere burden upon the community in the workhouses and infirmaries. In the second place there is at present no proof that the children of these physically defectives are any more liable to the diseases and deformities of their parents than are the children of the healthy. With comparatively few exceptions all their defects are acquired, and in the present state of our knowledge the inheritance of acquired defects is to be denied as not proved and improbable. What is much more probable is that the crippled father, being insufficiently educated in a trade, is able to earn but poor wages, so that he and his children are in want, perhaps under the circumstances of poverty his disease recrudesces, and his children are infected. Here the lack of training will itself have brought about the evil. I am certain that the proper training of these children is in the interest of the community and should be undertaken.

II.

DISEASE AND DEFORMITY OF THE SPINE.

The diseases from which the children in the London Invalid Schools suffer may be classified as follows :—

I. Tuberculous Diseases—

    (a) Of the Spine.

    (b) Of the Hip Joint.

    (c) Of the Knee Joint.

    (d) Of other Bones and Joints.

    (e) Of the Lungs.

    (f) Of the Glands.

II. Paralysis—

    (a) Infantile Paralysis

    (b) Spastic Paralysis.

    (c) Progressive Paralysis.

III. Various Deformities (including those which are congenital, those due to rickets, and many others).

IV. Heart Disease.

V. Various Chronic Illnesses of which Chorea is the most important.

VI. A few children with Defective Sight, Hearing, etc., and Delicate, Nervous and Backward Children, many of them admitted temporarily for observation.

The most important of all these are the tuberculous diseases. These together account for just about half the total number of crippled children in the London schools.

Tuberculous Disease.

Tuberculous diseases are caused by a very minute organism, the tubercle bacillus, which is present in the diseased tissues and in the discharges from them. It is thus present in the expectoration of consumptive persons and in the matter from tuberculous wounds. If consumptives are allowed to spit upon the ground or upon the floor, these tubercle bacilli may live in the dust, after drying has taken place, even for a period of many months. So that the dust-laden air of a house in which consumptive people live is often continually infectious to others. The same must be said of a tuberculous wound; the matter from it, especially after drying, is infectious. On account of these facts consumptive children, if they cough and spit, and children with discharging tuberculous wounds, have to be excluded from school. These are undoubtedly a danger to their healthy school-fellows.

Tuberculous disease also occurs in cattle, and in cows very often affects the udder; as a result tubercle bacilli in the living virulent condition are frequently to be found in milk. Recent investigations have shown quite clearly that the tuberculous disease of cattle is a slightly different disease from that of man, and that the bacilli which cause these two diseases are not identical. But it is also now clear that it is possible for men to become infected with that form of the disease which occurs in cattle, and evidently infected milk is a possible prolific source of such infection. Fortunately, this method of infection is much less common than would be expected. Men and children are generally infected from a human source. Over and over again we see a consumptive father or mother infecting the rest of the family one after the other. But we must remember the possibility of infection with tuberculosis from milk, and of course this is much more likely to occur in children than in adults.

In adults tuberculous disease shows itself most often in the lungs, as consumption. In children it also occurs in the lungs, but it is then very often an acute and rapidly fatal disease. As a chronic disease it is more common in children as an affection of the spine, bones, joints, and lymphatic glands. Slight cases of tuberculous disease of the lungs in children are extremely difficult for even the most expert physician to diagnose. Hence we find very divergent statements as to the prevalence of this form of disease in school children. Whilst some school doctors find it extremely common, others consider it so rare as hardly to exist at all. Really both find the same class of pale, thin, delicate children, often with large tonsils, enlarged glands in the neck, and perhaps some doubtful indication of disease in the lungs. Whether these children actually have or have not got consumption, seems a comparatively minor point. We have found out that if they are put to live a hygienic life in an open-air school, as a rule they steadily improve. If they have consumption, they fight it, and are cured; if they have not, their physique is so much improved that they are no longer liable to fall a ready prey to the infection. Our duty seems clear; we should extend our system of open-air schools so that all these delicate, possibly consumptive children, can be taken in hand and brought up to the normal standard of health.

Of the more evident cases of tuberculous disease of the lungs in children it is hardly necessary for me to speak. These children are very properly excluded from school, either because they are too ill to attend, or because they are infectious to others.

The most important crippling tuberculous diseases in children are diseases of the spine, hip joint, knee joint, and other bones and joints. I propose to take these in order, at the same time briefly considering the other deformities of the spine, hip, knee, etc., which are common in school children.

DEFORMITY OF THE SPINE.

The spine forms the main central support of the trunk. It lies close under the skin in the middle line of the back. It consists of a number of small bones (vertebræ) jointed firmly together, but allowing a small amount of movement between each pair. Each vertebra consists of a main solid mass lying in front (the body), and behind this an arch, forming a ring when seen from above, behind this arch ends in a point (the spinous process). This series of arches form a canal in which lies the spinal cord, a part of the central nervous system. The

21

bodies of the vertebræ are joined to each other by discs of elastic gristly material, which allow a little movement. The movement between any two vertebræ is small, but that of the whole spine is considerable, consisting of the sum of all these smaller movements. The movements are carried out by masses of muscle lying upon either side of the spine.

The healthy spine is concave backward in the neck and loin, convex backward between the shoulders. This last curve is the only one that is present in the baby; the others appear as soon as the child assumes an upright position. The neck and loin are the most movable parts of the spine; the intermediate part to which the ribs are fixed allowing comparatively little movement.

There are many defects of the spine which are not due to tuberculous disease; in which, in fact, there is no actual disease present at all—only deformity. It is important that you should have these clearly separated in your minds from instances of tuberculous disease. The most frequent of such spinal deformities in children are : —

Kyphosis, or round back, an increase in the natural curve in the region of the spine lying between the shoulders. The causes of this deformity are general muscular weakness and bad habits of standing and sitting. Short sight, uncorrected by glasses, deafness, and the presence of adenoids, are all contributory causes. Round shoulders are usually accompanied by a flat chest and prominent stomach. The treatment after the correction of any defect of sight, etc., is by remedial exercises. Spinal jackets are not required, and are, in fact, detrimental.

Lordosis, or hollow back, an increase in the natural curvature of the region of the spine in the loins. This deformity is usually secondary—that is to say, it is the result of some deformity elsewhere. Most often it is the result of the correction of a kyphosis by muscular effort, the spine becoming upright as the result of the correction of one curve by a second. Very often, however, lordosis is the result of deformity of the hip joint as, for example, in congenital dislocation. Lordosis itself practically never requires to be treated.

Scoliosis, or lateral curvature of the spine. In about one quarter of all people the spine is not quite straight, but deviates a little to one side. Very occasionally this deviation becomes so great as to be noticeable; the condition is then called scoliosis. Scoliosis is not always the same deformity; many varieties occur, but cases as a rule fall into one or other of the two classes. In the first class the spine is simply tilted a little to one side so that the opposite hip becomes prominent and the shoulder of the same side high. In the second variety there is a double curve first to one side and then to the other, the spine becoming S-shaped. In this latter variety, in addition to the prominent hip and high shoulder, the ribs usually project behind to form a hump upon one side, and the breast may form a similar projection upon the other. The first of these varieties is usually of little importance, readily cured by exercises and does not lead to severe deformity. The second is very important, requires expert treatment by massage and exercises with often prolonged recumbency and in some few cases the provision of a spinal support of some sort.

TUBERCULOUS DISEASE OF THE SPINE (SPINAL CARIES).

The tubercle bacillus when it affects the spine lodges in the front of the body of the vertebra and there causes inflammation. The bone is gradually softened and destroyed, being replaced by a soft cheesy material. This may occur in one bone or in several adjacent bones.

The first symptoms to which this gives rise are the same as those which occur from inflammation anywhere. They are pain and stiffness. The pain may not be in the back at all; it is often felt in the chest, stomach, or down the arms or legs. The stiffness is caused by a tight contraction of the muscles around, which endeavour thus to hold the spine stiff, so that movements which would be painful may be avoided. This rigidity of the spine may cause peculiar habits and attitudes which ought to lead to a careful examination of the child's back by a surgeon, without waiting for the deformity which will subsequently arise. Such a child sits still instead of playing, will not stoop to pick up toys, or when made to do so stoops carefully with hand on knee. He will not jump and runs stiffly; he may further have a tendency to stand always with one hand resting upon a piece of furniture, or failing this upon his knee. When the disease is in the neck the pain may be felt in the head (headache), and the only peculiar attitude may be a raising of the shoulders so that they are very square, and a tilting of the chin either forward or forward and to one side. If the disease is lower down the pain is felt in the chest or pit of the stomach, and in addition to the squaring of the shoulders there may be a tilt of the spine forward or to one side. Any of those peculiar attitudes and any disinclination to run, jump, and play naturally, coming on in a previously healthy child ought to lead to an immediate careful examination of the child's spine. If spinal caries is present it is curable at this stage without any considerable deformity resulting.

The next stage in the disease is the giving way of the softened bone in the front of the vertebræ so that these bones fall together and the spine, instead of its gradual curve, now makes a sharp angle which projects backward. Because this deformity is the almost invariable result of this disease as it is at present treated, spinal caries is often called angular curvature of the spine. The resulting curve is that seen in the large majority of those whom we call hump backs.

The softened bone may break down further and form an abscess which then extends away from the spine in various directions. The abscess may come to the surface in the neck, in the back, in the loin, in the groin, or even well down in the thigh. It may have extended a considerable distance from the spine before it reaches the surface. Such an abscess always requires careful medical treatment, but does not always require immediate operation. Many such abscesses disappear again if the child can be put completely at rest upon its back.

Occasionally such an abscess forms inside the canal in which the spinal cord lies. This cord may then be pressed upon, and as a result the legs become paralysed. This paralysis is first shown by the child dragging his feet or shuffling as he walks; he becomes unsteady and eventually may be unable to walk at all. Frequently there is also incontinence of urine.

24

The onset of any such symptoms of paralysis of course necessitates immediate medical treatment, the principal item of such treatment being again complete rest.

The treatment of spinal caries during the active stages is by securing absolute rest in the recumbent position with the spine as immobile as possible. This is best secured in a country hospital where the child is kept fixed upon a frame, is well fed and carefully nursed. Such treatment may have to last from six months to three years, or even longer. Unfortunately there is not sufficient hospital accommodation to secure this ideal treatment for all the poor children in London who suffer from spinal caries. Many of them have to be treated at the hospitals as out-patients. They are then kept lying on a double Thomas's splint or in a Phelps's box. Children who are lying down in this apparatus are, where possible, allowed into school because their surroundings are usually better in school than at home. It is perhaps hardly necessary to say that it is essential that they should be kept lying continuously in the splint or box. It is useless for them to lie down in the box whilst at school if they are allowed up and about immediately they get home.

Most of the children in invalid schools are, however, in the cured or quiet stage of spinal caries. It is the practice of most surgeons to provide some sort of spinal support at this stage. This may take the form of a poroplastic (felt) jacket, of plaster of paris, or of a metal support; in many cases, however, a support is not provided and is, in fact, not necessary. The jackets which many of these children are found to be wearing at school are useless, and occasionally they are even harmful. The requirements of a good jacket are that it should be rigid and that it should support the spine for a considerable distance above and below the seat of the disease. All jackets should fit firmly on the hips, as they must take their support from this point, and whenever the disease is at the level of the shoulder blades or higher the jacket ought to have a head support added to it. A further requirement is that the jacket should be at least as straight as the child in his best, most erect, position. An old jacket is not infrequently found to be keeping a child in an unnecessarily bent attitude.

Spinal caries, like all tuberculous diseases, is very liable to recur. It is therefore necessary for you to know what symptoms should lead you to suspect that the disease is again active and to send the child immediately to see his doctor. These symptoms are :—

(1) General ill-health, specially loss of weight, and a tendency to tire after very slight muscular or mental exertion. It is a very good rule to consider any child with spinal caries to be doing well so long as he is fat, to look upon him with suspicion and keep him under careful observation so long as he remains thin.

(2) Stiffness resulting from spasm of some of the spinal muscles, and giving rise to special attitudes and movements; and

(3) Pain.

The particular attitudes and the regions to which the pain is referred have been already described. The recurrence of these attitudes in a child who was previously doing well is most suggestive of renewed disease. In particular the use of a support, such as the chairs or desks in standing, or the resting of the chin upon the hand, is important, as is also the development of a lateral tilt of the whole spine, or of the neck (wry neck). Children with active disease in the region of the root of the neck often grunt loudly in breathing, and children with disease lower down often keep one thigh bent a little, so that they lean forward to that side in walking. All these symptoms should indicate immediate return to medical supervision, and if the children are not temporarily removed from school they should be kept recumbent whilst such symptoms persist.

Many children who suffer from spinal caries die; altogether about 30 to 40 per cent. of them die before they grow up. The remainder, however, are likely to live to a fair age, and should, if properly educated and given a suitable trade, be self-supporting. Paralysis and abscess, although they make the child's chance worse, do not destroy it. Paralysis, if properly treated, will nearly always completely recover.

The important points to be emphasised under disease and deformity of the spine are : —

(1) The difference between tuberculous disease and deformities which do not result from this disease.

(2) The symptoms of activity of spinal disease.

(3) That whilst the disease is active the child should be recumbent, and should, if possible, be got away to a country hospital.

(4) The symptoms of commencing paralysis.

III.

DISEASE AND DEFORMITY OF THE HIP JOINT.

Anatomy.—The hip joint is a ball and socket joint. The socket is a very deep one, and the joint is strengthened by very strong ligaments and by powerful muscles which surround it. Any displacement or dislocation of the joint is therefore uncommon. The movements are very free. They are :—

Flexion, or bending forward, which can be carried out up to the point at which the thigh touches the front of the abdomen.

Extension, or bending backward, to slightly beyond the point at which the limb makes a straight line with the trunk.

Abduction away from the opposite leg.

Adduction across the opposite leg.

Rotation in and out—that is, turning the foot in or out with the leg straight.

Circumduction, a combination of all these movements.

The nerves which supply the hip joint are branches of those which extend down to and supply the knee joint and the parts around it. Consequently pain in hip joint disease is often felt as if it were due to something at the end of those nerves that is in the region of the knee.

TUBERCULOUS DISEASE OF THE HIP JOINT.

This disease is the same in nature as spinal caries. It may originate in the bone or in the smooth membrane which lines the joint (synovial membrane). In a severe case the bone

28

practically always becomes diseased. It is then liable to soften and become to some extent destroyed as occurs in the spine.

The earliest symptoms of disease of the hip joint in children are : (1) A slight limp, the weak leg taking a shorter step and thus being saved at the expense of a longer step upon the sound limb; (2) pain, which is often, in fact usually, referred to the knee; and (3) rigidity of the muscles, causing the limb to be held in some fixed attitude.

In the very earliest stage as a rule there is only pain in the knee after walking, and a very slight limp. At this stage careful examination will often reveal clear evidence of disease to the doctor, and these symptoms in a child should always lead to careful examination. Very often it is only possible to make certain of the presence or absence of tuberculous disease by keeping the child at rest and examining at intervals for some weeks.

In the next stage the hip is held in a fixed position by the contraction of some of the muscles. The hip first becomes flexed, abducted away from the side, and the foot turned out, a very characteristic walk being thus produced. The pain is much more severe, specially if any attempt is made to move the joint, and the child often cries out with pain in the night whilst asleep. The abduction of the limb away from the side causes tilting of the spine and makes the affected leg appear longer than the healthy one.

This stage is usually temporary; sooner or later the hip becomes adducted towards the other leg and the foot may be turned in. The bone in the neighbourhood of the joint may become destroyed so that the limb actually becomes shorter than the healthy one. In addition, however, to this actual shortening, which is seldom more than an inch or an inch and a half in amount, the limb appears much shorter on account of the adduction. If the child is made to lie straight the adducted leg would lie across the sound one, in order to make the legs parallel the lower part of the spine is tilted, the hip bone (pelvis) being tilted up on the diseased side; the diseased leg thus appears much shorter than it really is. The deformity in hip joint disease is usually divided into three stages : in the first there is abduction, the limb being apparently lengthened; in the second there is adduction, the limb being apparently shortened; in the third there is actual destruction of bone, so that the limb is really shortened. In this third stage part of the shortness of the limb is *real*, due to destruction of bone; part is *apparent*, due to the faulty position. The importance of this fact lies in the possibility of treatment; shortening which is due to destruction of bone cannot be made good, shortening which is due to a bad position can be improved in the majority of cases by surgical treatment. In a large proportion (60 per cent.) of cases in the third stage one or more abscesses occur.

The proper treatment of tuberculous disease of the hip is by rest in bed or on a frame until the disease is cured; with this rest the deformity can generally be corrected by hanging a weight extension on to the limb. The treatment, as in the case of spinal caries, is best carried out in bed in a country hospital, and from six months to three years or more will be required. Owing, however, to the lack of sufficient hospital accommodation many of the children with hip disease have to be treated as out-patients at the hospitals. Some of these are kept lying down on frames, many are allowed to get about in a Thomas's hip splint.

The best result obtained in the treatment of tuberculous disease of the hip joint is a complete return to the natural condition with perfect movement. This is very rare indeed. The next best result is bony ankylosis—*i.e.*, the complete obliteration of the joint by bone, with a good position. In this result, although all movement is necessarily lost, a good firm leg with no possibility of the development of subsequent deformity, results. The worst result is ankylosis in a bad position, or union of the bones by fibrous tissue allowing a little movement. These are not nearly as good as firm bony union; a straight, stiff hip is much more useful for walking than a weak or deformed movable joint.

Operations have to be performed occasionally for abscess connected with hip joint disease. The only other operation done is that called excision. In this an attempt is made to cure the disease rapidly by removing the head of the thigh bone. Although it often hastens the cure, it does not always do so, and it nearly always leaves a weak joint so that the child walks very badly, dropping over greatly at each step upon the weak leg. It is therefore, as a rule, a bad operation, and it is much better to be patient and adopt the longer method of treatment.

The deformity resulting from hip joint disease is usually that described previously as the third stage, with flexion adduction and shortening which is partly real, due to destruction of bone, partly apparent, due to mal-position. When the disease is soundly cured the apparent shortening can generally be lessened or got rid of entirely by the operation of dividing the bone near the hip joint and bringing the two legs parallel (osteotomy).

As in spinal caries, hip disease is liable to take on renewed activity when it has long been apparently cured. The symptoms of such recurrence will be : (1) Pain in the hip or knee, and specially pain at night during sleep; (2) a diminution in the movements of the hip; (3) an increased limp due either to increased pain or to an increase in the deformity; (4) the development of an abscess.

Our duties in school, then, to children with disease of the hip joint are : (1) To watch those who are being treated as out-patients and see that they are carrying out the treatment properly; (2) to watch for recurrence of active disease or increase of deformity; and (3) to refer all those with bad persistent deformity for an opinion as to the possibility of improvement by operation.

The Thomas's hip joint splint is named after H. O. Thomas, a Liverpool surgeon. It consists of a central bar reaching down the back from the level of the arm-pits to the ankle with rings of a softer metal around the body, the thigh and the leg. It should be straight except for one curve opposite the buttock, and the child lying in it should lie flat on the couch. It should always be used with an iron patten on the opposite foot and with crutches. A child fixed in a Thomas's hip splint must always stand or lie down, and never sit. Sitting in this splint has the effect of bending it, so that it no longer lies flat upon the couch. It will then be holding the hip fixed in a deformed position. Such bent splints are a frequent cause of bad results in the treatment of hip joint disease.

Congenital Dislocation of the Hip Joint.

This is a deformity of the hip present at birth in which the proper socket for the hip is not fully formed, and the upper end of the thigh bone is dislocated upwards and backwards. It is much more common in girls than in boys, and is often present on both sides. If one side is affected the limb is short and the child lunges to the side in walking; if both sides are affected a waddle is produced. There is usually no pain. In every case, if possible, an attempt should be made to secure surgical treatment by the method known as " Lorenz's bloodless method." There is a good prospect of improvement or of complete cure if the operation is done before the age of 7; it should preferably be done, however, at $2\frac{1}{2}$ to 3.

If the hip is not replaced by operation, the deformity as shown by the gait usually becomes a little worse as the child's weight increases. But the condition, although it thus disables, is not due to disease and never affects the health or threatens the child's life.

Septic Arthritis of the Hip.

In childhood there may occur an acute blood poisoning, due to those bacteria which produce abscesses and erysipelas, and this may affect the joints. During the acute stage the child is very ill and a fatal result is not unusual. If, however, recovery occurs a deformity will be left. When the hip is affected an abscess forms in the joint, the head of the thigh bone is destroyed, and, as a rule, the joint becomes dislocated. The deformity that results with the scar of an abscess make the condition resemble tuberculous disease. But it differs from tuberculous disease in that when recovery has once taken place and the wounds have healed there is not the same liability to a recurrence of the disease. In the majority of cases nothing can be done to improve the deformity.

Coxa Vara is a deformity due to bending of the neck of the thigh bone. It is most often due to an accident. It is not due to or accompanied by any disease, and so does not threaten the child's life. In some cases it is necessary to keep the child at rest for a very long time, even for one or two years, in order to prevent the deformity becoming severe. But the ultimate result is almost certain to be good. The child will grow up strong, and although he will be lame, he will be able to do a great deal and to earn his living.

Disease and Deformity of the Knee Joint.

Anatomy.—The knee joint is a hinge joint protected and covered in front by the patella or knee cap. The movements which occur in it are extension until the thigh and leg are in a straight line, and flexion or bending until the back of the thigh and leg are almost in contact. In addition, when the knee is bent a small amount of twisting movement (rotation) can occur.

Tuberculous Disease of the Knee Joint.—The commonest disease of the knee joint in children, as in the case of the spine and hip, is tuberculosis. The disease most often commences in the ends of the bones, spreading later to the joint. In the bones it may commence as a single small patch or as a diffuse inflammation.

In the early stages there may be only a very slight limp, or it may be noticed that the knee is swollen before any limp or pain has appeared. Tuberculous disease of the knee is often remarkably free from pain. The only constant early sign is swelling; pain and stiffness are usually present also, but may be absent. Every case of persistent swelling of the knee joint in a child should be suspected of being tuberculous disease until its nature has been proved. In later stages deformity appears, the knee usually bends (flexion), and the leg becomes deviated outward (knock-knee), usually also the movements of the joint become less free or the joint may become quite stiff. As in the case of hip disease, an abscess not infrequently forms.

The treatment of tuberculous disease of the knee is by rest. In the more acute stages the child is kept in bed, the leg fixed upon a splint and a weight extension hung upon the foot. Later both rest and weight extension can be secured by the use of a Thomas's knee splint. Complete rest to the knee is required for at least six months and may be necessary for two or three years.

Operations are not infrequently done for tuberculous disease of the knee: (1) Abscesses, if they form, may have to be opened or else punctured; (2) in the early stage if the disease is confined to a small area in the bone this can be removed by operation and the disease thus cured with much greater rapidity; (3) some surgeons perform the operation of excision, *i.e.*, the removal of the ends of the bones and of the entire diseased joint. This is a very effectual operation in adults, but when performed in children it often leads to much subsequent deformity.

Tuberculous disease of the knee should not lead to deformity. In the cured condition the knee should be either straight and freely movable or straight and firmly fixed. Whenever a deformed knee has resulted from disease further treatment should be carried out. Nearly all the badly deformed knees found in school children as the result of tuberculous disease are the results of the operation of excision. The deformities found are bending (flexion), knock knee, bowing at the knee, and shortening of upwards of five or six inches. These, with the exception of the last, can all be corrected by the use of apparatus or by further operation. Where operation is required it is often better to postpone it until growth is almost or quite completed.

Thomas's knee splint consists essentially of a ring which surrounds the upper end of the thigh and upon which the child should sit comfortably, and of two side irons down the inner and outer sides of the limb. These end below, in the form of splint used in London, in a heavy ring which reaches the ground well beyond the foot. The limb is hung between the side irons and pulled upon by extension straps. An iron patten fixed upon the other boot makes this limb the same length as the splint. Crutches may be used, but are not essential. The weight of the body is thus carried direct from the ring round the thigh through the side irons to the ground, none of it being borne by the limb itself, so that it is possible to allow the child to walk about and yet to have the diseased knee entirely at rest.

In the Calliper knee splint, the lower ring is removed and

34

the side irons are turned at a right angle and fixed into a socket in the boot. With this splint the weight is carried directly down to the boot without passing through the limb.

These knee splints require careful supervision and adjustment; it is essential that they should always be long enough to prevent the foot reaching the ground. Children wearing them can stand, sit, or lie down, and can be allowed considerable activity.

Other Diseases of the Knee.—The same forms of blood poisoning already mentioned in speaking of the hip also affect the knee. They often lead to amputation through the thigh. When recovery takes place, however, without amputation, a stiff knee (ankylosis) results. In these cases the knee should be straight, if it is not, further surgical treatment, by apparatus or operation, must be sought.

Hæmophilia (bleeding), although it is a rare disease, when it occurs frequently affects the knees. It is almost confined to boys and tends to affect all the boys of a family. The symptoms are bleeding from the nose, mouth, etc., persistent bleeding from small cuts, bleeding under the skin producing painful bruises, and bleeding into the joints, most often into the knees and elbows. When the joints are affected they become swollen, hot, and painful. Rest is essential until the swelling has gone down. A certain amount of enlargement of the joint usually persists. Bleeding in these cases has to be stopped by firm pressure; in persistent cases the local application of chloride of calcium in a powder with pressure by a pad over it may succeed. There is always a risk of bleeding to death in children with hæmophilia, and medical assistance should be secured without delay if bleeding is not quickly controlled.

Congenital Syphilis inherited from parents is rare in school children. It most often affects the eyes so that many of the children are to be found in the blind schools. Swelling of both knees with painful swelling of the shins occasionally occurs.

Knock Knee and Bowing of the Knee are usually due to rickets and not to disease of the knee joint.

Tuberculous disease of the other bones and joints is much more rare than is that of the spine, hip, and knee. The principles on which treatment is carried out are always the same—that is to say, rest until the disease has ceased, the removal of small patches of disease in the bone, and the appropriate treatment of abscesses. I need not allude to those conditions in detail.

IV.

DISEASES OF THE NERVOUS SYSTEM.

The nervous system consists of two main parts: (1) Central, including the brain and spinal cord; (2) Peripheral, consisting of nerves which connect this central part with the muscles, the skin, and the organs of sense, such as the eyes, nose, ears, etc.

The *Central Nervous* system is composed of the brain, enclosed in the skull, and of the spinal cord continuous with the lower part of the brain, and lying in the canal formed in the spine by the arches of the vertebræ. It serves for the reception and recognition of all sensations of whatever sort (sight, hearing, touch, pain, heat, etc.); it also originates all movements.

The Peripheral Nerves are therefore of two chief kinds: (1) Those which carry sensations from the skin, eye, ear, etc., up to the brain; and (2) those which carry impulses (or directions) from the brain to the muscles, and originate movements. The first kind are called *sensory* nerves, the second are called *motor* nerves.

Every nerve consists of great numbers of very tiny fibres running side by side. Each one of these fibres carries a sensation from some particular spot to the brain, or else carries an impulse from the brain to a particular part of a particular muscle. Moreover, each of these fibres, when it enters the spinal cord, runs upwards in it, and ends in its own special place in the brain. Consequently, every spot in the brain has its own particular purpose or function, and we

37

are able to point to a special part of the brain as the centre for vision, or for hearing, or for the origination of movements of the hand, etc.

It is with the motor nerve fibres that we are chiefly concerned at present. These originate at a part of the surface of the brain which is called the motor area; those for the right leg, arm, and side generally originate on the left of the brain; those for the left side originate on the right side of the brain. Every one of these motor nerve fibres starts as a branch from a cell lying on the surface of the brain; it then runs as a continuous fibre through the brain to the spinal cord, where it crosses over and reaches the opposite side. In the spinal cord this fibre ends at a level which depends upon the part of the body for which it is destined—for example, those for the muscles of the arm end in the lower part of the neck, those for the legs end only when they reach the lowest part of the spinal cord. Each fibre ends by dividing into a large number of fine branches. Surrounded by these fine branches lies a second cell similar to that in the brain; from this second cell a second fibre originates, which leaves the spinal cord in the motor nerve, and runs down in it to the muscle; so that the impulse sent from the brain to the muscle, directing it to contract, is interrupted at a cell in the spinal cord on its way. It is as if a telegram had to be sent from a principal office, along one wire to a sub-office, and then from the sub-office along a second wire to the final destination.

This is the simplest possible description of the tract along which a motor nerve impulse passes: actually, the arrangement is often very much more complicated. There are, however, always these two sections or segments in the work; they are called the upper and lower motor segments.

The life and activity of each nerve fibre depends upon its attachment to the cell from which it originates, just as the use of a telegraph wire depends upon its attachment to the electric battery. If the cell dies or is injured, or if the nerve fibre is cut off from it, the use of the nerve fibre at once disappears, and the muscle fibre to which it runs becomes paralysed.

There are, then, two chief places in the central nervous system where paralysis can originate: (1) Disease of, or injury to, the cell in the brain or the nerve fibre starting from it—*i.e.*, the upper motor segment; (2) disease of, or injury to, the cell in the spinal cord or the nerve fibre starting from it—*i.e.*, the lower motor segment. These constitute the two great classes of paralysis.

I.—Disease or Injury of the Lower Motor Segment (Infantile Paralysis) (Anterior Poliomyelitis).

In Infantile Paralysis there is an acute disease, in the course of which the motor cells in certain parts of the spinal cord are injured. During the next six months to two years some of these cells and their fibres recover, but some die, and the muscle fibres which they supply are left paralysed. After this period no further muscle fibres will recover, but those which have recovered may become much stronger as the result of proper use. During this period of recovery the proper treatment is by massage and electrical stimulation. After this period such treatment is of much less use.

All muscles carry out some definite movement of a part of the body. As a rule each muscle or group of muscles has its opposing muscle or group, which carry out the opposite movement—*e.g.*, the muscles behind the thigh (hamstrings) flex the knee joint, those in front of the thigh extend the knee joint. These form two opposing groups.

When a group of muscles becomes paralysed there is a tendency for the opposing group to contract and to become permanently shorter; thus, if the extensors of the knee are paralysed, the flexors become contracted, and the knee becomes permanently flexed. In this way infantile paralysis may lead to much deformity, which is entirely due to contraction of certain muscles. Throughout the treatment of infantile paralysis one has to guard against this contraction of muscles. The children with infantile paralysis in school have generally passed the period of recovery. The degree of paralysis which they show is permanent, and can only be lessened by increasing the strength of the muscles which have recovered. The treatment of these children consists of :—

1. Correction of all deformities or contractions.

2. The application, when necessary, of such an apparatus or instrument as will (*a*) enable the limb to be used in its

natural way—*i.e.*, in the lower limb enable it to be used for walking; this enables muscles which have partly recovered to resume their natural work; (*b*) prevent any contraction coming on.

With regard to special regions : —

(1) Paralysis of the spinal muscles leads to very severe curvature of the spine, and necessitates the application of a support. Fortunately it is rare.

(2) Paralysis of the arm does not require the use of an instrument, but can often be improved by surgical treatment.

(3) Paralysis of the lower limb in the large majority of cases requires the application of some form of walking instrument. The exceptions are : (*a*) Very slight cases, children who can walk naturally without support; (*b*) very severe cases, where the limb is quite useless.

Whenever it is possible, by the application of an instrument, to bring a paralysed leg into use, the instrument ought to be obtained. But for these severe cases the instrument is expensive, and requires to be well made and well looked after; it is better amongst the poor to provide such expensive instruments only in cases where the parents are sufficiently careful and can be relied upon to look after them well, leaving other children to walk with crutches. When a leg is completely useless—*i.e.*, when it cannot be swung forward and backward—it is better to amputate it through the thigh.

The proper care and treatment of these badly paralysed limbs is one of the most difficult branches of surgery, and as a result the practice of different surgeons with regard to them differs very considerably. The principles which I have stated are those which I personally always adopt, and I consider that it is most important to provide whenever possible such an instrument as will enable the limb to be used as nearly as possible in the natural way, and specially such an instrument as will prevent contractions arising. Instruments are often very expensive, but it is sometimes possible to provide cheap but efficient forms which will serve the purpose, although because they are a little unsightly or inconvenient they would not satisfy the parents of well-to-do children.

Children with badly paralysed limbs may suffer severely from chilblains. To guard against these the leg should be kept very warmly clad and leather leggings reaching to the knee should be worn. When chilblains have once arisen they must be kept clean, fomented if inflamed, and then treated with a simple ointment—zinc oleate ointment is very effectual. Persistent chilblains on a badly paralysed leg form a good reason for advising amputation.

II.—DISEASE OR INJURY TO THE UPPER MOTOR SEGMENT (SPASTIC PARALYSIS).

The cell in the brain or its nerve fibre may be injured or destroyed by:—

(*a*) An acute illness which affects the brain cell and injures it, just as the acute illness in infantile paralysis injures the spinal cord cell.

(*b*) An injury to the surface of the brain, occurring at birth. (This, again, injures the cell.)

(*c*) Destruction of or pressure upon the nerve fibres in the spinal cord, as in the pressure which occurs occasionally in spinal caries.

In *Hemiplegia* the injury is to one side of the surface of the brain, and the opposite side of the body is paralysed. Usually the arm is most affected; the leg, trunk, and face being less severely paralysed.

In *Paraplegia* the top of the brain of both sides is affected, and the paralysis affects both legs.

In *Diplegia* both sides of the brain are extensively injured; both legs, arms, and sometimes the face also, are paralysed.

In these spastic paralyses, due to injury to the upper motor segment, the muscles are not lost and do not waste. They remain capable of carrying on their movements, but they are not kept properly under control. They may be found in one or other of two principal conditions:—

(*a*) Spastic Contraction—that is, the muscle contracts and remains contracted, but is not permanently shortened, so that

41

by steady pulling for a few minutes it can be made to give way. This contraction produces a deformity which differs from that produced by infantile paralysis in being thus corrected by steady pressure.

(b) Inco-ordination—that is, the muscle is capable of carrying on its work, but does so in an irregular, jerky, or shaky way, because it is not properly under control.

A further condition—*Athetosis*—sometimes occurs. In it there are constant movements of the limb, which are not capable of being controlled. This is most common in the arm in hemiplegia.

The treatment of spastic paralysis differs very greatly from that of infantile paralysis. It consists :—

1. In training the use of muscles, by putting them into regular action—*i.e.*, the chief treatment is in the way of education of the muscles.

2. In stretching constantly, and in some cases in the lengthening (by division of their tendons) of muscles which tend constantly to contract.

In spastic paralysis, it must be remembered that the defect is usually in the brain, and that, as a consequence, most of the children show some mental peculiarity. Nearly all are highly emotional, and many show varying degrees of mental defect. They have often a vacant expression, and may, if the face is affected, keep the mouth constantly hanging open with saliva dribbling from it. They present a difficult social problem, as many, specially those with paraplegia and diplegia, are quite incapable of being trained so as to be self-supporting. They are not, as a rule, sufficiently defective to require segregation in an asylum, so that many of them drift into the workhouses and infirmaries. It would perhaps be better and more economical to provide permanent homes for them from an early age, where they could do such work as they are able. It must not be thought, however, that all these children are useless; some of them are capable of learning and doing a great deal, and, in hemiplegia particularly, a skilled trade may be learnt.

Progressive Forms of Paralysis.

Infantile paralysis and spastic paralyses account for nearly all the paralysed school children. But there are other rare forms of paralyses, of which some tend to steadily progress as the child grows.

The most frequent of these is *Pseudo-Hypertrophic Paralysis*. This occurs in boys almost exclusively; it commences at about 7 or 8, with an unsteady gait. The calves are generally noticed to be unusually large; gradually the walking gets worse; in two or three years the boy loses the power of walking altogether; he gradually becomes bedridden, and usually dies before adult life is reached. The disease tends to run in families.

The other forms of progressive paralysis, such as Friedreich's Ataxia, and Peroneal Muscular Atrophy, are extremely rare.

V.

RICKETS.

Rickets is a disease of infancy usually limited to the fiist eighteen months of life. Amongst the poor it is so common that it is said that 80 to 90 per cent. of the children of this age attending a children's hospital suffer from this disease. In the large majority of cases, however, the evidences of active disease have disappeared before the end of the second year, and the child soon after outgrows the deformities which have remained.

The most important result of rickets is the production of deformities of the bones. These arise because the new bone formed in the process of growth is imperfect and soft, owing to an insufficiency of lime salts in it. The bones give way as the result of pressure, and the resulting deformity depends upon the way in which pressure is exerted. Thus, sitting with legs crossed may cause curvature of the tibiæ; standing may cause knock-knee or bow-leg, and sitting or standing may cause curvature of the spine.

As a rule the disease ceases, and the bones gradually grow straight. Sometimes, however, the disease does not cease, and sometimes the deformities have become so severe that they do not right themselves. It is those cases of " continued rickets," and of rickets with severe deformity, which come to the special schools.

Continued Rickets.—Rickets has a very marked effect upon the general growth, therefore all these children are below the normal in stature. They generally show some

44

rickety deformity such as knock-knee or bow-leg; in addition they have a peculiarly shaped head—high in front and long —and they show the evidences of active rickets. The latter are certain constitutional symptoms—pallor, listlessness, and profuse perspirations; also enlargement of the ends of the bones, best seen at the wrists. As long as this enlargement of the bones exists, the rickets must be considered to be active.

The proper treatment for these children is correct feeding. The simplest rules that can be given for their diet are to cut down all starchy foods to the least possible quantity, to forbid potato altogether, and to give plenty of meat, eggs, and milk. The only starchy foods which I allow are milk puddings and a little bread.

The prevention of deformity is best carried out by curing the rickets by proper feeding. The old-fashioned method of applying splints to prevent walking is now largely abandoned. In my opinion it seldom does good, and it may do harm, by making the muscles weaker and flabbier by preventing them from being used.

The correction of deformity is necessary in most children who have any considerable curvature of a bone left at the age of 6 or 7. This curvature may right itself, but it will seldom do so completely after this age. The operation of division of the bone (osteotomy), or of breaking the bone (osteoclasis) is so safe and so satisfactory that it should always be carried out in these cases.

Occasional cases of curvature of bones from a congenital defect, either local or general, and from other diseases such as congenital syphilis, must be distinguished from rickets; surgical correction of these curvatures may or may not be advisable.

AMPUTATIONS.

Children who have lost a leg should, as a rule, be provided with an artificial limb at some time during their school life. It is the custom of many surgeons to delay ordering the artificial limb until full growth is attained because of the expense entailed by alterations on account of growth. This, I consider, is wrong for several reasons. In the first place as soon as the child has his peg leg and is able to get about without crutches he is able to join in all sorts of games that he would otherwise miss, and these games have a distinct educational value. In the second place the fact that he can get about without crutches makes it much easier to get him work when he leaves school. And in the third place an artificial limb is often at first very uncomfortable; the child has various inducements in the shape of participation in games, etc., to make him anxious to discard his crutches, and in addition pressure can be brought to bear upon him in school. It is by no means uncommon to see an expensive artificial limb provided for an adult and never worn on account of discomfort. As to cost, a peg leg should cost from 30s. to £2, and should last two years or more; allowance for growth can be made by replacing the peg by a longer one. New pegs can be turned by any good carpenter at a trivial cost.

CLUB FEET.

Club feet may be congenital, *i.e.*, present at birth, or if acquired subsequently, are as a rule due to paralysis. They should never be left uncorrected, as correction by surgical means is easy and safe during childhood. The earlier the correction is carried out, the easier it is, and the better is the result. Simple correction is never sufficient. The subsequent provision of an instrument is essential, otherwise the deformity is practically certain to return. Therefore the provision of instruments ordered for these children is urgent. Club feet as a rule require several years' careful observation by a surgeon after correction has been carried out.

HEART DISEASE.

Anatomy.—The heart consists of two sides (right and left), and each side of two chambers (auricle and ventricle). The auricles are thin-walled, and not very strong; the ventricles have very thick powerful walls. The walls of the heart consist of muscle, and the whole constitutes a powerful and complicated pump. The direction in which the blood flows in the heart is regulated by valves, each of which consists of two or three flaps, which swing aside to allow the blood to flow forward, but close together, and prevent it flowing in the reverse direction.

The blood naturally flows from the great veins into the right auricle. By the contraction of this it is pumped into the right ventricle. The powerful right ventricle forces it through the pulmonary artery into the lungs, where it is purified by taking up oxygen from the air. From the lungs the blood collects again into the left auricle by the pulmonary veins. It is pumped by the left auricle into the left ventricle, and by the latter—the most powerful part of the heart—it is finally pumped into the aorta, and thence passes all over the body. There are valves between the right auricle and right ventricle, and between the right ventricle and pulmonary artery; and similarly between the left auricle and ventricle, and left ventricle and aorta.

Disease, such as rheumatism and chorea, causes a chronic inflammation of the valves, which are apt to become thick and hard, and to move imperfectly. As a result of this, either (1) the valve flaps do not close completely, and allow blood to flow in the reverse direction; or (2) the valves are stiffened, and the opening between auricle and ventricle is narrowed. One or other of these changes occurs in valvular disease of the heart.

The result of these changes is to upset the heart's regular pumping action by throwing a greater strain upon it. In children who are doing well, however, the muscular tissue of the heart increases, and makes up for this; so that, although the heart is large, and the signs of valvular disease, (such as murmur) are present, the child remains well, and is able to do almost as much as a normal child. In these cases we say that compensation is good. When a greater strain is thrown upon this heart by exertion or by illness, the compensation fails. The heart has not a sufficient reserve force, its action becomes rapid and irregular, and the child is obviously distressed.

Most of the children in school come under the class of well compensated heart cases. They may live practically a normal life, but—

(a) Whilst ordinary exercise, play and drill is good for them, sudden over-exertion, such as running upstairs, is bad.

(b) They require the greatest care to prevent recurrent attacks of rheumatism, each of which, by causing fresh disease of the valves, may make the heart worse.

There are a few badly compensated cases. You should know these by the medical officer giving directions that they are to be kept quiet. You can judge them for yourselves to some extent; they are often a bad colour—blue or pallid—get out of breath easily, and sometimes have large ends to the fingers. These children should never be allowed to run, nor to do anything which makes them out of breath.

The children who are liable to fainting attacks are particularly those with disease of the valves at the root of the aorta. These also are liable to sudden death. In spite of this latter fact, it is necessary to keep them in school, as many of them live well into middle life. On the whole, children with heart disease do badly; one-half of the deaths in our invalid schools occur amongst them. Repeated attacks of rheumatism or chorea, causing progressive changes in the heart, are the most serious causes of these fatalities.

Congenital Heart Disease means that there is some original defect in the structure of the heart. Nearly all the children are very " blue," particularly in cold weather. With very few exceptions, these blue children die before reaching adult life. The occasional instances of children with congenital heart disease who are not blue and have no symptoms, may be treated as practically normal children.

Children suffering from heart disease sometimes return from country holidays much the worse for their stay. This is because they have not been under proper supervision, and have been allowed to over-exert themselves and do too much.

It is a good rule never to send a child suffering from heart disease away, except after a report from a doctor who knows the child, and who also understands the sort of home to which he is to be sent. Children with severe heart trouble should, as a rule, only be sent to convalescent homes where they are used to taking heart cases.

CHOREA.

Chorea, or St. Vitus's Dance, is a chronic disease which is very common in children, and is characterised by irregular involuntary movements. When these movements are present the child should, as a rule, be excluded from school, and further, should be kept very quiet at home, as far as possible out of contact with other children. Children who are convalescent from chorea, and those in whom repeated attacks have occurred, are often admitted to the invalid schools. It is found that they are able to attend these schools, where they are kept quiet, and not urged to work too much, without any great liability to recurrence of the disease. If they are returned to the ordinary schools, where they compete with healthy children, a fresh attack often comes on. These children are often extremely nervous and highly strung, and even in the interval between attacks of chorea they may be extremely fidgety. They have to be humoured to a great extent, and must often be allowed to do just that amount of school work that they feel inclined to carry out.

Occasionally a habit spasm in a fidgety child simulates chorea. Habit spasm is, however, as a rule, a single invariable movement such as a particular twitch of the face or a particular hand or arm movement. In chorea the movement varies, being perhaps first in the face, then in the right arm, then, if the right arm is restrained, in the left arm, and so on. The distinction of habit spasm from chorea must be made by the medical officer. It is important, for habit spasm should be constantly corrected; choreic movement must never be interfered with at all. All choreic children in whom movements recommence must be referred to the medical officer for exclusion from school as soon as possible.

The other deformities and chronic diseases from which

children in the invalid schools suffer are so many and various that it is impossible for me to go into details with regard to them, or to give directions for their care. The only rule I can lay down is, when in doubt as to the health of a child, or as to the possibility of improvement in a case of deformity as for a doctor's report as soon as you are able to get it. Some comparatively small treatment carried out during school life may make a great difference to the child's future, and no trouble should be spared if this treatment can be secured.

THE INCEPTION AND DEVELOPMENT OF AN INSTITUTION FOR NEGRO CRIPPLED CHILDREN

Elliot White

THE INCEPTION AND DEVELOPMENT OF AN INSTITUTION FOR NEGRO CRIPPLED CHILDREN

ELLIOT WHITE
Philadelphia, Pa.

An account of the House of Saint Michael and All Angels may well begin with an extract from the note book of Sister Sarah, to whose zeal and devotion this Home for Colored Cripple Children owes its foundation:

Having learned this evening of a destitute crippled negro child in the lower part of the city, I at once set out to minister to it. After difficulty in locating the house to which I had been directed, I found it to be occupied by several families. Ascending rickety stairs, and through a narrow, dark, musty passage, I entered a small, dark room entirely destitute of furniture. The atmosphere was sickening. On rags in one corner of this closet (it might be called) a boy of about nine lay on the floor. Beside him was a piece of stale bread and a tin cup with some water. I spoke, but received no reply. I knelt by his side, taking his crooked fingers in my hand, but they were cold and stiff. I passed my fingers over his forehead, and through his crisp hair, but he felt it not. The angel of death had borne the spirit of this weary child from a world in which he had known nothing but sorrow, pain and want. The angels rejoice over the recovery of one penitent sinner. Do they weep over the victims of cruelty and wrong?

Cases like this—for this was not the only one of its kind—led to the establishment of the House of Saint Michael and All Angels. There was the more special need for a home devoted to the care of cripples of African descent, because they were debarred by reason of their color from some of the charitable institutions of Philadelphia qualified to help them.

Work was begun by Sister Sarah (Kirke), with the help of

Mrs. Helen Loyd. A small house, No. 4012 Ludlow Street, West Philadelphia, was rented and opened in August, 1886. The name, 'House of Saint Michael and All Angels,' was suggested by a friend, in remembrance of the passage in the Psalm, "He shall give His angels charge over thee." Sixty dollars was secured for the rent. There was but little furniture. The kitchen was provided with a small oil stove, with some tomato cans to cook in. A kitchen table was made of boards resting on barrels. The first inmates were a boy who had lost both feet from exposure to cold, and two little minstrels sent from the almshouse. Food was begged from the markets and groceries. In October, it is noted, the house was enriched by the gift of 'a pot and a tea kettle' and in November 'two table cloths, cups and three plates' were received.

The Sister was an earnest believer in prayer, and signal answer to her petitions occurred the Christmas after the Home opened:

As the first Christmas approached it seemed as if man had forgotten us, although a few small gifts came, but food was lacking; in fact, the first stage of starvation seemed approaching. Supper time of Christmas Eve had come; not a crust, while many have bread to spare. In the twilight the children were sent into the yard to play. Soon they returned, seeking their evening meal. Nothing: but, equal to the emergency, the Sister provided amusements to engage their attention. This continued till late evening, when suddenly a vehicle stopped at the door. A loud knocking ensued, doubtless with the supposition that all had retired and were asleep. The prayer of faith had been answered; for before the door stood an express wagon fully loaded, *all* for our house; everything and indeed more, supplies of every kind that lasted for weeks, besides the things to make the great Festival a joyous one in the eyes of the children, such as they had never before known.[1]

Work of such heroic self-sacrifice was bound to rally friends to its support. A check for a thousand dollars was received and set aside as the nucleus of a fund for a permanent building. The

[1] The writer of this sketch is indebted for the above quotations to *The Life of One of God's Saints*, by Rev. H. B. Wright, Rector of St. Asaph's, Bala, Pa.

Guild of Saint Michael and All Angels was organized. A small paper called the *Cripple News* was published monthly and widely circulated. Friends were raised up in these and other ways. The following anecdote will show how interest grew from small beginnings: Miss Cora Roberts visited the Home with her class of Sunday school scholars. When about to leave she asked what she and her class could do, and was informed that an additional crib was greatly needed. This was furnished immediately. Some weeks after, this lady with her class returned and was much pleased to see the bed occupied by an interesting little cripple boy. It was proposed that the bed be endowed. Miss Roberts bravely set to work and had raised almost enough money when death called her. Friends made up the deficiency, and the cot now bears her name.

The small house on Ludlow Street was soon filled to its utmost capacity. One evening a boy appeared, asking to be taken into the Home. His clothing was thin and ragged; he had hobbled on a crutch from South Street, several miles away. His mother, he said, was dead, and the woman with whom he had been staying would keep him no longer. The house was then overflowing and he could not be received. With tears streaming down his cheeks, the boy turned away. His body was taken the next morning from the river.

The need of larger quarters was manifest. The case of the boy excited widespread sympathy. The Guild attacked the problem with great energy, and in less than a year sufficient money was added to the original gift of one thousand dollars to justify the purchase of a commodious house on North 43d Street, near Haverford Avenue. Children now began to be sent from all over the country, many of the cases being full of interest. One, a little girl, whose legs had become crooked and stiff from having for nearly two years been tied daily in a chair to be safe and out of the way while her mother toiled at the washtub. Another child was ticketed and expressed from Georgia. Another, paralyzed and helpless, was sent in a basket from Hagerstown, Md., with a bottle of milk to feed it on the way. Two girls and a boy came from Mrs. Buford's Hospital in Virginia. One of the girls was blind. She was treated at the Wills Hospital and her sight restored. The other, seventeen years old, was a great sufferer from bone disease. The boy had club feet. He was treated successfully and returned home without crutches. He afterward married and prospered to the extent of being able to purchase a house and ten acres of land. One child was left on the doorstep, covered with sores and quite helpless.

Again more room was called for. The house adjoining was purchased, and more land, which furnished an admirable playground.

A very generous benefactor of the work was Mrs. Pauline E. Henry. A copy of the *Cripple News* fell into her hands; she read, became interested, and visited the Home. The small chapel fitted up in the house was not at all adequate, and she offered to erect a suitable one on part of the property. This was done in 1889. The Mission Chapel of Saint Michael and All Angels fronts on Wallace Street. The building, designed by Mr. William Masters Camac, is of great beauty and was furnished completely by the donor. It was erected in loving memory of Mrs. Henry's adopted daughter, Margaret Connor, and its use limited to colored cripple children and as a mission church for colored people. Its seats must be kept free. Mrs. Henry died in May, 1905, leaving in her will bequests for the keeping of the property in repair, and also a fund to augment the salary of the chaplain or priest in charge. Thus the Home ministers not only to the children within it, but also to the colored people in the neighborhood.

Upon the retirement of Sister Sarah the management of the Home was given over, after a brief interval, to the Sisterhood of Saint Margaret, an order of Sisters in the Episcopal Church, founded in England in 1855 by Dr. J. M. Neale, the noted hymn writer, and the American branch established in Boston in 1873. Three Sisters are assigned to this work.

REPORT OF WORK
AMONG THE CRIPPLED CHILDREN
OF THE TENEMENTS OF NEW YORK CITY

REPORT OF WORK AMONG THE CRIPPLED CHILDREN OF THE TENEMENTS OF NEW YORK CITY

Published under the Auspices of the Guild for Crippled Children of the Poor of New York City, 1904 [1]

The training of atypical and defective children to useful citizenship is attracting the attention of thoughtful people in increasing measure. The community owes it to them and to itself to make them as nearly as possible self-supporting and altogether self-respecting, to save them from misery, vice and crime, and to add them to the ranks of the productive and helpful.

Work for the manual, mental and moral training of cripples was begun in Italy many years ago, and through its inspiration the Industrial School for Crippled and Deformed Children was founded in Boston in 1893; its beautiful new building in St. Botolph street has just been completed. In New York the work was begun by the Rev. Dr. J. Winthrop Hegeman, who founded The Guild for Crippled Children of the Poor in 1898. The work carried on by the Guild and its Auxiliaries through their schools and otherwise has grown in importance and efficiency, and several other organizations have taken up various phases of the work.

Our managers, feeling that efficiency would be gained by the cooperation of the different societies interested, invited them to

---

[1] This is the first of a series of reprints of documents of historical interest in the development of provision for cripples. The present report, which is now out of print and very rare, gives a synthetic account of all work for crippled children in New York City in 1904. Much light is thrown on the early beginnings of organizations which, since that time, have broadened and enlarged their work to a degree not then considered possible.

a conference-dinner, donated by one of our Board, in January, 1903, and last spring to a meeting at which the question of co-operation was discussed. It was voted to organize a series of conferences to which each society should send two delegates, and at which views should be exchanged on practical topics connected with the work. The Guild also voted to publish, in lieu of its own fifth report, this joint report, to which all have been invited to contribute. We also contemplate holding in the near future a joint exhibition of what has been accomplished in manual training by the different schools. Our Vice-President, Dr. Hegeman, was instrumental in starting a Guild for Crippled Children in Syracuse, and there are good prospects of doing similar work in other cities. There are many phases of the work that remain to be developed, such as the relation of the Cripples' School to the home, training for the older children, industrial or farm communities for adolescents or adults, employment for cripples after leaving school, the place of the convalescent home, instruction for cripples in hospitals, the relation of the public school system to the work, summer outings and camps and many others.

The Guild wishes to acknowledge valuable help received from its many friends, from the Charity Organization Society, from several of the settlements and their devoted workers, from many hospitals and dispensaries, and from its sister organizations. In addition to its own special work, in the school, in the home, in the country, and in co-operation with the hospitals and dispensaries, it appeals for closer fellowship, for a broad and disinterested handling of present problems, and for earnest and enlightened study of new problems as they arise. If our information and experience is made mutually available and our enthusiasm contagious, the cause of the helpless and neglected cripple will appeal with irresistible force to an intelligent public.

HENRY LING TAYLOR, *President.*

REPORT OF SECRETARY OF GUILD FOR CRIPPLED CHILDREN OF THE POOR OF NEW YORK CITY

The object of this little volume is to describe in a brief way all the known efforts that are being made in New York City in behalf of the crippled children of the tenements.

The first beginnings of the school and manual-training work were made by a few individuals who were deeply interested in this defective class. It was then taken up in a co-operative way by the Children's Aid Society and by the Guild for Crippled Children, the latter organized, and afterwards incorporated (May 1, 1900) to do this special work, since which time each has been working independently.

Of the other societies mentioned in this report, the Hospital work, the Ethical Culture Society Visiting Guild and the House of the Annunciation go back several years, while the Darrach Home and the Wm. H. Davis Free and Industrial School are outgrowths of the above mentioned co-operative work, each now, however, being upon an independent basis. The Orthopedic Hospital also has Crippled Children among its patients.

The special objects and methods of the several societies will be found in the following pages. Fuller information of each can be secured by sending for the annual reports to the various addresses given.

The object and method of the Guild can best be expressed in the words of our Constitution:

OBJECT

The object of the Guild is to secure the co-operation of congregations of all denominations and of societies and individuals in helping the poor to an intelligent care for their Crippled Children who are not otherwise provided for.

METHOD

We propose to effect this by helping parents to obtain for their children such surgical and medical treatment as they may need, nourishing food and suitable clothing, to establish shcools and teach the children trades, to entertain them at our seaside homes, and by whatever means may be necessary to improve their condition.

The Guild has now two strong and flourishing Auxiliaries, each of which is autonomous, having independent control of its funds. Each Auxiliary is represented on the Board of Managers, to which it presents at the monthly meetings reports of its work.

Steps are now being taken by us to start a third school on the lower West side, which it is hoped will in time develop into another Auxiliary.

The Guild is also aiming to secure a closer co-operation upon the part of the various societies, hoping thus to have the city covered in a more systematic and effective way. The work for crippled children is yet in its infancy. There are hundreds, in all probability, as yet unreached, and the methods employed can doubtless be improved and extended.

Towards these greatly desired results, it is hoped that this combined report may in some degree contribute.

CHARLES B. CHAPIN, *Secretary.*

AUXILIARY II OF GUILD FOR CRIPPLED CHILDREN

This school was started by the Guild on Thanksgiving Day, 1900, in a room kindly given free of charge in the Clark Neighborhood House, corner Rivington and Cannon streets, with some thirteen children, and Miss Marie Phillips as teacher.

It was not, however, until the following spring that the work was vigorously developed. This came about in answer to an appeal by Dr. Chapin and through several parlor meetings. A committee of women was then organized, of which Mrs. Daniel P. Hays was made the chairman, Miss Steinberg the secretary, and Mrs. Mark Ash the treasurer.

Over a thousand dollars were privately raised by the Committee, necessary school supplies were purchased, and arrangements for outings for the children made for the early summer. By the middle of July twenty-two children had been sent for a longer or shorter time to various places in the country.

On October 23d the Committee was formally organized as Auxiliary II, with officers and board of directors.

The school is now comfortably housed at 29 Montgomery street, the number of children on the register being seventy-five, and the average daily attendance from sixty to sixty-five. There are over one hundred on the waiting list.

In the building, which is a three-story house, arranged in comfortable class-rooms, a janitor is employed, who is assisted by his wife and one servant.

A corps of teachers is also employed, as follows: one in elementary work, one in kindergarten and two in manual training; also a general superintendent, who, in addition, teaches the deficient children. The children are brought to the school daily in stages, and from 9:30 A. M. to 3 P. M. they are given instruction, with an intermission for dinner, which is served in the house.

The results attained in the school are most encouraging. Some children, whose infirmities are not too great, are fitted for the public schools, and thus given an opportunity to associate with other children and to receive an education which they could not otherwise obtain, and which will enable them to take their place with other citizens of our great city in building its future. Others are given a trade, by means of which they can earn a livelihood and relieve the city of the expense of their support.

The physical needs of the children are, of course, provided for. A trained nurse is employed at the house, who daily looks after their needs, and two physicians attend whenever necessary, to prescribe for them and see that their braces are properly adjusted, and that they receive the requisite medical attention.

In addition, an eye specialist and a nose and throat specialist are called in when required. Mothers' meetings are regularly held at which various kinds of instruction are given and a social hour is enjoyed.

The manual-training work at the school is one of its important and encouraging features. The boys are taught caning and basketry, thus giving them a trade by which they can earn their livelihood. There is also a work-room for overgrown girls, too old to attend the elementary classes, where they are taught all kinds of sewing and basketry.

For three months in the summer they are taken to Long Branch, N. J., where in every possible way they are cared for and instructed.

The Auxiliary has nearly seven hundred members. It raises and disburses its own funds.

Officers and Board of Directors—President, Mrs. Daniel P. Hays; First Vice-President, Mrs. David Leventritt; Second Vice-President, Mrs. Julius Hart; Third Vice-President, Mrs. Henry Goldman; Treasurer, Mrs. S. Weinhandler, 326 West 108th street; Recording Secretary, Mrs. Jas. J. Franc; Corresponding Secretary, Miss Gertrude Sinn.

MRS. DANIEL P. HAYS, President.

AUXILIARY III OF GUILD FOR CRIPPLED CHILDREN

On February 26th, 1902, Auxiliary No. 3 opened the Day Home and School for Crippled Children at 2111 Madison avenue. The work of the initial six months was of the most perplexing character and proved beyond possibility of doubt the imperative need of schools for crippled children. Comparatively few pupils were secured at first, but among these were some who, though too crippled to attend public school, had been able to hobble down to the doorsteps and the curbstone, where they had established the only communication possible for them with the outside world. The instruction received there was from the idle, corrupt men and women who loiter about such places. The lessons thus learned are difficult to forget, and make ineffaceable scars on the moral character of the pupils, while their unused brains and hands become less and less capable of responding to any effort for improvement which the future may hold for them. Daily contact with these boys and girls impressed upon us our inability to obliterate the effects of this "door-step education," and forced us to realize the necessity of providing wholesome means of education, and an encouraging mental and moral atmosphere for cripples *while very young*.

Sixty pupils have been enrolled since Auxiliary No. 3 started, although 34 is the greatest number on register at any one time.

Our sub-title "Day *Home* and School" suggests the things we try to do for the children beyond and above formal teaching. The great holidays of the year are made real home festivals in the school, and justice and courtesy are held in as high respect as proficiency in arithmetic. A hot dinner is given each day and a wagonette carries the children to and from the school.

The three months "summer outing" given each year has proved its value by the number of children who have been enabled to enter public school on their return to the city in the autumn.

The expense of maintenance for 1903 was nearly $4,000. That included rent, conveyance, food, fuel, salaries of matron, teachers, maid, janitor, and the "summer outing," with all its extra demand of cots, bedding, etc. Our salaried teaching corps has been admirably reinforced by volunteers. More money is needed, however, to secure the proper amount of manual training.

The object of Auxiliary No. 3, as expressed in its Annual Report, is, "To provide a day home and school for such crippled children of the poor as are, by reason of their physical limitations, unfitted to attend public schools; to raise them mentally, morally and physically to a better condition, and to so educate their hands that they may become in a measure self-supporting; to brighten their lives by enabling them to keep their own self-respect and to win the respect of others."

Officers—Mrs. Merle St. C. Wright, President; Mrs. William Cunningham Savage, First Vice-President; Mrs. William Houston Kenyon, Second Vice-President; Mrs. Leander A. Bevin, Third

Vice-President; Mrs. Robert Emmett Clarke, Recording Secretary; Mrs. John Hutchinson, Jr., Treasurer; Miss Mary H. Kenyon, Corresponding Secretary, 32 West 68th street.

MRS. MERLE ST. CROIX WRIGHT, *President*.

SCHOOLS FOR CRIPPLED CHILDREN UNDER THE AUSPICES OF THE CHILDREN'S AID SOCIETY

The first school for crippled children in New York was opened in the Henrietta Industrial School of the Children's Aid Society, in the year 1898.   The need of such a school was presented to the writer by that noble woman, Miss Darrach, and the first class was organized experimentally, so little was the necessity understood at that time.   Within a year it had grown in importance far beyond our first intention.   There were thirty-five cripples in attendance and fifty enrolled.   The visitor of the school discovered these children living in the tenement houses in a state of pitiable neglect, their wounds and deformities uncared for, and the children growing up without education or training of any kind.   They were brought to school in a comfortable wagonette, and many of them came in the most destitute condition.   They were washed and their wounds dressed, and their dirty rags replaced before they were fit for the school-room. Here they spend the day, have a good, wholesome meal at noon and such other nourishment as individual cases require.

Since then three additional schools for crippled and deformed children have been organized in the buildings of the Children's Aid Society, and they have become of such necessity to the happiness, to the health and welfare of these little unfortunates, that it is hard to believe that such neglect was permitted until so lately.   There are now 206 crippled and deformed children in these schools, who are brought in our five wagonettes in the morning, having to be carried down the tenement house stairs by our attendants, and returned again in the afternoon to their homes.   This outing, in contrast to their former condition of hopelessness, is a change which brings happiness to these children to an extent difficult to realize. The cheerful school-rooms, the lessons, the manual-training work, and later on the industrial training, the care and attention of trained nurses, the sanitary comforts, the cots, wheel-chairs and appliances, and best of all, the affection which now surrounds them, is a contrast to their former state of neglect so touching to the heart that no one can visit these classes without being deeply moved.

At the Children's Summer Home of the Children's Aid Society there is a comfortable cottage for the use of these little ones during the summer, and everything is done for their happiness that ingenuity can devise.

C. Loring Brace, Secretary.

CRIPPLED CHILDREN'S CLASSES

THE RHINELANDER SCHOOL OF THE CHILDREN'S AID SOCIETY NO. 350 EAST 88TH STREET

In our classes for crippled children are enrolled over 90 little unfortunates. Most of these children represent the lowest element of the East Side of the city. Coming to us uncouth and entirely ignorant of either moral or mental training, our work among them becomes a labor of love, interest and duty. The keen sense of their physical deformities, and the cruel treatment many of them receive from their parents, tend to make their dispositions both bitter and vindictive, and it is entirely by means of love and kindness, and assuring them of how much they can do, not only for themselves, but for those even less fortunate than they, that we are able to overcome these sad traits in the lives of these little victims of circumstance.

For all this beautiful charity we are indebted to the late Mrs. Evan T. Walker and her sister, Miss Watson.

The subject of cripples becomes more interesting and requires deeper thought each year. To educate these children in the best manner which will aid them in the future, is a problem which all who are interested in these little unfortunates are endeavoring to solve. During the past year some of our older girls were taught to cut and make their own dresses, to make little worsted hoods for baby brother or sister, and other articles needed in the home. We hope to enlarge this work during the coming year, particularly in the dress-making department. If these girls could make not only their own clothes, but those of their younger brothers and sisters, they would be doing a good share in aiding their families until they became competent to fill some position that would in time make them self-supporting.

Our class has now been in existence for four years, and it is very gratifying to note the progress made mentally and physically by these little sufferers. Many who upon entering the class were considered mentally incapable of being taught, have developed wonderfully under the teacher's patient guidance; thus showing that such children's minds were simply dormant, and required but encouragement and a little kindness to arouse them. Even in the case of children who are mentally deficient we have found great improvement, especially morally.

K. REA STACKPOLE, *Principal.*

CLASSES FOR CRIPPLED CHILDREN

AVENUE B SCHOOL, 537 EAST 16TH STREET, AND PHELPS SCHOOL, 316 EAST 35TH STREET, OF THE CHILDREN'S AID SOCIETY

In February, 1900, an Auxiliary Board of Managers of the Children's Aid Society opened a Class for Crippled Children in the Society's Avenue B School, No. 537 East 16th Street. There were at first but three children; before the close of the school year there were fifteen in the class. The following year the attendance more than doubled. In January, 1902, the same Auxiliary Board opened another class in the Society's school at 316 East 35th street, and in February of the same year a trade department, for girls over 14 years of age, was opened in a shop owned by the

Society, adjoining the school in East 16th street. Between 70 and 80 children are now in attendance in the classes started by this Auxiliary Board.

The Children's Aid Society provides the educational side, and the Auxiliary Board raises, by subscriptions and donations, money for the omnibuses, nurses, and any relief that it is found necessary to give.

The work of the Auxiliary Board is divided into two parts, the educational and the relief. The Chairman of the Educational Committee has personal supervision of the classes, and the Committee meets the teachers once a month, after school hours, to talk over the work and the needs of the individual children. The trade department is looked after by a sub-committee of the Educational Committee. The Chairman of the Relief Committee keeps track, through the trained nurses, of the physical condition of the children and of their home conditions. This Committee holds mothers' meetings at the 16th Street school, on these occasions uniting the two classes, and members of the Committee make visits to the families when invited to do so.

Every effort is made to make the classes like regular schools. The courses of studies are planned to bring each child as nearly as possible to the standing it would have in public school, and whenever anyone is physically able to attend public school, the transfer is made. The nurses do no dressing of wounds, etc., at the schools. Anything of that kind that is required the nurses do in the homes, and they show the mothers how to care for the children, and insist upon the regular attendance at their dispensaries, with a proper carrying out of the surgeons' directions. In some cases the nurses must take the children to the dispensaries, but every effort is made to leave the responsibility to the mother or guardian.

The aim of the teachers is to make the children better able to "hold their own." They try to teach the children how to study, how to find things out for themselves. Is there any better "tool" to give them for this purpose than a thorough training in reading, writing and arithmetic?

In the girls' trade department, lamp-shade making, plain sewing and embroidery are taught, and again the aim is to make them self-reliant, and whenever possible, after a certain time, the girls are encouraged to take places outside. Experiments have been tried without success in the line of trades for the older boys; in the meantime they are given manual-training, and a social club has been formed, in order to hold them together until some practical plan can be thought out. Here, likewise, the effort is to make them less dependent, and thus better able to cope with whatever may be in store for them, be it in the school or out in the world.

This plan to make them help themselves is carried into the homes as well; when clothes, food, etc., are donated to the classes, they are sold to the families at low figures. The proceeds from these sales go to buying, by the quantity, articles of food and clothing most needed, thus enabling the families to buy their small quantities at reasonable rates.

MABEL IRVING JONES,
Chairman Educational Committee.

CRIPPLED CHILDREN'S CLASSES

HENRIETTA SCHOOL OF THE CHILDREN'S AID SOCIETY (SUPPORTED IN PART BY MISS SPENCE'S SCHOOL SOCIETY),
225 WEST 63d STREET

Officers—Miss Amy Ellis, President; Miss Natalie Munde, Vice-President; Miss Dorothea Draper, Secretary; Miss Alice Agnew, Treasurer.

Directors—Miss Anita Peabody, Miss Catherine Dodge, Mrs. W. F. Dominick.

The third year of the school for crippled children under the management of Miss Spence's School Society, in co-operation with the Children's Aid Society, has been interesting, and on the whole, full of encouragement. About fifty-two children remained on the roll during the year, and the average attendance was good. In spite of their disabilities, the children are always cheerful and most appreciative of the school and the hot dinners.   During the year, under the guidance of a very efficient trained nurse, the appearance of the little ones improved decidedly, children and mothers co-operating with the nurse in her efforts to teach them cleanliness, and to impress upon them the importance of attending the clinics and hospitals regularly.   Physical improvement has been marked in several cases.

The fortnightly meetings for the mothers were most encouraging, the women coming together to sew, chat and drink a social cup of tea.

And this year, owing to our enlarged rooms, a sewing and trade class for the older girls has been successfully started.

Through the kindness of a friend, the loan of an old farm-house at St. James, L. I., was secured rent free for July, August and the first part of September.   Sufficient money was finally raised to keep thirty children there during this time, under the care of the trained nurse and an assistant.   In a few special cases the child was kept for the entire ten weeks; but the majority went for a fortnight at a time, the house being only large enough to accommodate ten children at once.

Thus in spite of some discouragements, we cannot but feel that much happiness has been given to these little cripples, and that our efforts to educate and train them to some degree of usefulness will not be without results.

AMY ELLIS, *President.*

THE WILLIAM II. DAVIS FREE INDUSTRIAL SCHOOL FOR CRIPPLED CHILDREN

This school opened on September 17th, 1900, at 434 West 57th street, with twenty children.   Its present quarters are at 471 West 57th street, and the work has grown to such an extent that there are seventy children on the roll-book, with an average daily attendance of sixty.

It was incorporated in July, 1903.

Every morning the wagonette owned by the Society makes its rounds to pick up the children who cannot walk. The driver carries the children from the rooms to the wagonette, and a nurse is in attendance to take charge of them to and from the School. Many of the children are encased in plaster, some have iron braces on their limbs, others have jury-masts to support their heads. Their faces are pinched and aged with suffering, yet, withal, they are wonderfully happy.

The School is absolutely non-sectarian, and admission is open to every crippled child without regard to race, creed or color. The advantages given are the same as in the public schools— kindergarten, primary and grammar classes, besides manual training. At noon a hot, nourishing dinner is served to the children, every afternoon a simple service is held in the assembly room, a psalm is read, the Lord's Prayer repeated, and hymns and songs sung, and at four o'clock the children are returned to their homes.

MANUAL TRAINING A SPECIAL FEATURE OF THE SCHOOL

This branch of the work has advanced gradually from basket weaving and fancy iron work to wood carving for the boys, while the little girls are taught fine sewing and Indian basket weaving. Skilled teachers are employed, so that weak, helpless little fingers and halting minds may be coaxed over the hard places.

In the manual-training classes the school has demonstrated one great thing in the four years of its existence, which is that crippled children may be trained to become self-supporting. Many make encouraging progress in the manual-training class. One boy, little more than an infant, carries home each month "the price of the rent," as he calls it. Several of the other boys earn enough to buy their own clothes and pay for their braces. One boy has earned $50 since last September, and thinks he is not making enough at that.

There is a "Penny Provident" station at the School—mothers and children are encouraged to bring in their pennies, the largest amount received at one time being twenty-five cents—most of the deposits have been one, two and three cents at a time.

When a dollar has been saved a regular bank account is started for the depositor in a Savings Bank, thus inculcating habits of thrift.

Mothers' meetings are held every Thursday, at which sewing lessons are given and talks on hygiene, and then a social half-hour is enjoyed.

A splendid summer work is done by the School at Warren, Mass. The children throughout the entire year also receive careful and constant medical attention.

The Society has two hundred and fifteen active and fifteen life members.

Officers—President, Mrs. Arthur Elliott Fish; Vice-Presidents, Mrs. William S. Hawk, Mrs. George Joseph Smith, Mrs. Clinton L. Bagg, Mrs. George F. Cummings, Mrs. Frank Scott Gerrish, Mrs. Chester B. McLaughlin; Treasurer, Mrs. Edward Davis Jones; Corresponding Secretary, Miss Florence Guernsey; Secretary, Mrs. Hugh Reid Lawford.

MRS. ARTHUR ELLIOTT FISH, *President.*

THE DARRACH HOME FOR CRIPPLED CHILDREN

The Association of the Darrach Home for Crippled Children was organized in October, 1900, to provide a home for orphaned, friendless, or deserted little cripples who do not require hospital treatment and who are not suffering from chronic organic disease. Its aim is to receive such children who, on account of their deformities, cannot be sent out for adoption, and are not admitted to the ordinary asylums, and through the co-operation of our clinics and hospitals to provide them with the best surgical treatment and to see that they receive a common school education through our public schools and other institutions, supplementing such instruction by a technical training adapted to the capacity of the individual child, and intended to enable him to become wholly or in part self-supporting.

An important factor in laying the foundation of health and strength is the "fresh-air work." The children are taken to a mountain camp on the shores of Lake Sunapee, New Hampshire, from June to October. A teacher of manual-training goes with them, and a part of each day is spent by the children in such delightful occupations as fine sewing, embroidery, fancy work, cane seating, basketry, pyrography, etc., carried on in the open air under the pines and birches.

The dormitories are tents, except in very stormy weather, when their little occupants seek the shelter of the near-by cottage. The benefit of the summer outing is shared by more than the "Home children," as the Guild extends its hospitality to poor crippled children from the tenements.

At the present time there are twenty-one children in the summer Home, fifteen of whom are the permanent charges of the Association.

The "Work" of the "Home" is supported entirely by voluntary contributions and through the co-operation of other societies acting as auxiliaries to the Association. It is non-sectarian, the children receiving their religious instruction through the churches to which they respectively belong.

Officers—May Darrach, M.D., President; Mrs. J. F. Raymond, Vice-President; Mrs. Wyatt-Hannath, Treasurer.

MAY DARRACH, M.D.

ORTHOPEDIC WARD OF POST-GRADUATE HOSPITAL

The Orthopedic Ward of the New York Post-Graduate Hospital has been in existence twenty years. The Ward was first in the original Hospital in 20th street, then it was in a small room up five flights of stairs, with the late Dr. Phelps and one nurse caring for the children to the best of their ability. In 1894, when the Hospital moved to its present building, five ladies who had previously interested themselves in the work begged that the crippled children might have a ward to themselves, where they would be properly cared for, offering to become responsible for all expenses except those usual for a hospital—heating, lighting, medical attendance, etc.—to which the Hospital consented.

The Orthopedic Ward, in charge of Drs. Warren O. Plimpton and Henry Ling Taylor, consists of one large room containing 18 beds, with a small kitchen attached, a reception ward with four beds, a small ward for very sick children, with four beds, an endowed room with two beds, a room for the head nurse, a bath-room, linen closet, and an "operating" room, where the children's wounds are dressed. The large operations are performed in another room downstairs. The twenty-seven beds are always full, with a long waiting list ready to take any vacant bed as soon as it is ready. The little children are most kindly taken care of. Miss Leadingham, the head nurse, is an unusual woman; she not only superintends every little detail, but finds time to "mother" the children as well, calling each child by name, and knowing as much as possible of their home history, in order to take more interest in them.

During the spring and summer a weekly drive is provided for such children as are able to go out. A kindergarten teacher is also provided twice a week, who is able, in cases where they remain a sufficient length of time, to teach them to read and to give them some little education.

We raise our money for supporting the Ward by subscriptions, donations and annual dues from the Ladies' Committee. There is a President, Vice-President, Secretary and Treasurer and committee of twelve ladies. We intend extending our committee to fifty members.

Anyone interested in seeing how the crippled children are cared for can visit the Ward any afternoon between two and four o'clock and will be cordially received.

(MRS. ROBERT) SARAH GIBBS THOMPSON,
President Ladies' Committee.

HOUSE OF THE ANNUNCIATION

The work at the House of the Annunciation, for Crippled and Incurable Children, was commenced by the Sisters of the Annunciation, who were incorporated in the same year, in 1893, at 73 West 94th street, New York. After some years that house found too small, and the present house, 518 West 152d street, purchased in its stead.

Our wards are fitted up to accommodate 20 patients, and at present we only take girls between the ages of four and sixteen. Several children have been cured while with us. We aim to help them spiritually, morally and physically. They are taught the rudiments of a good, plain English education, sewing, and light housework. No charge is made for the care of them. The internal management of the House is entirely in the hands of the Sisters and their helpers. The officers at present are Rev. Edward Wallace-Neil, Sc.D., President; the Mother Superior, Treasurer, and Sister Rebecca, Secretary.

There is an Advisory Committee of three gentlemen, who assist in various ways in the business of the House. We have a place in the country, Sister Elizabeth's house, Riverbank, Conn., where we go with the children for the summer. There we have about fifty acres on a high hill overlooking the Sound, where the stay benefits the children very much.

THE MOTHER SUPERIOR.

VISITING GUILD FOR CRIPPLED CHILDREN

SOCIETY FOR ETHICAL CULTURE

The Visiting Guild for Crippled Children was organized thirteen years ago, for the purpose of taking charge of those little children whose physical infirmities debarred them from attending school.

Its object is to visit the chronic sick in their homes, and to give them such instruction as they are fitted to receive; to aid them in procuring work; and to render them such service as will add to their well-being and comfort.

This work, faithfully carried on by a number of our active workers, has been in most cases highly satisfactory, as not only the child's mental, moral and physical welfare was carefully looked after, but also the morals and the home life of the entire family were often raised from a low order to a plane of respectability. Employment was often secured for either the father or mother of the family, and those children who were strong enough and able were taught some sort of work whereby they could earn some money.

We have for a number of years been in active co-operation with the prominent orthopedic hospitals in the city, insisting that the mothers take the children regularly to the dispensaries, and also frequently entering children in the hospitals, for operations and treatment.

Since the many schools for crippled children have been started in various parts of the city, we have made it a point, if the child resides within calling distance of the school stage, to enter it at the school, as there it is looked after from 10 until 3 o'clock, five days in the week, which is preferable to our system of visiting for a few hours, twice a week. However, we never lose sight of these children, some of whom we have been caring for during the past seven or eight years. This still leaves us with the worst cases to be looked after—those who are not even able to attend these schools.

We have taken the children to the country each summer for a longer or a shorter time. Now we have a beautiful permanent summer home at Hawthorne, Westchester County, with twenty-four beds.

A winter home for discharged hospital cases has also been opened at 9 West 124th street, as an experiment. This home has fifteen beds.

Since 1895 the Guild has cared for seventy-seven children, thirteen of whom have died, thirty-seven have entered various schools, and twenty-seven are still being cared for. This does not include the children in the Home on 124th street.

The membership list consists of 151 associate members, who pay annual dues, and 54 active members who give personal service. Most of the latter are young girls, who have done excellent work, especially in the fine spiritual influence they have exercised upon the backward minds and characters of the cripples.

Officers, 1903–1905—Mrs. E. Strauss, President, 308 West 94th street; Mrs. I. N. Seligman, Vice-President, 36 West 54th street; Mrs. F. Hermann, Treasurer, 20 East 80th street; Miss F. Benjamin, Secretary, 251 West 95th street; Miss J. Jacoby, Financial Secretary, 112 East 70th street; Miss E. Lawton, Auditor, 176 West 87th street.

HOSPITAL FOR RUPTURED AND CRIPPLED

42D STREET AND LEXINGTON AVENUE

A brief and comprehensive description of what is being accomplished at the Hospital of the New York Society for the Relief of the Ruptured and Crippled Children might best be obtained from a review of the work of a single year, statistical mostly, but so explanatory as to be easily understood.

The records of the Out-Patient Department show that 11,226 persons presented themselves for treatment for the first time, and that 34,222 continued visits were made by patients already under treatment; making a grand total of 45,448. These people were cared for and treated by a corps of surgeons averaging twelve daily.

This department is separated into sections, for the treatment of orthopedic and hernia cases; subdivisions being provided for the different requirements of each section. A commodious operating room is an adjunct of this department.

The Hospital proper during the year cared for 975 patients, with a daily average of 201.5; the total days treatment being 73,554. 722 operations were performed, of which number 45 per cent. were cured, 49 per cent. were improved, 5 per cent. un-improved, and less than 1 per cent. died.

Apparatus and braces of various kinds, aggregating 11,003 in number, were applied; a well-appointed gymnasium for physical training, in charge of competent calisthenic teachers, was in daily operation; a daily school and kindergarten, which is one of the corporate schools of the Board of Education, is conducted. While there is no regularly organized Sunday School, the children are all provided with Sunday-school lesson papers, and every Sunday dear friends of the Hospital come and teach them in such way as they may be prompted.

When discharged, the parent or guardian of each child is given a printed circular instructing him to call at stated intervals; thus providing a way for every child who has ever been here to keep in touch with the Hospital if he will to do so. By this means a large number of children have been practically wards of the Hospital, surgically speaking, until maturity.

Statistics are useful in bringing to light the vast number of children, in our community, suffering for the most part quietly and patiently from distortions of body and limbs, with but little of the brightness of hope to cheer them; but most inadequate to express results obtained in the prosecution of such a tremendous work as this institution is doing.

Science to prune and brace and train the poor little shrunken forms into a development of symmetry and grace; earnest and loving hearts and hands to minister to their material comfort; devoted teachers to stimulate and train the neglected minds and stagnant brains into an activity that will transform from ignorance and vice into moral purity and beauty; a Christian atmosphere, bringing the little lives in touch with the Master who gave Himself for them all—these agencies are working ceaselessly, and, only in the fullness of time will the fruitage of such blessed service be manifest.

S. H. LE ROY, *Superintendent*

EDUCATION OF THE CRIPPLED CHILD

Charlton Wallace

EDUCATION OF THE CRIPPLED CHILD.*

BY CHARLTON WALLACE, M.D.,

Orthopedic Surgeon East Side Free School for Crippled Children; Assistant
Orthopedic Surgeon Hospital for Ruptured and Crippled; Lecturer in Orthopedic Surgery, New York Polyclinic Medical School and Hospital.

America has been remarkably forward in its public care for
the mental and physical uplift of the normal child, and perhaps the
rapidity of the advance in this respect has, through its concentration on the child in general, somewhat retarded the awakening of
public conscience to its duty toward the crippled child.

In the public school, among normal children, he is at an immense disadvantage. His physical inequality and moral depression, consequent upon comparison with his more fortunate fellow,
have a distinct adverse effect on his mental capacity and a
tendency to lower his ultimate general efficiency.

The cripple has not had a fair or a just opportunity to work
out the best that is in him; and it is for this fair chance that we
are working. His full and free development is our goal.

The physical condition of the crippled child must be brought
up to its highest standard, if mentally he is to be capable, if
morally he is to be uplifted, and if industrially he is to add his
quota to society. He must be guarded against overexertion, allowed
periods of rest, and have overzealous consideration always.
Medically, it must be made easy for him to secure the treatment
that his condition requires, and, supplementally, it should be seen
that the body is properly nourished, looking toward ultimate cure.

In the public school, difficulties are many for the cripple. He
must transport himself laboriously to and from school, climb stairs,
sit on benches ill-fitted to his comfort, encumbered as he is with
mechanical apparatus. The discipline and uniformity of the system does not permit of due consideration. Medically, the school
interferes with the proper clinical attention; or reversely, the
clinic interferes with the school, and thus neither is entirely successful in its ministrations. At present it is found impossible
for the public schools to take over what naturally should be
parental duty, but which, through sheer inability, ignorance or in-
difference, is so frequently neglected, namely, the duty of providing food for the proper nourishment of the body, which, in adding

---

* Read before the Orthopedic Section, New York Academy of Medicine, April
15, 1910.

strength to the resistance of the child, daily assists in the cure and furnishes sufficient bodily warmth so that open-air treatment may be successfully carried out.

Mentally, the care should be very different from that of the normal child in the public school. Much individual attention should be given, hence groups should be small. Classification is difficult, and demands careful thought and discrimination. The crippled child is, on the average, 2 years older than the normal when he enters school. Constant irregularities in attendance and mental variations, due to physical ups and down, make him ever a problem and candidate for new classification. Thus, it is to be seen that the instructor's work lies with the individual, and this is not practical in the public school class-room as constituted today.

Following the purely mental training of the class-room, the crippled child demands an efficient course of a practical nature. To offset his infirmity, he must be carefully prepared for some special work which he is fitted to do, so that he may maintain himself and hold self-respect throughout adult life. The normal child is equipped to fight physically, and thus to survive, if "fittest." The crippled child, being unfittest physically, must depend upon dexterity in his struggle. Through skilled industrial training we are emphasizing and developing in the cripple that quality in which he may excel, and thus diminishing in the eyes of the world and in the mind of the child himself the handicap of his infirmity. In industrial training, as in mental, the unwisdom of putting a cripple in a normal class is plainly seen. Consideration, full opportunity and individual attention are not possible; and, besides, occupations for them are of a special, adaptable type, which often could not be taught successfully in a general class.

It is easy from the foregoing to see how interactive are all of these educational factors. A combination of them results in an intense moral stimulus. The enforced introspection of the cripple makes him old before his time, makes him philosophical and thoughtful, so that he is fit soil for the germination of moral forces through the influence of these uplifting agencies. Repression, physically, mentally and industrially, bring about depression morally, because every hope is taken away. Uplift him in these respects, and you uplift him morally, give him happiness, make his aspirations higher, his accomplishments greater, and society better.

The history of the training of cripples is of too recent beginning to be very extensive, but at present universal effort in this respect is being put forth. We have, as one of the earliest examples, the "Danish Clinic School and Craftsman," in the suburbs of Copenhagen, which was organized in 1874. It has a clinic which admits all classes of patients free, and supplies them with apparatus or shoes. There is a trade school for male and female, in which are taught wood-carving, wood-engraving, book-binding, brush-making, carpentry, housekeeping, dressmaking, weaving and sewing. The course is three and one-half years for males, and two years for females. In the evening there are classes in Danish, history, writing, arithmetic, drawing and modeling. The clinic maintains a shop in Copenhagen, where many of its graduates find employment, and situations are procured for the others. There is a home where the pupils live while attending the clinic and school; also, a seaside hospital for those demanding that type of treatment. In our own country the Boston Industrial School for Crippled and Deformed Children is the pioneer, having been organized in 1893. Chicago has recently opened a school of this kind. The Widener Memorial Industrial Training School for Crippled Children is working along these lines, and is wonderfully complete in its equipment; but it borders on the hospital plan, and does not rightly belong here, time will not permit of our treating of the admirable schools carried on in many hospitals for cripples, notably the Hospital for Ruptured and Crippled, which has had a school since its foundation, 1863.

New York, within the last ten years, has come to the front in an effort to give the crippled child an education which shall be broad and practical enough to make him a competent worker. It now has 11 schools for crippled children, with a seating capacity of 696. which accommodation has need to be speedily increased. We find that during the last five years the Hospital for Ruptured and Crippled has admitted to its out-patient department 18,401 new cases under fourteen years of age. Within the next five years a large proportion of this number will seek schooling, and a great many will be forced to go into the regular classes of the public schools, unless private or public philanthropy furnishes more accommodations of this special sort.

Having considered in outline the needs and wants of the crippled child educationally, let us proceed to their practical development, taking as a prototype the East Side Free School for Crippled Children, which was organized Thanksgiving Day, 1900, with 13 children, and now has an enrollment of 183. The aim of this school from the beginning has been to advance the physical, mental, moral and industrial conditions of such unfortunate children. The physical and industrial departments are carried on by private philanthropy, the Department of Education assuming responsibility for the class-room teaching.

For the past two years the school has occupied the modern six-story building erected for it through the generosity of Mr. Emmanual Lehman and his children. It is complete and up to date in every respect. The class and industrial rooms are large and light. There is a roof garden adapted to every season and sort of weather, a kitchen and dining-room, and a well-equipped dispensary and large elevator.

The school is divided into a kindergarten and seven special grades. The work is conducted as it is in the public schools, with special reference to the individual child. The teachers coöperate with the medical department, and are ever on the alert for over-exertion, fatigue or sign of other discomfort in any child.

The ethical development constantly follows the intellectual. The children are taught to consider each other, to be helpful, one to another, the stronger assisting the weaker in the games and tasks. Every effort is made to keep them happy, cheerful and contented. Their playground is the roof, and their games are supervised. Frequent entertainments are arranged, in which the children are encouraged to excel. Improvement in the homes is brought about by friendly visits and suggestions. Mothers' meetings are held, where instruction is given in the care of the child, with direct reference to the crippled child, and emergency aid is supplied to the families, when needed.

In the 1906 report of the Copenhagen school we read: "The close connection between clinic and school has proved to be of great benefit to the patients. It was to have been desired that other countries which have followed our example had realized this, instead of founding the school separately from the clinic." The East Side Free School has been modeled on the Copenhagen plan, and its experience concurs with these findings. Through the dispensary it has been proven to the satisfaction of those concerned that such a course is of the greatest advantage to the patient, because:—

(1) The treatment is closely followed and continuously maintained.

(2) Irregularity in therapeutic measures can be prevented, so that the child may not be obliged to suffer through lax tendency of its guardians.

(3) Fatigue and time spent in attending outside clinics are eliminated.

(4) Uninterrupted attendance upon classes is preserved.

In considering the physical care of the children it is self-evident that the transportation to and from school must be furnished on account of faulty locomotion, the danger of street crossings, and the desire for prompt attendance. Three large stages are employed in this work, each making two trips before and after school. Two able-bodied men are in charge of each wagon, to carry the children up and down stairs at their homes.

In the school rooms thorough ventilation is insisted upon as necessary for tissue upbuilding and the proper growth of the child. The windows are kept open constantly, the temperature varying in winter from 55° to 60° F.

An underfed, poorly nourished child cannot stand the fresh air without becoming chilled; but when supplied with the requisite food, fresh air is a powerful factor in the healing process. The East Side Free School for Cripples realizes that without sufficient nourishment every other element in the treatment is futile. Upon arrival and departure, each child is given bread and butter and milk, and at noon a hot dinner, consisting of meat, vegetables, bread and dessert, with special diet for those for whom it has been prescribed.

Personal hygiene is given due consideration as an agent in toning up the system, increasing the resistance against disease and for bodily comfort. Each child has two baths a week, and all are taught to care for their teeth.

The simpler forms of medication are given, and a competent medical man has them under observation. There are also in attendance a rhinologist, oculist and dermatologist. Operations for adenoids and tonsils are performed elsewhere when required.

All of the orthopedic work except the operations is done at the school. Braces are furnished and repaired; plaster of Paris bandages are applied, and carefully selected exercises of the simpler form are prescribed and given in the school-room by the teachers, under the supervision of a physical instructor specially conversant with orthopedic exercises. A trained nurse is in constant attendance, whose duty it is to readjust braces, to overlook the orthopedic welfare of the child and to supply his immediate physical wants.

The class- and work-rooms are furnished with desks and chairs adjustable to the comfort of the individual. The health of the children is further benefited by a stay in the country during the summer vacation. Our benefactors, the Lehman family, have recently purchased land and are constructing a summer home at Oak Hurst, N. J., which will be ready for occupancy this summer, and will accommodate 100 children. Tuberculous cases remain throughout the entire summer, and the others go in relays. The school building is kept open, and the pupils in the city are taken to the roof garden for six days in every week.

Froude, in his short study, "The Essay on Progress," says: "Labor is the inevitable lot of the majority, and the best education is that which will make their labor most productive." In such a spirit was our work-room organized, and it is carried on with the idea of making it the ultimate end, the post-graduate course of every school pupil. In 1904 the work-room was open to 3 girls, to whom embroidery was taught, the average wage being $1.75 per week. Now 12 girls are doing embroidery, fine white and fancy art work, which has a ready market, and from its sale they are paid according to their skill, the maximum wage being $10, the minimum $2, and the average $4.66 per week. A book-bindery and basketry shop was opened two years ago, where 8 boys work at a maximum of $4.50 per week. The products of the workshop sold this year for $4,309.19. Of this $2,421.85 were paid to the workers in wages; materials having cost $1,332.96, leaving a balance over expenditure of $554.38. At present we have no need for other trades. The policy has been to work up to perfection those already installed, and, as more of our children at the school arrive at the working age, it will mean the enlargement of the industrial department and the broadening of its scope.

Five years ago there were 56 children on the registry, and up to the present date we have entered 297. Of the 114 who have left the school, 70 moved from the district, 14 were discharged, 12 died, 6 secured employment outside, 5 were placed in homes, 4 in hospitals, and 3 married. Of the remaining cases, 5 are cured and there are 10 whose lesions are about healed. Of these 297, 140 suffered from tuberculosis of the bone.

This work represents a clear vision of possibilities for the cripple. What has been accomplished worked itself out from day to day, as experience indicated. It clearly points the trend such work should take, and is submitted as a suggestion for future effort. The friend of the cripple must now take up this work, and intelligently, with broad sympathy, unselfish devotion and generous coöperation, bring it to its ultimate solution.

The Board of Education is awake to its duty toward the crippled child, and is honestly putting forth every effort toward betterment in his education. It has freely coöperated with private charity, seeking in this manner to bring to the crippled advantages which under its own present plans are impracticable.

The model presented is representative of this work in the other schools. Of the 11 schools in New York City 2 are entirely under private philanthropy and 2 wholly under the Board of Education, while 7 are conducted by a combination of the Department of Education and private charity. The enrollment of the 11 schools is 632, divided into 44 classes, an average of 14 pupils per teacher. Eight of the schools have industrial departments, in which altogether 10 different trades are taught, namely:—

(1) Sewing and dressmaking. (2) Embroidery. (3) Tapestry-weaving. (4) Leather-tooling. (5) Hand-carving. (6) Making of jewelry. (7) Brass work. (8) Book-binding. (9) Basket-working. (10) Carpentry.

Of the 3 schools that have no industrial department 1 is a kindergarten of the Association for the Aid of Crippled Children. This society is generously coöperating with the Board of Education by transporting its children to one class or another in the public schools, as well as to its own kindergarten and to the Manhattan Trade School for Girls, thus manifesting its interest in the industrial training. The second is the Boat School, for tuberculous cripples, carried on by the young women of Miss Spence's School society. This is a new departure, the classes being held out-of-doors, where the rest cure is combined with their mental training. The last school is the class in the public school at Grand and Essex Streets, which has been recently organized and has an enrollment of only 12.

We can, therefore, say that the schools are practically one, as regards the realization of the value of industrial training. Having noted this common idea, we foresee that there will come a day when industrial plans and aims will be unified, each school will give and gain, and advance will be such as never before.

In all such development there are clearly indicated certain

points that must be worked out. The first is that the output must have a ready market—that is, it must be something the public wants. Second, it must compete with like products purely through merit, or, in other words, it must be as good as the best of its sort. Third, the method must be business, and not charity. So much for the product of our crippled labor. These possibilities of realization will surely be brought about.

But what of our cripple when he becomes a "master-workman," when we can teach him no more in our industrial school! Having brought him so far, we are obliged to take him farther in order to accomplish that which we have stated as our end, namely, to give him the opportunity to become self-respecting and self-supporting throughout adult life.

Two ways to accomplish this suggest themselves:—

(1) By a special employment bureau through which his labor may be sold in the market, with the conditions, in the long run, exactly similar to those which surround any workingman; or,

(2) We, ourselves, can be his employer through a shop which shall be started on a firm business basis, having at first the backing of wealth, but which will ultimately become a self-supporting coöperative undertaking, managed by the crippled and for the crippled.

How inclusive this plan may be made and how much we might still have to depend upon the outside labor market are questions which the future will settle. At least some such plan is an ideal for us all to look forward to, think about and work for.

CRIPPLED CHILDREN IN CONNECTICUT

John P. Sanderson, Jr.

Crippled Children in Connecticut

John P. Sanderson, Jr.[1]

Hartford, Conn.

Alice, aged seven, crippled as the result of infantile paralysis, had for several weeks been living in the almshouse of one of our larger cities. Her mother died in June, leaving the father, and three small children all under nine years of age. Less than two months later the father died. The Department of Charities asked our assistance in providing for the crippled child. From all sections of the State similar appeals come to us for attention.

In 1898, six years after its founding, the Connecticut Children's Aid Society established a 'Home for Incurables' at Newington, five miles south of Hartford. Mrs. Virginia T. Smith, the founder of the Society, was secretary and supervisor of the Home until her death in 1903. Her work was marked with singular success, but many of her advanced opinions brought bitter criticism.

Her report as Chairman of the Committee on Preventive Work among Children at the National Conference of Charities, held at St. Paul in 1886, indicates her remarkable understanding of the need for a constructive program in children's work throughout the country. Her committee recommended:

First, that it shall be our aim, through laws made to that effect, to remove, when practicable, to proper surroundings and to the benefit of family homes, all neglected and outcast children.

Second, that asylums, temporary homes, and institutions may be simply a means by which we shall accomplish this object.

Third, that the boarding-out system for babies and young children may be an additional means for the promotion of this object.

Fourth, that a thorough system of investigation and visitation be inaugurated as necessary to the success of the work.

[1] Executive Secretary, Connecticut Children's Aid Society.

Fifth, that we secure, if possible, a thorough system of classification, which will protect innocent children from the dangers of being committed to correctional institutions.

From the very origin of the Connecticut Children's Aid Society the placing of children in family homes has been emphasized, but the urgent need in the State of institutional care for crippled children forced the Society to establish its Home.

The original law "concerning the commitment and support of poor children of sound mind who are cripples or who are afflicted with any non-contagious disease" refers to the 'Home for Incurables', which unfortunately is the name still appearing on the commitment blanks. Undoubtedly a bill will be introduced at the next General Assembly, changing the name to 'Home for Crippled Children'.

Following the death of Mrs. Smith in 1903, Miss Josephine Griswold, who had been associated with the former secretary since the beginning of the work, became secretary, and during the next decade the work of the Society developed rapidly. Following Miss Griswold's death in 1914, Miss Elizabeth A. Holcomb became secretary of the Society and Mrs. Susan J. Crane, one of the incorporators, became supervisor of the 'Virginia T. Smith Home for Incurables'.

The last six months have marked a general reorganization of the Society. The former secretary strenuously urged the Directors to bring about this reorganization and graciously resigned in order that it might take place. The Society now has three distinct departments of work:

First, a Department of Advice and Inquiry with Miss Maud Morlock as supervisor. This Department makes inquiry regarding every application both for placement of children in family homes and for commitment to the Home for Crippled Children.

Second, a Department of Placing-Out, which carefully places and supervises children in private homes throughout the State. Miss Holcomb remains with the Society in the capacity of supervisor of this department.

Third, the Home for Crippled Children at Newington. The former supervisor of the Home resigned recently after fourteen years of faithful service, and Miss Constance Leigh, a graduate nurse with special training in institutional work, has taken charge of the Home.

Inventory has been taken and some surprising conditions have been revealed. For many years Connecticut has suffered through lack of adequate facilities for her feeble-minded. Almshouses have looked to county homes for help, and the latter have naturally not cared to open their doors to this mentally deficient class. Consequently, as a means of last resort, many of the feeble-minded with little or no physical disability have been committed one after another to our Home for Crippled Children. The need of a careful survey of all the children in our care became evident, and as a basis upon which to reconstruct the work, this survey was made. A group of three physicians with the writer gave considerable time to this classification. We preferred to consider not only whether or not the child was to remain in our Home, but, if discharged, what disposition was to be made.

Every child was, therefore, entered under one of the following four classifications:

1. Can go home.
    a. Those not to be benefited by further treatment at the Home.
    b. Those not a public menace.
    c. Those whose family are able to care for them.

2. Can be placed out in private homes.
    a. Those who can be treated as well medically, etc., out of the institution.
    b. Those who cannot get proper care at home.

3. Should go to the School for Feeble-Minded or other State institutions.
    a. Those who are a public menace.
    b. Those who are chronically mentally defective.

    i. Idiot.
    ii. Imbecile.
    iii. Moron, etc.
    c. Those requiring special type of education.

4. Should be retained at the Home for Crippled Children.
    a. Those who can soon be sent home or boarded out and require medical or surgical treatment for condition which would improve mental or physical condition.
    b. Those who are not lacking in capacity to learn.

The findings of the Commission may be classified as follows:

To be discharged as patients and retained as help	4
Group No. 1	2
Group No. 1 or 2	13
Group No. 1 or 3	1
Group No. 1 or 4	1
Group No. 2	3
Group No. 2 or 3	1
Group No. 3	26
Group No. 4	67
	118

In other words, sixty-seven of the 118 were definitely considered eligible to remain as patients at the Home, four to be discharged as patients because of age and temporarily employed as help, and forty-seven were definitely classified as not belonging in our Home for one of the first three reasons cited above.

Meanwhile the Directors of the Society clarified the situation by the adoption of a resolution "recommending that the Home provide for crippled children of sound mind and no others and that the Executive Secretary be empowered to bring about as rapidly as possible such changes as are recommended by the Commission."

Next, the question of relieving the Home of these forty-seven has been demanding the greatest amount of attention. In the majority of cases cooperation has been asked of the organization, public or private, through which the child was originally committed, and after an explanation has been made on our part all interested have usually united in an effort to transfer the child to a suitable home pending institutional care later, if necessary.

We have urged the towns to make application for the commitment of feeble-minded children to the State School for Feeble-Minded at Lakeville, even though the latter is known to have a waiting list of several hundred. Perhaps in this way the State will quickest come to a realization of the problem and meet its needs.

In every case the Society has urged the removal of the child to be discharged, basing its claim on the justice to the other crippled children entrusted to its care. We are now nearing the completion of the task; twenty-seven have been returned to their parents or near relatives; nine have been returned to public charities departments; seven have been committed to the Training School for Feeble-Minded; and one has been provided for in a private hospital, making a total of forty-four removed.

Finally, we are about to begin. The three teachers who refused to return unless the feeble-minded children were removed will be with us at the opening of school. The daily program in the school will give more emphasis to manual training; more care is being given to the individual needs of each child admitted; and through the efforts of the visiting staff of the Society, great care is being taken to discover the important points in the history of every case, so that, if the child is accepted, the family history will be known and proper treatment and care can be given.

Meanwhile, the children under our care are thriving. Nature has provided a bountiful supply of good air and sunshine in the hills of Newington where the Home is most attractively located. The boys' house accommodates forty-five, the girls' house fifty-four, and a small hospital has three wards of six beds each, making a total capacity of 117 children.

The Children's Aid Society is entrusted with a most responsible work for the crippled children of Connecticut. Its inheritance is of the best. Perhaps this inventory which has been carried on during the last few months will help to produce larger dividends in the years to come.

THE HISTORY OF A HOSPITAL
FOR CRIPPLED CHILDREN IN THE FAR WEST

Ann B.L. Stedman

THE HISTORY OF A HOSPITAL FOR CRIPPLED CHILDREN IN THE FAR WEST

Ann B. L. Stedman
Seattle, Wash.

The history of the Children's Orthopedic Hospital of Seattle resembles that of almost all charitable institutions for children, in the fact that its inception came from the heart of a good woman seeking to better the condition of little children, whose burden of pain, deformity and environment cried aloud for help.

In January of 1906, a few women were invited to come together to discuss the necessity and advisability of caring for the crippled children of the Northwest. So far as could be learned, at that time, there was no orthopedic hospital west of the Mississippi, north of San Francisco. The situation was gone over carefully and the natural call of women to care for the helpless was so in evidence that organization began at once. The immediate need proved so pressing, applications coming as soon as the organization became known, that beds in a general hospital were engaged and the orthopedic charity for this immense Northwest territory was begun.

Officers, trustees, advisory board and standing committees were formed and elected; surgical staff with assistants appointed. Memberships—active, associate and junior—were instituted, and at the end of eighteen months work was well under way in a small bungalow with a capacity for twelve ward beds. This was called the Fresh Air House and was the upward turning point for many boys and girls who otherwise would never have known the joy and privilege of being alive and well to enjoy all that fresh air and scientific treatment means to a body greatly improved or free from deformity.

The inspiration of the work proved so true that the Fresh Air House was filled immediately. Applications came pouring in from all directions, and a waiting list that has never been wiped clear was established. Many patients remained for such extended periods of time that the necessity for a larger building became apparent at once. To this end, every effort was made to raise money for a permanent institution. The city of Seattle was districted. In each district a guild was formed with officers and members drawn from the membership of the general association—hospital membership carrying the privilege of guild membership. The guilds are wholly independent in their work and means of raising funds for whatever they select as their individual responsibility. For instance, one guild maintains a bed at $250 a year, and also raises money to purchase material which its members make into bed gowns for all the patients in the hospital.

In December, 1910, the actual excavations for the new building began. September, 1911, saw this building completed and dedicated. It represents an investment of $125,000 and would have been opened free of debt could all the pledges have been collected, but the outstanding $5,000 was raised within a year. Since that time every penny given has been applied directly to the care of patients, with the exception of the salary of a bookkeeper, who is paid $15 a month. Women who love the hospital perform all duties connected with its administration.

Beginning with nothing in January, 1906, in January, 1915, the Association had a membership total of 650, an investment of $125,000 and *no* debts. The fireproof building is two full stories, and an above-ground basement, 103 feet frontage, 46 feet deep, a floor area of 4,350 square feet. Exterior of brick with cement trimmings, walls and ceilings of hard plaster, floors cement, some left natural, some covered with raecolith and some with battleship linoleum. There are four inside wards, a large porch ward, three private rooms, together with all the regulation hospital equipment of operating room, dressing room, diet kitchen, baths, toilets, out-patient department, store rooms, laundry, ice machine room, dining rooms, kitchen, store and refrigerating rooms and so forth. All are equipped with latest improvements and kept up to a high state of efficiency.

Strictly speaking, a dispensary has not been established, although the out-patient department cares for that line of work, both in the part of the building set aside for that purpose and in the homes of patients.

The Fresh Air House has been converted into a nurses' home, fitted up attractively and made as comfortable and homelike as possible. In this house the Superintendent has a suite, the pupil nurses a dormitory, the graduate nurses on day duty sleeping porches, dressing rooms and baths. The Association also owns a second cottage where night nurses and maids live in comfort, surrounded by all that makes life outside hospital walls as bright as possible. In this house the lectures are given and a study-hall for pupil nurses is provided.

The grounds are most attractively treated, while ample space is allowed for play for all patients able to be moved out of the building.

The hospital's capacity is fifty beds, but by careful management in selecting children who are so placed in casts they cannot interfere with each other, two are sometimes in the same bed and there have been fifty-eight in-patients at one time. This, however, occurs infrequently, yet demonstrates the need of such a hospital as the Children's Orthopedic.

Seattle, of course, sends more children than any other one place, but many other localities have been represented—all the Northwest States, Alaska and India.

From Alaska we have had many children. The intermingling of races, remoteness and consequent lack of care, produce distressing results. A girl of mixed blood suffering from tubercular hips was sent to us from Kodiak two years ago. She was completely cured and through the same influence that sent her to the Children's Orthopedic Hospital she was placed in a California training school. She developed a remarkable voice but was so unhappy in the school that she has been sent to New York City to continue her training.

A few months ago a telegram was received from Kodiak asking if the sister of this girl could be sent to us. A prompt reply was wired to send her immediately. Within the week this girl of eight arrived in care of the steward of an Alaska boat. She was so frail and emaciated even a photograph could not be taken. The same tubercular condition as her sister's, only worse, is yielding to care and treatment. A complete cure is expected within a year.

Infantile paralysis spares no locality, but we little dreamed that India would send a case. The son of an English clergyman heard of the Children's Orthopedic Hospital from a Seattle physician who was traveling in the Orient. The eight-year-old son, paralyzed from the hips down, came this long distance with only his Hindoo servant, aged 16, to care for him on the trip. Immigration laws were strict, papers had to be drawn and signed. Eight months was the limit of time he could remain in the United States. The case looked dark from every standpoint, but at the end of the allotted time, Noel could stand without support and walk with crutches.

The nationalities follow a wide range. Our very first cure was a colored girl with tubercular joints, who came to us from the County Farm in a dying condition. Japanese, Chinese, Swedes, Norwegians, Esquimos, every combination and mixture, are also received.

The territory called the Northwest includes: British Columbia, Alaska, Washington, Idaho, Oregon, Montana, North Dakota and so forth. An entire family moved from Michigan to Seattle to put a child in this hospital; several from California with the same mission.

Affiliation with other hospitals has been worked out and it is planned to enlarge and improve this branch of the training school. School is in session every day, also kindergarten. The city supplies the school teacher, but the Association pays for the kindergartner. Sunday school also is provided by interested members of the Association. Manual training is to be installed and handicraft of salable quality is now produced. The profits of the sales go to the child who made the article sold.

The out-patient department is of great social and educational value, carrying into homes, where ignorance and waste had been the rule, enlightment and economy, making for improved citizenship as well as for health.

A boy who had been an in-patient a year begged his mother to go to the hospital and learn how to make soup such as he had enjoyed while under treatment. In so far as possible, careful account is kept of patients for as long a period as is needful, renewing casts, and so forth, but the distressing cases are those who are compelled to return to homes too remote to reach except by infrequent letters.

In 1913 a dental staff was appointed with necessary equipment. This has been of the greatest advantage and assistance towards the health and happiness of the patients. Under the direction of the chief, two dentists are on duty at a time, examining and correcting the teeth of each child. Eye, ear, nose and throat specialists, neurologist and radiologist give of their time and skill.

From the patients, payment in part or in full is expected when this can be afforded, but free treatment is gladly provided for those who need it. And the charity case is always given precedence in the ward when several apply and only one can be admitted. Sixty-eight per cent. of the treatment is free to destitute children.

Support may be given in several ways. First, to be depended upon are membership, active, $10 and up; associate, $5 and up; junior, $1 per annum; $250 names a free bed for one year. The gift of $5,000, which the Trustees will carefully invest and use only the interest thereof, will endow a ward bed in perpetuity; $7,500 will name and endow a bed in a private room in perpetuity; $10,000 names and establishes a ward, and a $50,000 gift would endow a ten-bed ward in perpetuity.

Bequests, endowments, and so forth, are placed in first class investments; only the interest being used in the working fund. The cost of maintenance per month approximates $1,500. This is covered by the memberships, interest on investments, patients' fees, donations of all kinds—money, clothing, provisions and hospital supplies being included. One generous firm of wholesale druggists has for several years furnished all drugs free of charge. What this means to the hospital can be understood when the value frequently passes the $100 mark a month. From this large contribution, gifts range through every form of supply to the very personal and touching gift from a woman of small means but large heart, who goes to the hospital one afternoon of each week. She is hailed with hand clapping and shouts of pleasure, for she is the 'Story Telling Lady.' In each ward she tells the same story so that every child has the same knowledge and joy, but to the very sick child she brings a personal little story that is told quietly and sweetly at his bedside. Who can judge of the far-reaching influence of this one woman, who gives of heart and time?

Once a year the Junior Guild, under the direction of the Ways and Means Committee, gives an entertainment for the children of Seattle. This entertainment is free not only in that the performers give their services but those who attend give only as they feel inclined. This supports what is called the 'Christmas Bed' at $250 a year; any surplus goes into a fund to endow the bed in perpetuity.

Old patients send new patients on and on. The far reaching effect of eight years' effort cannot be measured. Nebraska has recently answered the call of the crippled child, meeting half way between Mississippi and Pacific the outstretched hands of those asking help to straighten crooked bones.

Until eugenics are more fully understood and regulated, deformity will come into the world; until the end of time accidents are unavoidable. The care of the crippled child comes to us with the appeal of humanity and protection, the world hears it and the response is immediate, bringing into existence these charities that so appeal to the hearts of all who care for the uplift of the conditions of children.

A STUDY OF THE CHARACTER
AND PRESENT STATUS OF PROVISION
FOR CRIPPLED CHILDREN
IN THE UNITED STATES

Douglas C. McMurtrie

A STUDY OF THE CHARACTER AND PRESENT STATUS OF PROVISION FOR CRIPPLED CHILDREN IN THE UNITED STATES

Douglas C. McMurtrie
New York

The care and education of cripples is a comparatively new subject, at least in comparison with provision for other types of the physically handicapped. But the need was a real one, the demand urgent, and the growth has been proportionately rapid. In 1890 there were but five institutions for crippled children in the United States; since then special institutions for their care have multiplied sevenfold.

The development in each locality has, however, been independent of work elsewhere, and there has been practically no interchange of experience. Many have been making the same mistakes, meeting the same obstacles, achieving the same successes, without knowing of each other's efforts. The field of work for cripples was one, therefore, which peculiarly invited a careful and exact study in order to set forth for mutual benefit the fruit of experience up to the present time.

This opportunity for valuable service was grasped by the Child Helping Department of the Russell Sage Foundation when it entered upon a study of the institutional work for crippled children in the United States. An exhaustive report[1] of this investigation has just been published. Its findings are of such importance as to warrant detailed consideration.

The book presents a comprehensive survey of American institutions for crippled children, which is accurate and reli-

[1]EDITH REEVES. Care and education of crippled children in the United States. Introduction by Hastings H. Hart, LL.D. (Russell Sage Foundation Publication.) New York, 1914.

able.   The findings are in the main sound and conservative. The result is a credit to the ability of the investigator, Miss Reeves (now Mrs. Solenberger), and to the foresight and judgment of Dr. Hart, Director of the Department of Child Helping.

The investigation was first undertaken at the suggestion of Dr. Bradford of Boston to study primarily the matter of vocational training, but it was found necessary to cover first the field of institutional work.

The method of study was personal visitation of the individual institutions by the investigator.   All of the institutions (with the exception of one in the far West) were visited once and many of them twice.   After a general acquaintance with the field and its problems had been secured, definite points on which data were desired were decided upon, and on subsequent visits the information was carefully recorded.

After the completion of the field work, the statistics were compiled and the general deductions made.   Throughout the study, hearty co-operation was obtained from the officers of the individual hospitals and homes.

In all, sixty-four institutions were studied.   Of these, the work of thirty-seven, which make residential provision for cripples exclusively and are open all the year, is presented statistically in detail.   The work of the remaining twenty-seven is described, but is not represented in the statistics.

After a discussion of the scope of the study, the author passes to a consideration of three leading features of work for crippled children: (a) physical care, (b) special provisions for education, and (c) handwork and vocational training.   There is next presented in summary and detail the statistical findings, and finally, in one of the most interesting sections of the book a detailed description of each institution.

The thirty-seven institutions studied in detail were classified according to character in three groups, ten as hospitals, fourteen as convalescent hospitals or homes, and thirteen as asylum homes.   "This classification is not borne out by the names of all the institutions. Some of the early hospitals were organized many years ago as homes for crippled children, and the old titles have been retained since the institutions developed into hospitals. A number could easily be classed in either of two of the three groups. It has been necessary, therefore, to put each institution into the group whose general type it most nearly resembled." The institutions coming within each group are listed in the tables reproduced later in the present article.

The physical care of crippled children is generally acknowledged to be the feature of primary importance. If the proper surgical and convalescent treatment can be provided at an early enough age, a considerable proportion of crippled children can be cured and restored to a normal status. This automatically solves the problem of future care and vocational training.

This is clearly set forth. "All efforts in behalf of crippled children must be based upon sound policies of surgical treatment and general physical care, which aim to cure the diseases and correct the deformities of the children whenever that is possible, and to return them to conditions of living on a plane with those of children who have not been crippled. It is equally true that for the crippled children whose handicaps cannot be entirely removed, the first aim should be the elimination, in as large a measure as possible, of the difficulties which set them apart from children who have no physical defects."

And though the physical care seemed the feature of most moment, it seemed the best provided for. Miss Reeves found almost universally competent orthopedic service freely given, with the results of the work highly effective.

The nursing provision in the various institutions is discussed in detail, as also the visiting nursing in connection with dispensary work. This latter is coming to be most important, as it greatly increases the effectiveness of out-patient departments, but it is a field which should be much further developed. According to the findings at the time the study was made: "Only three out of the nine institutions [with dispensaries] recorded a number of visits paid to homes by visiting nursing which was commensurate with the size of the dispensary service, namely, the New York Orthopædic Dispensary and Hospital, the New Jersey Orthopaedic Hospital and Dispensary, and the Kernan Hospital and Industrial School in Baltimore." There are also interesting systems in other hospitals not among those tabulated.

The subjects of physical culture and gymnastics, dietary, living conditions, and provisions for quarantine are also considered as factors of physical care.

The important question of education receives adequate consideration. Miss Reeves reports a general recognition of the impracticability of meeting the educational needs of most crippled children in regular school classes attended by healthy children. In consequence, special classes for cripples have been opened in public and private day schools and in many residential institutions.

There is brought up one most interesting suggestion which would profit from further discussion by those engaged daily in the actual educational work. The point comes up in the following paragraphs:

Some of the problems which must be solved in the education of crippled children are produced by the fact that both curable and incurable crippled children are usually taught in the same special classes. A large proportion of crippled children can be cured or so far helped that in the course of time they will be able to re-enter regular classes in the public schools. Many of these temporarily crippled children find in the special classes a much needed opportunity to 'keep up' with their school work in so far as their physical condition permits. But there are also considerable numbers of crippled children whose cure is impossible, or possible only after years of treatment. These children need a complete system of education which will develop such powers as they possess.

The teacher of crippled children has to deal with some who are familiar with public school routine and have much the same point of view as the normal pupils, together with a large number who have never been able to attend the regular schools or to associate freely with other children.   It is not intended to suggest that crippled children can be divided accurately into the, two groups mentioned.   The crippled child may differ greatly or to only a slight extent from the normal, sound child of his own age in general strength and in point of view; and the graduations are numerous between: for example, a boy who has been a vigorous urchin until he lost a leg in a trolley accident at twelve or fourteen and, on the other hand, a child who has been paralyzed from the age of three or four, or one who has been fighting to overcome bone tuberculosis since an early age.   It is important that every teacher of crippled children should have an elementary knowledge of the different physical difficulties which have caused them to become crippled, and that she should know in the case of each individual child how long he has been in a handicapped condition, and in what degree his life has differed from that of a normal child up to the time when he entered her class.

The matters of schoolroom equipment and curriculum next come up, and there is then given considerable space to the public school classes for cripples. This particular field of work is an exclusively Anglo-Saxon development which is of unusual interest to continental students of the subject. The work along this line promises rapid extension.

One of the most difficult features in the care of crippled children has proven to be industrial training with a view to subsequent self-support. The author here points out that adequate training is far more important in degree to the crippled than to the normal child. "The success of such training for normal children is judged according to the ability of the trained pupils to take better positions and advance more rapidly than the untrained. The benefit of industrial training can be judged only by comparing those who are trained with untrained children who are also crippled. When crippled children who would otherwise fail as producers are able to earn part or all of their own living after special training, the value of that training must in many cases be judged by the difference between the measure of success they do attain and complete dependence."

One of the principal pitfalls in the choice of subjects for industrial work has been the persistence of the 'traditional' manual training subjects as, for instance, basketry, chair-caning, and the making of fancy articles. "The fact that it is hard to secure steady employment or reasonably good wages by making such articles outside the institution and away from the possibility of a 'charity' demand for the things made, has been too often forgotten." The study showed, however, the development of general discontent with these subjects, and a tendency to branch out into more practical lines. In the choice of occupations the prevailing wage scale of the trade is another important factor.

In the chapter devoted to statistics are presented summaries of the various totals and averages. The thirty-seven institutions studied in detail had a capacity of 2,474, with an average number of children under care during the year of 1,968. The average ratio of children to employees was found to be 2.3. The other tables concern floor space, cost of plant, current expense, salaries and wages, food cost per capita and per diem, sources of income, public funds, admission and discharge, school statistics, hand work, and dispensaries.

This statistical section will probably have a more restricted appeal than the earlier part of the book. The careful work on these details, however, should prove of very considerable value to those planning future developments. A humorous sidelight on this particular section of the study is the amazement engendered in the managers of the institutions by "their measuring every room in the building."

The tables of widest interest are probably those realting to the rules of admission and discharge. These are reproduced herewith.

RULES OF ADMISSION AND DISCHARGE IN 10 HOSPITALS

Hospital	Kinds of orthopedic cases taken and preferred	Physical and mental restrictions and preferences	Usual period of stay in institution
ILLINOIS Chicago Home for Destitute Crippled Children	All kinds	Feeble - mindedness, epilepsy, and lung tuberculosis excluded	Until dispensary care can be safely substituted
MAINE Portland Children's Hospital . . .	All kinds	None; cases of lung tuberculosis isolated	Until dispensary care can be safely substituted; average 97 days
MINNESOTA St. Paul State Hospital	All kinds	None	As long as benefited by hospital care; average one year
NEBRASKA Lincoln Nebraska Orthopedic Hospital	All kinds	None	As long as benefited by hospital care; average 250 days [a]
NEW JERSEY Newark Home for Crippled Children .	All kinds	Lung tuberculosis and feeble-minded cases not desired; sometimes taken	Transfer as soon as possible to dispensary; great demand for beds
Orange New Jersey Orthopædic Hospital and Dispensary .	All kinds	Lung tuberculosis excluded	Until dispensary care can be safely substituted; average 3 months
NEW YORK New York City Hospital for Deformities and Joint Diseases . . .	All kinds	Lung tuberculosis excluded	Until dispensary care can be safely substituted; average 6 months
Hospital for the Ruptured and Crippled	All kinds	None	Until dispensary care can be safely substituted; average 65 days
New York Orthopædic Dispensary and Hospital .	All kinds	Lung tuberculosis excluded	Until dispensary care can be safely substituted; average 50 days
WASHINGTON Seattle Children's Orthopedic Hospital	All kinds	Lung tuberculosis excluded	Until dispensary care can be safely substituted; average 44 days

[a] Aim to develop educational work and keep children until self-supporting.
[b] Plan to start visiting nursing.
[c] Some exceptions.

After care and visitation	Ages received	Age limit for discharge	Sexes received	Color restriction	Financial terms	Geographical restrictions and preferences
Through dispensary only	2½ to 11 [e]	12 [e]	Both	None	Usually free; maximum charge $5 a week [e]	Intended for residents of Illinois. Rule not strictly followed
Through dispensary and systematic visits by one agent of Maine Children's Committee	Any under 21 [d]	No rule	Both	None	Medical service free; patients pay for braces; board often free; maximum charge $1 a day	In-patients must be residents of Maine. Out-patients no restrictions
None	Any under 16	No rule	Both	None	Free	Minnesota children only
None	2 to 18; a few adults	No rule	Both	None	Free	Must have been resident in Nebraska one year
Through dispensary only	All	No rule	Both	None	Usually free; a few pay $1 to $10 a week	None
Through dispensary and systematic visits by one nurse (half time)	Boys 1½ to 16; girls 1½ up	Boys 16; girls no rule	Both	None	Usually free; maximum charge $5 a week	Preference given to New Jersey children
Through dispensary only [b]	All	No rule	Both	None	Usually paid for by relatives or city; some free; some private cases	None
One social service worker recently engaged	4 up [e]	No rule	Both	None	About 60 per cent paid by city; 20 per cent free and 20 per cent pay	None
Through dispensary and staff of 5 visiting nurses	2 to 14 and adult women [e]	No rule	Both	None	94 per cent free; occasional payments $4–$7 a week	None
Through dispensary and visiting nurse	Any under 16	No rule	Both	None	Usually free; maximum charge $10 a week	None

[d] Charter permits taking of adults.
[e] All ages treated in dispensary.

Convalescent hospital or home	Kinds of orthopedic cases taken and preferred	Physical and mental restrictions and preferences	Usual period of stay in institution
ILLINOIS West Chicago Convalescent Home for Destitute Crippled Children	Curable cases; no bed patients at present	Backward children received; but none obviously feeble-minded; no lung tuberculosis	At least until cured
MARYLAND Baltimore Children's Hospital School	Cases likely to be cured or distinctly improved	Lung tuberculosis and feeble-mindedness excluded [c]	Until benefited as much as possible
Baltimore Kernan Hospital and Industrial School for Crippled Children	All kinds	Backward children received, but none obviously feeble-minded; no lung tuberculosis	Plan to keep until as much benefited as possible [g]
MASSACHUSETTS Canton Massachusetts Hospital School	All kinds	Feeble-minded and epileptic cases excluded	Until benefited as much as possible
MICHIGAN Detroit Van Leuven Browne Hospital School	All kinds [b]	None	As long as they need a home
MINNESOTA Phalen Park, St. Paul State Hospital and School for Crippled Children	All kinds	Lung tuberculosis and feeble-mindedness excluded	Until benefited as much as possible [f]
NEW YORK Coney Island Sea Breeze Hospital	Tuberculosis of bones and glands only. Preference to bone tuberculosis	Because of great demand seldom take feeble-minded or chronic cases	Until benefited as much as possible
Garden City House of St. Giles the Cripple	All kinds	Very few feeble-minded cases; no new ones will be taken	Until benefited as much as possible, or as long as they need a home
Port Jefferson St. Charles Hospital for Crippled Children [a]	All kinds	None [d]	Until benefited as much as possible, or as long as they need a home
West Haverstraw State Hospital for Crippled Children	All kinds	Feeble-minded cases not often taken	As long as in need of convalescent care
White Plains Country Branch New York Orthopædic Hospital	Curable cases; especially bone tuberculosis	Lung tuberculosis excluded	Until cured and probability of relapse is past
PENNSYLVANIA Philadelphia Widener Memorial School	Permanent cripples, yet not absolutely helpless	Accept only those likely to become partially self-supporting. No lung tuberculosis, feeble-minded or backward children	Until 18 to 21 for purpose of industrial training
Pittsburgh Industrial Home for Crippled Children	All kinds	Preference to those likely to profit by industrial training. No lung tuberculosis, no feeble-mindedness	At least until benefited as much as possible; occasionally longer for purposes of education
Sewickley Sewickley Fresh Air Home	All kinds	Children with lung tuberculosis or markedly feeble-minded or epileptic, excluded	Until benefited as much as possible

[a] Department of Brooklyn Home for Blind, Crippled, and Defective Children.
[b] Occasional non-orthopedic cases. [c] Occasional exceptions as to feeble-minded.
[d] Feeble-minded children segregated. [e] This policy is not fully carried out because of demand for beds.
[f] May decide to keep for industrial training when organized. [g] Expect to employ visitor.
[h] Most institutions which have no formal system of after care keep in touch with many discharged children through correspondence and visits of the children to the institution.

RULES OF ADMISSION AND DISCHARGE IN 14 CONVALESCENT HOSPITALS OR HOMES (*continued*)

After care and visitation	Ages received	Age limit for discharge	Sexes received	Color restriction	Financial terms	Geographical restrictions and preferences
New institution; policy not definitely decided	4 to 14	No rule	Both	None	Free	Cases transferred from Home for Destitute Crippled Children, Chicago
None ᵍ	3 to 10	13	Both	White only	Usually free; maximum charge $7 a week	Preference given to Maryland children
Through dispensary and staff of 3 visiting nurses	Up to about 16	Undecided	Both	White only ᵖ	Usually free; maximum charge $14 a week	Preference given to Maryland children
None ʰ	5 to 15	No rule	Both	None	State, cities or towns. Parents pay $4 a week if able	Must be residents of Massachusetts
None ʰ	3 years up ⁱ	No rule	Both	White only	Usually free; maximum charge $5 a week	None
None ʰ	5 to 17 ʲ	Undecided	Both	None	Free	Minnesota children only
Visits by agents of the Association for Improving the Condition of the Poor	2 to 12	No rule	Both	None	Usually free	None
None ʰ	Up to 16	..	Both	None	Usually paid for by city	None
Visits by agent of Catholic Orphan Asylum Society	No rule ᵏ	No rule	Both	No rule	City cases at $.40 a day, others free or payment small	Most children from Brooklyn; none from Manhattan; a few from other states
None ʰ	4 to 16 ˡ	No rule	Both	None	Free; parents furnish clothing if able	Must be resident of New York State one year
None; if necessary would be supervised by nurses of city branch ʰ	3 years up ᵏ	No rule	Both	None	Usually free. A few pay something	None
Plan boarding home for discharged children who are partially self-supporting	4 to 10 ᵐ	21	Both	White only	Free	Preference first to residents of Philadelphia; second, Pennsylvania outside of Philadelphia; third, any other states
None ʰ	3 to 12 ⁿ	No rule	Both	No rule; no colored children yet taken	Usually free; maximum charge $1 a day	Pennsylvania children only
None ʰ	3 to 12 ˡ	No rule	Both	White only	Free	No rule; so far, all but one from Pennsylvania

ⁱ Occasional exceptions. ʲ Occasionally under five.
ᵏ Probably would not take boys over 12 years. ˡ Occasionally receive children under four years.
ᵐ All children must be indentured to the institution until 21. ⁿ Occasionally receive children over 12 years.
ᵒ If children remain after 16 they become "helpers" and may stay indefinitely.
ᵖ Colored children treated at city dispensary.

Asylum home	Kinds of orthopedic cases taken and preferred	Physical and mental restrictions and preferences	Usual period of stay in institution
CONNECTICUT Newington Virginia T. Smith Home for Incurables . . .	All kinds	Lung tuberculosis excluded [e]	Until benefited as much as possible; longer if they need a home
ILLINOIS Chicago Happy Haven	No children unable to attend public school classes for cripples	Lung tuberculosis excluded	As long as they need a home
Maywood Home for Disabled Children .	Cases not requiring surgical treatment	Feeble-minded, deaf and blind cases and those with lung tuberculosis, excluded	Until self-supporting or a good home is found
MASSACHUSETTS Hyde Park New England Peabody Home for Crippled Children .	All kinds	Lung tuberculosis and feeble-mindedness excluded	Until benefited as much as possible; or until self-supporting if they have not good homes
NEW JERSEY Englewood Daisy Fields Home and Hospital for Crippled Children	Curable cases, able to walk	Lung tuberculosis and feeble-mindedness excluded	Until benefited as much as possible; longer if they need a home
NEW YORK Buffalo Crippled Children's Home .	All kinds	Children with lung tuberculosis or markedly feeble-minded or epileptic excluded	Until benefited as much as possible; longer if they need a home
New York City Darrach Home . . .	All except helpless cases [b]	Lung tuberculosis excluded	As long as they need a home
House of the Annunciation for Crippled and Incurable Children . . .	All except meningitis; no long-time bed cases	Children with lung tuberculosis,[d] epilepsy, St. Vitus' dance or syphilis excluded	As long as they need a home
New York Home for Destitute Crippled Children [a] . .	Cases not requiring surgical care or nursing	Lung tuberculosis and feeble-mindedness excluded	Until age limit if they need a home
OHIO Cleveland Holy Cross House . . .	All kinds	Children with lung tuberculosis, known to be feeble-minded, or requiring special diets, excluded	As long as they need a home [e]
PENNSYLVANIA Philadelphia Children's House of the Home for Incurables . . .	All kinds of incurable cases	Children with lung tuberculosis or feeble-minded or epileptic excluded	Most cases permanent; transferred to adult department at various ages
Home of the Merciful Saviour for Crippled Children .	All kinds	Lung tuberculosis and feeble-mindedness excluded	Girls as long as they need a home. Incurable boys transferred to institutions for adults at about 16
House of St. Michael and All Angels	All kinds	Lung tuberculosis and feeble-mindedness excluded	Boys must leave at 10. Aim to place girls at service at about 18

[a] Institution closed since this study was made.
[c] Plan to take no feeble-minded cases.
[d] Possible exceptions in cases under four years, slightly affected.
[e] Do not plan to keep adult cases.

[b] Some exceptions.

After care and visitation	Ages received	Age limit for discharge	Sexes received	Color restriction	Financial terms	Geographical restrictions and preferences
By agents of Connecticut Children's Aid Society	2 years up [g]	No rule	Both	None	State pays $3 a week for one-half; a few free. Relatives or towns pay something for others, usually $1 a week	Connecticut children except in rare instances
None [f]	School age	No rule	Both	None	Usually free; 1 pays $4 a week	None
By agents of Children's Home Society	No infants. None over 8	No rule	Both	None	Usually free; parents may contribute to home	None
None [f]	To 12	No rule	Both	None	Usually free; maximum charge $3 a week	New England children
None [f]	3 to 10	Boys, 14, girls, no rule	Both	White only	Usually free; a few pay small amounts	None [j]
By members of a visiting committee, who also co-operate with other agencies	Up to about 16	No rule	Both	None	Usually free; per capita rate for county cases	None
None [f]	3 to 12 [b]	No rule	Both	White only	Usually free; a few pay a little	None
None [f]	4 to 16 [b]	No rule [i]	Girls only	White only	Free	None
None [f]	3 to 14	Usually 17	Both	White only	Free	None
None [f]	No rule	No rule	Both	White only	Usually free	Preference to Cleveland children; some from other cities and states
None [f]	Up to 12	No rule	Both	White only	Usually free; maximum charge $7 a week	First, Philadelphia, second, Pennsylvania, and third, other states
None [f]	2½ to 6	No rule	Both	White only	Usually free; a few pay small amounts	Preference to Pennsylvania children others taken
None [f]	2 years up	Boys, 10, girls, usually 18	Both	Colored only	Usually free; a few pay $1 a week	None

[f] Most institutions which have no formal system of after care keep in touch with many discharged children through correspondence and visits of the children to the institution.
[g] Adults not taken.
[i] Usually leave at 16.
[b] Occasionally under four.
[j] Receive mostly New York City children.

After the statistical tables there are appended detailed descriptions of the individual institutions. This section is a model of accuracy. Plans of several institutions are included.

It should also be noted that the book is fully illustrated with a large number of photographs of the institutions and their work. The index is carefully made and adequate.

The mechanical appearance of the book is good. It would be interesting to know, however, the reason for using two widely different faces of type in its composition. The typography is accurate. The authority for spelling employee as *employe* without an accent is not quite clear.

This brief outline of the contents of the book does not do the work justice. The report should be read by everyone interested in any form of work for crippled children, as it supplies indispensable information not otherwise available.

As has already been stated the results of the investigation are most creditable to the compilers. Some of the points of especial value have already been briefly touched upon. If the present review is to be in any way constructive, however, such defects as exist should also be mentioned. Several may be enumerated—of course, as matters of personal opinion only.

In the first place, the book was compiled on the basis of American experience only, without reference to foreign work. So long as this principle was adhered to the author dealt with a field in which she was the unquestioned authority. But on the subject of statistics a tempting English booklet effected an infraction of the rule and five tables based on an enumeration in Birmingham, England, are given an important place in the book. It is stated, without qualification, that "the one attempt to secure a complete and scientifically analyzed census of the cripples of a community . . . is the census of cripples in Birmingham . . ." The inaccuracy of this statement and the undue importance accorded the Birmingham tables become apparent when it is known that there was taken in 1906 a complete census of all crippled children in the German Empire, and that in 1909 there was published a most elaborate report of the enumeration in a quarto volume of 450 pages. This census was discussed extensively in the literature of the subject, and was widely known. It constitutes probably the most important statistical study of any defective class yet made. Any general excursion into the field of statistics of cripples should certainly include mention of it.

Second, the book does not seem to give to the dispensary work a due share of emphasis. To the foreigner, the outstanding feature of American work for cripples is the vast number of patients treated in the clinics of the various hospitals. It is the field of work that touches directly the interests of over ten times as many cripples as the residential institutions. Dispensary work is sometimes the forerunner of other types of provision, and when supplemented by an adequate visiting nursing service is most effective. There is some discussion of dispensary work in the main chapters of the book, and there is included a table outlining the work in nine institutions. But no conception of the magnitude of the aggregate work is given. Some large orthopedic dispensaries, as for instance those in Brooklyn are not mentioned at all. But they constitute factors which cannot be neglected in any appraisal of 'care for cripples in the United States.' It will be understood that this is a criticism on degree of emphasis only.

The third comment, along a similar line, concerns the omission of detailed statements of the work of organizations which do not actually own buildings. Some of these associations carry on most important work, and in a list otherwise so complete surely have had a place. The Association for the Aid of Crippled children, the Brearley League, the People's University Extension Society, and the Crippled Children's Driving Fund, in New York, and the Sunbeam Circle, in Cleveland, for instance, might profitably have been added. As these organizations are so few, their inclusion would have been all the easier. To be sure, their activities receive scattered mention in the text, but they are found missing on the general roster.

The last criticism is that the tables do not show clearly the years for which the figures are given. This is all the more important in that the report did not appear for quite a time after the field work was completed.

There has been purposely deferred any mention of the introduction to the book. This deserves and will repay careful reading and re-reading. In its preparation Dr. Hart went thoroughly into the questions concerning care for crippled children and in his consideration of them brought to bear his wide experience in other fields of social work.

This introduction gives an editorial survey of points at issue, shows sound judgment in the conclusions drawn, and makes a conservative prophecy for the future of the movement. In particular the further establishment of state hospitals is heartily commended.

In conclusion it may be confidently asserted that the publication of this volume marks a milestone in the progress toward more perfect provision for the crippled members of the community.

HISTORY OF THE NEW YORK SOCIETY
FOR THE RELIEF
OF THE RUPTURED AND CRIPPLED

Oliver H. Bartine

HISTORY OF THE NEW YORK SOCIETY FOR THE RELIEF OF THE RUPTURED AND CRIPPLED

OLIVER H. BARTINE
New York

Vast strides have been made both in medicine and surgery, but no branch in the hospital field has grown as rapidly and developed as much as the work in orthopedic surgery and the care of the ruptured and crippled.

The first work done solely for the ruptured and crippled was under the guidance of Dr. James Knight in the year 1842. After working among the crippled poor of the city for years, he determined that an institution should be founded to relieve their suffering, realizing as he did how very inadequately the crippled and ruptured could be cared for in their own homes or even in the hospitals of that day. In December 1862, he, with the aid of a few men of prominence and means, organized the original society that has been known from that date as the New York Society for the Relief of the Ruptured and Crippled.

For twenty-four years Dr. Knight, the founder and chief of the hospital, carried on the work of the institution, which grew and increased in such a surprising manner that one wonders why the work was not done years before. In 1887 after Dr. Knight's death, Dr. Virgil P. Gibney was appointed his successor, and from that time to the present has been Surgeon-in-Chief of the hospital.

The original work of the hospital was done almost entirely by means of trusses and braces, gymnastics, and later massage, but very few operations were performed. Dr. Gibney, the present Surgeon-in-Chief, was the first to introduce the modern orthopedic surgery, and he had as associate, the late Dr. William T. Bull, who added to the efficiency of the Hernia Department,

by operating for radical cure. Dr. Wisner R. Townsend,[1] and
Dr. Royal Whitman, Associate Surgeons to the Orthopedic Departments, Dr. William B. Coley and Dr. John B. Walker,
Attending Surgeons to the Hernia Department, have been associated with Dr. Gibney in this work for nearly a quarter of a
century. The statistics of hernia operations have grown so
that they are unsurpassed. No case of deformity or of hernia
need ever go unrelieved.

From March 1, 1863, the date of the incorporation of the
Society, the original building used for a hospital was Dr. Knight's
private residence, No. 97 Second Avenue, which was leased for
three years and then purchased by the Managers. There the
institution was in operation for seven years, until May, 1870,
when an up-to-date hospital, situated on the corner of 42nd
Street and Lexington Avenue, was completed. Here the benefi-
cent work continued from year to year with gratifying success.
In 1887 a fire destroyed the northwest wing of the hospital.
The trustees at once proceeded to reconstruct the destroyed
portion and to add an additional story to the main structure for
the purpose of utilizing it for play room as well as class rooms
for the school. The entire roof was planned for the children's
comfort as well as for fresh air treatment. In 1898 the extension
on 43rd Street and Lexington Avenue was completed. The
necessity for such a building was obvious if the efficiency of the
service in every department was to be enhanced. At this time
a female adult ward was opened and has been of incalculable
benefit in the In-Door Department. This additional building
met a long-felt want and the completed hospital building was
adequate for the needs of the Greater New York, and conformed
to the advances made in both Orthopedic Surgery and in the
Surgery of Hernia. The Building Committee took into account
the actual needs and incurred no expenditure that was not approved by the practical experience of hospital work. Fads,
fancies and experiments were not attempted and the Committee

[1] Died March 12, 1916.

kept well within the appropriation of the Board of Managers. In 1911 the New York Central Railroad acquired the hospital property in order to complete their terminal and this necessitated the construction of the present building which the society moved into on November 29th, 1912. The Board of Trustees selected the present location because of the air and light, of the high ground, of its proximity to the surface car lines penetrating every part of the city and Greater New York, of the nearness to the railroads in order that the patients would be able to reach the hospital by the payment of a five-cent fare from practically every portion of the city, and of the ease with which the doctors and friends of patients, etc., would reach the hospital with a minimum amount of delay and inconvenience.

The Out-Patient Department from the beginning has been an important feature and its daily attendance has constantly been increasing. A machine shop, where the braces for both the out-door and in-door patients could be made, has always been an integral part of the hospital. Of course, the original brace shop was crude as compared with the elaborate work done to-day, but the institution has always done its own iron and leather work in the manufacture of braces and trusses.

Any one who believes that a special hospital cares only for its specialty is vastly mistaken. Almost from the beginning this hospital has had a full staff of consultants as well as a regular attending staff, and at present there are experts in every branch of medicine and surgery connected with the institution, so that patients have at their disposal the leading specialists of this city.

Soon after the incorporation of the society a school was opened and today it is one of the recognized schools of New York City. Here the children are taught during their course of treatment, thus enabling them to reenter their classes in the city schools when discharged from the hospital.

A word must be said of a recent branch of the Out-Patient Department: namely, the Social Service Department. This social service work is somewhat original and different from that in other institutions. The workers are in the dispensary every day and they talk to the patients and the parents, discuss home conditions, family life and come in close touch with them. In this way we learn of the actual home condition of the patient and can then care better for the physical condition. The social workers then see that the treatment is followed up in their own homes, and if money is needed to meet an immediate necessity this is supplied, if clothes are needed these are provided, and if a sojourn in the country would assist in restoring them to health they are placed in country homes.

The most noticeable feature of our present building is the sun, light, space and fine ventilation throughout the building. The wards have loggias or porches opening from the ward so that bed patients may be wheeled out and kept in the sun and air the entire day. Over the entire building is a very fine roof garden where the children spend most of their days. The top floor is devoted to the school rooms and assembly hall and they are all large and sunny and so attractively equipped that the children love to attend school.

The building has its own plant for heating, ventilating, lighting, refrigeration, a complete laundry and kitchen, equipped with the most modern apparatus. A brace shop where all the work of both in-door and out-door patients is done; an X-Ray department, laboratory, gymnasium, hydrotherapy, artificial sun-ray, electrotherapeutic, mechano-therapy, massage and baking department, in connection with a very large and unusually fine dispensary. The building contains a very fine operating suite, nine light, large wards and quiet rooms, with their special dining rooms, diet kitchens, pantries, dressing rooms, toilets and bath rooms, assembly room and Solarium, as well as a modern dental department.

The treatment of the patients continues under the supervision of Dr. Virgil P. Gibney, the Surgeon-in-Chief, and it is interesting to note that the present Board of Managers include nine sons and grandsons of the earlier Board. The traditions of careful management of the affairs of the institution which were strictly adhered to by the original board of trustees have been continued up to the present day and it is a source of extreme pleasure for one to be associated with them in this, one of the greatest of all works, the relief of the suffering.

The work done in improving the condition of patients suffering from paralysis is remarkable. Unfortunately, in this branch of the work a cure is rarely possible, but by judicious and skillful treatment the condition of practically every paralyzed patient can be improved. It is no uncommon sight to see a child who was carried into the hospital in a totally helpless condition, or who got about only with the assistance of crutches, walk out of the hospital after some months' treatment wearing a light steel brace and able again to take an active part in the struggle for a livelihood.

Deformities of all kinds are corrected. Club-foot, bow-legs, knock-knees, wry neck, curvature of the spine, old fractures and dislocations, flat feet, and various bone diseases all come under the heading of orthopedic surgery, and are treated in this hospital. Congenital dislocation of the hip has been treated at the Hospital for thirty years, with a large percentage of cures. Congenital dislocation of the hip was formerly an incurable condition, and the treatment afforded by this hospital marks one of the advances of surgery.

During the past few years great strides have been made in the treatment of tuberculosis. Not only can this be said of pulmonary tuberculosis, but also of the disease in the bones and joints, the usual form in which it attacks children.

Tuberculosis is much more prevalent among children than is commonly supposed, the majority of people associating the name of the disease with a hacking cough and chills and fever, as seen in the infected adult. In children, on the contrary, the disease more frequently lodges in the bones and joints, and, as a result, we have spine disease, hip disease, knee joint disease, etc. Not many years ago, before it was known that the condition was due to tuberculosis, the affected bones and joints were said to have 'white swelling' and the disease was supposed to be incurable, amputation occasionally offering the only possible chance of saving the life of the child. Nowadays, if the disease is recognized early enough, the patient can be so completely cured that often no traces whatever of the disease are left, and the child becomes a healthy, useful member of society. When one considers that many cases of deformity seen on the street could have grown up straight and strong, if the cripple had only had the benefit of treatment, only then is the true greatness of the work appreciated.

Of course, the treatment must extend over many months and sometimes even years, but it is one of the chief aims of the Surgeon-in-Chief and associates to so arrange the treatment, that it interferes as little as possible with the ordinary routine of life. For example, it is rarely the custom to keep the child confined to bed for any length of time. He is immediately placed in some fixative apparatus such as a light plaster of paris bandage or brace, which allows him to get about and gain the benefit of exercise. This plan also allows him to continue to occupy his place in the hospital school, so that his education in no way suffers by his enforced separation from home.

A part of the routine treatment is the exposure of the children to the air and sun for several hours daily on the roof garden. This feature combined with the administration of good nutritious food, goes far to assist the more active surgical treatment. During the summer those children who can leave the hospital go to homes by the sea or to the country for the benefits of fresh air and a country life. As necessity for operation arises, the patient comes under the skilled hand of the Surgeon, and the results are uniformly good.

FRONT VIEW OF THE HOSPITAL BUILDING

WAITING ROOM OF THE OUT-PATIENT DEPARTMENT

LEATHER SHOP FOR THE MANUFACTURE OF ORTHOPEDIC APPLIANCES

SEWING ROOM FOR THE MANUFACTURE OF ORTHOPEDIC APPLIANCES

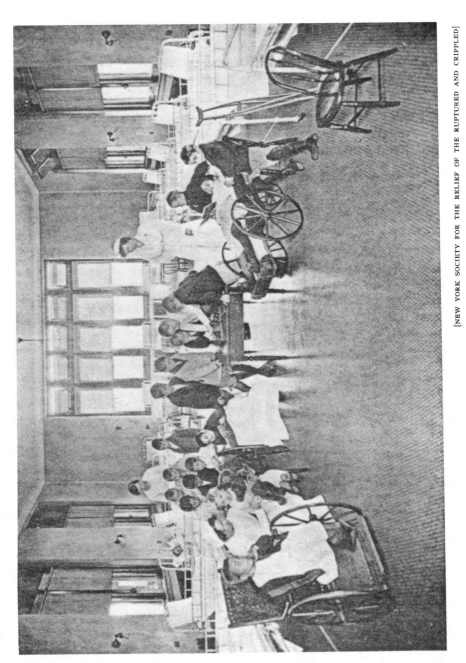

A WARD FOR BOYS

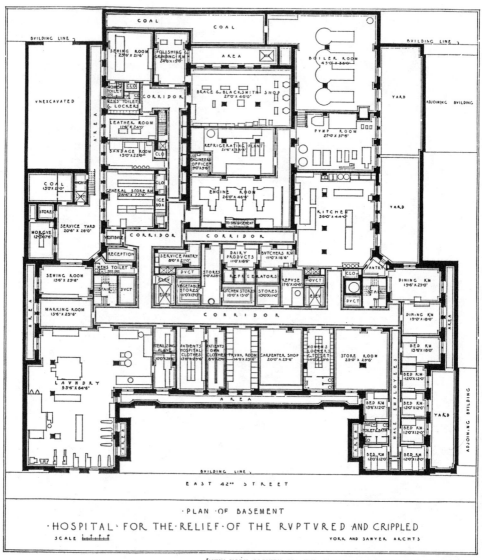

PLAN OF BASEMENT

HOSPITAL FOR THE RELIEF OF THE RVPTVRED AND CRIPPLED

SCALE

YORK AND SAWYER ARCHTS

PLAN OF BASEMENT

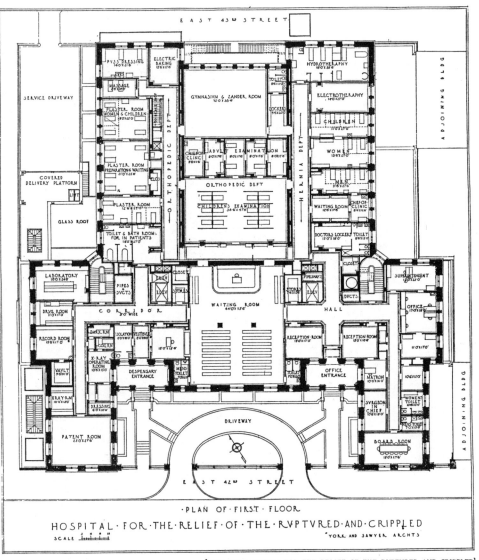

·PLAN·OF·FIRST·FLOOR·

HOSPITAL·FOR·THE·RELIEF·OF·THE·RVPTVRED·AND·CRIPPLED

SCALE ┠┼┼┼┼┨   ⁎YORK·AND·SAWYER·ARCHTS

PLAN OF FIRST FLOOR

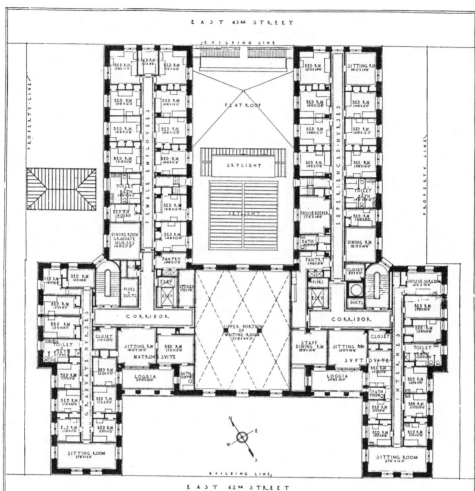

PLAN·OF·SECOND·FLOOR

HOSPITAL·FOR·THE·RELIEF·OF·THE·RVPTVRED·AND·CRIPPLED

SCALE

YORK·AND·SAWYER·ARCHTS

PLAN OF SECOND FLOOR

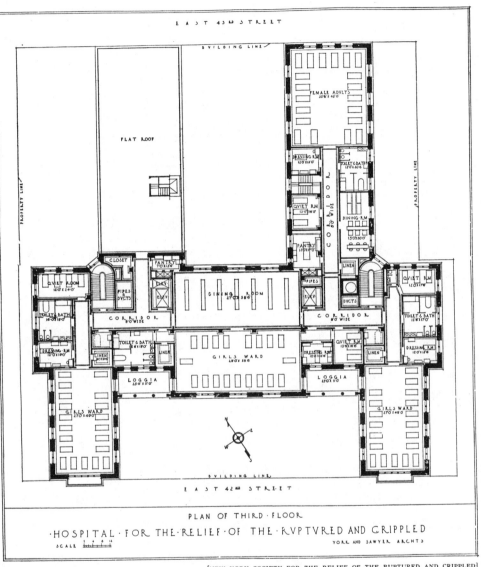

PLAN OF THIRD · FLOOR

· HOSPITAL · FOR · THE · RELIEF · OF · THE · RVPTVRED · AND · CRIPPLED

SCALE

YORK AND SAWYER ARCHTS

PLAN OF THIRD FLOOR

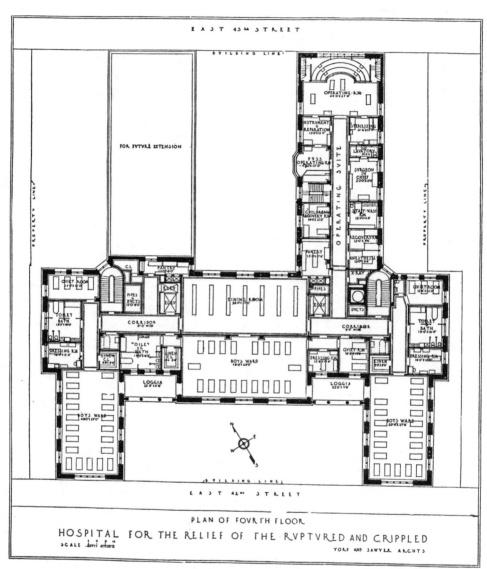

PLAN OF FOVRTH FLOOR

HOSPITAL FOR THE RELIEF OF THE RVPTVRED AND CRIPPLED

SCALE

YORK AND SAWYER ARCHTS

PLAN OF FOURTH FLOOR

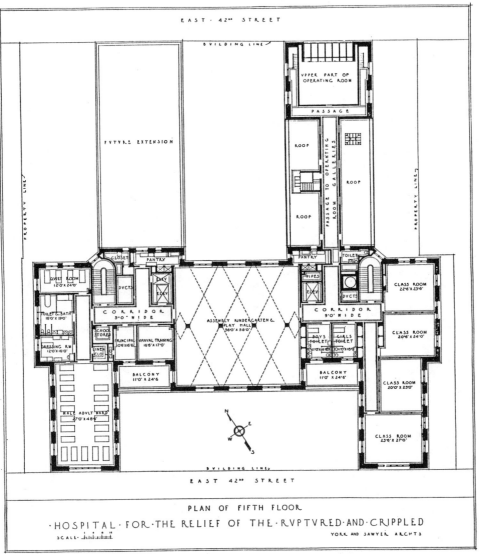

PLAN OF FIFTH FLOOR

·HOSPITAL·FOR·THE·RELIEF·OF·THE·RVPTVRED·AND·CRIPPLED

SCALE

YORK AND SAWYER ARCHTS

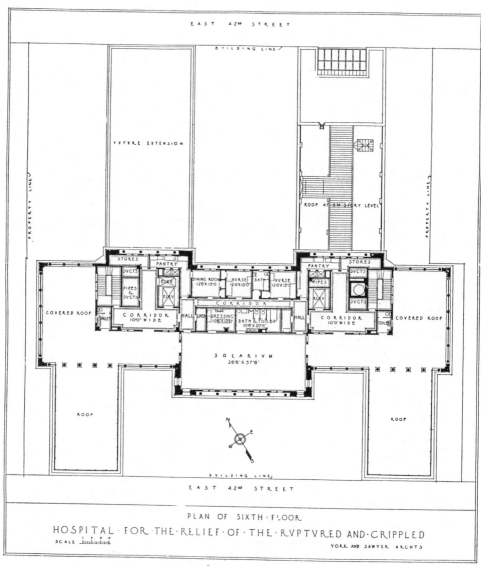

PLAN OF SIXTH FLOOR

HOSPITAL · FOR · THE · RELIEF · OF · THE · RVPTVRED · AND · CRIPPLED

SCALE

YORK AND SAWYER ARCHTS

PLAN OF SIXTH FLOOR

TWO CASES
CRIPPLED BY INDUSTRIAL ACCIDENTS:
A COMPARISON OF METHODS OF AFTER-CARE

Grace S. Harper

TWO CASES CRIPPLED BY INDUSTRIAL ACCIDENTS; A COMPARISON OF METHODS OF AFTER-CARE

GRACE S. HARPER
Boston, Mass.

A study of the following industrial accident cases brings out sharp contrasts in their social and legal management and presents a challenge of unfairness against the Massachusetts Workingmen's Compensation Law in relation to industrial minors. Some of the conditions under which compensation is enforced and the method of controlling the amounts granted under varying circumstances are here illustrated.

Plans for the vocational future of these boys have involved the added problems of character and education.

Howard (Case A), a 16-year-old boy of American parentage, in October, 1913, was sent for vocational guidance to the King's Chapel Bureau for the Handicapped, Boston. He had caught his hand between the rollers of a press. Efforts to stop the machine were fruitless as the automatic guard was out of order. The hand was amputated as a result of the injury received.

Thus, through the carelessness of some individual in not attending to a defective machine guard, this boy of only 16 years deprived of the most useful member of his body, his right hand, was forced to face the problem of earning a livelihood without any special training.

After a few months of idleness following his injury, he had become restive concerning his future and thus came to the attention of the Bureau for the Handicapped.

My first impressions of him were unusually favorable. He was strong, muscular, of good height, and manly in appearance and bearing. His manner was quiet and his conversation showed seriousness of purpose. Further knowledge of him through friends and teachers proved him to be a boy of unusual character. They spoke especially of his loyalty and squareness in all dealings in the club to which he belonged.

An acceptance of responsibility towards his family had made him ambitious to get on in the world. His mother and sisters needed him to take the place of a worthless and unprincipled father, from whom, even at this youthful age, he had been called upon to protect them. His grandmother spoke with pride and with sadness of their former hopes that some day Howard should go to the Institute of Technology and study to become a mechanical engineer.

The surgeon who amputated his hand marvelled at his courage as he faced the ordeal and at his consideration for his family. He quoted him as saying, "Of course I know what this will mean to me all my life but if I show it, they will feel badly at home."

Guiseppe (Case B) came from an environment quite different from Howard's. Moreover, he had a weaker inheritance to fall back upon at a time when he specially needed good counsel and guidance from his parents. He was the oldest of five children of an Italian laborer. His father's work was casual, often making it necessary for his mother to go to work in a shoe factory. The home was poor and forlorn. There had been little chance for discipline, though the mother evidently tried to do the best, as she saw it, for her children. Guiseppe was a well built, healthy looking boy when I first saw him. He had just come from the hospital where his hand had been amputated as a result of injury from catching it between the roller and plate of a press. He was neat in his dress and had a pleasant, though not very responsive manner. His character was not strong, neither was it vicious, and as far as could be learned, he had no very bad habits. Not having completed his grammar school course when he went to work, he had tried to make up for this by attending evening school up to the time of his injury. This may be fairly judged as an indication of ambition at that time.

We had inquired into Guiseppe's case and had learned his rights for compensation, while he was still in the hospital. Finding that he had automatically accepted the provisions of the act and so could not go to law about it, this was explained to him and his parents. But our explanation had not the slightest effect upon their efforts to take the case to court. From one cheap lawyer to another, he and his mother appealed, each lawyer taking up the case only to find that nothing could be done about it. Friends spurred this ignorant mother and boy on to think that large sums of money could be obtained. Some said $10,000 was the least he should settle for, others remembered a similar case where the injured man had obtained $18,000 and so on.

Friends offered to start Guiseppe in business when he should get his money. A fruit store, a real estate business, a pool room and other easy money-making schemes were suggested, until the boy and his mother came to believe that a life of luxury and ease was in store for them. Owing to their vacillating and unsympathetic state of mind, almost nothing could be accomplished, almost nothing beyond showing a disinterested friendship for the family. So after a few weeks the case was temporarily dropped.

When, at last, none of the lawyers had been able to help him (as will be seen by an explanation of the terms of the act) the inevitable acceptance of what the law provided came about. The weekly payment of $4 was arranged for and the mother appealed to the former employer begging him to take back the boy. There was nothing in the factory which he could do without special training, except errands, so as errand boy he was re-employed at $5 a week. After two months he was discharged for petty lying and 'lack of ambition.'

The Massachusetts Workingmen's Compensation Act provides for the compensation of injuries arising out of and in course of employment.

When the Act became law in 1912, three common law defences were abrogated, viz: assumption of risks, fellow servants' fault and contributory negligence. This means that it shall not constitute a defence on the part of an employer, that an employee assumed the risks incident to the occupation when he entered it. Likewise that injuries resulting from a fellow workman's carelessness or injuries to which the employee's negligence has contributed, unless wilfully so, cannot be defended on these grounds. But employers are still allowed a choice of insuring under the act or retaining common law rights. Likewise the employee can accept compensation as provided for by the act, or have recourse to common law rights.

To protect the masses of ignorant workingmen who stand little or no chance against the experienced counsel secured by industrial concerns, also to eliminate the expenses of litigation, the acceptance of the provisions of the act becomes automatic unless otherwise signified by the employee. When he wishes to retain common law rights an employee must state this to his employer in writing at the time of "contract of hire,", i. e., on date of entering on employment. In both cases presented here, the boys came automatically under the provisions of the act, neither of them having forseen the possibility of accident.

Before he was sent to us for assistance, Howard's case had nevertheless been undertaken by an able lawyer and a suit for $20,000 had been brought against the firm in whose employ the boy was when the accident occurred. The suit was based on the illegality of a contract entered into by a minor, and denied the validity of the automatic waiving of a contract by a minor who was not in a position by law to make one. But if this defense is declared invalid by the Supreme Court of Massachusetts, the boy has forfeited all right to compensation for the injury since suit deprives him of the automatic compensation payment.

The maximum compensation payable for the loss of a hand was in this case and at this time, $2200 under the law, but the probable compensation for a normally healed stump of hand was $500 to $1000.

Under the Massachusetts law Guiseppe had received $200 for the loss of his hand. This represented $4 a week for a period of 50 weeks. In addition he had been paid $4 a week during the period of total incapacity which was 50 weeks. When re-employed the amount of compensation had become 50c. a week or 50%[1] of the difference between present and former wages. Therefore at the time of Guiseppe's second application to our Bureau for the Handicapped he was receiving but 50c. a week (as he had lost a job) and had to overcome the deteriorating effects of nearly a year of aimless loafing.

As will be seen by the chart, the cases of the two boys were alike in many respects, namely: age, occupation, wages and the nature of accident, which in both resulted in amputation of the right hand. The automatic inclusion of both under the Compensation Act was another point of likeness.

When Guiseppe returned to us, the two boys were then in the hands of our Bureau ready to be guided in the selection of a vocation, in case means could be found to provide the special training necessary. Guiseppe's employer was an unusual one. He had not only given him an artificial hand but also gave the necessary money for vocational training. Telegraphy was chosen for both boys and they were placed in the same school. At the end of eight months, Howard had made so good a record that he was given employment in a telegraph office at $8 a week.

Guiseppe had attended the same school fairly well and showed intelligence in his work. But he needed my constant supervision, as he had made poor associates during his idleness and was frequenting a pool room in the neighborhood. In spite of having had the same advantages as Howard, he had not the character to persevere in practice and to acquire the speed necessary for obtaining a position as telegrapher. For the

[1] In 1914 this became 66⅔%.

Factors Involved	Case A	Case B
Nationality	American	Italian
Age	16 years	17 years
Education	Graduate of grammar school at 14 years.	Left school in seventh grade at 14 years.
Character	Strong character, very ambitious, courageous, industrious.	Ambitious, selfish, smooth and plausible, petty liar, deceitful in small things.
Accident	Crush of hand, caught between rollers of rubber mixing press.	Crush of hand, caught between roller and plate in printing press.
Result	Amputation of right hand.	Amputation of right hand.
Wages	$6.00 weekly.	$6.00 weekly.
Relation to Workingmen's Compensation Act	Automatically included.	Automatically included.
Maximum Compensation payable	Loss of hand, $200 $4 weekly, not to exceed 500 weeks, 2000 ——— Total $2200	Loss of hand, $200 $4 weekly, not to exceed 500 weeks, 2000 ——— Total, $2200
Action taken	*Compensation refused.* Suit filed for $20,000 Basis of suit: Illegal for minor to *make a contract*, therefore cannot waive a contract; so has rights to "common law."	*Compensation accepted.* At time of discharge as errand boy the full amount of compensation due him was: Loss of hand, $200.00 $4 weekly for 50 weeks 200.00 50c. for 250 weeks, 112.62 ——— Total, $512.62 (Less interest if paid in a lump sum)
Vocational Guidance and Supervision	*Special fund raised for training* *Source:* Boy's Club (unknown to boy personally). *Reason given:* Because of boy's fine character.	*Special fund raised for training* *Source:* Former employer. *Reason given:* Personal gift on account of interest in boy's condition.
Selected Vocation	Telegraphy.	Telegraphy.
Vocational Results	*While in training:* Intelligence = Excellent Industry = Excellent Faithfulness = Excellent Application = Excellent *Length of time to complete course:* Seven months. Practice without pay—two months. *Present job—night work—$8 a week.*	*While in training:* Intelligence = Fair Industry = Fair Faithfulness = Variable (Constant need of watching) Application = Poor *Length of time to complete course:* Nine months.

year spent in idleness had unsettled his mind and had made steady, plodding effort seem an impossibility to him. Such deterioration of character is only what may be expected when a person's handicap is used as a source of interest and pity.

Of interest on this point, was the attitude of Howard's lawyer. He clearly appreciated the significant loss to a boy's character that is bound to come through enforced and aimless idleness; he desired to assist in preventing any such loss. He felt the urgent need to have him employed and learning a trade preparatory to self-support, even at the risk of losing his case if the boy were self-supporting at the time of trial and therefore not as much an object of pity as is often presented to a judge.

It is too soon to say that Guiseppe's opportunity has been wasted, even though at the present time he is not keeping up the practice requisite for acquiring speed. When business conditions improve and more telegraphers are needed, he may find the incentive to work which he seems to lack at the present time. But suppose he does not. Who can say what success he might have shown had he been placed in the school *immediately* after the injury and before the attitude of his family and friends had had a hand in his undoing? It takes most unusual courage to settle down to an uninteresting régime after being in the limelight of attention from one's neighbors, from friends, and even from strangers. Petting and sympathy are so unsparingly lavished on the victim of an accident, that his habit of mind becomes fixed, with an assumption of the right to support from others as its logical conclusion.

It may be argued that Howard had such character that he would have succeeded under any circumstances. I doubt this. If no means had been found to secure special training for him, he would in all probability have been forced to return to some unsatisfactory kind of work in order to help out with the family expenses. What hope and ambition for the future can there be in such a position as is open to a young boy who has lost his right hand? How many years might there be ahead of him before he could learn bookkeeping, for instance, with his left hand, and in the short sessions of an evening school? Many a boy of strong character has lost his grip through an accident which shattered his dreams of success and substituted a reality of long, weary hours of left handed labor before he could hope to advance.

Special provision for vocational training should be made for minors who become crippled as the result of injury. This training should follow immediately after recovery from accident or crippling disease. The masses of chronic idle will be increased if the maimed are forced to rely on such casual and unskilled jobs as may be available. And when an injured employee does return to an unskilled job or even to his former occupation, another danger must be recognized when judging his suitability, physical and mental, for performing such work. As was seen in the case of Guiseppe, when taken back by his former employer and paid $5 a week, his rate of compensation through the State law, was reduced to 50c. weekly. Later he was discharged, a result which might have been foretold. Petty lying on two occasions, and lack of ambition were the causes of his being considered undesirable. He had then foregone his right to more than 50c. weekly compensation.

Who is responsible for a lack of industrial ambition on the part of a boy placed in a job leading nowhere? When he was employed after his accident, nothing was known of his character as shown in his previous employment. Nothing had been asked, because he had the physical requirements for feeding a press. Could his petty lying affect his press work? Presumably not. Look at the pity of it all from this standpoint. Here was a boy who had an industrial value in spite of his faults, while he was physically whole. He was then tried under a physical handicap in a position requiring qualifications which he did not possess and which no one took the trouble to find out about. It was obviously unfair to him, and this his employer afterwards appreciated. So much for the story—as it relates to character and vocational guidance.

Now consider its financial and political side. Having held a job stands to the insurance companies as evidence of ability to work and therefore re-instatement of the former rate of compensation is not obligatory on their part. This ruling left the boy with the munificent sum of $510 as compensation for the loss of a right hand, not to mention the mental suffering involved. The loss of the hand is represented by $200, this being $4 a week for 50 weeks. Added to this he received $4 a week for the 50 weeks before re-entering employment, making $400. Fifty cents a week for the remaining 250 weeks (300 weeks being the limit for partial incapacity payments at that time)[2] less interest if paid in a lump sum, brought the total to $510. Financially he was worse off for having tried to resume work for which he was unsuited.

All injured persons who make an honest effort to return to work for which they afterwards find themselves unfitted are apt to fall into the same plight. What more obvious result than that those with the best of intentions will be reluctant to undertake work which, if unsuitable, will leave them with a financial loss. But if they do not work they degenerate. Therefore they should be allowed time to prepare for suitable work whenever possible.

Another point which may be mentioned here is the injustice of giving equal compensation for the loss of a hand or a foot. From a point of view of incapacity there is no comparison between the two. An artificial foot can be manipulated with great facility and ease, and is less of a hindrance to normal exercise than is often supposed. Furthermore it does not present any evidence of its maimed condition to the casual observer. But the loss of a hand, especially the right, not only incapacitates one for any but special employment, but also draws attention to a maimed condition, about which many persons are extremely

[2]This has now been extended to 500 weeks.

sensitive. An empty sleeve creates an uncomfortable pity in most people, and an artificial hand produces an uncanny feeling in others. Thus the pity of some, the squeamishness of others, are alike prejudicial to the victims of any accident whose effect cannot be concealed.

I should like to draw attention to one other point: that the potential values of minors should in some way be taken into account when rates of compensation are being adjudged.

During the early working years, a boy who is apprenticed to a trade with the hope of becoming an expert, skilled workman in that trade, starts at a very low wage. His pay is lower by far than that which is given in many unskilled jobs to a boy of the same age, but in which there is no opportunity for advance.

A boy who has the making of a master printer in him, receives the same compensation if injured, as the one who started as a lumper and may always remain an unskilled laborer. By the time he is 21 years old this potential printer is earning a much fairer wage as a basis of estimated worth, than he was earlier, and the unskilled man is in the same position as before.

An adjustment in this relation might be based on a recognition of training for skilled work in which the minor might reasonably anticipate a future, as against an unskilled job presenting no possibilities for advance.

To bring about a fair adjustment in the compensating of minors, the factors just mentioned should be given serious consideration.

To sum up the points referred to in these cases:

1. A period of enforced idleness after injury almost inevitably results in a loss to character which may result in chronic dependence.

2. This should be obviated by provision for vocational training as soon as is possible after a crippling injury.

3. The potential value of minors should be given consideration in the provision for compensation.

4. The amount of compensation for the loss of a hand should exceed that for the loss of a foot, in proportion to the difference in resulting incapacity.

THE HISTORY OF THE FEDERATION
OF ASSOCIATIONS FOR CRIPPLES

Katharine W. Ambrose Shrady

THE HISTORY OF THE FEDERATION OF ASSOCIATIONS FOR CRIPPLES

Katharine W. Ambrose Shrady

The attempt to amalgamate the work of associations for cripples had its inception in 1908 when the Russell Sage Foundation through its Social Research Committee, co-operating with the Bureau for the Handicapped of the Charity Organization Society, began an investigation of the possibilities of employment for cripples. It was found that women and girls were quite well provided for, but for men and boys without technical training it was extremely difficult to procure employment. As the result of the investigation by this joint committee, an article by Miss Eleanor H. Adler and Miss Serena G. Marshall appeared in *The Survey* of April 30, 1910, making a strong appeal for the establishment of trade schools for crippled men and boys. One of the best trade classes in New York was the outgrowth of this appeal, and since then another fully equipped trade school for men and boys has been established. It was also shown by this investigation, as well as by the practical experience of those actively interested, that overlapping and lack of co-operation prevented the attainment of the best results. There are many agencies doing friendly visiting in the city, and a crippled person being somewhat conspicuous, rarely escapes attention. It is a great waste of time and energy, and not productive of the best results, to have a number of persons giving advice to the parents of a crippled child as to its training and general treatment. It is also true, that there was little knowledge among workers as to what associations other than their own were doing to advance educational methods; also an absence of harmony in the interchange of information, between societies that might otherwise have been working together along progressive lines for the benefit of cripples.   In this way associations frequently wasted valuable time dealing with problems which had been satisfactorily solved by others.   There was no central bureau, where information could be obtained pertaining exclusively to cripples. The logical and systematic way of meeting this want, was through a federation, as being better adapted to do such work than any other existing agency.   It was therefore, in response to the wide-felt need for co-operation, that representatives of twenty or more associations met in New York in February, 1912, and discussed plans for organizing a federation of associations for cripples.   A committee known as the Amalgamation Committee was formed, which consisted of Miss Dorothy Bull of the Brearley League Industrial Classes for Cripples as Chairman, Miss Florence S. Sullivan and Miss Dorothy Truesdell of the same society, Mrs. Henry B. Barnes and Miss Edith M. Bond, of the Association for the Aid of Crippled Children, Mrs. Henry Goldman and Mrs. Moses Heinemann of the Crippled Children's East Side Free School, Miss Helen Sturgis and Miss Elizabeth K. Lamont of Miss Spence's School Society, Mrs. Ernest Strauss and Miss J. F. Benjamin of the Ethical Culture Visiting Guild for Crippled Children, Mrs. John M. Galloway of the New York State Branch of the Shut-In Society, Mrs. Spencer Lathrop of the Harlem Day Home and School, Mrs. B. E. Martin and Miss Spelding of the Darrach Home for Defective Crippled Children, and Miss Eleanor H. Adler of the Bureau for the Handicapped.   During the ensuing year frequent meetings were held.   A sub-committee, of which Miss Florence S. Sullivan was Chairman, was appointed to consider in detail, and report on the various phases of industrial training for cripples, the advantages and importance of a central shop for the sale of work-room products, and the advisability of allowing cripples to compete with regular factory workers, or work in shops by themselves.   The committee suggested ways of improving the training of cripples for commercial and industrial life, and recommended the employment of an expert investigator who should report in writing from time to time upon all questions relating to the home life, work-shops, industrial schools, and eleemosynary institutions for cripples.   As a result of these preliminary meetings, the Federation was formally established in January, 1913, and its first general meeting was held on the twenty-third of that month.   The following April at its second general meeting, a Constitution was adopted and committees appointed.   Officers were elected at the first annual meeting held December 10, 1913.

The Federation began with fifteen of the leading associations and societies of Greater New York as members, and is in active co-operation with thirty-two other similar organizations.

Its general object is to co-ordinate the work of the various societies interested in cripples by the establishment of a central bureau, where a complete registry is kept of all homes, schools, hospitals, aid societies, fresh air agencies, and industrial schools, so that cripples may be referred there for information, if they require industrial training, positions adapted to their abilities, or work in their homes.   An executive or field secretary is employed to investigate all cases that are brought to the attention of the Federation.   She has also made a complete survey of the forty-seven institutions and associations in Greater New York and immediate vicinity which includes a history of the work carried on by each agency, and the number and kind of persons benefited.   A list of summer homes and fresh air opportunities offered exclusively for cripples has also been compiled.   The Federation is intended as a clearing house of information and a registration bureau, and is in no sense a relief agency.   Its function is to refer persons to the organization best suited to their needs.   Frequently the question is asked, "What benefit does an association derive by joining the Federation?"   The greatest benefit outside of the varied information which it classifies and places at the disposal of all, is the opportunity it affords of improving the general condition of cripples. It would be impossible for the earnest, experienced members of fifteen leading associations to meet and discuss plans and methods, without some advancement resulting therefrom. Organizations do not surrender any of their individual rights by federating, and their specific lines of work are conducted as independently as if they stood alone. Common-sense methods are followed, and only where benefit will result is co-operation desired. Federation has a tendency to broaden the attitude of those interested, so that instead of being devoted to one given line of work, they will endeavor more fully to help the individual cripple by placing him where he can derive the most benefit from the training he receives. For example, if a boy of artistic and technical gifts has been taught to embroider on linen, work of the very highest excellence, and it is discovered through the Federation that this boy can be taught the more suitable trade of engraving on copper, silver and gold, it surely is a step in the right direction to place him in the school where he may be taught engraving. In the short time that the Federation has existed, instances have frequently occurred where it was found advisable to transfer pupils from one school to another, better adapted to their needs. The possibilities of this have been learned through membership in the Federation. There will always be those who prefer not to unite with others to do the greatest good for the greatest number, for fear that they will not receive recognition or due credit, but the person who loves to work for cripples, primarily to help the individual, will not be restrained by selfish considerations from joining with others to accomplish this purpose.

The importance of a central shop where work done by cripples may be sold, has been strongly urged by those in charge of trade schools. It is conceded that at present there are difficulties which prevent the carrying out of such a plan. Schools, for instance, that are not endowed and depend for maintenance on voluntary support and the output of their work rooms, cannot afford to risk any diminution of revenue by an experiment of this nature.   On the other hand, it is urged by those who advocate the central shop, that by requiring the workmanship to reach a certain standard of excellence, a larger market would be created, and thus through increased demand, loss from competition of individual schools, would be counterbalanced.   Much benefit has thus far resulted from industrial exhibits under Federation auspices.   This was satisfactorily tested in New York last December, when the industrial departments of six leading associations gave an exhibit and sale, of the output of their trade classes.   At least two of the schools displayed art embroidery on linen and silk that is not surpassed by similar work in any other country.   The effect of this excellence was to set a standard for other exhibitors which cannot fail to improve the quality of their work.   Another significant feature of the combined sale, was the receipts of individual associations. In every instance they reached a perfectly satisfactory figure, and in the case of one of the largest schools, was several hundred dollars ahead of the amount customarily received from this source.   It is felt therefore, that the central shop open for a period of several months each winter, if not all the year, will naturally be evolved from the combined sale and exhibition, given under social auspices for two successive afternoons annually.   The value of the Federation to societies whose work is along purely educational and social lines, is the opportunity afforded at Federation Conferences, for the discussion of leading questions.   The problem of separating and training mentally defective cripples is one that is brought home daily to teachers and managers of industrial schools.   It has been a much discussed subject, presenting many dilemmas, but it is expected that a practical solution will be effected through the efforts of the Federation's Committee on Legislation, which is now studying the question.   No greater opportunity has yet been offered the Federation to demonstrate its usefulness in a practical way.

Although so much is now being done throughout this country and Europe to ameliorate the general condition of cripples by giving them special training to make them self-supporting, there has been an absence of literature relating to these subjects, mainly because no suitable mediums, such as a magazine or news bulletin, existed. It is with the intention of meeting this need that the AMERICAN JOURNAL OF CARE FOR CRIPPLES, a quarterly magazine, is now to be published under the auspices of. the Federation. By this means it is intended to keep informed, those who are seeking to improve the methods of helping their afflicted fellow-beings who are handicapped by accident or disease. To make the JOURNAL successful the Federation bespeaks the support of those throughout the world, who are interested in bettering the condition of cripples.

EDUCATION AND CARE
OF THE CRIPPLED CHILD

George Newman

EDUCATION AND CARE OF THE CRIPPLED CHILD [1]

SIR GEORGE NEWMAN, M.D.
Chief Medical Officer, Board of Education, Great Britain.

INTRODUCTORY

Schools for Crippled Children provide for the education of those who require special training owing to chronic disease or severe deformity, and are therefore incapable of deriving benefit from the training provided in the Public Elementary School. The power to provide such education is furnished in Section 1 [1a] and Section 2 of the Elementary Education (Defective and Epileptic Children) Act, 1899, and the Board is empowered to recognize day and residential schools for cripple children whether established by Local Education Authorities or by voluntary governing bodies. The first school to be recognized under the Act of 1899 was the Tavistock Place Special School which was certified in April, 1900. The school, which is maintained by the London County Council in premises belonging to the Passmore Edwards' Settlement, had been conducted for some years prior to this by a Committee which had been called into existence through the efforts of Mrs. Humphry Ward.

The extent to which cripple children exist in the area of an Authority is based on information derived chiefly from three sources. In the first place they come to the knowledge of the School Medical Officer in the course of medical inspection both of routine groups and special cases. Secondly, the school teachers become aware of cases among children in attendance at school,

---

[1] This is the section on cripples in the *Annual Report for 1914 of the Chief Medical Officer of the Board of Education*, London, 1915, p. 170–186. It contains a deal of unusually interesting data. The official paragraph numbers have been omitted in the present publication.

and in the ordinary course of events, in an area in which the School Medical Service is properly administered, they would refer them for examination by the officers of the School Medical Service. Thirdly, the School Attendance Officers learn of cases not in attendance at school in their visits to the homes particularly in those areas in which they are responsible for the systematic scheduling of all children of school age. It is important that they should report all such cases to the School Medical Officer in order that, as far as practicable, he may bring them under the supervision of his department with the object of securing amelioration of their condition or of bringing them eventually within the educational system.

NUMBER AND CLASSIFICATION

There are at present insufficient data to allow of an accurate statement as to the number of cripple children in England and Wales for whom special provision should be made. Dr. Priestley (Staffordshire) reports that of 16,000 to 17,000 children under supervision 545 are 'cripples'. The figures include 180 paralytics, 82 cases of tubercular bone disease, 78 of rickets, 47 of other deformities, and 28 of physical injuries. The remainder are attributable to developmental defects.

Dr. Chetwood, the School Medical Officer for Sheffield has made a special inquiry into the number of crippled children in the city, and reports that the total number is 527. Of these, 201 are on the registers of the three Day Special Schools, 107 are noted as either at the present time or likely soon to be fit for such schools, 110 are in attendance at ordinary schools, and 109 are considered at present as unfit to attend school. A considerable number of these latter will probably be admitted to the new residential Memorial Hospital for Cripple Children to be opened in the autumn.

Dr. Hamer (London) furnishes a classification of the defects of 3,631 children attending the Council Schools during 1914. The classification includes children other than cripples proper:

Tuberculous diseases	1,145
Infantile paralysis	625
Spastic paralysis	170
Other forms of paralysis	54
Congenital deformities	220
Various deformities	399
Heart disease	705
Other chronic diseases	285
Other defects	28
Total	3,631

As the result of a special inquiry made in Birmingham in 1911 into the condition and circumstances of all known cripples in the city from the age of 5 years and upwards, the causation of the crippling in 828 cases over 16 years of age was found to be:

	Cases	Per Cent.
Tuberculous disease in	206	24.9
Accident	133	16.1
Apoplexy or birth palsy	116	14.0
Infantile palsy	73	8.8
Rheumatism in different forms	72	8.6
Congenital deformity	47	5.7
Venereal disease	39	4.7
Miscellaneous	142	16.7

The causation of the crippling in the case of 721 children under 16 years was determined as follows:

	Cases	Per Cent.	Males	Females
Tubercular disease	285	39.5	147	138
Infantile paralysis	175	24.3	115	60
Rickets	73	10.1	26	47
Congenital deformity	71	9.8	38	33
Apoplexy	33	4.6	15	18
Birth palsy	25	3.5	14	11
Scoliosis	13	1.8	7	6
Pseudo - hypertrophic muscular paralysis	5	0.7	5	0
Progressive muscular atrophy	2	0.2	0	2
Rheumatic	3	0.4	0	3
Necrosis of bone	5	0.4	2	3
Rheumatoid arthritis	2	0.3	0	2
Fragilitas ossium	2	0.3	0	2
Flat foot	1	0.1	1	0
Achondroplasia	1	0.1	1	0
Accident	25	3.5	14	11

The following represents the causation of crippling in the case of cripples who have passed through the Red Cross Street Special School, Bristol, since 1900. It will be observed that tuberculosis was responsible for approximately three-fifths of the cases:

Cause of Crippling	Boys	Girls	Total
Paralysis (chiefly infantile paralysis) . . .	22	16	38
Tuberculosis:			
Spine	25	10	35
Hip	22	11	33
Knee	2	5	7
Foot	—	1	1
Ankle	—	2	2
Elbow	—	1	1
Several joints	—	2	2
Deformity:			
Leg	2	—	2
Foot	1	2	3
Hand	1	—	1
Amputation, leg	3	—	3
Rickets	3	3	6
Congenital hip disease	—	4	4
Total	81	57	138

At the Heritage School of Arts and Crafts at Chailey the causes of crippling in the children admitted since 1903 were as under:

Causes of Crippling	Boys	Girls	Total
Paralysis (mainly infantile)	21	9	30
Tuberculosis:			
Spine	24	10	34
Hip	22	15	37
Leg	1	—	1
Knee	5	3	8
Foot	1	—	1
Ankle	1	—	1
Amputation, leg (disease or accident) . . .	17	2	19
Amputation, arm	3	—	3
Deformity (congenital)	4	—	4
Miscellaneous	6	2	8
Total	105	41	146

Speaking generally it is probable that between half and one per cent. of the children of school age are in greater or less degree disabled by crippling disease. The chief cause is tuberculosis.

NATURE OF SPECIAL PROVISION REQUIRED

There is a certain proportion of cases of comparatively trivial deformities or of results of previous disease for which special treatment need not be considered. Such children may quite suitably attend the ordinary public elementary school. For the remainder special provision is required, and among the type of children selected will be those suffering from the following defects:

1. *Tuberculous Disease of the Bones or Joints.* There are three chief forms, spinal caries, hip disease, and disease of other joints. In many non-pulmonary tuberculous cases the disease is quiescent, but attendance at the Special School is desirable in order that the child shall be kept under supervision to avoid the risk of relapse. In the other cases the resulting deformity renders attendance at the Special School desirable in order that the child may be prepared for a suitable career.

2. *Paralysis* commonly takes one of three forms, cerebral spastic paralysis, infantile paralysis, or muscular paralysis. It must be of such a degree of severity as to interfere definitely with instruction in an ordinary school or liable to be affected adversely by the conditions of an ordinary school.

3. *Deformities* (kyphosis, scoliosis, rickets, etc.) of the trunk or limbs which are progressing, or which require observation or are under treatment, or which are so severe as to make it inadvisable for the children to mix with ordinary children.

4. Defects, other than those producing crippling proper, include (a) *cardiac defects* in which compensation is imperfectly established. (Cases of fully compensated heart disease may, generally speaking, continue in attendance at the ordinary school provided care is taken in physical exercises and games. On the other hand, cases of uncompensated heart disease which require continuous rest and treatment should not be admitted to the special school until the condition has improved); (b) *Chorea*, more particularly in cases which are liable to recurrent attacks; and (c) a few miscellaneous chronic ailments of a medical character.

Among cases which are not as a rule considered suitable for admission are children suffering from deformities or paralysis combined with mental defect, blindness, or deafmutism, cases of rapidly increasing paralysis (*e. g.*, pseudo-hypertrophic muscular atrophy), epilepsy, lupus, active pulmonary tuberculosis, nephritis, neuropathic or merely delicate children, and children suffering from bad habits or offensive discharges.

So far as possible provision should be made separately for the tuberculous and the non-tuberculous cases. For those suffering from tuberculosis in an active form, and especially when associated with any form of discharge, provision should be made preferably in a Sanatorium School. Children otherwise healthy, but suffering from deformity, the result of past tuberculosis, can suitably be accommodated with non-tuberculous cases. In large centres of population it will probably be convenient to group the cripples together in a separate school; in small centres the accommodation may be shared with other delicate children. In still smaller areas, or in the case of children resident in the more scattered parts of county areas, it may be necessary to arrange for admission to a residential school. In any event, provision on the lines of an open-air school is preferable for the large majority of the children. In the case of many of the tuberculous children the disease, though apparently cured, may show signs of recrudescence, and many of the paralytic cases are delicate.

EXISTING CRIPPLE SCHOOLS

The total number of Cripple Schools at present certified by the Board is 61, providing accommodation for 5,005 children. The number of new schools certified during the year is four (situated in London (2), Bradford, and Sheffield). The majority of the Schools—57 in number—are Day Schools provided by large urban authorities, accommodating 4,773 children. The principal schools are in London, Liverpool, Birmingham, Bradford, Leeds, Sheffield, Bristol, Reading, West Ham, and Oldham. About 75 per cent. of the total accommodation lies in the area of the London County Council. About four-fifths of the children in these schools are cripples proper, the remainder being cases of various forms of chronic disease, mainly heart disease.

Residential Schools providing accommodation for 232 cripple children are established under voluntary committees as follows:

Name of School Date of Certification	Age of Children at the School	Accommodation	Average Attendance	Average No. on Books	Teaching Staff
1. Sussex, Chailey, The Heritage School of Arts and Crafts. May 1, 1904.[2]	8–15	90	84	89	4
2. Salford, The Greengate Dispensary, Grimke Ward. May 1, 1908.	5–9	15	14	14	1
3. Northumberland, Gosforth Home. November 1, 1910.	6–15	105	75	79	4
4. Gloucestershire, Stroud, St. Rose's Roman Catholic. March 25, 1912.	5–15	22	17	18	1

In addition, provision for children suffering from tuberculous bone and joint disease is available at the Sanatorium Schools.

THE AIM AND CURRICULUM OF THE CRIPPLE SCHOOL

The aim of the Cripple School is, in the first place, to provide adequate elementary training for afflicted children whose education has been seriously retarded owing to prolonged illness. Secondly, having regard to the comparative helplessness and frequent ill-health of these children, the Special School should ascertain the aptitude of the pupil and attempt to direct his efforts into channels which will be helpful to him in the choice and fulfilment of a suitable career. To accomplish these ends in any substantial measure it is of advantage that the period of school age should be extended; and authorities are empowered therefore to maintain children until the expiry of the sixteenth year, the Board's grants being payable until that age.

[2] Also certified by the Home Office as an Industrial School.

EDUCATIONAL ARRANGEMENTS

The curriculum of the Cripple School provides for instruction in elementary subjects and in manual training. The subjects of instruction are chosen to meet the special needs of the individual child, particularly as regards backwardness due to prolonged absence from school.

Elementary instruction follows the course adopted in the ordinary schools with the provision of individual attention to each child. This is possible on account of the small classes which do not exceed 25 in average attendance. In the London schools lending libraries are provided for the use of children in and above Standard III.

Manual instruction for junior children includes Kindergarten occupations, drawing, color work, needlework, knitting, raffia, cane and clay work. In the case of the London Schools a special art class is held for elder boys and girls, in which instruction is given by special visiting art teachers, with the object of encouraging the taste and inclination for higher craft work which it is hoped that many of the pupils will eventually undertake. To meet the requirements of such children the London County Council has established two schools for elder cripple girls at New King's Road, Fulham, and at Holland Street, Lambeth. At the former the subjects of craft instruction are drawing, dressmaking, blouse-making, embroidery and needlework, and, at the latter, drawing, fine needlework and embroidery and the making of children's garments. Consultative committees of trade experts are appointed to advise as to the instruction given in each school. No trade day schools have been established for elder boys, but in the newer special schools provision is made for preliminary instruction in woodwork and carpentry, tailoring and shoemaking.

At certain of the residential schools definite instruction is given in trade work to both boys and girls. At Chailey the boys are trained to a high degree of skill in design, cabinet-making, carpentry, and the manufacture of toys, and the girls in fine needlework, dressmaking, and in various branches of domestic service. The Gosforth Institute provides courses and instruction in tailoring and bootmaking and carpentry for elder boys and dressmaking and cooking for elder girls.

In the case of the Day Schools the children are conveyed to school in ambulances, which are in many cases specially fitted for recumbent cases. Couches and special reclining chairs are provided at the school. In order to meet the difficulty of distance at which many children live from the schools, the schools provide a midday meal. The children are not as a rule necessitous and can afford to pay. In the cases which cannot, the cost of the dinner is remitted totally or in part. The dinner is prepared in a kitchen provided as part of the school premises. A school nurse is attached to each school. Her duties include attendance with the ambulance on its rounds to collect the children from and return them to their homes, the superintendence of the midday meal, and attention to the cleanliness and minor ailments of the children at school.

MEDICAL SUPERVISION

Every child must be examined medically prior to admission to a Special School in order that the statutory certificate may be completed by a qualified medical practitioner approved by the Board of Education stating that the child is by reason of physical defect incapable of receiving proper benefit from the instruction in an ordinary Public Elementary School, but is not incapable by reason of such defect of receiving proper benefit from instruction in a Special School.

The Board's regulations applicable to Schools for Blind, Deaf, Defective, and Epileptic Children require (Article 24) that provision shall be made for the medical examination of every child at least once a year, in order to ascertain whether he is on the one hand, fit to return to the ordinary school or whether, on the other hand, he is incapable of deriving further benefit from education of any kind and ought accordingly to be removed from the school roll. In addition to these formal yearly visits prescribed by the regulations, it is most desirable that children requiring it should be kept under the observation of the medical officer as frequently as may be necessary. Moreover, in view of the fact that many of the children are under the care and attention of a nurse for dressings, electrical treatment, massage, or treatment by drugs, adequate supervision on the part of the medical officer of the work of the nurse is required. Steps also should be taken to ascertain periodically that the best is being done in the way of treatment for each individual case, whether treated at home or at hospital. In recommending children for return to the Elementary School, care must be taken not to re-admit too soon a convalescent child, especially if tuberculous. Recurrence in tuberculosis of the spine, hip and knee is so common that great care is necessary.

The duties of the school medical officer in regard to all cripple children in his area may therefore be summarized as follows:

1.   To ascertain their number and character.
2.   To examine, prior to admission, to a Special School.
3.   To inspect, periodically, the Special School.
4.   To supervise cripple children not admitted to a Special School.
5.   To arrange for after-care.

Speaking generally, the day cripple school system has justified itself and now needs extension; further provision should be made for technical and vocational training in both day and residential schools; and additional accommodation is required for hospital and sanatorium schools where systematic treatment and educational training may be provided.

MENTAL CONDITION OF CHILDREN ADMITTED TO CRIPPLE SCHOOLS

In the early days of the institution of Cripple Schools, it was not infrequently urged by those primarily responsible for their establishment that the children were generally of normal mental power, and indeed were not infrequently possessed of abnormal capacity for learning. With this in view it was urged that the curriculum for cripple children should be of a high standard, particularly as regards craft employment involving the exercise of considerable intelligence.   It became evident as the schools began to grow, however, that the high mentality of the cripple was an unsound view, and as long ago as 1907 the school medical officer for London furnished a report based on the examination of 1,080 children attending the Cripple Schools of the London County Council.   From the report it appeared that not more than 8.5 per cent. were up to the proper standard, and of the remainder who were below normal, 21 per cent. were stated to possess exceptionally low ability.

Dr. Hamer, in his report for 1914, reports a further inquiry by Dr. Williams into this matter as it affects a selected group of children, *i. e.*, those suffering from paralysis.   The results are shown in the following table, which indicates that the mental condition is better in the cases of spinal than of cerebral paralysis, and of the latter the cases of hemiplegia are better than those of spastic diplegia or paraplegia.

	Above Average	Average	Below Average	Definitely below Average. Almost on border line of Mental Deficiency
Poliomyelitis	63 (18.2%)	169 (48.7%)	89 (25.6%)	26 (7.5%)
Hemiplegia	6 (8.8%)	22 (32.4%)	21 (30.9%)	19 (27.9%)
Diplegia and Paraplegia	0 (0.0%)	10 (15.1%)	16 (24.2%)	40 (60.6%)

A more recent inquiry undertaken at two schools in the London County Council area shows that of 265 children on the rolls not more than 219, or 83 per cent., are normal, while the remaining 46, or 17 per cent. are retarded one, two, three, or more years. The retardation refers to elementary subjects only.   A similar inquiry at Red Cross Street Cripple School, Bristol, shows that 40 out of 166 children, or 24 per cent. are normal in elementary school attainments. According to the estimate of the head teachers respectively of the two schools for physically defective children in Birmingham, 136 of the children, out of a total of 230, are retarded two years and more in their school work. The retardation was estimated at four years in the case of 17 of the children. It is important to note that a proportion of the retarded cases are either normal or above the normal in manual attainments.

It may be asserted generally, therefore, that the large majority of children frequenting the Cripple Schools are mentally below normal, though not mentally defective. This is what one would expect. The afflictions from which they suffer involve long absence from school in early life, entailing not infrequently a complete sacrifice of all opportunity for education. Even when they come to school there is a heavy burden of school absence to reckon with. It is certain, therefore, that, given normal intelligence, there will be much leeway for the school to make up before the majority of the children can be regarded as normal in attainment. The great disparity in the mental capacity of crippled children renders it especially incumbent to consider their educational requirements individually. There is some danger that the needs of the children who are more capable intellectually may be overlooked, and care should be exercised to ensure that they are afforded the opportunity of developing to their full capacity. In view of the small size of the classes, this end should not be difficult of attainment.

AFTER CARE

The arrangements for the supervision of the careers of cripple children who have left school is in the hands of after-care committees. These committees work in close association with the Local Education Authority, who contribute representatives to their governing bodies. The most important committees are those working in connection with the Schools of London and Birmingham. The duties of an after-care committee are:

1. To assist in securing employment, apprenticeship, or further education at the expiry of school age.
2. To supervise the cripple during the early years of adolescence, and to advise him in all matters affecting his welfare.[3]

It is an essential condition for the real success of after-care work that the cases should remain under supervision for a considerable number of years after leaving school. In a well-organized scheme it should not be impossible to secure a fairly good record covering a period of ten years, but this is found by experience to be impracticable owing to scarcity of sufficient voluntary workers and lack of funds. To these causes must be attributed the fact that a large proportion of cases are lost sight of shortly after leaving school; in fact, in London about 200 to 220 cripple children obtain employment for the first time each year. The number of old cases under the supervision of the association in 1914 was not more than 411, which points to the rapid and extensive leakage of cases from public or semi-public control after the expiry of school age.

Much remains to be done for the education and equipment of the crippled child, but it is evident that given good school training and adequate provision for after care that the majority of the boys can be properly placed in the industrial field. The same is not equally true for girls, and it would appear that some further provision is necessary after the expiry of school age. In the case of London there is a limited amount of workshop provision for crippled women and a great lack of opportunity for exercising the higher craft training provided by the schools. Whether the organization of home industries or the establishment of workshops for

[3] The whole of the after-care work is voluntary, and until 1913 no funds were available from public sources. In that year the Board of Trade expressed its willingness to assist the London After-Care Association for Physically Defective Children by a grant of 300*l.* per annum towards administrative expenses, on condition the Association undertook the responsibility of receiving applications from all physically defective blind and deaf children in London who apply and are fit for employment.

crippled women will best meet the case is a matter for After-Care Committees to consider in connection with local conditions. But it would appear to be certain that upon the present footing much time, effort and expense are wasted owing to lack of opportunity to follow up into adult life the excellent results of school training. The reports which are available on after-care effort do, in fact, point to a similar conclusion arrived at in the case of feeble-minded, and which I embodied in my Annual Report of 1910. "We need more effective and vigilant *after care*, which shall not consist merely in the collection of statistics but shall include the care and following-up of all cases, rendering assistance in obtaining occupation, promoting the welfare of, and maintaining a connection and interest with, the children who have left school by means of societies, clubs, and other friendly associations, with a view to continuing educational influences and preventing degeneration."

LONDON

The official reports of the London Council Education Committee point to the same conclusion. It is stated that of 218 ex-pupils who left for employment in the year ended March 31st, 1911, 189 were known to be in employment at the corresponding date in 1912, and not more than 165 at the same date in 1913, showing a leakage of 53, or 25 per cent. in two years. The returns from individual schools are in some instances quite satisfactory, but frequently the information obtainable points to a serious leakage.

Among the more gratifying results the London County Council Brook Green school may be quoted, where in the period 1902–1914, 75 per cent. of the boys who left are stated to be in satisfactory employment. Of the girls at this school who have left during the same period a satisfactory account cannot be given of more than 25 per cent. The London County Council Haverstock Hill School shows for the period 1904–1915 a record of 45 per cent. of girls and 60 per cent. of boys satisfactorily placed. The New King's Road Special School for elder girls—a trade school—is disappointing in its results. In the period 1908–1915 not more than 36 per cent. of leavers are fully accounted for.

The fact appears to be established that girls generally come off less well than boys. This is attributed to varying causes: the difficulty of obtaining employment in what must necessarily be a restricted field, the power to overcome the disabilities of ill-health, which seems to be weaker among girls than boys, and the not unnatural tendency of parents to keep their crippled girls at home rather than allow them to face the rigors of the industrial world.

Among the trades in which boys are placed are tailoring, cabinet-making, wood-carving, basketry, boot-making, printing, engraving, watch-making, ticket and sign and facia writing, trades connected with the manufacture of articles made from precious metals, jewelry-making, manufacture of electrical instruments, tapestry weaving, saddlery and office work. Girls are placed at dress-making, millinery, fine needlework, embroidery, feather manufacturers, corset-making, laundry work, domestic service and office work.[4]

BRISTOL

A special inquiry into the present status of all crippled children who had passed through the Special School since 1900 was kindly undertaken by Miss Townsend acting through the Head Teacher of the Red Cross Street Special School and the Secretary of the local branch of the Guild of the Brave Poor Things. The following is a summary of the results:

Present Status	Tuberculous Children			Not Tuberculous Children		
	Boys	Girls	Total	Boys	Girls	Total
At work	33	23	56	21	16	37
Out of work				2		2
Helping in home		1	1		5	5
Too ill to work	4		4	3	1	4
In Institution	1	2	3	1	4	5
Dead	13	1	14	3	1	4
Lost sight of	1	1	2		1	1
Totals	52	28	80	30	28	58

[4] These quotations in smaller type are from reports of local education authorities.

The wages earned are as under:

Wages	Tuberculous Children			Not Tuberculous Children		
	Boys	Girls	Total	Boys	Girls	Total
Under 5s.	1	1	2		2	2
5s. to 10s.	2	6	8	3	3	6
10s. to 20s.	7	5	12	2	4	6
20s. to 30s.	1		1	2		2
30s. and upwards	2		2	1		1
Apprenticed	9	6	15	9	5	14
Not known[5]	9	3	12	5	3	8
Total	31	21	52	22	17	39

Since 1900, 53 boys and 16 girls have been apprenticed by the local branch of the Guild of the Brave Poor Things. The principal trades to which the ex-scholars are apprenticed are as follows:

Boys: Cabinet-making, boot-making, tailoring, ticket-writing (formerly), watch-making, jewelry repairing, engraving, mechanical dentistry and wood-carving in furniture factory. *Girls:* Millinery, dressmaking, and waistcoat-making.

The usual apprenticeship fee is from 10*l.*—25*l.* in the case of the boys' trades and 2*l.*—5*l.* in the case of the girls. In the majority of the cases the whole of the premium is repaid by the workers. Out of 42 cases in which the apprenticeship has been completed 30 are earning a living, 6 have died, and 4 have drifted into desultory occupations. Mechanical dentistry is considered to be the most hopeful trade for boys. Watch-making is now less good than formerly. In the case of girls, the long hours of work in girls' trades, the small remuneration during apprenticeship, the long distances from their homes to the dressmaking establishments (involving expense of transit), are causes militating strongly against apprenticeship, and most of the girls go into factories which are usually nearer their homes and where the hours are shorter. Speaking generally in the case both of boys and girls poverty is found to be a serious handicap to apprenticeship, though the Guild reports

[5] Applies chiefly to those who have set up in business on their own account or who are at work with parents.

that often every effort is made by the family to do the best possible for the invalid child.

BIRMINGHAM

Particular attention has been paid in the city of Birmingham to the problems of the crippled child. The Cripples' Union was formed in 1896, its work embracing systematic visiting and reporting, lending spinal carriages and bath chairs at a small charge, giving Hospital and Dispensary Notes, sending cripples away to the Woodlands and other Homes, granting milk and other nourishments free, or at a nominal charge, finding employment when possible, teaching home-bound adults some light handicrafts, and giving parties and entertainments in winter and summer. An active *After-Care Committee* follows up all children as they pass through the Cripple Schools. On the committee are representatives of the Special Schools Sub-Committee, the officials connected with the Special Schools and the Head Teachers of these schools, together with a few additional members. Further, there is a Special Schools' Care Employment Committee, a Sub-Committee of the After-Care Committee and including members of the Cripples' Union. This Sub-Committee concerns itself with children up to the age of 18 years only.

In 1911 an exhaustive inquiry by a special Committee of the Special Schools' Sub-Committee was made into the condition of all cripples in the city of Birmingham. The results were tabulated as they related to adults and to children under 16 years of age respectively. A cripple was defined as "a person whose (muscular) movements are so far restricted by accident or disease as to affect his capacity for self-support." The Committee found that there were in the city 1,001 cripple adults (546 males, 455 females)—over 16 years of age. Of these 1,001:

214 (128 males, 86 females) were able to go to work under ordinary conditions.
145 (84 males, 61 females) would be able to attend a Central Workshop.
111 (30 males, 81 females) were able to do remunerative work at home.
531 (304 males, 227 females) were unable to do any remunerative work.[6]
1,001 *Total.*

[6] The capacity of these 1,001 cripples for supporting themselves was stated to be as follows:—176 (99 males, 77 females) are self-supporting; 156 (86 males, 70 females)

are not self-supporting, but do not require help; 144 (54 males, 90 females), are not self-supporting, do not require help at present, but will want help later on; 191 (95 males, 96 females) are not self-supporting, and require help; and 334 (212 males, 122 females) are being maintained by the Guardians in their institutions.

There were also found in Birmingham 697 cripple children (males, 371; females, 326) under 16 years of age. The capacity of these was estimated on the same lines as in the case of the adults, with the following results:

230 (115 males, 115 females) likely to be able to go to work under ordinary conditions.

191 (110 males, 81 females) likely to be able to attend a Central Workshop.

42 (22 males, 20 females) likely to be able to do remunerative work at home.

57 (24 males, 33 females) likely to be unable to do any remunerative work.

177 (100 males, 77 females) impossible to estimate their future capacity.

697 *Total.*

Since its formation the After-Care Committee has dealt with 565 cripples who have passed through the Special Schools and in regard to whom the following information is available:

108 are doing remunerative work. Of these, 52 males are earning wages varying from 1s. 6d. to 24s. per week (average 9s. 5d.), and 56 females are earning wages varying from 1s. to 21s. per week (average 6s. 5d.).

7 youths assist in their fathers' businesses.

4 girls assist their mothers or other relations in business at home.

44 are living at home and doing no work.

68 are unable to attend school owing to physical or mental incapacity.

69 have been lost sight of—57 during school age and 12 after school exemption age.

130 have been transferred to ordinary schools.

42 have been transferred to special schools for the mentally defective.

42 are in institutions.

51 are dead.

565 *Total.*

Of the 273 cripples who have left school and whose whereabouts are known, only 39.5 per cent. are earning wages, and only 25 (19 males and 6 females) earn as much as 10s. per week. Of special interest are the facts bearing on the wage-earning capacity of cripples. This is summarized in the accompanying two tables:

Males

Age	Total Number	No. in Employment	Percentage Employed	Highest Wage	No. Earning 10s. per Week or more	Average Wage
				s.		s. d.
16–30	142	56	39.4	30	28	10 5
30–45	121	24	19.8	30	18	15 3
45–60	168	25	14.8	35	20	17 2
Over 60	115	6	5.2	15	3	10 2
Totals	546	111	20.3	35	69	12 7

Females

Age	Total Number	No. in Employment	Percentage Employed	Highest Wage	No. Earning 10s. per Week or more	Average Wage
				s. d.		s. d.
16–30	157	56	35.6	11 0	6	6 1
30–45	103	16	15.5	12 0	2	5 5
45–60	107	9	8.4	12 6	1	4 0
Over 60	88	1	1.1	1 0	0	1 0
Totals	455	82	18.0	12 6	9	5 8

CHAILEY

Of 103 boys discharged from The Heritage School of Arts and Crafts, Chailey, since its foundation, 83 are reported as engaged in work, 5 have died, 1 is in hospital, and in the case of 14 satisfactory information is not to hand. Of the workers all are engaged as carpenters or cabinet-makers with the exception of 12. Of these, 3 are draughtsmen, 1 works on a farm, 1 in a garden, 1 at watch-making, 1 at boot-making, 1 as a casual worker, and 3 work at miscellaneous occupations. Of the carpenters and cabinet-makers 24 earn from 10s. to 15s., 13 from 15s. to 20s., 9 from 20s. to 25s., 5 from 25s. to 30s., 6 30s. and over. In 14 cases the wages are not reported. Of the 36 girls discharged from the school 30 are at work, 3 have died, 1 is at an institution and 2 proved unsatisfactory. Sixteen of those at work are engaged in fine needle-work and earn in nearly every case from 10s. to 15s. weekly, 7 work as maids in different capacities, earning from 12l. to 24l. a year, 3 are engaged in dressmaking or machine work and 4 work at home. The period of training at Chailey of those who have left extends in most cases over a period of 2–4 years.

THE PREVENTION OF CRIPPLING

There can be little doubt (a) that greater attention to hygiene in infancy coupled with (b) the effective treatment of the disease in its earlier stages will do much to prevent many of the cases of crippling among children. This is particularly true of all cases due to tuberculosis. The onset of this disease in infancy and early childhood, and often before the age of compulsory school atten-dance, leads to the result that children do not come within the purview of the school medical service until the disease is well advanced and has already led, or inevitably will lead, to perman-ent crippling. No pains should be spared by the School Medical Officer to become cognisant of these cases at the earliest possible stage. In a properly organized school medical service it should not be difficult to obtain cognizance of all cases at least at the age of five years. At this age all children not in attendance at school on account of ill-health should be reported to the School Medical Officer who can then take steps to follow up the cases in such ways as may appear desirable. But even before the age of compulsory school attendance by the supervision of children in the babies' classes and by the utilization of the visits of School Nurses and Health Visitors and School Attendance Officers to the homes, it may reasonably be expected that earlier knowledge of the occurrence of these defects will be forthcoming than has been the case up to the present. Further, directly and indirectly through such organizations as Schools for Mothers, Crèches and Nursery Schools, and through visiting in the homes, particularly in connection with the Notification of Births Act, few cases should escape early detection. The need then arises for taking prompt and effective remedial measures. In this connection attention may may be drawn to the action taken at Brighton where special efforts are made to ascertain the occurrence of cases of joint and bone tuberculosis in their earliest stages, when sanatorium treatment is offered at the Borough Sanatorium.

In considering the question of prevention, there is, it must be admitted, one disquieting feature. In the large majority of the cases of crippling due to paralysis the condition is the result of an attack of *infantile paralysis*, an acute specific fever which appears to be on the increase, to become more epidemic in form and for which, at present, no preventive measures seem availing. The resulting crippling, however, will in many cases be much modified and lessened in proportion to the character and amount of effective persistent treatment during the early months following the onset. The two chief desiderata in regard to treatment of paralysis are (a) the recovery of every possible muscle affected, by rest, massage and applied exercise, and (b) the prevention of deformity.

It is important to note among the many results of medical inspection that improved attention to the physical welfare of children in early life is resulting in a marked diminution of *rickets*. Dr. Butterworth, Lancashire, points to a steady decrease of this defect among both entrants and leavers. Thus, among 5 year old boys, a percentage of 5.5 in 1909 has fallen to 2.2 in 1914, the corresponding figures for girls being 3.1 and 1.3. Among 12 year old children the percentages for boys were 2.4 in 1909 and 0.8 in 1914, and for girls, 0.8 in 1909 and 0.3 in 1914. Dr. Scatterty (Keighley) points to a similar result, the percentages for 1908 to 1914, being 8.8, 6.6, 4.6, 3.1, 3., 2.4, and 2.3 respectively. School Medical Officers who have given attention to the matter appear to agree that rickets is more prevalent among boys than girls. The Special School should improve the condition of the rachitic child in three ways, (1) remedy malnutrition, (2) improve general physical and mental condition, and (3) strengthen the muscles by applied exercises.

THE TRAINING OF THE CRIPPLE SOLDIER

It is hoped that the experience gained by some Authorities in 15 years' administration of cripple schools may be of timely use in helping to provide for crippled soldiers. Their numbers will be large; they will in many cases be unable to follow their old trades; they will have to be taught anew the means of earning a livelihood and their claim for consideration will be pressing. Many are already returning home, and no time is to be lost if they are to be saved from a condition of lifelong inactivity and poverty. The work already organized by Mr. C. Arthur Pearson for Blinded Soldiers at St. Dunstan's Regent's Park, will serve to show what can be done in a short time. Fifty soldiers are now receiving instruction in new trades. Workshops are being erected and residential accommodation being provided for 120 men. They are being taught carpentry, boat-repairing, mat-making, basketry, and poultry farming, bee-keeping, market-gardening, and massage. Special attention is given to recreation, including rowing and swimming.

A similar effort, though unhappily on a much more extensive scale, is required for crippled soldiers.

In order to make appropriate provision in particular areas or in suitable circumstances, four steps may be taken as follows:

1. A complete register of crippled soldiers should be formed, suitably subdivided into those who are trainable and those who are not.
2. Local Education or other Committees should coöperate with the military authorities on the one hand and ameliorative agencies on the other, with a view to organizing a scheme of training.
3. Day and residential technical classes should be established, and the subjects should include carpentry, cabinet-making, toy-

making, tailoring, boot-making, horticulture, etc. Provision should also be made for the apprenticeship of students to craft trades of higher type, watch-making, engraving, working in precious metals, etc.

4. After-care supervision would be necessary, and in many large towns considerable experience has now been gained in this work.

Schools for the instruction of cripples, if established by Local Education Authorities, can be recognized for Grant under the Board's Regulations for Technical Schools. The Board is therefore in a position to assist movements of this nature not merely in advising as to the scope and nature of schemes of instruction, but by affording financial aid.

TRAINING FOR CRIPPLED BOYS
AND CRIPPLED SOLDIERS

Douglas C. McMurtrie

TRAINING FOR CRIPPLED BOYS AND CRIPPLED SOLDIERS. ILLUSTRATIONS FROM THE DAY'S WORK AT THE HERITAGE SCHOOL OF ARTS AND CRAFTS, CHAILEY, SUSSEX, ENGLAND

DOUGLAS C. MCMURTRIE
New York

The work of the Heritage School of Arts and Crafts, at Chailey in Sussex, and the establishment of military wards in conjunction with it, has been well described by Mrs. Kimmins in a recent issue of this journal. Since the time her article was written public interest in the enterprise has broadened and the work has been considerably enlarged.

The illustrations, to which this brief note forms an introduction, give an excellent idea of the day's work at this interesting institution. The crippled boys demonstrate to the newly-crippled soldiers that physical handicaps can be overcome with proper training, and afford the men much encouragement through the early period of their progress, which is necessarily slow.

When the men first arrive from the London hospitals basket work and other light occupations. Later they engage in wood-turning and cabinet-making, and, when stronger still, attempt work in the fields. Other occupations available are toy-making, rug-weaving, stencilling, sketching, brass and copper work, bookbinding, leather work, and so forth.

The present activity in which both soldiers and crippled children play the principal rôles, well exemplifies the motto of the school: "The courage to bear and the courage to dare are really one and the same."

The school, which was founded for the industrial training of crippled boys and girls, has been in successful operation for some years. Most of its pupils are drawn from London; some of them are graduates of the special classes for physically defective children in the public schools of that city. The London County Council has frequently awarded to such children scholarships at Chailey in order that their education may be continued along practical lines.

HERITAGE SCHOOL OF ARTS AND CRAFTS, CHAILEY, SUSSEX.

AN EXHIBITION OF ROLLER SKATING

HERITAGE SCHOOL OF ARTS AND CRAFTS, CHAILEY, SUSSEX

IN THE HAYFIELD—REGAINING CONFIDENCE AND STRENGTH

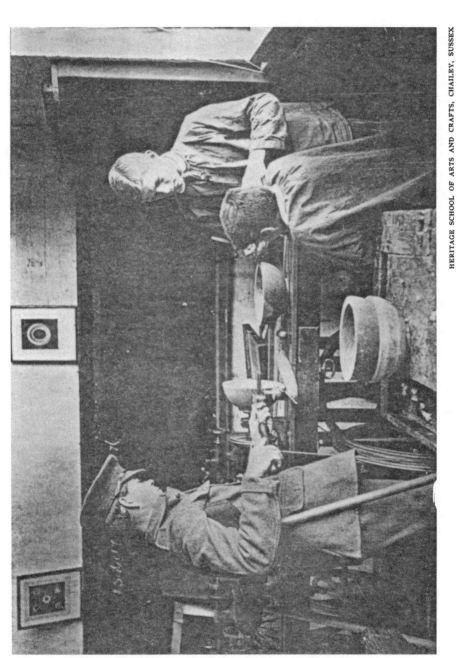

HERITAGE SCHOOL OF ARTS AND CRAFTS, CHAILEY, SUSSEX

CRIPPLED BOYS INSTRUCTING A CRIPPLED SOLDIER IN THE ART OF WOOD-TURNING

HERITAGE SCHOOL OF ARTS AND CRAFTS, CHAILEY, SUSSEX

GOOD EXERCISE AND GOOD FUN COMBINED

HERITAGE SCHOOL OF ARTS AND CRAFTS, CHAILEY, SUSSEX

A COMPANY AT SALUTE

HERITAGE SCHOOL OF ARTS AND CRAFTS, CHAILEY, SUSSEX

CRIPPLED BOYS MAKING WOODEN TOYS

HERITAGE SCHOOL OF ARTS AND CRAFTS, CHAILEY, SUSSEX

READY FOR A RACE

HERITAGE SCHOOL OF ARTS AND CRAFTS, CHAILEY, SUSSEX

BOYS AT WORK IN THE HAY FIELD

HERITAGE SCHOOL OF ARTS AND CRAFTS, CHAILEY, SUSSEX

THE ELEMENTS OF MILITARY TRAINING

THE RECEPTION OF DISTINGUISHED VISITORS

HERITAGE SCHOOL OF ARTS AND CRAFTS, CHAILEY, SUSSEX

HERITAGE SCHOOL OF ARTS AND CRAFTS, CHAILEY, SUSSEX

THE BOYS HAVE LONG BEEN ACCUSTOMED TO WORK IN THE GARDEN

HERITAGE SCHOOL OF ARTS AND CRAFTS, CHAILEY, SUSSEX

A BIT OF EXERCISE IN THE OPEN AIR

THE HISTORICAL DEVELOPMENT
AND PRESENT STATUS
OF CARE FOR CRIPPLES
IN SWITZERLAND

Wilhelm Schulthess

THE HISTORICAL DEVELOPMENT AND PRESENT STATUS OF CARE FOR CRIPPLES IN SWITZERLAND[1]

WILHELM SCHULTHESS, M.D.
Zürich, Switzerland

It is a conspicuous fact that in Switzerland, where relatively much has been done for the care of orphans and the mentally defective, the cripple has been largely neglected. The only explanation for this lies probably in the fact that, in general hospitals for children founded during the last thirty or forty years, provision has been made for a certain number of crippled children, thus minimizing the need for their special medical treatment.

For a long time the *Mathilde Escher-Stiftung*, founded in 1864, remained the only institution of its kind. From the first, however, it received not only cripples but also other children afflicted with chronic diseases impairing their capacity for physical activity. The first rule of the institution read:

The asylum is open to mentally normal but physically weak or sickly girls who are not able to attend public school. Those excluded are idiots, epileptics, and children who require hospital care; also orphans and abandoned children who may receive care in other appropriate institutions. Such latter may in special cases, however, be admitted for a limited period.

The eighth rule read:

The institution provides for the children's lodging and, according to agreement, clothing. It also provides instruction, medical care

[1] WILH. SCHULTHESS. Die Krüppelfürsorge. (Hülfsgesellschaft in Zürich, 112. Neujahrsblatt.) Zürich, 1912. A translation of Chapter V of this work: Die Entwicklung und der Stand der Krüppelfürsorge in der Schweiz. Translated and edited by Douglas C. McMurtrie. The three concluding paragraphs of the original version are omitted.

and, in general, everything that appertains to the physical needs of the children. The pupils will, with God's help, be taught to become honest women and Christians, and will, within the limits of their capacities, learn to provide for their own support.

Set forth in these rules we find actually the modern program of care for cripples: education, medical attendance, and occupational training. The specifications of diagnosis, however, do not quite correspond with the modern tendencies of the work.

Crippled children predominated, however, from the start, and the Rev. Schäfer, who visited the institution in 1871, was so impressed as to lead to the inauguration of his first efforts to care for cripples. The institution formed part of the St. Ann Foundation whose objects were, in the main, religious. The school connected with the institution, and designed primarily for its inmates, was also open to children from the outside. Thus we find here a first attempt towards a special class for cripples. Later, the services of a house physician were secured, but he was not an orthopedic surgeon and, in accordance with the spirit of the time, his services were demanded only in cases of acute disease. The care of cripples as such, or orthopedic treatment was not considered, largely because of deficient facilities at the institution. During latter years about twelve pupils were provided for.

For various reasons, and largely on account of the realization by the administrative board that the time was ripe for reconstruction of the institution along modern lines, the asylum was closed for several years, while plans were being prepared for the erection of a new building designed to meet all requirements.

The administrators of the fund joined hands with a newly organized committee for the foundation of a Swiss institution for the care of crippled children, in order, through joint effort, to find a suitable locality. The Mathilde Escher board wished to have their building in the immediate vicinity of the prospective institution in order to utilize its facilities and service for cases needing orthopedic treatment. The committee sold to the asylum board part of the land it had acquired in Balgrist, Zürich V. On that ground there has been erected and equipped a house for twenty-five children. This was opened in November, 1911.

The children live two or three in a room and use in common a number of public rooms, a living and dining room, a classroom, and a gymnasium equipped for orthopedic purposes, and especially for the treatment of scoliosis. This latter technical equipment was needed as the Swiss institution was not to be opened until some time in 1912. The house is surrounded by extensive porches and a large court provides ample space for exercise.

The staff consists of a house matron, a nurse, a teacher, two maids, and a porter. The medical work is under the supervision of a woman physician, Dr. Charlotte Müller. The orthopedic work is in charge of the present writer.

The institution is under the control of a committee consisting of men and women. The pupils so far accepted have been all orthopedic cases. The gymnasium is made good use of. Although the home has been open but a short time, the great demand for such institutions has already become apparent. On the other hand, it has become plain that a modern institution of that type cannot be run without medical direction.

From the prospectus and admission requirements the following may be quoted.

1. The first rule is the same as already stated.
2. The age of admission is that of school attendance—6 to 16 years.
10. The first quarter or half year, in each doubtful case, is a period of probation, followed by definite acceptance, or rejection in favor of some other institution.

Rule 8 is the same as the early one already cited.

In addition to the institution just described is the *Hospice Orthopédique*, founded in Lausanne in 1876. It has accommodations for thirty-six children and has for years employed the services of a physician, Dr. Nicod, who devotes himself entirely to orthopedic cases. Whereas in the Mathilde Escher institution education was in the foreground, at Lausanne the medical features are emphasized. There is some elementary instruction but no provision for occupational training.

The first rule of the institution reads: *L'Hospice orthopédique est destiné aux enfants atteints d'une difformité réclamant un traitement orthopédique.* (The Hospice Orthopédique is designed for children with deformities which require orthopedic treatment.) Only children under twelve years of age are accepted.

The institution has grown out of an enterprise formerly conducted by Henri Martin. At present it treats a hundred children annually, and publishes each year regular medical reports in which the work is graphically presented.

Further than this, crippled children are taken care of in hospitals for children at Zürich, Basel, Bern and Geneva, and in the children's sections of other hospitals. In such work, however, there is, of course, no possibility of prolonged or permanent care or of occupational training. Elementary instruction is given at several institutions by professional or volunteer teachers.

Most closely related to the modern institutions for the care of cripples, however, are the *Kinderheilstätte*, founded by Dr. Christ, at Langenbruck near Basel, the *Heilstätte für rhachitische und skrofulöse Kinder* at Aegeri, and the *Kindersanatorium* at Rheinfelden. At Langenbruck and Rheinfelden many cases of bone tuberculosis are being treated, while the institution at Aegeri devotes itself particularly to rachitis.

A considerable number of smaller institutions in Switzerland, mostly charitable foundations, are concerned with so-called incurable children, and in them cripples are often cared for. There may be mentioned the *Anstalt für Kinderpflege* in Lindenbach, Zürich IV, the *Kinderheim* at Chur, the *Asile d'enfants incurables Eben-Hézer* at Lausanne, and so forth. It should be noted, finally, that in a number of institutions for mentally defective or backward children cripples are received in individual cases, but care only, not medical treatment, is provided for them.

Nowhere in Switzerland do we find a well equipped free orthopedic hospital or dispensary in conjunction with the requisite organization and facilities for education and industrial training.

The advances in orthopedic science have been manifested only in the establishment of several private orthopedic institutes, which are not in a position to offer care and education to more than a very small percentage of crippled children.

Under such conditions, and in view of the activities of neighboring countries, especially of Italy and Germany, the establishment of a new institution in Switzerland became a necessity—a point of national honor.

The first public steps toward a realization of that need were taken by Rev. I. Kägi, director of the *Diakonissenhaus* at Riehen and by Dr. Zollinger, secretary of the educational bureau at Zürich. The former issued in 1903 a small pamphlet, *Zur Krüppelpflege*, in which he briefly outlined the status of care for cripples and emphasized the great need for new institutions. The latter adverted to the problem in a lecture delivered during the winter of 1904-1905 before the *Gesellschaft für wissenschaftliche Gesundheitspflege* (society for the scientific conservation of health), in which he called attention to the contributions made to this field at the school hygiene congress at Nürnberg. Later a small committee was organized in Zürich with the aim of taking active steps to encourage provision for cripples. The sum at the disposal of this committee was, however, limited to 10,000 francs which were placed by a lady at the disposal of the present writer to be expended for any purpose at his discretion. Soon, however, another generous donor contributed 50,000 francs to the committee, being prompted to the gift by the Rev. Ritter, who died in 1906. At once, a larger committee was formed and financial appeals were issued. Thus were laid the financial foundations for a Swiss institution.

The contributors soon organized themselves into the *Schweizerische Verein für krüppelhafte Kinder* (Swiss society for crippled children) on June 23, 1909.

A number of members undertook to continue the solicitation of contributions. The community responded enthusiastically to these efforts on behalf of cripples, and the capital of the institution reached the total of 470,000 francs. Among the contributions were several large gifts, one amounting to 55,000 francs.

The selection of a site for the institution proved a laborious task, it being difficult to find in the neighborhood of Zürich a plot of adequate size. The committee was determined to locate near the city on account of the consequent convenience to physicians, mechanics, teachers, and visitors to the dispensary, to remain within the city limits on account of building facilities, water, electricity, and gas supply, and sewerage features often defective outside of cities.

A modern institution for cripples is a very different thing from what it is conceived to be by people who are accustomed to associate it only with the care and incidental occupation of children. When, however, there is considered the technical equipment necessary to proper treatment, the required service by a medical specialist, an orthopedic mechanic (if indeed one is not regularly connected with the institution), and the various classes of artisans and professional people who are called upon as teachers—all of whom should be near at hand; and finally the desirability that individual children during certain hours should be sent to the city's public schools: the impracticability of operating an institution in the country becomes obvious. This issue is emphasized because the committee has been criticized on the ground that an institution could have been erected in the country at much less cost.

A relatively uncongested locality was another prerequisite, mainly on account of the cripples who have been or may be suffering from bone tuberculosis, and to whom sunshine is of such major importance.

From the outset, the committee was determined to combine with the resident hospital an out-patient dispensary, to provide for patients who, after leaving the institution, would return for the inspection of braces, the adjustment of appliances, massage, corrective gymnastics, and so forth. An office, where information would be available, regarding other provisions for care and regarding occupational opportunities, was considered another necessity. All these purposes would be served by the establishment of an orthopedic dispensary.

This division of our new institution embraces a gymnasium, two dressing rooms for men and women, six rooms for examinations, the application of bandages and plaster casts, massage, and radiography, and one special room for photography. In the basement are a supply room, an orthopedic workshop, and a room to be used eventually for medico-mechanical apparatus for which there may not be space in the gymnasium. On the first floor are fitted up several rooms for patients or pupils, particularly those male patients who must be provided with apparatus. Above this section is a small apartment for the physician. The porch situated on the top of the gymnasium provides accommodation for 'sun cure' cases.

The dispensary should make it possible to provide particularly for the many children suffering from spinal deformities.

For hygienic reasons, principally to prevent the transmission of children's diseases to the resident patients, the dispensary is located in a separate building.

The main building consists of a square structure and an annex which houses the kitchen (below) and the operating rooms (above). The ground floor includes, in addition to the kitchen, a spacious foyer, a dining room for about fifty persons, a living or work room for the pupils who are not confined in bed, an office with a waiting room, and a schoolroom.

On the first floor is the operating division, consisting of a waiting room (which is also used for the application of plaster casts to inmates), an operating room with large window space, washrooms and lavatories for the surgeons, and a room for instruments and the sterilization of bandage materials. On the same floor twenty-nine children can be taken care of in four rooms. There is a bathroom for the patients.

On the second floor, above the operating rooms, is a large room the use of which has not been determined, but which will probably be used as a dormitory or playroom. On the southwest side is a ward for twenty-nine patients. There is also one extra room.

On the third floor are the sleeping and living rooms for servants, the house-mother, and the attendants.

The top floor also contains three small isolating rooms which are provided for infectious or suspicious cases which may thus be promptly separated from the other children in advance of their transfer to appropriate hospitals. Infectious cases are, of course, removed from the institution as soon as their character is definitely ascertained.

It will thus be possible to provide for at least fifty-eight children, and if beds are placed in the large hall referred to the number can be increased to sixty-eight or seventy.

For workrooms there can be used the so-called living room on the ground floor and rooms in the basement as yet unapportioned which can be heated and provided with large windows. The ground, first and second floors are all surrounded by wide porches which cover almost three quarters of the southwestern and southeastern sides of the house, thus providing ample space for fresh air treatment.

Regarding organization, it may be said that the institution is controlled by representatives of the *Schweizerische Verein für krüppelhafte Kinder* (Swiss society for crippled children). The directorship is vested in a physician (the present writer) assisted by a resident house physician. The general supervision of the patients and the household staff is in the hands of the house-mother. The specialized care of the children, especially the sick ones, is performed by a number of nurses from a Swiss sisterhood.

The institution is designed primarily for natives of Switzerland from all parts of the country.

THE CARE OF THE CRIPPLED
IN NORWAY

I. Rummelkoff

THE CARE OF THE CRIPPLED IN NORWAY.

By Iv. Rummelhoff, Oslo, Norway.

THE two corner-stones of modern care of the crippled are special surgical orthopædic treatment, and training for self-support (in school and elsewhere). The doctor and his helpers must first do their part, reducing the infirmity as far as modern skill and appliances can ; and next, the special teacher and the school must take up the task and carry it on until the cripple is entirely or partially independent and self-supporting.

How far a cripple requires the support of the community depends on a number of circumstances that may be summarized as follows: (1) The nature of his infirmity, (2) its degree, (3) the individual qualities of the cripple, and (4) the conditions under which he lives.

When we discount all the cripples who for one reason or another have no claim on the support of the community, there remain " such persons as are crippled in body or in limbs, but are fairly well-equipped mentally, are neither blind, deaf, nor dumb, and are without definite moral defects; whose infirmity is of the kind and the degree that will, considering the social and economic conditions which they labour under, make it extremely difficult for them to lead a more or less normal life."

This definition is used by a committee of experts who, some time ago, brought forward a proposal as to the lines on which the care of the cripples of Norway should in the future be carried out. This committee also emphasizes the necessity of keeping in view that one is dealing, not with a special case of disease, but with an individual human being; and in this the psychical factors play no small part. We have latterly begun to consider the many problems that

meet us in our care for the crippled from a more
psychological standpoint, whereas we formerly
approached the task too much from its material side.
The physical cure, wrought by special surgical treatment and by training for work, means far more to
the individual than his mere bodily and economic
restoration; his worth as a human being is thereby
raised, and his intellectual gifts are brought into
play.

The Handicraft School for Cripples, started in
Oslo in 1892, was the first organized effort on behalf
of the crippled in Norway. The school had an
extremely modest beginning, at first with only one
pupil; but it was carried on by two sisters, Agnes
and Nanna Fleischer, in a manner that aroused both
admiration and enthusiasm at home and abroad. As
early as 1894 the school gained a silver medal at the
great exhibition in Antwerp and, three years later, a
gold medal at the exhibition in Stockholm.

The leading personality in the work for the crippled in Norway, from its first foundation, when the
handicraft school was opened in 1892, until her death
in 1909, was Miss Agnes Fleischer, herself a cripple
and otherwise of weak health. As she lay in her
wheel-chair, with its board serving at once for the
telephone, writing materials, and meals, she maintained constant communication with those interested
in the care of the crippled both at home and abroad.
In loyal co operation with her sister, she directed
the internal and external management of the handicraft school and its accommodation for boarders with
a steadiness of purpose and an energy that compelled
the greatest respect. She was moved from room to
room through the various storeys of the building, or
out into yard and garden, so as to keep an eye on
everything; and whenever any hitch in discipline or
in other respects occurred, those concerned had to
appear before her and give account of themselves.

She had an inborn administrative faculty which
gave her a position of peculiar authority; and her
own fate naturally led her to choose this field of
work. She suffered from an affection of the spine

with paralysis, which confined her to her bed for the
greater part of her life, and on the rare occasions
when she was on her feet she was obliged to use
crutches.

In 1896 the annual sale of work held by the
Misses Fleischer's Cripple School, as it was generally
called, was visited by our king at that time, Oscar II.
His Majesty was so much struck by the beautiful
articles of work exhibited, that he immediately gave
a large order for the palace, and subscribed a considerable annual sum of money towards the support
of the school. Two months later the Misses Fleischer
received the joyful news that the king and queen
had agreed that the jubilee gift, received by them
from the Norwegian people, should be applied to the
advantage of the crippled.

With these funds a new and, for that time, a well-
appointed handicraft school for cripples was built;
it was named after the queen, " Sophia's Memorial,"
and has been carried on for many years with from
fifty to sixty pupils each year.   But of far greater
importance is the fact that this magnificent gift laid
the foundation of the great *Central Institute for
Crippled* in Oslo, which will henceforth be the
nucleus of this work in Norway.   This Institute,
when fully finished, will have room for 300 cripples,
and will be supplied with every resource that modern
provision for the crippled now commands.   To begin
with, our cripples will here receive special surgical-
orthopædic treatment and after, or simultaneously
with this, a training such as is required by anyone
who is to lead a contented life as a self-supporting
member of the community, and who is not to become
a burden to others.   In many cases there are, as is
well known, only two roads open to the cripple ; either
he must remain all his life a financial burden on his
relations or on the public, or else, as all experience
shows, he may, by means of skilled treatment and
teaching in a cripple institute, become not only independent but a prosperous taxpayer.

When the Central Institute is fully finished, it
will contain workshops for the following handicrafts :

the making of bandages, orthopædic and ordinary
shoes, brushes, baskets, painting, watches, metal
engraving, carpentry, bookbinding, toys, wood
carving, knitting, weaving, tailoring, dressmaking
and plain sewing. Various other kinds of work may
be taken up by degrees, and individual cripples may,
under the supervision of the Institute, be settled
with employers in the town ; the latter will be greatly
helped by the advantageous situation of the Institute.
There will thus be the best opportunity of supplying
each inmate of the Institute with the training he or
she may desire and be best fitted for.

The Institute will have a central and dominant
site, high and free in a large park, with a view over
the town and fjord. Beside the workshops already
mentioned, with boarding accommodation for boys,
men, women and girls respectively, the Central
Institute includes a clinic and polyclinic. It should
specially be noted that the teaching of handicrafts in
the Institute is not only of importance for the training of the pupil, but will always play a prominent
part in the economy of the whole Institute ; for
when once all is in working order, a considerable
financial surplus is expected from the sale of handicraft. In the first story and facing the street there
will be attractive sale and showrooms for the work
produced at the Central Institute. It may be of
interest in this connection finally to mention that
the Institute will be carried on as an independent
foundation under public control ; and that the
necessary building funds will be obtained through
grants from the Storting and the Town Council
of Oslo.

It would indeed be a fatal error to believe that
a cripples' institute—how complete it may be—is
sufficient in itself or that the facilities and opportunities it offers to cripples be sufficient in our
time. It requires to be built out with various
organs and institutions.

The Central Board for Cripples was established
upon an Act of the Storting for the purpose of
organizing and practising the care for the cripples in

war and peace in co-operation with the existent and
coming institutions. The said Board is conducted by
a representative of the private Cripples' Institution,
of the State Insurance Board, and one representative
for the sanitary staff of the Army. The Central
Board which was organized during the war when it
was possible that Norway might be drawn into the
war, was in the beginning assigned to the Ministry
of Defence, but has later on been transferred to the
Ministry of Social Affairs.

The Central Board immediately recommended
the various communities throughout the country to
elect *Municipal Cripples Committees*, each consisting
of three members, of which one should be a physician,
the other a man or a woman interested in social
affairs and the third the Inspector of State Insurance.
The aim of this was to establish a unity of the
organizational care for the cripples all over the
country. The object of these committees was to
help and assist the cripples within each community
with advice, especially in obtaining the necessary
treatment and training and also an appropriate
occupation.

This recommendation met with great success.
Although no provision to that effect was found in
the law, about 93 or 94 per cent. of the total number
of communities complied with the invitation.
Only a few communities declined, but they have
later on followed suit.

A guide for these municipal cripples' committees
giving details of their sphere of work was shortly
after published together with a schedule of the
cripples in each district. This schedule should at
the same time serve as a register of the local
committee, and a copy of it should be used as a
report to the Central Board. The guide also gives
instructions as to how the committees should trace
the cripples residing within each district and advises
them regarding facilities for their treatment and
training.

The arrangement of establishing such local
cripples' committees was an excellent administra-

tive principle. The organization is inexpensive and
efficient. The members receive no remuneration for
their work. Of course, not all the committees have
accomplished equally good results, but many of them
deserve the greatest credit for their unselfish and
excellent work, especially those composed of women.
On account of various circumstances, it has proved
difficult to obtain the results which were expected to
begin with. At that time we reckoned on getting
the Central Institute within a short time, also the
law concerning cripples. The shortage of physicians
during the first years also handicapped the development. But these unfortunate conditions are now
improving.

*The first Registration of Cripples. The Cripples and
the Census of* 1920.

The first thing which the committees had to do
was to proceed to a registration of the cripples.
About 50 per cent. of the communities responded to
the call, and about 3,400 cripples were listed. We
found that more statistical material was desirable,
and on the schedule to be filled out for the general
Census 1920, a special item for infirmity was
inserted. It was limited to men and women under
65 years of age, and only the severe cases of
infirmity among children were included.

Of the entire population, amounting to about
2·7 millions, 8·891 were cripples under 65 years of
age, a number very nearly corresponding to that of
all the deaf, blind and mentally defective of the
same age. Of the male cripples, 2·092 (43 per cent.)
were self-supporting wage-earners, whilst 1·529 (31
per cent.) were provided for privately. Of the
women, 631 (16 per cent.) earned a living wage, and
1,007 (25 per cent.) were supported privately.
There were 1,106 men and 48 women employed on
farms or in fisheries, 890 men and 427 women in
industrial work, and 436 men and 75 women were
occupied in various departments of business. In
459 cases the deformity was accompanied by other
defects, such as blindness, deafness or dumbness.

The greater number (about 41 per cent.) had been crippled by disease. The crippling in 20 per cent. was due to cerebrospinal meningitis, in 9·7 per cent. to tuberculosis, and in 3·5 per cent. to rheumatism. The crippled at birth represented 22, and 18 per cent. had been crippled by accidents.

The loss to the community—from a purely financial point of view—will, with regard to the crippled, chiefly depend on: (1) The loss of the cripples' earnings for a greater or less number of years; and (2) the public or private outlay in support of the cripple during this period.

According to our Census in 1920, the crippled men had been in this condition on an average for sixteen years, the women for nineteen years. From a purely economic point of view, effective care of the crippled in our country, with its 2·7 million inhabitants, may be relied on to yield an annual profit to the community of about 4 million kroners. This amount is probably below rather than above the result to be expected. But to this we must add all the moral and ideal values which are to be gained by an effective organization of the work, and which cannot be expressed in figures or in financial estimates. We have, moreover, long left behind us the question why, and are now concerned only with how an effective care for the crippled is to be carried out.

As a sort of central guidance the Central Board during the last years has been available for the individual cripple and for the various organs of the cripples' care as well. A great number of questions have been submitted to the Central Board touching special cure, possibilities of training and occupation, purchase of prosthesis, infirmity chairs and carriages, assistance in applying to other institutions for stipends, free tuition and various allowances, assistance in obtaining work, application for gratuitous legal services, assistance in obtaining work from the same employer in whose service he became infirm, application to public institutions, help to set up in business, purchase of horses on the instalment plan, purchase of materials, sale of ready-made articles, &c.   Later on, we expect to appoint a travelling secretary who will act as a guide in co-operation with the Central Board and the other organs of the cripples' care.

The Board has published ten pamphlets in about 63,000 copies, as enclosures to the *School Magazine*, *Medical Magazine*, *Cripples' Magazine*, *Sunbeam* and a number of other periodicals.   In this way, the pamphlets are scattered around into the various circles.   The expenses have been covered by advertisements and the daily newspapers have shown much courtesy.   The Central Board has distributed between 50 and 100 articles to the press.   A list of them has been inserted in the report published on the occasion of ten years' activity of the Board.   The magazine *Sunbeam*, specially printed for the cripples, deserves great credit for its excellent articles for the cripples' sake.

The Importance of Early Special Treatment.

This is a point which we seize every opportunity to emphasize.   The surgical and orthopædic resources of to-day can often effect an entire or partial cure in many cases which were formerly more or less hopeless, and the patient is thus enabled to support himself entirely or in part.   Instead of being " on the parish " he becomes self-supporting and a taxpayer. With regard to defects at birth or those acquired in childhood, such as malformation of arms and legs, club-foot, pointed-foot (talipes equinus), lameness, paralysis due to cerebro-spinal meningitis, and limbs deformed by acute or chronic affections, it is of the greatest importance that the cripple should receive special treatment as soon as possible.

Many such cases, which in childhood appear insignificant and which cause no alarm for the future, may become worse with the child's growth, so that schooling, training and therewith the capability of self-support, are hindered or rendered impossible, if special treatment is not given at the right time.

Many cripples avoid, instead of seeking, a cure for their infirmities; and their relations frequently fail to realize their duty in this respect. The public authorities are thus obliged to do their utmost to obtain information as to such neglected cases.

Cripple Children of an Age to attend School.

These are as far as possible placed in the ordinary schools, since it is most desirable, for the child and the adult cripple alike, that they should be assimilated in social life and not isolated. In order to ensure the educational rights of crippled children, steps have been taken to introduce into town and country school-laws resolutions clearly enforcing the conveyance to and from school, or the lodging, of such cripples as by lack of means are prevented from attending the ordinary schools. For children who are too severely crippled to be placed in these, the necessary teaching is provided either in their own homes or in special school-homes for the crippled. It may possibly be objected that crippled children, when placed in the ordinary school, may be hardly dealt with by their healthy fellow-pupils, or may prove hindrances to the teaching in their class; to which we reply that competent and experienced teachers in our country give it as their opinion that this is, as a rule, no longer the case. On the contrary, touching instances are often met with of the care shown by healthy children for their crippled fellow-pupils, whom they try to help in all possible ways. The opportunity thus afforded the ordinary child, of learning whilst at school to care for less fortunate fellow-beings, is of course of great value and importance.

Start-help for those who become crippled as Adults.

All experience teaches us how important it is that a man having become crippled in adult age as a result of an accident or illness, as soon as possible be directed into activity so that he hardly will have time to stop and reflect upon his infirmity. The longer time passes, the greater power and resolution of mind will be required by him. Consideration should also be added to the psychological fact that it is easier to get people interested and make them ready to help where the infirmity is fresh in mind, else such unfortunates are apt to be "forgotten." A "reconstruction plan" should therefore as soon as possible be drawn up.

In most of the cases only a "push" is sufficient to make the cripple absorbed by his daily work and the duties and privileges therein embodied. By means of goodwill much can be accomplished by only replacing and reassigning the infirm from one job to another—for instance, if a mail-carrier has lost a foot, he may be assigned to a job at the post office ; if a slaughterer has got his arm damaged, he may be placed in the shop or the like. In some cases it will be necessary to make many attempts before the right position is found, and it requires patience and ability as well. But it is essential to success.

In order to get in the quickest possible touch with the invalid, it is required in Norway that all cases, in which he is allowed a high indemnity by the State Insurance—of 50 per cent. and more—should be notified to the Committee located in his district. In case of necessity, the Committee are also notified, regardless of the infirm being covered by the Insurance.

When a pupil is dismissed from the Cripples' School, the Committee in his home district will be notified so that they can be prepared to help him to get suitable work, &c.

No one is in a better position to encourage the invalids than one who has himself been in a similar condition, but has overcome the difficulties. What he often needs most is to get his mind restored so that his self-confidence will be awakened enabling him to look forward to certain aims and prospects. A physician said once to a war-invalid : "I have no more medicine for you. You must go out in fresh air and sunshine, and mix up with other people. You need more to practise the word 'I must' than for want of one hand or a foot."

Means of Livelihood for the Cripple.

As has already been shown, great weight is laid on the need of affording the cripple every possible opportunity of choosing the employment most in accordance with the nature and degree of his infirmity, as well as with his inclination and his powers. In our country we are agreed the training in handicrafts, which formerly dominated this work, is no longer sufficient. In this connection it may be of interest to quote the following from Henry Ford's book, "My Life and My Work": "When work is divided according to the laws of economy, there will always be plenty of positions in which the partially disabled can perform one man's work and earn one man's wage. From an economic point of view it is therefore a waste of power to regard the crippled as a burden on the community. In modern specialized industry there are more positions for the crippled than there are cripples to fill them." In Ford's works there are, as is well known, ten thousand employees with various physical defects. In our own country we have many instances of the crippled obtaining good positions other than in handicrafts or industrial work; as clerks, teachers and the like, or, in the case of women, as housekeepers, teachers in cooking, schools, &c. Not a few have done well on the land, or in such outdoor work as poultry farming, garden work, bee-keeping, and market-gardening. Such work has been proved to be specially suitable for the one-armed, or those suffering from other defects of the upper limbs; and for these various appropriate prostheses have been constructed. In many cases, consideration for the general health of the cripple indicates outdoor work as preferable to sedentary employment in workshop or office.

Through the Central Board cripples have for many years received scholarships for training them in studies, for attending teachers' schools, commercial schools, &c., aggregating an amount of about 50,000 kroners. These scholarships have given good results and many of the students have secured pro-

8

fitable positions. Also one of the Swedish pioneers
for the cripples' sake, the late Professor H. A. Walter,
said once: "It seems that the infirmity in many
cases brings about an improvement of the intellectual
faculties." Much of the mentality which comes
naturally to the able-bodied must be fought for by
the disable-bodied by using every muscular and
mental effort available. A blind man gets a sharpened hearing and sensibility, the deaf man's sharpened
visual sense enables him to "read from the mouth,"
and in a similar way the faculties of a disabled man
become intensified as a sort of compensation of his
or her lost limbs. They must reflect and act syste-
matically in cases where others need not, and it is
only natural that such forethought develops the
personality and enables him to perform work requiring
mental abilities.

The Duties of the Government and the Communities in Employing Cripples.

It is a question which has been much at issue
lately. Through the Ministry of Social Affairs, the
Central Board in the autumn of 1925 urged upon the
Government's various administrative branches to
appoint disabled persons in positions which they
could fill as well as able-bodied. A similar recommendation was made to the various communities.
The Ministry acted with much courtesy in the
matter and recommended it to the proper authorities.

The State as well as the communities have
interest in and are under obligation to help such
disabled persons to get a position suitable to his or
her physical and mental abilities, and a great number
of positions are available, but to fill these are often
preferred men of giant type. This is the sort of
economy that breaks nuts with a steam-hammer, and
the result is often that such a man is discontented.
The scattered efforts hitherto made in this direction
have, as a rule, proved particularly successful. In
the postal service alone there are about three or four
thousand positions, as post office officials, postmen,

and the like, which in many cases could be well filled by the one-armed or by those otherwise disabled. It is to be hoped that a systematic survey will soon be made as to what positions would preferably suit them. Time will certainly show that the functions of the Society will be carried out in proportion to each man's ability and physical strength, but no compulsory measures will in Norway bring any good results.

Superintendence of the Cripple's Work.

This is an important, but hitherto much neglected task, as is also the care of pupils and patients who have left the Institute. Experience has, however, taught us that the cripple is often, and naturally, ill-fitted to act alone and without supervision immediately on leaving the Institute. He may often find it difficult to produce work at a price and of a quality to bear the strain of competition, and may perhaps prove unable to vie with the handicraftsman whose work is only a by-product in addition to his other employment. The Municipal Cripple Committees have in this an important and interesting problem. Some of them have taken up the task of helping the cripples to procure materials and to find a sale for their finished work.

Nursing and Work Homes for Helpless and Homeless Cripples.

In spite of all the resources and all the experience of the present day, there will always remain a number of cripples whose defects and infirmities are so extreme that they can obtain the necessary care and attendance only in homes specially fitted to their need. There are, for instance, those who from birth or from later causes suffer from most serious defects or paralyses of various kinds. Few are so hard hit by fate as these, and yet it has been proved that even these, when they receive the necessary help, can often carry out various forms of work, not only as a pastime, but as a means of support.

Of not least importance is the relief given by these homes to the family and relations of the sufferer, in cases where housing difficulties and small means render the strain of nursing such an invalid for years almost intolerable. Unlike our ordinary old-age or nursing homes, which afford little or no opportunity for paid work, these cripple homes in different parts of the country will be combined nursing and work homes.

In contrast to the general provision for cripples, which on the whole, and in accordance with the existing conditions in our country must depend on the State and the municipalities, these homes for helpless and homeless cripples will be started and carried on by private means; and it is first and foremost our cripples themselves who are striving to build these homes, one in each division of the country. Everything will be simply, inexpensively and practically arranged, without any extravagance either in administration or otherwise.

In order to bring about the necessary firmness and authority in the management, superintendents are—upon the order of the public authorities—appointed for the various homes, said superintendents being representatives of different sorts of work.

In spite of the poor financial conditions prevailing, more than 100,000 kroners have during the last couple of years been donated to these homes. Besides, the Storting has appropriated 50,000 kroners of the funds of the "lottery" destined for the home at Northern Norway. A fully equipped building has been bequeathed by testament to serve as a cripples' home in one of the other parts of Norway.

Our Cripples' own Organizational Work.

They have formed their own unions, one for each part of the country, and they have shown a rapid growth. This summary would be incomplete, if their important work in this line was not mentioned.

The soul of this movement, which was started four to five years ago, is the cripple Torolf Sandvik of Bergen.

He is himself lame in both legs and partially paralysed in his back and one arm, after an attack of cerebro-spinal meningitis at the age of 10, thirty years ago. Sandvik, by training a woodcarver, now edits a paper for the cause of the Norwegian cripples, entitled *Sunbeam* (*Solglimt*), which, after less than four years, has 4,000 subscribers, a rate of progress unexampled for a paper of this kind in our country. *Sunbeam* is first and foremost our cripples' own organ and adapted to the cripples themselves, but it also has a number of fellow-workers from other camps, and is read over the whole country.

The numbers of members of the cripple unions already exceed 1,500, and to these we may add a number of young people's unions, sewing societies, childrens' clubs and the like, all working on behalf of the cripple unions and their aims. The unions have first and foremost concentrated their activities on building the above-mentioned homes for helpless and homeless cripples, but they have also given valuable help to propaganda for improved provision for cripples as a whole, and especially the cripples' right to be helped towards self-help. The unions hold their annual meetings each summer, and these have been attended by as many as 100 to 200 cripples, some of whom have come from great distances. These gatherings have done much to stir up the public conscience, and it has been a joy to witness the sympathy and helpfulness shown by the people at large.

Last summer a 17-year-old boy, lame in one foot, came to the cripples' meeting at Trondhjem in a motor-driven three-wheel bicycle—automouche— which only is operated by the hands. He managed to drive from Asker near Oslo across the mountain Dovre (1,000 meters above sea), a distance of about 600 km., in three days. In the beginning of September, 1926, he drove from Oslo to the cripples' homes in Stockholm, Gothenburg and Copenhagen, a distance of about 1,400 km.

There is splendid co-operation between the cripples' unions, the Central Board for Cripples, and the other institutions taking part in this work.

When a man lately bequeathed a large amount of money to this cause, without having mentioned which branch of the work was to benefit thereby, all the authorities agreed that the sum should be employed by one of the unions for a home for the crippled, since all held the opinion that the legacy would thus bear the most fruitful results. Most important has been the deliverance of the cripple from his or her isolated position, in which egoism of thought and interest threatened to stifle all development and, in place of this, the inspiration of common interests and of fellowship in the lot of others. In this way the individual has grown both in his own self-respect and in the eyes of his fellow-citizens; and this, together with our cripples' own work for daily bread, has, beyond all else, contributed to raise them to a higher level than was theirs before.

An Annual Sport Day all over the Country will be Instituted for the Benefit of Helpless and Homeless Cripples.

This is expected to take place each autumn under the name of "Norges Fotball-forbunds dag for Norges vanföre." (The Norwegian Football League's day for the Cripples in Norway.) On September 5 this year matches were held in fourteen different places in Norway, with great attendance. The *King* and the *Crown Prince* were among the onlookers to the great match in Oslo; 60,000 tickets were sent out. *Roald Amundsen's* and *Fridtjof Nansen's* appeal to Norway's sporting youth: "The building of homes for the cripples is just something for those who enjoy health and physical strength," was printed on each ticket and shown on all the moving picture programmes. The "day" was an excellent "awakener" for the cripples' sake. Addresses on the same subject were delivered from the broadcasting stations, and articles were published in the Press.

The Law Concerning the Crippled.

A proposal for the enforcement by law of the care of cripples has lately been brought forward by a

committee of experts appointed by the Department
of Social Affairs.   The most important measures for
the insurance of systematic care of the crippled are
here collected in an act which is simply entitled
"The Law Concerning the Crippled."   This act is
in substance as follows:—

The present voluntary form of organization for
cripples with a Central Board for cripples embracing
the whole country, and Municipal Cripples' Committees in each town and district commissioned to
advise and help the crippled, is to be enforced by
law.   The central ruling body, whose task it is, in
conjunction with other institutions that are or may
be formed, to organize and lead the care of cripples,
shall be appointed by the Department of Social
Affairs.   The work of members of the Municipal
Cripples' Committee shall be unpaid and the position
shall be honorary.   We shall thus have the necessary
organs for effective care of the crippled throughout
the entire country.

Doctors, who, in the pursuance of their calling,
observe a cripple, are to give the Committee concerned notice thereof within a month, together with
information as to the nature of the defect observed ;
and similar injunctions are given to midwives, clergy,
teachers, parish nurses or those otherwise serving in
the district.

Cripples or persons apparently in danger of
becoming crippled are, on receiving notice from the
Central Board or the Committee concerned, obliged
to let themselves be examined by the doctor whom
the said authorities assign.   The doctor's fee is to
be paid by the cripple's parish without right of
refund.   If the cripple has claims on no particular
parish, the expenses will be paid by the State.

Crippled children between the ages of 7 and 18
may be summoned by the Central Board, after conference with the local school authorities concerned,
to share in the curriculum of the ordinary school ;
or, if necessary, to become pupils in the schools for
crippled children that are or may be founded by the
public authorities.

Every cripple whose need of medical treatment, &c., is not otherwise provided for, has a right to treatment in the cripple institutes or school homes for the crippled supported by the State; as also to special orthopædic treatment inasmuch as the cripple is judged by due authority to require such, and a place is vacant for him or her.

The expenses of the cripples' journey to and from the cripple institutes and special orthopædic centres, &c., and of maintenance in these, as also of the outlay on bandages and prostheses, are to be borne by the parish to which he belongs, and if this is a country district, by its council. The County Council can ordain that an amount not exceeding one-third of the whole sum shall be refunded by the district concerned. Expenses of clothing shall be borne by the home parish. If domicile cannot be proved, expenses will be met by the State.

Expenses in supplying invalid cycles, carriages and the like are not referred to in the law, but are expected to be covered as hitherto by the unions, legacies and other private institutions. Expenses incurred by the municipality or State may be entirely or partially reclaimed from the cripple or any relatives responsible for his support, in so far as the Committee concerned find this to be reasonable in consideration of his or her financial position.

Expenses of conveyance and lodging incurred by doctors, members of the Central Board and secretaries, on journeys in connection with this law, will be paid by the State. None of the expenses mentioned in this law will be considered as pauper relief, unless the person concerned is without Norwegian citizenship or rights as a native of Norway. The handicraft work of the cripple institutes will be carried on unhindered by the decisions of the Handicraft Law. When needed, contracts concerning time of apprenticeship and the like may be made for the pupils at the handicraft school of the Institute.

In the proposed Bill for a " Cripples' Law " an elastic system has been adopted, which would adjust itself to the various conditions and which necessitates no new positions. The Bill is looked upon favourably by all parties concerned. The Medical Director has strongly recommended it, and the County Councils and City Councils have approved it. But not all have as yet expressed their opinion. Unfortunately, it is to be feared that it will pass some time before the Law takes effect on account of the financial situation.

In all countries and not least in Norway, it is found that the crippled have a unique power of inspiring others with increased energy and activity, their strength of will and their perseverance make them centres of light in town and country alike. At such a time of economic depression and privation as that which the world is now passing through, this stimulating educational influence is an asset of the greatest value. In our propaganda on behalf of the crippled we therefore constantly bring forward the fact that it is as much in the interest of the whole community as of the crippled that the Central Institute and the law for the crippled should be supported. These two objects are in our opinion the foundation-pillars of the future of the cripples' cause in Norway.

As an example of the cripples' longing for activity and work, let me cite the following from one of the first annual reports issued by the Cripples Training School in Oslo.

" The pupils show great energy and love of their employment. They are so keen over their work that they generally leave it with reluctance at the interval between classes ; and when school hours are over, they often ask leave to remain at work so as to finish some article."

Our great poet, Björnstjerne Björnson, has given happy expression to a cripple's craving to make the most of life, when, in Magnhild, a crippled girl says : " What would have become of me in the world if you had not come to the school and taught me the very work that suits me ? Without you I should

have been a burden on others, or I should have
worked without gladness. Now I seem to be joining
in something that is always growing."

Co-operation between the various Countries on the Field of the Cripples' Care.

Finally I take the opportunity to emphasize the
importance of an organized co-operation between the
various countries for the exchange of experiences,
plans and improvements on this field. Each country
has much to learn of the other countries and the
co-operation has hitherto been too scattered. It
should be given a more concise and firm form and all
countries should participate—not only some of the
nations who took part in the World's War.

When one knows that one of the results of this
war was to leave ten million cripples, and that the
number of " peace " cripples is also to be counted in
millions, one realizes the extent of this problem, both
economically and from a humanitarian point of
view.

As far as the Scandinavian countries are concerned, the co-operation is in progress and a committee has newly been appointed to prepare the
organization of a Nordic Cripples' Society.

The time has come to institute a permanent
international clearing house for the cripples' care.

There can be little need for us to express here how entirely
we are in agreement with our contributor, Dr. Rummelhoff, in
his most admirable and constructive proposal of an international
clearing house for the discussion and practice of all that may aid
the cause of the cripple. We would ask our readers to ponder
upon Dr. Rummelhoff's article, and when they have grasped the
inspiring programme in Norway let them post it on to some
friend. It is in our opinion one of the most valuable, most
practical, and most informative contributions we have had the
good fortune to print in this Journal. In the name of ourselves
and our readers we thank Dr. Rummelhoff, and we wish him the
achievement he deserves.—THE EDITOR.

CRIPPLEDOM IN SOVIET RUSSIA

Henry Turner

CRIPPLEDOM IN SOVIET RUSSIA.

By Professor HENRY TURNER.

Director of the Orthopædic Department of the Military Academy of Medicine in Leningrad.

" I have no home, no kin, no kind, not made like other creatures or to share their sports or pleasures."—BYRON.

THE DEFORMED TRANSFORMED.

THE insufficiency of medical aid equipment in relation to the vastness of the Russian country, and the geographical peculiarities of some of its remote parts being, inaccessible during some periods of the year, have always been a source of crippledom in its most various and fantastic forms. Cripples constitute a considerable proportion of the multitudes of pilgrims swarming in the direction of holy shrines, some influenced by the hope of cure, others attracted by practical considerations based on the psychology or the religious enthusiasm of the crowd. The picture of a church porch beset by mendicants and cripples, stretching out their hands to the congregation streaming out of service on a holiday, has often been a subject for a masterly artist's brush. The cripple still finds resources in such surroundings. On the other hand the busy crowd of a large city does not feel disturbed by the sight of a human paralytic crossing a muddy street amidst trams and motor cars, nor does the passer-by pay much attention to a fellow-traveller with deficient lower limbs, steering an improvised self-made vehicle on small wooden wheels along the sidewalk.

The term " Cripple " (Kalexa) is very familiar in Russia, and mention is often made of " wandering cripples " (Kaliki perechoshii) in the ancient legends. Continuing to exist as an inevitable accessory of society, cripples were left to depend upon liberal alms generally coming from the common people. There were no regulations or institutions for the care of this numerous destitute class, which, according to calculations of some authors, contained about 165,000 persons not having reached the age of 15.

The humanitarian ideas of national institutes for crippled children promoted by the Danish Pastor Knudsen gradually began to leak in the direction of Russia via Sweden and Finland. The first small " Asylum for Cripples " was established in 1890 in one of the remote parts of Petersburg by a small society of benefactors presided over by our elderly philanthropist M.M. Semenov. An anonymous gift of £4,000 (now known to have come from a Mr. Mereshkovsky) served as a foundation for the enterprise. The number of the inmates of the asylum at the beginning did not exceed 30. But the limits of its work continued to increase through the pecuniary support of an increasing number of members of the committee and other contributors. The Society came into the possession of a small wooden tenement to which a small chapel, specially built, was soon annexed. But the construction of the building containing two stories could not answer the demands of a national institute. Lack of sunlight and closeness of the compartments were serious drawbacks. As to the demands which the Asylum had to face from the first start, there was no possibility of gratifying even a small part of candidates desiring to enter the home. Children of all ages, amputated victims of railway or tram accidents, creeping paralytics, subjects gravely deformed by rickets, or physically handicapped by congenital defects, were brought by parents anxious to be relieved from a useless and cumbersome member of the family.

To this variegated compound was inevitably admitted a sufficient number of sufferers from late results of bone tuberculosis, deformed about the hip, spine or knee, some of them with discharging fistulas of long standing. The overcrowding of such different disabilities under the same roof could not but produce disastrous effects and reflect upon the admirable intentions of humanitarian benefactors. Healthy, robust children, with amputations or congenitally deficient, arriving from the country, were easily affected by the close atmosphere of the asylum; constant proximity to tuberculous comrades with poorly bandaged fistulæ helped them to succumb to the deadly disease. Thus would succumb some previously healthy case. Admitting the obvious grave error committed in concession to urgent necessity, the superintendent took steps for combating the evil by the isolation of tuberculous cases.

The next step was towards the training of the cripple. Special attention was given to the organization of the home according to the accepted functions of an educational institute. Measures for moral development were very effective in the hands of experienced and devoted teachers. Provisions for education were made. A Finnish instructress was appointed to teach craftwork selected for suiting different cases of physical deficiency. The list of occupations is too well known to be here enumerated. From many years' observation I must emphasize the interest taken by crippled children in handwork, which must be accepted as one of the principal factors in maintaining their morale. Their capacity to adapt deformed limbs to different employment, and doing such work as carving with their feet, has been marvellous, a living reproach to those who cling to the old traditional belief that the cripple is incapable of taking his place in the world's activities.

As to equipment for alleviating and correcting the children's deformities, the Institute had recourse to the Orthopædic Clinic of the Medical Academy directed by the author. The successful results of operations which restored function or lessened physical deficiency were duly appreciated by the children, and " When is my turn ? " was the general cry of the throng as they saw the surgeon, some hopping on one leg, others using their hands for froglike locomotion.

A gift of £2,000 as a part of capital bequeathed by a deceased Mrs. Kouschin in Moscow for charitable purposes gave new energy to the Committee, and hastened the plan of building a stone house adjoining the old wooden building. The foundation was of a

commercial character, as the five-storied house
ultimately intended for the purpose was leased to a
large town school. This measure secured the budget
of the Institute which had to be content with its
former dwelling in expectation of better times. The
outbreak of the Great European War brought unexpected hindrances to the further growth of the
home. The multitude of war invalids needed special
help. An appeal, headed by the motto "There is a
time to kill and a time to heal" (Ecclesiastes iii)
was made by the author in the medical press, urging
the necessity of organizing special institutes for
treating war cripples, supplying them with prostheses
and re-educating their working abilities. Several
establishments sprang up at that time of which some
few continue to exist in the central towns. Foremost among them stands "The Prosthesis Institute
of Leningrad" under the directorship of Dr. H.
Albrecht, former Assistant of the Orthopædic Clinic.
The number of appliances furnished by this establishment during the current year exceeded 2,500, of
which one half consisted of artificial legs.

The temporary decay of the Cripple Hospital for
Children came to be evidenced very acutely during
the first years of the revolution. Heavy financial
stringency, and the substitution of the experienced
staff of tutors by new elements, weakened the
system of upholding the *moral* and physical level of
the patients. It is difficult to describe the sudden
change in their behaviour and character after the
stoppage of handwork and other useful occupations.
Forced inactivity produced roughness of manners,
disobedience and tendency to crime. The yearning
for occupation was written in the dull eyes of the
children.

This short period of decay is now ceding to a new
wave of regeneration. Great progress has been
achieved by procuring a summer residence for the
Hospital in the outskirts of the town, where many
buildings have been forsaken by their previous pro-
prietors. A few months' sojourn in a sandy, elevated,
country place, partly covered with pine trees, has

had an immediate beneficial effect on the standard
of health of the cases of the forsaken town dwelling.
Primitive-built solaria confirmed the energetic healing
capacity of the northern sunray, and blackened the
skin of the emaciated children to a degree equal to
that seen in the bathing places of the Crimea.   The
healing effect of sun and air upon rickety and tuberculous cripples has been amply demonstrated.

Upon taking possession of its new town building,
now   abandoned   by   the   Municipal   School,   the
Hospital has been able to broaden its field of action
and to provide more comfort and sanitation for the
crippled children, the number of which has risen to
100.   An operating theatre and outfits for photo-
therapy have been added to its equipment.   An outdoor department will distribute assistance to the
inhabitants of the district.   It is the intention of the
Institute to establish a filial department out of town.
Medical aid is provided by two resident physicians
and one chief officer.   Orthopædic help is given by
myself and my staff of assistants.   The necessary
financial means for sustaining the Institution are
provided exclusively by the Government.   The future
of the Institute's activity is assured.   I must emphasize the satisfaction felt by me in my co-operation
for its welfare.   It seems as if nature tries to com-
pensate the physical handicap of cripples by endowing them with superior intellectual development.
Their sensitiveness to the services bestowed upon
them is generally very acute.   In conclusion to this
brief survey, may I say how the cripple children
on reaction to treatment bring to my memory the
final act of a drama of Ibsen ("Little Eyolf"), in
which some unfortunate parents having suddenly
lost their deformed and neglected son, decide to exchange their formerly empty existence for a life dedicated to cripples with the intention "to develop the
rich capacities concealed in their souls and to
demonstrate by their own life how great is human
responsibility."

Greetings to the *Cripples' Journal.*

STATE PROVISION FOR CRIPPLES
IN HUNGARY

Emerich Ferenczi

State Provision for Cripples in Hungary[1]

Dr. Emerich Ferenczi

Consulting Expert on Social Legislation for the City of Budapest

Count Stefan Tisza, the prime minister, inaugurated the welfare work for disabled soldiers in the kingdom of Hungary. His first move was to take a census of war cripples, including soldiers still drawing pay and civilians drafted into military service. The first census, on December 1, 1914, included only those actually in Budapest, the second, on March 31, 1915, covered all the Hungarian states.

On February 1, 1915, the prime minister called a conference to consider the duty of the state and of private charity toward these men. A small executive committee was appointed under the presidency of Count Kuno Klebelsberg, secretary of state. Its function was confined, at first, to the organization of medical treatment and re-education for lamed and crippled soldiers. On the other hand, the finding of employment for these cripples was considered to be the duty of private charity and was handed over to a committee of the Hungarian Red Cross, composed of representatives of the principal private societies. The government committee established several institutions for re-education and convalescent care, but it soon became evident that they must extend their responsibility to internal ills as well as external and must, in fact, cover the whole field of social welfare for war cripples. Therefore, in September, 1915, both the committees were dissolved and there was created a Royal Hungarian Department for Disabled Soldiers, which should direct the entire work.[2]

Before we take up the legal basis for the social care of war cripples, we must mention another provision in the same law dealing with the care of disabled soldiers. In the statute dealing with public expenses for the first six months of the fiscal year 1914-1915 (Statute XV of the year 1915), there is a provision relating to the support of war cripples; and of needy families who are dependents of war cripples including persons drafted for special service. These classes of persons are entitled to an extra subsidy in addition to the military disability pension, for as long as the war lasts and for six months after the war (Statute LXVIII of the year 1912).

War cripples and their families are entitled to a disability pension according to law (Statute L of the year 1875, Austrian law, December 27, 1875). This pension, however, is so exceedingly small that it will not support a family, even with the addition of the supplementary allowance which is none too generously apportioned. In order for a man to claim a disability pension, his earning capacity must be reduced by not less than twenty per cent. In that case, the pensions are as follows: Private, 72 kronen; lance-corporal, 96; corporal, 120; leader of division, 144; sergeant-major, 168; officer's deputy, 214. To this may be added, in given cases, the mutilation allowance which ranges from 192-288 kronen. Thus our military pensions are graduated ac-

[1] Translated from the Zeitschrift für Krüppelfürsorge, Leipzig, 1916, ix, 145-153.

[2] Professor Dr. Spitzy speaks, in an article which appeared in the Zeitschrift für Krüppelfürsorge, Leipzig, 1915, viii, 187-190, of the Austrian government having decided to transfer to the separate states the care of its disabled soldiers. He includes Hungary among the states as a matter of course. But again he seems to imply that the work for disabled soldiers in Austria and Hungary is maintained under common direction

and he mentions Budapest among the 'Austrian' state capitals. Now we know that the 'Wiener orthopädisches Lazarett und Invalidenschulen" (Vienna Orthopedic Hospital and Cripple School) was established as a national institution, and was, therefore, under the Austro-Hungarian military authority, not merely the Austrian. On the other hand, the work in Hungary was initiated by the Hungarian legislature. It is true that it had the moral and financial support of the Austro-Hungarian military authorities and was to that extent national. But it developed independently along lines of its own and on a quite different basis from similar work for disabled soldiers in Austria.

cording to the military rank of the wounded man. This principle, however, is untenable and in direct contradiction to the democratic character of our army. I must emphasize the fact that the present supplementary allowances to disabled soldiers are not made according to this very rough classification but according to the degree to which earning capacity has been impaired.

The following table presents a summary of the annual allowances to disabled soldiers, over and above their military pensions, in accordance with Section 7, Statute xv, year 1915.

Order of Rank	The Amount of the Pensions According to the Present Law	For the Disabled Soldier			For the Disabled Soldier's Legal Wife	For Each Child of a Disabled Soldier (Even if Illegitimate)	For the Father, Mother, Grandfather and Grandmother of the Disabled Soldier
		Class A. If His Earning Capacity With-in His Former Occupation Has Been Impaired by at Least 20 Per Cent., But Less Than 50 Per Cent.	Class B. If His Earning Capacity With-in His Former Occupation Has Been Impaired by 50-100 Per Cent.	Class C. If He Is Unfit to Pursue Any Gainful Occupation			
	Crowns	*Crowns*	*Crowns*	*Crowns*	*Crowns*	*Crowns Per Capita Ranging According to Discretion of Authorities*	*Crowns Per Capita*
Infantryman	72	60	120	180	60	36–60[3]	60
Lance-Corporal	96	60	120	180	60	36–60	60
Sergeant	120	60	120	180	60	36–60	60
Leader of Division	144	60	120	180	60	36–60	60
Sergeant-Major	168	60	120	180	60	36–60	60
Sergeant-Major of Staff	192	60	120	180	60	36–60	60

[3] For each child of a total invalid.

The social measures taken by the kingdom of Hungary [4] for the welfare of war cripples, are authorized by Article 8, Statute xv, of year 1915, and by the decree of the prime minister on September 4, 1915. These provisions apply to all soldiers who have received in the present war an injury which decreases their earning capacity, whether it be a mutilation, laming, stiffness, or any other result of a wound. If there is any hope that their earning capacity may be restored through re-education or convalescent care, they are placed under medical treatment and fitted to pursue their former trade or a new one. A special decree is called for to answer the question how far this statute applies to those suffering from other injuries than those mentioned.

Convalescent care and re-education is provided in the public institutions established by the

[4] See also an article by the author in *Pester Lloyd*, December 8, 1914, entitled 'The Economic Future of the War Cripple'. This article was one of the first to arouse interest in the subject.

Hungarian Department for Disabled Soldiers in the military institutions and in those maintained by the Hungarian Red Cross. In Croatia and Slavonia, medical care and vocational training for war cripples are provided in establishments founded and maintained by the Kroatisch-slavonisch Landeskommission zur Heilung und zur Unterricht der Kriegsinvaliden (Croatian-Slavonian Public Commission for the Medical Care and Training of Disabled Soldiers).

Artificial limbs and orthopedic appliances are furnished gratis to wounded men who apply for them. Soldiers who refuse to make use of such appliances or to take advantage of the re-educational opportunities lose all claim to aid, even though they are adjudged in need of it by the board of examiners. The only exception is in favor of men who have been in active army service for ten years. Boards of examiners are to be established in Budapest,[5] Pozsony, and Kolozs-

[5] This board has already been named.

vár. The president and members of these boards are appointed by the prime minister, who selects them from among medical and industrial experts. A similar board will be established at Zagreb, in Croatia.

The costs of convalescent care and training are assumed by the military authorities. The period of provision for any one soldier cannot exceed one year. The Hungarian prime minister has just issued a decree, regulating the activities of the Department for Disabled Soldiers. According to this, disabled soldiers are defined as those lamed, mutilated or suffering from internal disabilities. The duties of the Department for their benefit include the establishment, the maintenance and direction of sanatoria, re-educational schools, workshops for the manufacture of prosthetic appliances and plants for practical and industrial training. The department initiates, directs, subsidizes, and supervises the private institutions for disabled soldiers. It also manages the funds of the institutions, solicits subscriptions for them, secures employment for the men, and organizes private endeavor in their behalf.

The department appoints expert supervisors to direct the sanatoria for convalescent care, the prosthetic workshops, the re-educational schools and the industrial workshops. There is also to be formed a Rat für Invaliden-Angelegenheiten (Council for War Cripples), consisting of thirty-six members, to be appointed by the prime minister, who will himself act as chairman. The duty of the council will be to keep alive public interest in the welfare of war cripples.

Three types of institution are to be provided: Sanatoria for convalescent care, prosthetic workshops, and re-education schools. The sanatoria have a medical staff, made up of director, head physician, department heads, and subordinate physicians. The director is the official head of the institution and directs the work of the civil staff. The head physicians, as chiefs of departments, are members of the committee on admission and discharge; they also prescribe the work for the subordinate physicians. The subordinate physicians examine and report on individual cases.

The staff of the re-education schools consists of the superintendent, the directors of the courses in elementary, high school, and general subjects, and the teachers of these courses. A director of industrial work, shop foremen, a director of supplementary courses, and a physician are also employed. The superintendent's duty is to organize the instructional workshops; to determine the daily routine; and oversee all branches of the work. The directors of courses are also responsible for having the teachers investigate thoroughly the economic status of the men. The director of industrial work is responsible for the business management of the workshops. The foremen must awaken a love of work in the men and accustom them to the practical requirements of employment under commercial conditions, even during their period of training.

The question of admission and discharge is brought before a committee consisting of the supervising officials of the institute. This committee, however, can give no more than a recommendation; the actual decision is in the hands of the superintendent. The men are assigned to the convalescent homes or to the re-education schools by the military authorities, in agreement with the Department for Disabled Soldiers. Their admission must then be passed on by the committee. The director has jurisdiction over their discharge and acts sometimes without consulting the committee, notably in cases where a man has been fitted to resume military duty and there is no need for further care.

If a wounded man has sufficient property of his own to support himself and his family, or if his previous earnings enable him to do so, nevertheless, he cannot be discharged without the approval of the committee. Wounded men may also obtain their discharge by appearing before the military board of examiners. In the latter case the discharged patient receives a certificate.

There is also provision for the establishment of industrial workshops for disabled soldiers who cannot properly be placed in commercial employment. Such workshops will provide the men with a means of livelihood under special conditions whereby their remaining productive capacity may be most economically utilized.

At a recent session of the House of Representatives, February 15, 1916, the prime minister gave the following report on the work for disabled soldiers up to date. The Department for Disabled Soldiers, in cooperation with the prime minister, keeps a constant record of Hungarian citizens who have suffered physical injury and are, therefore, unfit for further military service and in need of convalescent care. The report for September 30, 1915, gave the number disabled through external injuries as 28,932, through internal injuries, 5,810. Beside these, there were 7,900 cases about which a final statement could not be made.

The comparatively small number of internal injuries seems surprising at first. The reason for this, according to Count Tisza, was that, up to the present, but little attention had been paid to them and during the war, only the more serious cases were retired from active service. At present, the primary necessity is to defeat the enemy and every other consideration must be subordinated to it. But it is greatly to be feared that, on demobilization after the war, we shall find a large number of men suffering from internal injury or disease. The social and economic future of these men should be also, in our opinion, a matter for national apprehension.

The government is planning that the institutions which it erects shall not only meet the present need, but be of permanent service. After the war, they will be of special use in treating tubercular soldiers and later still can be used for the intensive treatment of the tubercular among the whole population. So far there have been organized two military institutions for the treatment of organic and internal diseases. The one at Beszterczyebánya, for tubercular patients, contains 2,400 beds; that at Rózsahegy, for other internal diseases, has 1,800 beds.

We are now in process of organizing a thoroughly equipped sanatorium for tubercular cases. It will be situated in the Taetra Mountains, where the climate is especially suited to the purpose, and the patients will be sent there in regular turn. We are also planning a large independent public sanatorium.[6] Besides this, we have arranged to have departments for tubercular patients in as many of the public hospitals

as possible. In this undertaking, the government counts on the generosity of the Hungarian municipalities, organizations, and private citizens.

Up to the present, the number of disabled men is only 29,000, but this number will, of course, be constantly increasing up to the end of the war. The central institutions where these men can be cared for are all to be newly equipped to meet their special needs and the number of such institutions must be constantly increased. This increase cannot be very rapid in Hungary, according to the prevailing opinion, because such institutions can serve their end only when they are completely equipped and under expert medical supervision.

In planning for these new institutions, Budapest is the first location to be considered. It has a large number of hospitals which can be adapted to the purpose; it offers the best opportunities for medical treatment and industrial training; it has facilities for thermal treatment (at Csasarfurdo, on the right bank of the Danube). For these reasons, four institutions for convalescent care have been established in Budapest, accommodating 4,500 patients. There is also one at Pozsony, accommodating about 1,000. To date, 4,400 patients have been discharged from these institutions at the conclusion of the treatment. Of these 2,059 have been completely cured and 2,300 partially cured.

In contrast to the medical and technical side, the social side of the work for disabled soldiers in Hungary is still undeveloped. However, we would point to the extensive effort to supply the demand for artificial limbs, a demand which can hardly be met by private manufacturers. The Department for disabled soldiers has established prosthetic workshops in the public technical schools for the metal trades in Budapest and Perrony. For these workshops it has drafted men, partly disabled workers who come under its jurisdiction, partly soldiers assigned by consent of the ministry of war. The workshop in Budapest began work in March, 1915, with three workers; at present, it has 125. Up to December, 1915, it has produced 2,446 prostheses and orthopedic appliances. Its weekly production is 100 pieces.

[6] One of our prominent manufacturers has already donated 750,000 kronen for this purpose and the city of Budapest has turned over a piece of woodland.

Each soldier who has had a limb amputated receives at public expense two artificial limbs: one for practical and one for aesthetic purposes. Men whose arms have been amputated receive, in addition to the arm prosthesis, the tools to fit it required by their particular trade. In city occupations, the artificial foot can serve both purposes, aesthetic and practical. In the Spring of 1916, a permanent prosthetic factory is to be erected, where all future repairs will be made free of charge. This will meet the request of the Hungarian Union for the Control of Unemployment.

It is not always possible to force impecunious disabled soldiers to submit to training. Therefore, the above mentioned legal statute deprives those who refuse it of their right to the disabled soldier's allowance. We cannot feel that this statute answers the purpose, since it is not calculated to force men either to study or to work, when they are definitely unwilling. If the allowance is withdrawn, society must, nevertheless, support the disabled man, in the form of a pauper or a mendicant. In cases like this, penal labor colonies are the proper educational corrective.

The largest school of the Department for Disabled Soldiers is in Budapest, at Pozsony, with about 700 pupils. The school is principally industrial, the most popular workshops being those for shoemakers, tailors, harness makers, wainwrights, locksmiths, and carpenters. Although ninety per cent. of the pupils come from agricultural occupations, the main purpose is to make them self-supporting tradesmen. This proceeds from the mistaken idea that when disabled men are in competition with sound ones, they lose their interest in work and their self-confidence suffers. But this idea does not take into account the relatively more precarious economic status of small tradesmen. Shop keeping is particularly hard for farmers who have great difficulty in acquiring commercial perspective and experience.

Other schools similar to that at Pozsony are to be established at Kassa and Kolozsvár. At our schools the illiterates are given elementary schooling in addition to their trade training; opportunities are likewise offered for continuing interrupted courses at the elementary and high schools. Some of the schools have introduced courses in typewriting, stenography, and bookkeeping. So far, we have not enlisted for reeducation purposes either the excellent public or private trade schools or the employers, notably the great industrial leaders. To agricultural instruction, we have given the least attention of all.[7] The department has sent about 100 soldiers to existing agricultural schools, but it is only beginning to equip special schools of this sort for disabled soldiers. Two such have just been started, one at Beszterczebánya and one at Debreczen. Blind soldiers are cared for at the Budapest Institute for the Blind, which has 140 beds. The trades offered are: Carpet weaving, chair caning, brush-making, and massage.

The archbishop of Kalocsa, with the cooperation of the department, has established a colony for disabled soldiers who are no longer capable of holding their own under standard conditions of commercial employment. The principal occupations are carpentry, bee-keeping, fruit-raising, gardening, and poultry-raising. A private donation of 100,000 kronen has just made possible the founding of another agricultural colony in the county of Szolnek. But the question of state-

[7] In answer to the question by Deputy Count Albert Apponyi, the prime minister made a statement about the experience of Germany in this respect which was unnecessarily pessimistic. He said: "Agricultural education does not play as important a part as we had originally supposed. A great many cripples are no longer fitted for farm work and are forced to change to industrial work. Only those owning their own plot of ground should take up agricultural training. For such men, instruction can be given along two lines. One is the training of men to the use of their prostheses. This is of particular use where it is an arm that is lost, for with training, a man may attain a fair degree of working capacity on his own estate, where it does not matter if he works more slowly. The other is the training of crippled farmers in agricultural branches. Efficient management of their small property will give them and their families a better income than ever before. For example, horticulture has been little practised locally in the past, but fine results were obtained last summer at Kecskemét, Pozsony, Kalocsa, and Goedoelloe, though only 230 cripples registered for the course. The number of registrations should be greatly increased this summer."

The prime minister will shortly suggest to the minister of agriculture that several agricultural schools which are well adapted to this work should give courses for crippled farmers during the summer vacation. Private philanthropy is also giving attention to this question.

Another question by Count Apponyi as to what measures were being taken for the settlement of war cripples on the land —the only way in which, according to Count Tisza, they could be retained in agriculture—remained unanswered.

supported colonies for disabled soldiers is, unfortunately, still in abeyance. The government does not mention the subject at all, though it constitutes the principal problem in Hungary where from seventy to eighty per cent. of our disabled men were agricultural workers.

Recently Deputy Count Albert Apponyi asked the prime minister whether the Disabled Soldiers' Council was yet organized. The prime minister replied that he had the matter under consideration and that the organization would soon be effected. He believed, however, that this council would not play a rôle of much importance until later. But would it not be reasonable to suppose that this council would have a voice in deciding such fundamental matters as the national program?

As to employment, the department has placed, to date, 500 disabled soldiers. This is an exceedingly small number. It would seem that soldiers who have not been at the re-education schools do not apply to the department at all. In the opinion of the prime minister, private charity could very well combine work along this line with the work it already does for the care of orphans. Private charity in Hungary has shown an inspired devotion and a warm sympathy and these could best express themselves through one central organization, open to every volunteer who is able and willing to help.

Opinions may differ as to the advisability of combining two such basically different functions as vocational guidance for disabled soldiers and aid for widows and orphans. But it is certainly a fault in our welfare work that it has hitherto been too bureaucratic. We have accomplished enormous, sometimes astounding, results on the medical and technical side, but we cannot extend our activities to social provisions for disabled soldiers. We make no provision for men whose support is temporarily assured, either because they have a little property or because they can practise their former trade. Although such men constitute the majority of our war cripples, we make no effort to provide them with vocational guidance, much less re-education or further training. So far, the only vocational advisers appointed by the department are doctors and elementary school teachers, and these only in the hospitals and the re-education schools. No effort has been made, either, to extend the work by getting the local authorities and the private societies to establish branches.

The chief mistake made in the organization of work for disabled soldiers in Hungary is that the state insists on centralizing all social problems and dealing with them in a strictly official and bureaucratic way. Many local and trade groups, such as agricultural associations and printers' societies, have volunteered their services to the government in Hungary, as in other places. Their help has not been made use of, and the very fact restricts our work for disabled men in the cases where it is most needed. The result is that we have not enough re-education schools properly equipped to take care of the men who are not able to earn their own living.

I have made an intensive comparative study of the different phases of the problem and the needs indicated. The results were presented in a lecture to which I can still refer you. It was delivered by request of several societies of political economy, at the Chamber of Commerce and Trades, Vienna, October 25, 1915, and was entitled: *The Restoration of the War Cripple to Industrial Life—in Germany, Austria, and Hungary* (Die Wiedereinstellung der Kriegsinvaliden ins bürgerliche Erwerbsleben in Deutschland, Österreich und Ungarn)[8].

[8] Published as the second pamphlet of the Austrian Society for the Control of Unemployment. (Vienna and Leipzig, 1916.)

THE LITTLE CRIPPLES AT MUNICH

THE LITTLE CRIPPLES AT MUNICH [1]

I was living in Munich some twenty years ago, with a dear friend, since dead, then a studiosus with the great Kaulbach of the 'Babel' and 'Hunnen Schlacht' epics. The laureate of mythic terrors had been minded to enact Æsop for a time, and make the world indebted for many a long laugh over his visible embodiment of the life and reign of 'Reynard the Fox'. That history was not yet published, but its fame had already spread abroad among sympathetic *cognoscenti* and the Magister's Bohemian court.

Down by fair Loch Starnberg, where the Alps stand afar, guarding the sleeping waters from the winds fierce from buffetings with the snow peaks, the Magister resided that summer; and it occurred to my friend and other studiosi, that it would be a famous joke to get a lot of masks of the chief characters in 'Reynard', incontinently appear with them at the cottage by the lake, and give the Magister a zoological ovation. The idea was adopted by acclamation. Every one's friend—Count P——, poet, musician, painter, caricaturist, volunteered the text and choruses. Then for the masks. Some of the men set to work to accomplish their own metempsychosis. For the rest, the difficulty remained till somebody, suddenly inspired, cried, "Why, let the little cripples make them."

"What do you mean?" said a young Berliner, suspecting persiflage.

"Mean?—the *Krippelhafter Knaben*, in the Asylum down by the Isar; they are wonderful chaps, equal to anything that is to be made out of paper and glue."

---

[1] The second in the series of reprints of documents of historical interest in the development of provision for cripples. The present document is the first known article in English describing constructive work for crippled children. It originally appeared in the *Dublin University Magazine*, 1872, lxxx, 322–328.

My friend was constituted 'Mask Committee', and I accompanied him on his official visit. We found the Asylum—a fine old house, that must have seen gay doings two centuries ago. The director, Herr Mayer, received us; my friend stated his business, gave the sketches of the desired masks, and was delighted to find the director at once enter into the humor of the thing. A clever draughtsman, too, Herr Mayer. We had forgotten two or three of the heads; but from my friend's hints he scribbled down notes for them, and they ultimately proved among the best. He showed us a quantity of the work done by the boys; masks and properties for theaters, and every conceivable kind of elegant toys in papier-mâché. "Some of the boys," he added, "are veritable little cobolds; but, with an artistic outlet for the spirit, good instead of evil comes of it." Herr Mayer invited us to revisit the institution; but it was long ere I could do so.

The masks were made; 'the parts' learned; a glorious May morning dawned, and, *omnes*, each with a duplicate head and packet of paper lanterns, started for a sixteen-mile tramp to the lake. There, in the forest behind the Magister's cottage, a throne and canopy of state were improvised, garlands wound, flags set waving, lanterns hung ready. A monstrous fox's head was laid at our hero's feet, with due ceremony, and he, *en bon prince*, said he 'would be delighted' to appear as Kaulbach, Rex Vulpinus, in the evening. The Magister's beautiful Frau conjured a bevy of pretty girls out of the earth; *pittores et scriptores* came, whence I know not, to enact our Greek chorus; and by evening a merrier party was assembled under the beech-trees than I can hope ever to see again. The Great King sat enthroned, a fox-bush his sceptre; his lieges—lions, crows, cats—paid homage in rhymes worthy of Thomas Ingoldsby. A rookery overhead got up an indignation meeting at the laughter and noise we made. The bright eyes of the Dryads in muslin shone through the glinting lights, laughing the sentimental moon out of countenance. How many of our fiercest *carnivori* got their claws for ever clipped somehow under the trees that night! But all this concerns us not here: the paper lanterns have long since burnt out; some of the bright eyes will shine on earth no more; and the masks, after some carnival roystering, went the way of human cuticle.   Their ghost leads me back to my story.

This summer, finding myself in the Bavarian capital once more, I resolved to pay that long-promised visit to the 'Krippelhafter Knaben Anstalt'.   Certain facts and figures regarding it I may perhaps as well note down here, though I did not learn them until after my visit.

In 1832, a private gentleman, Herr von Kurtz, having had his interest aroused in the forlorn condition of poor crippled boys, resolved to be the pioneer of their amelioration.   Unfortunately, his own means were not large; but friends came to his aid, and he had soon some rooms fitted up in his residence for the reception of a limited number of boys.   With some of the number he accepted a maximum payment of ten pounds per annum.   He had a tutor for their instruction in the usual branches of the public elementary schools, and gave the greater part of his own time to their instruction in various light industrial occupations.   After twelve years of unobtrusive usefulness, the attention of the government was, in 1844, drawn to Herr von Kurtz's establishment.   Its name and fame had spread abroad; but, having given it a firm basis, he not unwillingly consented to relinquish its management to the State; and, by an Act passed the same year, the 'Krippel-hafter Knaben Anstalt.' became a public institution, received a State endowment of £1800, and a regularly-appointed staff— namely, an inspector, resident director, a Protestant and a Catholic chaplain, a schoolmaster, industrial master, and medical adviser; a matron, female servant, and porter, for domestic duties.   The education provided was to include, besides the three R's, a glimpse into geography and history, singing and elementary drawing; religious instruction being left to the care of the visiting chaplains. Pupils to pay £10 a year towards their maintenance; and all sur-plus revenue from subscriptions and bequests to be devoted to founding free scholarships.   In 1850, a further donation of £1800

was made by the State; and at the present time the institution
possesses a capital of £6000. It maintains an average yearly of
twenty-six lads, at an outlay of £450. The immediate wants of
the pupils absorb but a small moiety of this; the work done by
them brings in a considerable sum yearly. But the staff is necessarily an expensive one; happily capable of taking the much extended duties to be imposed on it when the larger asylum now
proposed is completed.

In all simplicity, I went in search of the old grey House of the
Masks; to find, alas! all its little Robin Goodfellows gone, and,
greyer than ever, looking abashed at its change of fortune, now
harboring unphilanthropic 'long swords, saddles, bridles', and
such military belongings.

After various inquiries, I got at last on the right track, finding
that my right destination was No. 13, Staubstrasse. After a long
walk, traversing the flowery twin cemeteries, and passing finally the
little red-brick Franciscan church of Sorrows, with its life-size cruci-
fix gazing haggardly at the loiterers by the wayside, I found myself
in front of No. 13, Dust Street, named so, mayhap, by the monks,
as a grim glorification of their own mortifications and grey peas.

A two-storied white house, No. 13, standing above a sloping
grass plot, among fuchsias and standard roses; no institutional
dignity about it, or sign of its destination, except it were in the
accidental apparition under a window-curtain of two pale little
faces, which disappeared again as suddenly.

My appeal to the bell was responded to as though I had been
a one-eyed Calendar, with connections among the genii of the
'Arabian Nights'; the garden-gate opened, untouched by visible
hands, with a weird, sharp click. Taking this, however, for an
invitation to enter, I entered, and was aware of a great black dog
—a dog with a double nose!—bounding towards me to do the
honors. He snuffed at first suspiciously through those terrific
nostrils; seemed not dissatisfied with the result, and took me under
his protection to the back door, though I suggested the front
entrance. A little, old woman, neat as a fairy godmother, evi-

dently the housekeeper, appeared. I expressed my desire to see the Herr Director, if he was disengaged. Smiling benevolently, she "was sure he would rejoice"; bade me enter, and disappeared, leaving me in charge of my double-nosed friend.

A few moments, and the Herr Director descended the stairs— not the Herr Mayer of my recollections, but a gentleman of some thirty-five years of age, whose face at the first glance might predicate an artillery officer, or, at the second, an artist. He received me in the most courteous manner; informed me my old acquaintance, his predecessor, had long left, and was now head of a famous firm for art manufactures; then added, "I shall be no less happy to show you our little place, and what our boys can do."

My visit was made in the afternoon, and the Director explained, as he led the way to the schoolroom, that all school tasks were accomplished before the twelve o'clock dinner hour, so the boys were now busy at their manufactures; the schoolroom being turned for the time into a workshop. I followed my guide through a door to the right, and found myself in a veritable factory, some forty feet in length, but of scarce sufficient height, and certainly failing in proper ventilation, though well lighted by five windows. The resident master, a kindly, intelligent-looking gentleman, was in charge of some twenty-eight boys from nine to fifteen years of age, all occupied at the low square tables standing in double rank down the room. Cardboard slips and scraps of bright-colored papers strewed the floor; boxes and watchcases and every possible application of Bristol board in process of manufacture at some of the tables; at others sat little workmen, blowing an accompaniment to the singing of their wire saws, blowing the dust away, in fact, from the delicate tracery as they carved it.

All were dressed in the clothes of the asylum; dark cloth trousers and waistcoat, and that most practical of working garments, a belted stout blue linen blouse.

There were boys with crutches placed against their seats, ready to hand; boys with irons round their thin ankles; lame boys, indeed, of every variety; boys half paralyzed; others with their ten fingers so crumpled and twisted by a cruel freak of nature, it seemed miraculous they could ever learn the functions of human hands; hunchbacked boys also were there, perhaps occupying the best vantage-ground for success. Scrofula lies at the root of most of the deformities which these unfortunates have had born with them, the hunchback is rarely of the number: scrofula saps all the vital functions, and though acute but in one limb, debilitates all the others more or less. One small Quasimodo was by special permission this afternoon copying some foliations, and with the care and accuracy of a medieval illuminator. As he sat at work his head quite disappeared below the heaped shoulders, and I felt something like a shock on beholding the weird beauty of his pale face as it turned with a quiet, self-reliant pride to meet the Director's eyes. One must not look for the bashfulness and pretty *gaucheries* of childhood within the realms of crutches; such things vanish with the first consciousness of an exceptional destiny.

"I make all the boys learn drawing," said the Director; "the accuracy of touch and precision of visual measurement given by it is of the greatest use in supplying any natural manual deficiency. I never allow a boy to attempt any more delicate kind of our work until he can handle a pencil freely."

We moved on to a table at the far end of the room, where a boy about ten years old, straight in shoulder and limb as boy need be, stood deeply engrossed before a glue-pot and great pile of cardboard slips. Surely he was no cripple.

"How does the box get on?" asked my companion.

"All right, sir; see, sir!" And the boy held out a little box, the bevelled lid neatly papered by hands with but two fingers on each. A short time before the boy could do nothing but eat with those maimed hands; now he could write prettily, draw a little, and use edge-tools with perfect accuracy and skill. His affliction had been far surpassed by one of his predecessors, who had one finger only on each hand; but so well too had he applied himself to circumvent his deficiencies, that he became quite famous in the

institution for his handiwork, and is now earning his living outside its walls. What must the fate of such a boy have been if he
had not met with the patient care, the unwearied help and encouragement given there!

Glueing processes seemed to involve the most absorbing satisfaction to the operators: three little hunchbacks, with a big glue-
pot between them, were evidently in a sort of seventh heaven
while building the walls of a giant bonbonnière. Its prototype,
made by them, was a wonder of card architecture; its ivory-like
columns supporting a fantastic cornice, the wall behind gorgeous
with plaited silk, the lid a marvel of fairy ingenuity—Seugnot
frères would have held it a *chef-d'œuvre*. The designs for these
things are all made by the Herr Director. A great glass case,
occupying one end of the room, was filled with a multitudinous
display of pretty things of the kind, and still more artistic brackets,
crucifixes, card-trays—delicately carved *au jour* in various woods.
Whilst looking at them, I mentioned the old masks that had at
first brought me acquainted.

"Traditions of those famous specimens of zoology still exist,"
said the Director, "among the boys, and the very moulds for the
masks are preserved in a store closet. We occasionally have such
things to make still in carnival time. I am very glad when such
an order comes, the boys take such delight in the work. But as
we endeavor to make the institution self-supporting as much as
possible, our industries must be ruled by the demand outside.
Papier-mâché for room decoration was largely made here at the
time you speak of, now it is never asked for except in this form."
And he took down a stag's head, very carefully moulded, to be
afterwards fitted with real antlers. The papier-mâché so employed is, however, of a peculiar kind, and, though perfectly light,
will bear any amount of rough usage with impunity.

I inquired if the boys generally followed the trades thus learned.

"Not in the majority of instances," was the reply; "but the
end chiefly sought by the institution is obtained when the boys
achieve the manual dexterity the employments here give. On

their leaving, if of very poor parents, they are apprenticed from our funds to some suitable trade, and we have no difficulty in finding good masters for them.   By the first statutes made, no boy was admitted to the asylum under twelve years of age; but as preference is given to the poorest candidates, it was soon found expedient to relax the rule.   The task of their physical education especially is far easier when commenced quite early.   Parents too often trade on a child's deformity; the poor creature is driven out to beg until it grows to like the occupation, and better things for it are soon almost impossible.   The vanity thus engendered is a strange moral phenomenon."

Among other instances, the Director mentioned the following as an illustration of it.   An unusually clever little hunchback had been admitted into the institution: he was ten years of age, and had been accustomed to rove about the country alone for weeks together.   The first time he went to church, no sooner was he within the walls than he dropped suddenly to the ground, his limbs fell out of joint, and he commenced foaming at the mouth.   The more the crowd gathered round him the worse he grew.   The master brought him home quite terror-stricken.

"I," said the Director, "suspected a trick, accompanied him myself the next Sunday, and took him sharply by the collar just when he was prepared to fall.   My touch prevented the fit, and he afterwards confessed he always "took one when he got among a lot of people—it was nice to have them all looking at him." With judicious treatment he became one of the best boys in the institution.   "By judicious treatment," added the Herr, "I do not mean moral instruction merely; nothing, we find, tends so much to raise the boys' self-respect as physical education; the gymnastic ground, drill exercise, and plentiful bathing have a wonderful effect.   The gymnastic feats some of those crippled little creatures perform would puzzle many a boy sound in mind and limb; it is above all things, perhaps, their greatest delight— the only difficulty is to restrain them from overtrying their strength."

All the boys are under constant surgical supervision, and every medical alleviation is at their service; many have been restored, by careful treatment, to the complete use of their limbs. By singular good fortune the Herr Director is himself learned in orthopedic science, and has effected, since his appointment, some important improvements in the artificial limbs previously made in Germany.

Looking over a syllabus of the day's tasks, I was rather surprised to see stenography (short-hand) down among them. "An innovation of mine," exclaimed the Director; "its success with the lads certainly justifies it. It is a profession they may often be able to follow; requires no outlay of capital in its pursuit," he added smiling. "But you must see what we can do in it, though few of the lads accomplish more than sixty words in the minute." Then he summoned a little blue-eyed lame boy, carving an ink-stand, gave him a pencil and paper, and then rapidly read a paragraph from a newspaper. At the end of four minutes the boy had phonographed three hundred and sixty words, omitting none. "This is one of my best craftsmen, too," said the Herr. Then addressing him, "You must show that little picture-frame."

"It is in the cabinet workshop, sir."

"Then go with us there."

The cabinet workshop proved a small room, evidently devoted to tasks of great delicacy, for which the observance of strict order is of special necessity. Carpenters' benches lined the walls; boxes of tools stood about. But I had no time to look around ere the little stenographer took a frame from the wall, and held it smiling towards me. It was really an exquisite bit of work-manship. On a broad band of dark wood were inlaid a wonderful intaglio of scrolls, foliation, birds, and shells, in metal, ivory, and mother-of-pearl; the feathers in the birds' wings still awaited engraving. The boy flushed with pleasure at my praise.

"Who helped you to carve and inlay this?"

"Just nobody, sir."

The original, of which this was a copy, was a gem of French renaissance work, and had been brought by the Director from Paris for the purpose. Unfortunately, there is little demand for work of the kind in Munich.

We passed on to the great dining-hall, of the same dimensions as the schoolroom, and I learnt the following particulars of the bill of fare. For breakfast the boys have half-a-pint of milk and a white roll; for dinner, soup, meat, vegetables; puddings on the fast-days, instead of meat; and on Sundays and red-letter days, roast joints and beer. Stewed fruit is always an important item as an entremets. Supper consists of soup and bread and cheese, or some simple substitutes for the latter.

Then we passed upstairs. "Our dormitory," said the Director, regretfully, "does not fulfil modern sanitary requirements now our inmates have so greatly increased. The workshop downstairs was designed for an infirmary, but its position and north window make it quite inapplicable. Next Sessions we hope to get funds granted for rebuilding the place; then these deficiencies will be remedied, and space, I hope, provided for at least double the number of our inmates. The comparative expenses so involved will be actually on a diminishing ratio, as the staff of officials will need scarce any modification."

The dormitory door stood open, and very fresh and pleasant it looked; but the little beds were, perhaps, too closely ranked together. All had good horse-hair mattresses, feather pillows, blankets, linen sheets, and a plumeau above all. A little shelf pulled out of the bedstead frame to make a seat. A night-table with drawers for hair brush and comb stood by each. Wardrobes for the boys' clothes occupied one end of the room, and the washing apparatus the other.

The private apartments of the schoolmaster (the industrial master is non-resident) and of the Herr Director adjoin the great dormitory. I had a strange sensation as, accepting the Herr's courteous invitation, I followed him into his private domain, and found myself carried away by magic, as it were, from out the concentration of afflictions gathered together beneath our feet, into some calm, old-world Gothic sanctum for studious leisure. On shelves, enriched with curious carving, stood dignified folios and octavos, gorgeous with renaissance gildings, quaint ancient flagons, grim antique weapons and armor, multitudinous precious waifs of the past, from imperial seals of miraculous intricacy, cabinets and caskets where rich burghers of old kept their treasures, disinterred rings and relics, and carefully preserved gay tapestry, all hung, or niched, half hidden in the dark carved work that veiled the wall. In the center of the room the Present asserted itself in an easel bearing an almost finished oil picture. "I have not much time for such things now," said the Director, in reference to it; "but I let it stand there from month to month as a tacit promise to finish it some day." The subject was an antique gateway, with a peasant bridal passing beneath it—no indefinite amateur work—the colors too bright and transparent. Then, whilst talking of many things, my companion produced a portfolio of water and oil sketches, lightly touched, full of life and character, a chronicle gathered in old vacations of the strange, wild region of the Bayrischer Wald. Then I lingered too willingly over other portfolios of rare engravings, till I felt I must linger no longer. Bidding farewell to the tranquil little Cosmos of art, I descended with my kind guide to the ground floor once more. From the schoolroom came a great humming and buzzing of excited talk and shrill laughter. My double-nosed friend sat gazing at the schoolroom door in eager expectancy. "The boys are going to drill," explained the Herr Director. Another moment and out they all came, forming at once in line. They were presently marshalled on the grass-plot outside, under direction of the drill-master, and performing 'platoon' with the precision and gravity of veteran grenadiers. When drill was over, they hurried off to the gymnastic ground, and I soon saw such terrific centrifugal spinning, such trapeze tricks, that made me imagine all that limping, maimed humanity was endowed by sudden magic with the agility of monkeys. But I could delay no longer, so after a grateful farewell to the kind Herr Director, the little green gate swung behind me once more, whilst the double-nosed mystery gazed after with pensive, doubting eyes.

Here my task closes; but I cannot lay down my pen without briefly telling the story, learnt by me some days subsequently, of one of those crippled boys of the Anstalt I had visited. A poor woman was left widowed some thirty years ago with many children, one a cripple. Her commune sent him to the asylum, paying his fees. From almost helplessness, by careful treatment, he soon was able to develop an unusual artistic taste and dexterity. He left the institution at fifteen, an accomplished art workman, helped to support his mother and younger brothers for some years, and is now a celebrity in his native country, complimented by royalty, sought by theater managers, whenever a public festival needs graceful decoration. Not a rich man, perhaps, but one of the happiest in his simple independence; unwearied in the work he loves, as only the born artist loves the work his genius makes a part of himself. But for that Cripple's Home he must have been condemned to hopeless pauperism.

THE COPENHAGEN INSTITUTION
FOR CRIPPLES

Gustav Muskat

THE COPENHAGEN INSTITUTION FOR CRIPPLES

GUSTAV MUSKAT, M.D.[1]

Berlin, Germany.

Of all institutions for cripples, the one at Copenhagen, Denmark, is most noteworthy. By reason of the number of patients received and the good accomplished, it may be considered a model institution. For thirty-five years there has been in Copenhagen a society for the relief of the crippled and paralyzed. It was founded by Pastor Knudsen. By the aid of state appropriations and voluntary contributions, there was established a central bureau to which any Danish people who are in any way crippled or paralyzed may be brought. Some of the patients go to the institution of their own accord, others are sent there by local authorities. The railroad fare is granted either free or at a nominal price. Patients who are mentally deficient or who, because of their mental condition, could not enjoy the benefits of the institution are excluded. Also those presenting distinctively surgical cases, and those with open wounds are debarred.

The institution offers orthopedic treatment of various kinds. Professor Panum gives gratis his services as director of the surgical department. Appliances and supplies are furnished to patients either free or at a nominal charge.

Different types of apparatus—from the simple leather appliance for those suffering from flat feet to the complicated kinds used by the paralytics—are made in the departments of the institution. The industrial department for the making of

[1]GUSTAV MUSKAT. Das Kopenhagner Krüppelheim. *Deutsche medizinische Wochenschrift*, Leipzig, 1908, xxxiv, 426-427. A translation—with the omission of a few details not pertinent to American readers—of the above article. Translated and edited by Miss Dorothy Jacoby and Douglas C. McMurtrie.

appliances embraces rooms for plaster work, for leather work, blacksmithing, shoemaking, and the production of braces. Miss Thora Fiedler, for many years superintendent of the institution, deserves credit for having so organized the industrial departments that every bit of apparatus required can be made on the premises. Under these circumstances, not only is the expense much less than it would otherwise be, but also many of the cripples are given an occupation. Apparatus made in the workrooms is also sold outside at reasonable prices. The receipts thus realized are applied towards the maintenance of the institution. The extent of the apparatus work may be judged from the fact that one year's output was valued at approximately $15,000. And if these same instruments had been made outside the institution the cost would have been double this amount.

Another department which seems of the greatest importance is the one devoted to education. Industrial training in various trades is provided for patients after their limbs have been operated upon or they have been supplied with the required apparatus. The finer kinds of work are usually preferred as the patients do not usually possess great physical strength. At the time of my last visit in 1907 two teachers in the carpentry shop were instructing seventeen pupils, of whom a number were congenitally crippled in the lack of an arm or hand. There is no need of going into details regarding crippling of the lower limbs as the trades can be prosecuted without using them. Right handed and left-handed joiners' benches offer the pupils every opportunity for the development of their talents.

One patient holds a tool between the upper and lower sections of his arm, another has fastened to his fingerless hand, by means of a strap, a round block which he uses for a hammer, a third uses a tool for a finger.

Nine crippled students were working in the wood-carving department—and with remarkable results. In the evening they receive instruction in drawing and modeling.

After a certain period of instruction, the pupils must pass an examination by commission, just as normal trade students are required to do. The quality of the cripples' work and the way in which they succeed in later life is really surprising.

Younger children are given a regular primary school education, except that as much emphasis is attached to hand work as to language instruction and general training. Correct writing is considered of much importance.

In another department bookbinding and shoe-making are taught. Thirteen pupils were learning these trades. In addition to the sewing work there should be mentioned, in conclusion the department for fine fancy work in which are made old Swedish laces, copied from antique patterns. Many of these laces are sold, the proceeds going towards the expense of operation.

In all, fifty young men, thirty young girls, and twenty-five children were living in the institution. They pay a small sum daily for meals, washing, and instruction. In addition the Charity Society makes a yearly grant towards the expense of each patient. Cripples who live in Copenhagen sleep at home, but receive their meals and instruction at the institution.

Any eligible cripple is admitted to the institution. Those who are unable to do this, and who have received no outside financial assistance for five years, are admitted free.

Since the inception of the work over 11,000 patients have been given care.

The points most worthy of imitation in the conduct of the Copenhagen institution are: first, that chronic and essentially surgical cases are excluded; second, that mentally disordered patients are not admitted; third, the excellent system of instruction in the institution, whereby pupils are enabled to get a good general education and to learn a trade by which they can support themselves in later years.

It would be an excellent thing if, at the establishment of new institutions for cripples, the general principles of the work at

Copenhagen, were kept in view. If this were done not only temporary but also permanent assistance would be rendered to a large number of unfortunates. How similar institutions can be conducted in countries larger than Denmark, where the population and in consequence the number of cripples is greater, must be left to the future for solution.

MODERN METHODS OF CARE FOR CRIPPLES IN GERMANY

Konrad Biesalski

MODERN METHODS OF CARE FOR CRIPPLES IN GERMANY

KONRAD BIESALSKI, M.D.[1]

Berlin, Germany

Almost a hundred years ago there was in operation in Berlin an institution for cripples founded in 1823 by a Dr. Blömer, and providing the same features of care as the modern cripple-home, namely, hospital treatment, primary education, and industrial training. After existing for some years, however, the establishment was discontinued.

In 1832 there was established in Munich the present 'Königliche Zentralanstalt für Erziehung und Bildung krüppelhafter Kinder.' As this institution continued permanently, it must be considered as the real pioneer in the field of organized care for cripples—which is thus eighty years old.

During the early decades of this period very few institutions were started, but in 1886 an active movement, associated with the name of a protestant pastor, developed in northern Germany, the impetus being derived from the example of Pastor Knudsen in Copenhagen. The effort resulted in the founding of numerous institutions.

The greatest progress was made, however, during the last decade, this being due to the increased general interest in social

[1] KONRAD BIESALSKI. Die moderne Krüppelfürsorge in Deutschland. *Zeitschrift für ärztliche Fortbildung*, Jena, 1913, x, 155-159. An address delivered before a meeting of the English Royal Institute of Public Health, in Berlin, 1912. Translated by Douglas C. McMurtrie. Indebtedness is acknowledged to another version which has appeared in the *Journal of State Medicine*, London, 1912, xx, 595-604. Dr. Biesalski is the director and chief surgeon of the 'Berlin-Brandenburg Kruppel-Heil- und Erziehungsanstalt,' editor of the *Zeitschrift für Krüppelfürsorge*, and a member of the editorial board of this JOURNAL.

questions aroused by the legislative industrial reforms and the inauguration of state disability insurance. Another contributing factor was the rapid industrial development following upon the establishment of the empire, this bringing into circulation the money requisite for large measures of social amelioration. There was thus existent general sympathy with the needs of cripples and the ability to minister to them. The only thing still needed was the requisite initiative and a direction of the impulses toward the best means of practical expression.

These latter influences were provided by the census which was taken during 1906 of all cripples under sixteen years of age throughout the whole of Germany. This statistical inquiry showed the following important results:

(1)   It opened the eyes of the entire nation, from the highest officials in government departments to the lowliest village schoolmaster, to the fact that the cripple could be materially helped.

(2)   While former inquiries had only dealt with isolated districts, and were thus valueless for purposes of general application, by this inquiry were elicited and made possible of coordination the relations between the needs of and provision for cripples in each individual district. There was thus laid a solid basis for practical reform.

(3)   The statistical inquiry crystallized the vague conceptions of the term 'cripple' into a definite formula, and this definition has been accepted for practical purposes by the federated states of Germany and by all responsible authorities. It runs as follows: "A cripple in need of institutional care (*heimbedürftig*) is an invalid who in consequence of congenital or acquired nerve, bone, or joint disease (other physical defects also occasionally supervening), is hindered in the natural use of his body or limbs to such an extent that he is not capable of adjusting himself to his environment; this lack of harmony admitting of rectification only by appropriate treatment in an institution which, by virtue of its special facilities of a combined medical and educa-

tional character, offers the only possibility of developing his remaining mental and physical powers to their utmost economic value." This definition indicates that it is not mere physical defect which calls for charitable aid, but that the social and economic factors count as of equal importance. In our sense of the word, therefore, the severely deformed child of wealthy parents is not a 'cripple' as the father is quite capable of guarding him from social stress. But a girl, for instance, with only a slight degree of scoliosis, if she is at the same time an orphan, and a deaf-mute, and perchance also pthisical, is to us eminently a 'cripple.'

(4) In this way all units out of the vast army of cripples who were in no need of social protection were eliminated. A second distinction was made by dividing the remainder into two categories: the *heimbedürftig* and the *nicht heimbedürftig, i. e.,* those needing care in a resident institution, and those not requiring residential care. Whereas, in the past, all cripples had been regarded as institutional cases, the number of the latter was now reduced one-half by a process of exclusion, and the potential cost of treatment also diminished in consequence. This left workable numbers which could be dealt with if good will, energy, and a due regard to economy were brought to bear upon the task.

(5) Having defined the cripple as an invalid, the interest of the medical profession regarding his physical necessities was aroused. The orthopedic specialist particularly showed a willingness to come to the rescue.

All these factors united in the initiation of an enthusiastic movement throughout Germany which resulted in doubling the number of institutions for cripples in ten years.

The census of 1906 revealed the following facts:

In 1906 there were in the whole German Empire 100,000 cripples under the age of 16. Of these, according to expert medical opinion, 52,000 were in need of resident institutional care; 10,000 expressed their willingness to avail themselves of such treatment. The available beds, however, numbered only 3,000. This discrepancy has, fortunately, been largely overcome since that date. Though the population of Germany undergoes a yearly increase of three-quarters of a million—and this naturally increases the number of crippled persons—the institutional development has overtaken the cripple increase. While there were only twenty-three cripple institutions in 1902, we can to-day count fifty-three, and the number of beds has increased in ten years from 1,622 to 5,932.

About one-half of the existing homes are associated with some religious denomination—usually protestant, though there are some catholic; the other half are undenominational. In those of the latter type the practice of constituting the surgeon in charge as director of the institution is gaining in favor.

At the present time there is one helper to every 4.5 crippled children. This shows the excellent development of provision which has been attained. The average annual expenditure per capita is 415 marks, or slightly over one hundred dollars.

The feature in which the German institutions differ from those in some other countries, especially England, is that with us the larger proportion of the expense is derived from public funds. Even if we shall never dispense with the generous aid of private philanthropy—and we are far from wishing to do so if for no other reason than because of its moral value—the general trend of our efforts is to secure the necessary funds from public sources, instead of relying, as in England, mainly on private generosity. It is only in this way that economical administration and far-sighted organization can be rendered practicable. We are well supported by legislative action—e. g., in Prussia we have the so-called *Dotationsgesetz*.

In others of the federated states the socialization of care for cripples has been already introduced as, for instance, in Oldenburg, or the state makes yearly grants, directs the *Landesorganisation*, or takes an active part in the administration of a *Landesanstalt* for cripples.

In general what counts with us most in Germany in collecting funds for the care of cripples is the maxim: "Let us not be dependent on charity, but let us have financial security through the responsible co-operation of state and local authorities."

A good example of what a local council can accomplish is shown by the municipal authorities of Greater Berlin, who pay the regulation hospital grant for each crippled child placed in an institution. The late director of the Berlin Poor Law Board, Stadtrat Muensterberg, who was also known and respected in England, once said that the best way of helping a destitute patient was to make a healthy man of him, and this principle, which he derived from a profound knowledge of social conditions, he applied to care for cripples.

The municipal authorities of Greater Berlin have also, in conjunction with the *Landesdirektor* of the province of Brandenburg, rendered possible the erection of a new Berlin cripple institution, guaranteeing the interest and sinking fund for the capital outlay.

That care for cripples in Germany has met with such signal success in securing public financial support ensures it the best prospects for an established and prosperous future.

The aim of the institutional care is to make the cripple a self-supporting member of the community. This object should be internationally universal. But as regards the beneficiaries of care, there is some distinction to be made between English and German methods. In Germany, in accordance with the aforesaid definition, the term 'cripple' is held strictly to apply to individuals who exhibit functional disturbances connected with the movements of the body or limbs. But crippled individuals who also suffer, for instance, from tubercular glands, harelip, or rachitis in its most glaring form, or who are idiots or epileptics, are, generally speaking, excluded from the benefits of institutional training. It is true that the movement in aid of cripples maintains friendly co-operative relations with other provinces of social work—prevention of infant mortality, care for epileptics, deaf-mutes, or the blind, improvement of housing conditions, the prevention of intemperance, and the like—and that provisional care is taken of children who do not come, properly speaking, within the prescribed limits, until, at all events, some defect needing special treatment has received due attention. But the effort to care for cripples has its own field clearly delineated and any duplication of other social efforts can only react inimically to its own efficiency.

All the German institutions—of which the largest accomodates five hundred, and the average capacity being ninety-nine—are divided into three sections, the hospital, the school, and the industrial department. All three operate under one roof, under one management, and constitute an integral organization. This arrangement insures the most profitable employment of time, money, and energy, and achieves the best possible results.

The hospital section comprises an operating theatre, medico-mechanical apparatus, Röntgen laboratory, drill-hall, orthopedic workshop for the manufacture of iron braces and appliances. Every institution has a medical director and a number of assistants. The list of directors includes some of the most distinguished names in German orthopedic science.

The great advances in German orthopedic surgery since Hoffa first raised it to the rank of an independent science have always met with generous recognition in England and other foreign countries. But I may point out that modern modifications of the method of tendon-grafting first introduced by an Austro-German, and the new methods of nerve-operation in Little's disease in connection with the nerve-termini of either the spinal cord or of the periphery were first practised by German surgeons.

In the school section, the curriculum is designed in accordance with the scheme of the German elementary school, as only scholars of elementary school grade find their way into these institutions. In the Berlin institution an educational inspector is in charge of the school section but comes under the authority of the medical director. In the cripple school, instruction is also provided for backward children in the *Hilfsklassen* or special classes, for which specially trained teachers are selected. Continuation and trade classes are also arranged for the industrial pupils; these complying accurately with the legislative requirements. In general principle, the instruction is largely manual, *e. g.*, 'learning by heart' is avoided as much as possible and for this is substituted teaching by observation and the handling of concrete objects, by copying such forms in plastic material, and similar methods. This plan of instruction is especially suited to crippled children as it provides a certain amount of exercise for them.

In the industrial department, instruction is given in eighty-one different occupations, of which two-thirds are for boys. All the male students enter the trade school in their fourteenth year and, in compliance with the law, are entered on the Trade Registry. At the expiration of three years' apprenticeship they leave the institution as properly examined and qualified workmen.

In recent years, large and magnificent institutions with complete modern equipment have been erected in various localities. By far the most palatial of these is the institution at Munich, which has been erected by the Bavarian authorities. There are also new buildings projected at Berlin, Nuremberg, Beuthen, Cologne, Wiesbaden, and other places.

You will be astonished that I speak only of *institutions*, as though this comprised the only method of provision for cripples in Germany. As a matter of fact it is the method which in Germany is still predominant, and the majority of experts are probably of the opinion that it is the method yielding the best results. But that form of cripple care which has been developed in England with such excellent results—the 'ambulant' method of treatment in orthopedic dispensaries—is also gaining ground in Germany.

In 1902, next to nothing was done along such lines. Then

the 'Bayrische Genossenschaft des Johanniterordens' began the work of bringing crippled children from various parts of Bavaria to Munich, where they received treatment.

And since the statistics had strictly divided the cripples into two classes—'institutional' and 'non-institutional'—provision for ambulant treatment began to appear in every direction. Whereas in 1902 but 200 cripples, in two places in Germany, received ambulant treatment, there are now at least 36 institutions making such provision, handling 13,000 cases yearly.

The enormous expansion of care for cripples in Germany during the last ten years may best be gauged by considering that whereas in 1902 only 8% of all the cripples were cared for, the percentage to-day is 21.6. If the same rate of progress is maintained, it is within the range of possibility that in ten years more we may be able to say that, taking them as a whole, each crippled child in Germany is receiving its due share of attention.

It is true that we are still a long way behind the model arrangements of ambulant provision existing in London, and behind the admirable cripple dispensaries in New York and Milan; but we are on the right path and, as Germany has earned the reputation of making the best provision as regards institutional care, so we may hope that the time may not be far distant when ambulant provision for cripples may be equal to the demand.

In Berlin and other large cities, we shall also probably soon have to make arrangements for collecting children every morning by a special omnibus, taking them to centres where they can be treated, instructed, and fed, and returning them to their parents in the evening. We shall have to organize non-residential day schools for non-institutional crippled children, and non-residential continuation schools for those who have left school.

We are also backward in regard to cripples' labor exchanges, in which respect France is far ahead of us. It is true that a beginning has been made. There is a special society for this purpose in Berlin, in Munich the municipality has taken the matter up, and in Hamburg and Altona the cripples themselves have organized a union for self-help. But what we lack here is the French system of 'work depots', where the cripples can go every day to exercise their calling and pursue their trades without further trouble or expense. This also, however, we will achieve in time, so that we may make good our contention that properly organized care for cripples converts the recipient of alms into the tax paying citizen.

Now a word regarding the German organization for the care of cripples. Originally the work was entirely in the hands of religious directors who held periodical conferences—and still do, with most beneficial results. Three years ago the 'Deutsche Vereinigung für Krüppelfürsorge' was established under the presidency of Geheimer Obermedizinalrat Professor Dr. Dietrich, of the Prussian Ministry of the Interior, for the purpose of federating the various activities for the care of cripples in Germany, irrespective of their religious affiliation. This association counts among its members not only all the German homes and societies for cripples, but also a large number of public bodies, councils, social unions, and the like. It publishes the *Zeitschrift für Krüppelfürsorge* which, as managing director of the association, I had the honor of founding and now edit. Among the collaborators of the *Zeitschrift* you will find the name of the leading representative of orthopedic science in England, Mr. Robert Jones of Liverpool. The association has also published a guide to measures of care for cripples, *Leitfaden der Krüppelfürsorge*, which is acquired by public school authorities, schools, associations, and libraries, and serves as a practical book of reference. It also maintains a central office where advice and information are available to inquirers.

Every two years the association holds a convention. The first was held in Berlin, the second took place recently in

Munich under the presidency of Prince Ludwig of Bavaria, himself a physician and surgeon.

In order to promote lectures descriptive of the nature of deformity and the favorable prospects resultant upon proper treatment and care, the association has prepared several hundred lantern slides, and also a moving picture film, depicting the daily activity at the Berlin institution. By these means the facts are given wide publicity. Finally, the association arranged an exhibit demonstrating modern methods of care for cripples at the 'Internationale Hygieneaustellung' in Dresden, where it had a separate pavilion for the purpose. Over 300,000 persons visited the exhibit; on some Sundays there were 5,000 in a day.

By far the greater part of the exhibits are now housed in a small provisional museum in Bayreuther Strasse, 13. It provides the nucleus of a large museum on the care of cripples, which will be erected on the grounds of the new Berlin institution in the Grunewald Forest.

This in short, is what I have to tell you of the facts and principles of modern care for cripples in Germany. You will see that this province, small as compared with large social measures or the broad field of social hygiene, is permeated by a keen, healthy, progressive spirit. Many of the efforts made during eighty years' experience have justified themselves and will endure; others are still in the experimental stage; others again have had hardly time to manifest the first signs of young growth.

But the transactions of our two conventions have demonstrated the existence of a highly gratifying degree of earnest enthusiasm and a spirit of helpfulness. For my own part, and with me the pioneers of social care for cripples in Germany, I hold that so complex a mechanism would itself be crippled in its activities were it subjected to rigid uniformity and officialdom. I also think that by reason of differences in daily habits, social ideas, and even in climate and landscape, care for cripples in Germany will always tend to assume a form different from that of similar work in England, Norway, or Italy. But in spite of this, all countries may learn from one another and thus effect improvements in their own work.

It would, therefore, be a cause for gratification, were representatives from the domain of care for cripples in various countries to unite for the organization of an international congress. The feeling which must be common to all of us, and that inspires us in our work, must be the innate satisfaction inseparable from all efforts to lend a helping hand where it is most needed, together with the desire to give the innocently handicapped crippled child a new joy in life, and to assist him to a position of economic independence. If, therefore, the time should come when you receive from us a friendly summons to attend an international congress on the care of cripples, we earnestly hope you may see your way clear to accept an invitation most heartily extended.

A COMPILATION OF STATE LAWS RELATING TO PROVISION FOR CRIPPLED CHILDREN

Douglas C. McMurtrie

A Compilation of State Laws Relating to Provision for Crippled Children

Compiled by

Douglas C. McMurtrie

New York City

FLORIDA

Section 1186-j. State Board of Health to Establish Hospital for Indigent Crippled Children. That the State Board of Health be, and it is hereby authorized and directed to establish at some suitable and convenient location in this state a hospital for the treatment of indigent crippled children of this state. In such hospital indigent crippled children of this state shall be received and treated free of charge.

NOTE. Section 4, Chapter 6133, provides that the act shall take effect July 1, 1911.

Section 1186-k. Purchase of Site and Erection of Buildings, Equipment, Appropriation. That for the purposes of Section 1 [Paragraph 1186-j] hereof, the State Board of Health is hereby authorized to purchase a plot of ground and erect thereon a building suitable for such purpose, or to purchase a plot of ground with building already erected, in its discretion. For such purpose and for the purchase of suitable instruments, apparatus, furniture, fixtures, and other articles necessary for such an institution, the sum of twenty thousand dollars, or so much thereof as may be found necessary, is hereby appropriated, payable from the State Board of Health Fund.

Section 1186-l. Annual Appropriation, Proviso. That for the purpose of maintaining the hospital herein provided for, and of employing such physicians and attendants as are requisite for the conduct of the hospital, the sum of ten thousand dollars, or so much thereof as may be necessary, is hereby appropriated annually for the two years beginning July 1, 1911, payable from the State Board of Health Fund. Provided, that until the number of indigent crippled children, citizens of the State of Florida, shall be sufficient in number to warrant the State Board of Health to erect and maintain an institution of this character and nature, that the State Board of Health is authorized to arrange with any sanitarium or hospital in Florida to care for and treat the indigent crippled and deformed children of the state

and to pay for such treatment out of the funds of the State Board of Health, not in excess of the amount appropriated by this Act.

ILLINOIS

Section 279. Surgical Institution for Treatment of Children Authorized. Be it enacted by the People of the State of Illinois, represented in the General Assembly: There is hereby authorized to be established a surgical institution in and for the State of Illinois for the surgical treatment of children under the age of fourteen years, suffering from physical deformities or injuries of a nature which will likely yield to surgical skill and treatment, and which unless so treated will probably make such children, in whole or in part, in after life, public charges.

Section 280. Corporate Name. Said institute shall be known as the Illinois Surgical Institute for Children; and by such name shall be and constitute a corporation, under the laws of the State of Illinois.

Section 281. Purpose and Object. The purpose and object of said institute shall be to receive, treat and nurse such children whose parents or guardians may be financially unable to provide surgical treatment, as may be physically deformed, or suffering from injuries requiring surgical treatment, to the end that their physical disabilities may be removed, and that they may be thereby made able to become self-sustaining, instead of being, or becoming at some future time, public charges.

Section 282. Management and Control. The management and control of said institution shall be vested in the board of administration, and they shall faithfully see that the purposes of this act are fully carried out with all possible speed and expedition.

Section 283. Age, Admission, Transportation, Treatment. Any child under the age of fourteen, whose parents, or natural guardian, may be unable to furnish proper surgical treatment and who may be in need of the same, may be admitted to such institute, upon an order to that effect made by the county judge of the county in which said child may have had a legal residence for one year last past. The county treasurer of the county in which said child may have so resided shall, upon the order of said county judge, furnish said child with transportation from the place where said child may so reside to the place of said institution and return. The order admitting said child shall, when made, be filed with the superintendent of said institute, and said child shall be admitted thereto in the regular order of filing as soon thereafter as said institute can provide room, care and attendance therefor. Said child, if deemed feasible, shall be treated, nursed in said institute, until a recovery is effected, or it becomes apparent that further treatment will be of no avail, whereupon it shall be discharged and returned to its former place of residence.

Section 284. Said institution shall be located in that portion of Illinois which may be deemed most advantageous.

Section 285. Soliciting Donation of Site—Conveyance. Upon the taking effect of this act, the board of administration shall, by advertising in not less than four (4) of the daily newspapers published within the territory wherein the said institution shall be located, solicit the donation of a site for said home, describing the requirements thereof, which shall be a tract of land containing not less than one hundred and sixty (160) acres, convenient to railroad transportation, and suitable for such purpose, taking into account healthfulness of the location, water supply, drainage, and agriculture, and convenience of access both to those who will likely be inmates of said institution, and physicians and surgeons who may be required to treat the same; and if a location satisfactory to the said board of administration shall, within a time to be fixed by said board of administration, be offered to be donated for said purpose, they may, upon investigation finding the title to be good, free and clear, accept such offer, and cause proper conveyance thereof to be made for the purpose of such institution, in fee simple.

Section 286. General Superintendent to be a Surgeon. The said board of administration shall appoint a skilled and capable surgeon general superintendent, and may remove him for cause to be stated, first having given such officer a copy of the charges against him, and reasonable notice of the time and place when such charges will be heard, and an opportunity to defend himself.

Section 287. Officers, Employees, Compensation. All other officers and employees shall be appointed and removed as is now provided by the laws of the State of Illinois, and the compensation of the superintendent, officers, and employees shall be fixed from time to time by the board of administration.

Section 288. Physicians, Surgeons, and Internes; How Appointed. Assistant physicians and surgeons and internes shall be appointed to any vacancies in said surgical institute in either of said positions by competitive examination. Any graduate of any accredited school of medicine of Illinois or any regular trained physician or surgeon of the State of Illinois shall be eligible to take such examination. Said examination shall be specially held for this institute, and be conducted with especially (especial) reference to the surgical and medical treatment required by the children who may be patients in such institute. Appointments to such positions shall be made from those passing such examination in the order of grade standing, and in no other way whatsoever so long as there are eligible persons available as the result of such examinations. Any person passing such examination shall remain on the eligible list for two years.

Section 289. May Accept Gift, Donation, Bequest, etc. The board of administration may, from time to time, accept, hold and use for the benefit of said institution, or the inmates thereof, any gift, donation, bequest or devise of money, or real or personal property, and may agree to and perform any condition of such gift, donation, bequest or devise, not contrary to any law of the State.

Section 290. Rules and Regulations. The board of administration shall establish all needful rules and regulations for the management of said institute and the inmates thereof.

Section 291. Plans and Specifications. The board of administration shall cause to be prepared suitable plans and specifications for the building and improvements upon the site so selected, as may be necessary to carry into effect the purpose of this act. The principal building shall be of sufficient size and capacity to permit the proper treatment and care of at least fifty patients at one time; said building to be plain and substantial in its type of architecture; of approved design for the purpose for which it is intended, and shall be constructed of fire-resisting materials.

Section 292. To Be Submitted to Governor. The plans and specifications, when prepared to the satisfaction of the board of administration, shall be submitted to the governor, with a detailed estimate of the cost of each and every building and improvement proposed to be made.

Section 293. Approval of Governor, Notice for Sealed Bids. When such plans are approved by the governor, the board of administration shall cause not less than thirty days' notice to be given by publication in at least four daily newspapers, published in the State of Illinois, that sealed bids will be received for the construction of such building and improvements as the said board shall conclude to construct, at that time. Said notice shall specify when and the terms upon which bids will be received.

Section 294. Bid, Bond, Award. No bid shall be accepted which is not accompanied by sufficient bond in the penal sum of $10,000, payable to the People of the State of Illinois, with at least three good and sufficient sureties, conditioned that if his bid is accepted, he will enter into a contract with said school, by its corporate name, for the doing of the work, and will give bond required by this act, conditioned for the faithful performance of his contract. At the time and place specified in the notice and in the presence of such of the bidders as may appear, the bids shall be opened and the contract awarded to the lowest and best bidder, unless it shall appear that no satisfactory bid shall have been made, and if no satisfactory bid shall have been made, another notice shall be given in like manner for other bids until an acceptable bid shall be made. The trustees may accept bids for the particular portions of the work if they can be advantageously separated.

Section 295. Contract, Bond, Work How Approved. The contract to be made with the successful bidder shall be accompanied by a good and sufficient bond, to be approved by the governor before accepted, conditioned for the faithful performance of his contract; shall also provide for the appointment of a superintendent of construction, who shall receive not more than five dollars per day for his services, and who shall carefully and accurately measure the work done, and for the payment of the contractor upon the aforesaid measurement, and for the withholding of fifteen per cent. of the value of the work done and materials on hand until the completion of the building and for a forfeiture of a stipulated sum per diem for every day that the completion of the work shall be delayed after the time specified for the completion in the contract, and for the full protection of all persons who may furnish labor or materials by withholding payment from the contractor and by paying the parties to whom any moneys are due for service and materials, as aforesaid, directly for all work done or material furnished by them, in case of notice given to the board of administration that any such party apprehends or fears that he will not receive all moneys due; and for the settlement of all disputed questions as to the value of alterations and extras, by arbitration, at the time of final settlement, as follows: One arbitrator to be chosen by the trustees,

one by the contractor and one by the governor of the state, all three of said arbitrators to be practical mechanics and builders, and for the power and privilege of the trustees under the contract to alter changes in the plans at their discretion, and to refuse to accept any work which may be done not fully in accordance with the letter and spirit of the plans and specifications, and all work not accepted shall be replaced at the expense of the contractor, and for a deduction from the current price of all alterations ordered by the board of administration which may and do diminish the cost of the building. They may also make such other provisions and conditions in said contract not hereinabove specified as may seem to them necessary or expedient: *Provided,* that no condition shall be inserted contrary to the letter and spirit of this act, and that in no event shall the state be liable for a greater amount of money than is appropriated for said building and its appurtenances.

Section 296. Contracts, How Made. All contracts shall be signed by the president of the board of administration on behalf of the board, after a vote authorizing the president so to sign shall have been entered upon the minutes of the board; and it shall be attested by the signature of the secretary of the board and by the corporate seal. All contracts shall be drawn in triplicate, and one copy shall be deposited in the office of the board of public charities of this state.

Section 297. Vouchers. All measurements or estimates on account of work in progress shall show in detail the amount and character of the work estimated, and the estimates shall be paid from the State treasury only on the warrant of the auditor of public accounts on vouchers made by the said board of administration and approved by the governor.

Approved June 6, 1911.

IOWA

Section 254-b. Medical and Surgical Treatment for Indigent Children. Power of Court, Report. That any district or superior court of the State, or any judge thereof, sitting or acting as a juvenile court, as provided by law, may on his own motion, or on complaint filed by any probation officer, school teacher or officer, superintendent of the poor, or physician authorized to practise his profession in the State of Iowa, alleging that the child named therein is under sixteen years of age and is afflicted with some deformity or suffering from some malady that can probably be remedied, and that the parents or other persons legally chargeable with the support of such child are unable to provide means for the surgical and medical treatment and hospital care of such child, shall appoint some physician who shall personally examine said child with respect to its malady or deformation. Such physician shall make a written report to the court or judge giving such history of the case as will be likely to aid the medical or surgical treatment of such deformity or malady and describing the same, all in detail, and stating whether or not in his opinion the same can probably be remedied. Such report shall be made within such time as may be fixed by the court, and upon blanks to be furnished as hereinafter provided. The court or judge may also appoint some suitable person to investigate and report on the other matters charged in said complaint. [36 G. A. (S. F. 16, Section 1.)]

Section 254-c. Hearing, Duty of County Attorney, Order Committing Child to Hospital, Consent of Parent. Upon the filing of such report or reports, the court or judge shall fix a day for the hearing upon the complaint and shall cause the parent or parents, guardian or other person having the legal custody of said child to be served with a notice of the hearing, and shall also notify the county attorney, who shall appear and conduct the proceedings, and upon the hearing of such complaint evidence may be introduced. And if the court or judge finds that the said child is suffering from a deformity or malady which can probably be remedied by medical or surgical treatment and hospital care, and that the parent or parents, guardian or other person legally chargeable with his support is unable to pay the expenses thereof, the court or judge, with the consent of the parent or parents, guardian or other person having the legal custody of such child, shall enter an order directing that the said child shall be taken or sent to the hospital of the medical college of the state university of Iowa for free medical and surgical treatment and hospital care. [36 G. A. (S. F. 16, Section 2.)]

Section 254-d. Hospital Treatment at State University. It shall be the duty of the person in charge of the hospital of the college of medicine of the state university, or other person designated by the authorities in control of said medical college, upon such child being received into the hospital, to provide for such child, if available, a cot or bed, or room in the hospital, and such person shall also designate the clinic of the college of medicine at the state university hospital to which the patient shall be assigned for treatment of the deformity or malady in each particular case.

The said hospital shall not be required to receive any child into the hospital unless the physician or surgeon in charge of the department of said medical college in which such surgical or medical treatment is to be furnished shall be of the opinion that there is a reasonable

probability that the child will be benefited by the proposed medical or surgical treatment.

If the physician or surgeon of the clinic to which such child has been assigned for treatment declines to treat such child, he shall make a report, in duplicate, of his examination of such child and state therein his reason or reasons for declining such treatment; and one of said duplicates shall be preserved in the records of said hospital and the other transmitted to the clerk of the court of said county where said order committing said child to the hospital was entered.

When any patient has been admitted to the clinic for treatment the physician or surgeon in charge thereof shall proceed with all proper diligence to perform such operation and bestow such treatment upon such patient as in his judgment shall be proper, and such patient shall receive proper hospital care while therein. [36 G. A. (S. F. 16, Section 3.)]

Section 254-e. Treatment Gratuitous. No compensation shall be charged by or allowed to the physician or surgeon or nurse who shall treat such patient other than the compensation received from the university. [36 G. A. (S. F. 16, Section 4.)]

Section 254-f. Record of Treatment, Expense, Filing Statement. The superintendent of the university hospital, or other person designated by the authorities in control of the university college of medicine, shall keep a correct account of the medicine, treatment, nursing and maintenance furnished to said patient, and shall set forth therein the actual, reasonable and necessary cost thereof, and shall make and file with the secretary of the executive council of the State of Iowa an itemized, sworn statement, as far as possible, of the expense so incurred at said hospital other than the free medical and surgical treatment and nursing, as hereinbefore provided, and the said statement shall be made in conformity with rules prescribed by the executive council of the State of Iowa. [36 G. A. (S. F. 16, Section 5.)]

Section 254-g. Expenses, How Paid. The secretary of the executive council of the State of Iowa shall present the said statement to the executive council which, upon being satisfied that the same is correct and reasonable, shall approve the same, and shall direct that warrants be drawn by the auditor of state upon the treasurer of state for the amount of such bills as are allowed from time to time, and the said warrants shall be forwarded as drawn by the auditor of state to the treasurer of the state university of Iowa, and the same shall be by him placed to the credit of the university funds which are set aside for the support of the university hospital, and the treasurer of state shall pay said warrants from the general funds of the State not otherwise appropriated. [36 G. A. (S. F. 16, Section 6.)]

Section 254-h. Attendant for Child, Compensation, Compensation of Physician. The court or judge may, in his discretion, appoint some person to accompany such child from the place where he may be to the hospital of the medical college of the state university at Iowa City, Iowa, or to accompany such child from the said hospital to such place as may be designated by the court, the parent or parents, guardians or person having legal custody of said child, consenting.

Any person appointed by the court or judge to accompany said child to or from the hospital, or to make an investigation and report on any of the questions involved in the complaint other than the physician making the examination, shall receive the sum of three dollars per day for the time actually spent in making such investigation (except in cases where the person appointed by the court is a parent or relative or where the officer appointed therefor receives a fixed salary or compensation, in which cases there shall be no compensation) and his actual necessary expenses incurred in making such investigation or trip. The physician appointed by the court to make the examination and report shall receive the sum of five dollars for each and every examination and report so made, and his actual necessary expenses incurred in making such investigation, in conformity to the requirements of this act. The person making claim to such compensation shall present to the court or judge an itemized sworn statement thereof, and when such claim for compensation has been approved by the court or judge the same shall be filed in the office of the county auditor, and shall be allowed by the board of supervisors and paid out of the funds of the county collected for the relief of the poor. [*36 G. A. (S. F. 16, Section 7.*)]

Section 254-i. Returning Child, Expense, How Paid. The university hospital may in the discretion of the superintendent or other person designated by the authorities in control thereof, pay the actual, reasonable necessary expenses of returning the said patient to his home, and pay the attendant not to exceed three dollars per day for the time thus necessarily employed, unless said attendant be a parent or other relative or be an officer or employee receiving other compensation, and his actual, reasonable and necessary expenses incurred in accompanying such patient to his home, and such per diem and expenses shall be itemized and verified, and presented to and allowed by the executive council of the State of Iowa, in connection with the bills for hospital maintenance, as hereinbefore provided. [*36 G. A. (S. F. 16, Section 8.*)]

Section 254-j. Faculty to Prepare Blanks, Printing, Distribution, Report to Accompany Patient. The medical faculty of the university hospital shall immediately upon taking effect of this act prepare a blank or blanks containing such questions and requiring such information as may in its judgment be necessary and proper to be obtained by the physician who examines the patient under order of court; and such blanks shall be printed by the state printer and a supply thereof shall be sent to the clerk of each superior and district court of the State of Iowa; and the physician making such examination shall make his report to the court in duplicate on said blanks, answering the questions contained therein, and setting forth the information required thereby, and one of said duplicate reports shall be sent to the university hospital with the patient, together with a certified copy of the order of court. The executive council of the State of Iowa shall determine the number of such blanks to be printed and distributed to the clerks of the superior and district courts of the State of Iowa, and shall audit, allow and pay the bills of the state printer therefor, as other bills are allowed and paid for public printing. [*36 G. A. (S. F. 16, Section 9.*)]

Section 254-k. Patients in State Institutions, Authority to Send to State University Hospital, Authority to Pay Expense. The board of control of the state institutions of Iowa may in its discretion send any inmate of any of said institutions, or any person committed or applying for admission thereto, to the hospital of the medical college of the state university of Iowa for treatment and care as provided in this act without securing an order of court as provided in other cases, and the said patient so sent to the hospital of the medical college of the state university shall be accompanied by a report and history of the case made by the physician in charge of the institution to which said patient has been committed, or to which application has been made for his admission, containing a history of the case and information as required by said blanks, and the hospital expenses of such patient shall be paid as in other cases. State board of education for any such patient from the college for the blind and the board of control for any such patient from any institution under its control may pay the expenses of transporting such patient to and from the hospital out of any funds appropriated for the use of the institution from which such patient is sent, and may, when necessary, send an attendant with such patient, and pay his traveling expenses in like manner. [*36 G. A. (S. F. 16, Section 10.*)]

Section 254-l. Treatment Authorized, Experimentation Forbidden. It is expressly provided that no child under the terms of this act shall be treated for any ailment except such as is described by the order of the court, unless permission for such treatment is granted by the parents or guardians; and it is also expressly forbidden that any child shall be used for the purpose of experimentation. [*36 G. A. (S. F. 16, Section 11.*)]

MASSACHUSETTS

Be it enacted, etc., as follows:

Section 1. The governor, with the advice and consent of the council, shall appoint five persons who shall constitute the Board of Trustees of the Massachusetts School and Home for Crippled and Deformed Children, the purpose of which shall be the education and care of the crippled and deformed children of the commonwealth. The trustees shall hold office for terms of one, two, three, four, and five years, respectively, beginning with the first Monday of December in the present year, and until their respective successors are appointed and qualified; and previous to the first Monday in December in each year thereafter the governor shall in like manner appoint one such trustee to hold office for the term of five years, beginning with the first Monday in December of the year of his appointment, and until his successor is appointed and qualified. Any such trustee may be removed by the governor, with the advice and consent of the council. Any vacancy occurring in said board shall be filled in like manner for the unexpired term.

Section 2. The lands held by said trustees in trust for the commonwealth for the use of said school and home, as hereinafter provided, shall not be taken for a street, highway, or railroad, without leave of the general court specially obtained.

Section 3. The trustees shall be a corporation for the same purpose for which the trustees of each of the state insane hospitals are made a corporation by section twenty-three of chapter eighty-seven of the Revised Laws, with all the powers necessary to carry said purposes into effect.

Section 4. The trustees shall select a site for the school and home; and shall have power to purchase land therefor, subject to the approval of the governor and council, and to erect on such land suitable buildings to hold not less than 300 children and the officers, employees, and attendants, and to provide for the equipment and furnishing of said buildings: provided, however, that the expenditure for carrying out the purposes of this act shall not exceed $300,000. No expenditure shall be made for the erection of buildings except for plans therefor, until the plans have been approved by the governor and council, and no such approval shall be given unless the governor and council shall be satisfied that the cost of the real estate and the erection and completion of buildings and the equipment and furnishing of the same, so as to be ready for occupancy, will not

exceed $300,000. The trustees shall have authority to make all contracts and employ all agents necessary to carry into effect the provisions of this act.

Section 5. The trustees shall have the same powers and shall be required to perform the same duties in the management and control of the said school and home, as are vested in, and required of, the trustees of the various state insane hospitals under chapter eighty-seven of the Revised Laws, so far as said chapter is applicable.

Section 6. When the buildings constructed under the provisions of this act are so far completed that in the opinion of the trustees they may properly be used for the purposes of the school and home, the trustees shall notify the governor, who shall thereupon issue his proclamation establishing the school and home.

Section 7. After the establishment of the school and home the trustees shall receive no compensation for their services, but they shall be reimbursed from the treasury of the commonwealth for all expenses actually incurred by them in the performance of their official duties.

Section 8. The trustees may appoint and, subject to the approval of the governor and council, may fix the salaries of all persons necessary for the proper administration of the affairs of the school and home, and may incur all expenses necessary for the maintenance of the school and home.

Section 9. The charges for the support of the children of the school and home who are of sufficient ability to pay for the same, or have persons or kindred bound by law to maintain them, shall be paid by such children, such persons, or such kindred, at a rate to be determined by the trustees of the school and home. The board of such children as have a legal settlement in some city or town shall be paid by such city or town if such children are received at the school and home on the request of the overseers of the poor of such city or town. The trustees may in their discretion receive other children who have no means to pay for tuition and board; and the tuition and board of all such children shall be paid from the treasury of the commonwealth.

Section 10. There shall be a thorough visitation of the school and home by two of the trustees thereof monthly, and by a majority of them quarterly, and by the whole board semi-annually, and after each visitation a written report of the state of the institution shall be drawn up, which shall be presented at the annual meeting to be held in December. At the annual meeting the trustees shall make a detailed report of their doings to the governor and council, and shall audit the report of the treasurer, which shall be presented at said annual meeting, and transmit it with their annual report to the governor and council.

Section 11. The accounts and books of the treasurer shall at all times be open to the inspection of the trustees.

Section 12. The state board of charity shall have general supervision of said school and home, and may, when so directed by the governor, assume and exercise the powers of the board of trustees of said school and home in any matter relating to the management thereof.

Section 13. For the purpose of meeting expenses incurred under the provisions of this act the treasurer and receiver general is hereby authorized, with the approval of the governor and council, to issue scrip or certificates of indebtedness to an amount not exceeding three hundred thousand dollars, for a term not exceeding thirty years. Such scrip or certificates of indebtedness shall be issued as registered bonds or with interest coupons attached, and shall bear interest at a rate not exceeding four per cent. per annum. They shall be designated on the face thereof Prison and Hospitals Loan, shall be countersigned by the governor and shall be deemed a pledge of the faith and credit of the Commonwealth, and the principal and interest shall be paid at the times specified therein in gold coin of the United States or its equivalent; and such scrip or certificates shall be sold or disposed of at public auction, or in such other mode, and at such times and prices, and in such amounts, as the treasurer shall deem best. The sinking fund established by chapter three hundred and ninety-one of the acts of the year eighteen hundred and seventy-four, known as the Prisons and Hospitals Loan Sinking Fund, shall also be maintained for the purpose of extinguishing the bonds issued under the authority of this act, and the treasurer and receiver general shall apportion thereto from year to year an amount sufficient with the accumulations of said fund to extinguish at maturity the debt incurred by the issue of said bonds. Any premiums received from the sale thereof shall be paid into the sinking fund. The amount necessary to meet the annual sinking fund requirements and to pay the interest on said bonds shall be raised by taxation from year to year. (Revision of 1905.)

Section 14. This act shall take effect upon its passage. (Approved June 8, 1904.) Acts of 1904, Chapter 446.

Section 1. The name of the Massachusetts School and Home for Crippled and Deformed Children, established by Chapter Four hundred and forty-six of the Acts of the year Nineteen hundred and four, and located in the town of Canton, is hereby changed to the Massachusetts Hospital School.

Section 2. The act shall take effect upon its passage. (Approved March 20, 1907.) Acts of 1907, Chapter 226.

MICHIGAN

AN ACT making appropriations for the State Public School at Coldwater for the fiscal years ending June 30, 1914 and June 30, 1915, for the erection, furnishing, and equipment of two cottages and an industrial building for the reception, treatment, and education of dependent crippled children of sound mind between five and fourteen years of age, and for the temporary care and maintenance of certain blind children under the age of six years, and to provide a tax to meet the same.

The People of the State of Michigan enact:

Section 1. There is hereby appropriated out of any money in the State treasury not otherwise appropriated for the fiscal year ending June 30, 1914, the sum of $19,000 for purposes and by amounts as follows: For one cottage for crippled boys, $6,500; for one cottage for crippled girls, $6,500; for one industrial building in separate apartments for crippled boys and girls, $6,000. There is also appropriated for the fiscal year ending June 30, 1915, the sum of $6,000 for furnishing, heating, lighting, sewage, plumbing, sidewalks, and grading for the two cottages and industrial building, and for appliances, tools, apparatus, and other necessary equipment for said cottages and industrial building: Provided, That if the amount designated in this section for any one of the purposes stated be insufficient to complete the work or purchase, any surplus remaining after the completion of the other work or purchase specified in this section may, by obtaining the consent of the State Board of Corrections and Charities and Auditor General in writing before any expense in excess of the specific appropriation is incurred, be used in the account or accounts where such deficiency seems unavoidable, the intent of this proviso being to make the entire $25,000 available for the purposes stated herein if in the judgment of the State Board of Corrections and Charities and Auditor General it is deemed advisable to make the transfers for which provision is hereby made: Provided further, That the board of control may obtain money under this section before July 1, 1913, in such amounts as they may by requisition certify to the Auditor General are necessary for immediate use, which amounts thus advanced shall be deducted from the total amount appropriated when the appropriation becomes available.

Section 2. There shall be admitted as provided in Section 4 of this Act to the State Public School at

Coldwater, on and after the first day of July, 1914, or as soon as the buildings provided for in this act are completed and furnished, those dependent crippled children who have been declared dependent on the public for support as provided by law who are between five and fourteen years of age and of sound mind and have no chronic or contagious disease and are capable of acquiring a common school education and some trade or occupation. While in said institution they shall be taught the English branches. The boys shall receive manual training, the girls shall be taught domestic science and both classes may be taught any trade or occupation the board of control shall consider adapted to their condition. They may be retained in said institution such time during their minority as the board of control may determine and at all times may be placed in families on indenture or by adoption in the discretion of said board, and shall be subject to the same management and disposition as is now provided by law and regulation of the State Public School regarding other wards of said board except wherein provided otherwise in this act: Provided, That blind children who are under six years of age, of sound mind, and whose physical condition is normal except as to blindness, and who are dependent upon the public for support, and when there is room therefor, may receive temporary care and maintenance in the State Public School in the buildings herein provided, pending such time as arrangements shall have been made at the Michigan School for the Blind for the care of said children, when said children shall be removed thereto or to such other institution as may be provided by law therefor. Said blind children shall be committed to the State Public School in the same manner as prescribed by law for the commitment of normal and crippled children to said institution, and shall be subject to the same management and disposition as is now provided by law and regulation of the State Public School regarding other wards of said board, except wherein provided otherwise in this act: Provided further, That said blind children shall be removed from the State Public School as soon as preparations can be made and facilities furnished for their care, maintenance, and support at the said Michigan School for the Blind, or at some other institution: Provided further, That no blind children shall be committed hereunder to the said State Public School prior to the first of July, 1917, and the obligation to receive, support, and maintain them at such school shall cease on the first day of July, 1919.

Section 3. Whenever the judge of probate shall adjudge that any crippled child provided for in this act is dependent on the public for support he shall, under proceedings to have it committed to the State Public School, cause it to be examined by the county physician, if there be one, and if not, then by another reputable practicing physician and shall in no case enter an order on the journal of his court committing a child to said State Public School unless the physician making such examination shall certify, in writing, under oath, filed in said court, that the child examined by him is in his opinion of sound mind and has no chronic or contagious disease, and has not been exposed to any contagious disease within fifteen days prior to such examination; that it can care for itself without a personal attendant, and that it is mentally and physically competent to acquire a trade or occupation. The said certificate shall contain a diagnosis of the condition of the child examined, describing without technical language its special disability. A copy of such certificate shall be attached to the other papers required by law committing the child to the said State Public School.

Section 4. The dependent crippled children described in this Act shall be admitted to the cottages authorized to be constructed in Section 1 of this Act, and to any cottage or cottages that may hereafter be constructed for such purpose, when provision has been made for their support and education and for teaching them some trade or occupation: Provided, That before the judge of probate shall commit a crippled child to said State Public School he shall receive a written notice from the superintendent of said institution that there is room therein for the child and that provision has been made for its support and education and for its instruction in manual training and domestic science: Provided further, That if the facilities of the institution will permit, the board of control thereof may receive for instruction hereunder crippled children of school age who are not dependent; and may enter into such agreements and arrangements with parents or guardians of such children for the payment of compensation for the instruction and incidental maintenance and support thereof as may be deemed expedient and proper.

Section 5. The construction of the cottages provided for in Section 1 of this Act shall be especially adapted for the comfort, convenience, and recreation of crippled boys and girls and shall include dining rooms, kitchens, and bathing facilities including building for manual training in separate apartments to be situated near or in connection with said cottages: Provided, That said cottages and manual training building authorized by this Act may be used for children of sound mind and body when in the opinion of the board of control it will not cause discomfort to the crippled children.

Section 6. The said board shall employ competent teachers, cottage managers, and others well skilled in teaching domestic science, manual training, and education in the common branches, in order that said crippled child may acquire a trade or occupation, and become self-supporting. When the said crippled children are of sufficient age, education, and training, it shall be the duty of said board of control to procure for them, as far as possible, suitable employment at which they can support themselves.

Section 7. The several sums appropriated by the provisions of this Act shall be paid out of the general fund in the state treasury to the treasurer of the State Public School at such times and in such amounts as the general accounting laws of the state prescribe, and the disbursing officer shall render his accounts to the auditor general thereunder.

Section 8. The auditor general shall incorporate in the State tax for the year nineteen hundred thirteen the sum of nineteen thousand dollars, and for the year nineteen hundred fourteen the sum of six thousand dollars, which when collected shall be credited to the general fund to reimburse the same for the money hereby appropriated.

[This Act is ordered to take immediate effect.

Approved May 2, 1913.]

MINNESOTA

Section 1. That the donations tendered by the said city of St. Paul and certain of its citizens, are, and each of the same is, hereby accepted in behalf of the State of Minnesota for the purposes aforesaid, and the proper officials of the State of Minnesota are hereby authorized and empowered to accept any and all donations hereafter tendered to the state in aid and for the benefit of the state hospital for indigent, crippled and deformed children hereinafter described.

Section 1. Sanitarium and School. That the sum of fifty-five thousand (55,000) dollars or so much thereof as may be necessary, be and the same is hereby appropriated out of the moneys in the state treasury not otherwise appropriated, for the purpose of constructing and equipping upon the following described land in the city of St. Paul, in Ramsey County, Minnesota, to wit: All of the northeast quarter (N. E. ¼) of the southwest quarter (S. W. ¼) of section twenty-one (21), township twenty-nine (29), range twenty-two (22), reserving therefrom seventeen (17) acres of land taken under condemnation proceedings by the city of St. Paul for Phalen park, a building or buildings to be used pursuant to the provisions of Chapter 81 of the General Laws of the State of Minnesota for the year 1907, for a fresh air sanitarium and educational and industrial school building for the indigent, crippled and deformed children of the State of Minnesota, and to care for and educate such other indigent crippled persons as are unable to support themselves, and may be admitted to such institution by the board of control of the State of Minnesota.

Section 2. This act shall take effect and be in force from and after its passage.

[Approved March 31, 1909. *General Laws of Minnesota for 1909; Chapter 130.*]

Section 2. Establishment and Location. That there is hereby established a state hospital for indigent, crippled and deformed children of the State of Minnesota, which shall be known as the 'State Hospital for Indigent, Crippled and Deformed Children', and such hospital is hereby located upon the following described lands in the city of St. Paul, county of Ramsey, and State of Minnesota.

Section 3. Control and Management, Who May be Admitted. Said hospital shall be under the control and management of the state board of control, and said board of control is hereby authorized and empowered to make provision for the care and treatment in such hospital of indigent children who may have resided within the State of Minnesota for not less than one year, who are crippled or deformed, or are suffering from disease through which they are likely to become crippled or deformed, and such board is authorized and empowered to make the necessary contracts for the maintenance and care of such children in said hospital.

Section 4. Rules and Regulations. The said state board of control shall adopt such rules and regulations as said board may deem proper and necessary for the admission, discharge, care, treatment and education of such children.

Section 5. Repeals inconsistent acts.

Section 6. This act shall take effect and be in force from and after its passage.

[Approved April 2, 1907. *General Laws of Minnesota for 1907; Chapter 81.*]

NEBRASKA

Section 7234. Establishment and Location of Hospital. A hospital for crippled, ruptured and deformed children, and those suffering from diseases from which they are likely to become deformed, shall be established in the city of Lincoln, Lancaster County, State of Nebraska. (*1905 p. 382; Ann. 10040; Comp. 3729a.*)

Section 7235. Location of Hospital. The location of the hospital shall be on the grounds of the 'Home of the Friendless' in the city of Lincoln, Nebraska. (*1905 p. 383; 1907 p. 257; Ann. 10042; Comp. 3729j.*)

Section 7236. Admission of Children to Hospital. Whenever application for admission to the hospital is made by or on behalf of a patient in any county, the county physician of such county shall examine such patient and report the result in detail to the board of public lands and buildings. If the board deem such patient a proper subject for admission to the hospital according to the law, they shall issue to the county physician, for such patient, an entrance permit in due form: Provided, however, the entire cost of any examination as aforesaid and of conveying any patient to or from the hospital when not borne by his relatives or friends shall be paid by his county. Provided further, any child coming within the provisions of this article, who is supported by any county in this state, either at a poor house or elsewhere, may be transferred therefrom to said hospital. (*1905 p. 303; Ann. 10044; Comp. 3729a.*)

Section 7237. Admission of other Patients. Whenever the same can be done without limiting in any way the advantages of the hospital for the patient for whom the hospital is primarily designed, the board may in their discretion admit other crippled and deformed patients on such terms and under such rules as they may from time to time prescribe: Provided, however, all income from patients or from any other source whatever shall be turned into the state treasury and placed to the credit of the hospital fund described in the next following section. (*1905 p. 384; Ann. 10046; Comp. 3729β.*)

Section 7238. Funds for Hospital, How Used. Appropriation hereafter made, with any other moneys at any time rendered available to the board by gift or otherwise for the uses of the hospital, shall form a hospital fund which the state treasurer shall keep separate from all other funds. The board shall, during no biennium, make such outlays as to leave this fund in deficit at the close, and whenever and so long as patients are present in the hospital in such numbers as to make it reasonably certain that any addition would involve a deficit at the end of the biennium, no more shall be admitted. The state treasurer shall make payments from this fund on board's orders and vouchers in the same manner as is now usual in making payments from general funds. (*1905 p. 384; Ann. 10047; Comp. 3729g.*)

NEW YORK

Section 130. Establishment of the New York State Hospital for the Care of Crippled and Deformed Children. The state hospital, known as the New York state hospital for the care of crippled and deformed children, established at West Haverstraw, is hereby continued for the care and treatment of any indigent children who may have resided in the state of New York for a period of not less than one year, who are crippled or deformed or are suffering from disease from which they are likely to become crippled or deformed. No patient suffering from an incurable disease shall be admitted to said hospital. Said hospital shall provide for and permit the freedom of religious worship of said inmates to the extent and in the manner required in other institutions, by section twenty of the prison law. (*Amended by L. 1909, ch. 240, Section 72.*)

Formerly L. 1900, ch. 369, Section 1.

Section 131. Board of Managers, Appointment of. The governor, by and with the advice and consent of the senate, shall appoint five citizens of this state who shall constitute the board of managers of the New York state hospital for the care of crippled and deformed children. The full term of office of each manager shall be five years, and the term of office of one of such managers shall expire annually. The present board of managers is continued in office until the appointment of their successors. Appointments of successors to fill vacancies occurring by death, resignation, or other cause, shall be made for the unexpired term. Other appointments shall be for the full term. Failure of any manager to attend the regular meetings of the board for the period of one year shall be considered as a resignation therefrom, and his office shall be declared vacant by resolution of the board. A certified copy of such resolution shall forthwith be transmitted by the board to the governor. The managers shall receive no compensation for their services, but shall be allowed their reasonable traveling and other expenses. Such expenses shall be duly verified and paid by the treasurer of the board on the audit of the comptroller. Any of said new managers may be removed from office by the governor for any cause that he may deem sufficient, after an opportunity to be heard in his defense, and the vacancy may be filled as herein provided. Three members of the board shall constitute a quorum for the transaction of business.

Formerly L. 1900, ch. 369, Section 2.

Section 132. Powers and Duties of Board of Managers. The board of managers shall have the general direction and control of the property and affairs of said hospital, which are not otherwise specially provided by law, subject to the inspection, visitation and powers of the state board of charities. They may acquire and hold, in the name of and for the people of the state of New York, by grant, gift, devise or bequest, property to be applied to the maintenance of indigent children who are crippled or deformed or are suffering from diseases through which they are likely to become crippled or deformed, in and for the general use of the hospital. They shall—

1. Take care of the general interests of the hospital and see that its design is carried into effect according to law and its by-laws, rules and regulations.

2. Keep in a book provided for that purpose a fair and full record of their doings, which shall be open at all times to the inspection of the governor of the state, the state board of charities, or any person appointed by the governor, the state board of charities or either house of the legislature, to examine the same.

3. Make a detailed report to the state board of charities, in each month of October, in such form as said board of charities may require, and with such recommendations as said managers may deem expedient, together with a statement of all moneys received by them, and of the progress made in the erection of buildings for hospital purposes, if any, for the year ending on the thirtieth day of September preceding the date of such report.

4. Establish such by-laws as they may deem necessary or expedient for regulating the duties of officers, assistants and employees of the hospital, and make and enforce rules and regulations for the internal government, discipline and management of the same.

5. They shall appoint a surgeon-in-chief who shall be a person of suitable experience in the care and treatment of disabling and deforming diseases, and may for cause at any time remove him and appoint his successor. They shall also appoint a treasurer who shall have the custody of all moneys, obligations and securities belonging to the hospital.

Formerly L. 1900, ch. 369, Section 3.

Section 133. Powers and Duties of the Surgeon-in-Chief. The surgeon-in-chief shall be the superintendent of the hospital. He shall appoint and may remove an assistant superintendent, steward, matron, and such assistant physicians and surgeons, assistants and attendants as may be necessary for the proper treatment of the patients under the care of the hospital, and shall have power to fill vacancies as often as they occur. The assistant superintendent shall act as the assistant to the surgeon-in-chief, so far as the superintendence of the hospital is concerned, to such extent as said surgeon-in-chief may from time to time authorize and direct. The first assistant surgeon shall be clothed with all the authority and power of the surgeon-in-chief during the absence or disability of the surgeon-in-chief. Subject to the by-laws and regulations established by the board of managers the surgeon-in-chief shall have the general superintendence of the property, buildings, grounds, fixtures and effects, and control of all persons therein. He shall also—

1. Provide for ascertaining daily the condition of all the patients and proper prescription for their treatment.

2. Keep a book in which he shall cause to be entered at the time of the reception of any patient, his or her name, residence and occupation, and the date of such reception, by whom brought and by what authority committed, and an abstract of all orders, warrants, requests, certificates and other papers accompanying such person.

3. On or before the fifteenth of each month cause to be prepared by the assistant superintendent or steward, estimates in duplicate of the amount required for the expenses of the hospital for the ensuing month, including salaries and compensation of employees, which estimate shall be certified by him to be required for the hospital. One of said estimates shall be transmitted to the comptroller who shall, if he approve the same, issue his warrant for the amount thereof and transmit the same to the treasurer of the hospital.

Formerly L. 1900, ch. 369, Section 4. as amended by L. 1901, ch. 38, Section 1, and L. 1901, ch. 421, Section 1.

Section 134. Salaries and Compensation for Services. All surgical and medical officers of the hospital, except the surgeon-in-chief, shall render their services gratuitously. All salaries and compensation of officers and employees shall be fixed by the board of managers with the approval of the comptroller, president of the state board of charities and the governor, within the appropriation made therefor.

Formerly L. 1900, ch. 369, Section 5.

Section 135. Powers and Duties of Treasurer. The treasurer shall have the custody of all moneys, obligations and securities belonging to the hospital. He shall:

1. Open with some good and solvent bank conveniently near the hospital, to be selected with the approval of the comptroller of the state, an account in his name as such treasurer, for the deposit therein of all moneys, immediately upon receiving the same, and drawing from same only for the use of the hospital, in the manner prescribed in the by-laws, upon the written order of the steward specifying the object of the payment, approved by the surgeon-in-chief and subject to audit by the board of managers.

2. Keep a full and accurate account of all receipts and payments in the manner directed by the by-laws, and such other accounts as the managers shall prescribe.

3. Balance all accounts on his books annually on the last day of September and make a statement thereof and an abstract of the receipts and payments of the past year, and deliver the same within thirty days to the auditing committee of the managers who shall compare the same with the books and vouchers and verify the results upon further comparison with the books of the steward and certify to the correctness thereof to the managers at their next meeting.

4. Render statements quarterly in each year of his receipts and payments for the three months then next preceding to such auditing committee, who shall compare, verify and certify in regard to the same in the manner provided in the last preceding subdivision, and cause the same to be recorded in one of the books of the hospital.

5. Render a further account of the state of the books, and of the state of the funds and of the property in his hands, whenever required by the managers. Execute any necessary release and satisfaction of mortgage, judgment or other lien in favor of the hospital.

6. Such treasurer shall give an undertaking to the people of the state for the faithful performance of his duties, with such sureties and in such amount as the comptroller of the state shall approve.

Formerly L. 1900, ch. 369, Section 6.

Section 136. Official Oath. The surgeon-in-chief, treasurer, first assistant surgeon, assistant superintendent and steward, before entering upon their duties as such, shall take the constitutional oath of office and file the same in the office of the clerk of the county of New York.

Formerly L. 1900, ch. 369, Section 7, as amended by L. 1901, ch. 38, Section 2.

Section 137. Who May Receive Treatment. No patient shall be received except upon satisfactory proof made to the surgeon-in-chief by the next of kin, guardian, or a state, town or county officer under rules to be established by the board of managers showing that the patient is unable to pay for private treatment. Such proof shall be by affidavit. If there was an attending physician before the patient entered the hospital, it shall be accompanied by the certificate of such physician giving the previous history and condition of the patient.

Formerly L. 1900, ch. 369, Section 8.

Section 138. Donations. All donations made to the hospital may be received, retained and expended by the managers for the purposes for which they were given, or in such manner, if unaccompanied by conditions, as the board deems advisable.

Formerly L. 1900, ch. 369, Section 9.

Section 139. Managers' Report of Receipts. The managers shall make detailed report of all moneys received by them by virtue of this article, and the progress made in the erection of any buildings that may be hereafter from time to time erected, to the legislature, in January of each year, and also to the comptroller as often and in such manner as the comptroller shall or may from time to time require.

Formerly L. 1900, ch. 369, Section 10.

OHIO

Section 2073. A commission composed of the governor, auditor of state and three persons resident of the state, to be appointed by the governor, not more than . . . three members of which commission shall belong to one political party, is hereby established, and on behalf of the state is directed to select and purchase . . . a tract of land, in this state, . . . which tract shall be of such size as the commission deems advisable, and which shall be suitable for the location of a state institution, to be known and designated as the Ohio institution for the treatment and education of deformed and crippled children.

Section 2074. The commission shall adopt plans and specifications, prepare estimates of cost and construction, accept donations, let contracts for and cause to be constructed on such lands the necessary buildings and structures, at a total cost not to exceed that hereafter appropriated for that purpose, for the medical and surgical treatment and polytechnic and literary education of the crippled and deformed children of the state, under the age of eighteen years; for the purpose of purchasing the land herein referred to and maintaining the institution for the fiscal year ending June 30, 1918, there is hereby appropriated out of any money in the general revenue funds of the state, not otherwise appropriated, the sum of sixty thousand dollars; the purchase price of said land shall be paid by a warrant drawn on the auditor of state, signed by the chairman and secretary of said commission with the approval of the commission; and the further sum of thirty thousand dollars is appropriated out of such general revenue fund for the purpose of maintaining said institution for the fiscal year ending June 31, 1919.

Section 2075. The commission is also directed to purchase and provide all equipments, fixtures, appliances, and furnishings for such land, buildings, and structures and to make contracts, employ an architect and other agents and employees as it deems proper and necessary to carry into effect the provisions and purposes of this chapter.

Section 2076. The institution is founded for the purpose of caring for, treating and schooling the crippled and deformed children of the state, that they may be aided to live in physical comfort and be self-sustaining citizens rather than life-long charges upon the public. Children admissable to the institution shall be apportioned among the several counties of the state in proportion to population as shown by the next preceding federal census, but each county shall be entitled to at least two enrolments therein at all times.

Section 2077. The deeds of land purchased in pursuance of this chapter shall be executed in the name of the state and recorded in the records of deeds in the county wherein they are situated.

Section 2078. Before entering upon the duties of their office, the members of the commission appointed by the governor, shall take and subscribe an oath or affirmation faithfully to discharge all the duties required of them by this chapter.

Section 2079. The members of the commission shall be allowed their traveling and other necessary expenses incurred in the discharge of their duties. The accounts of expenditures, including expenses of the commission, when certified to by the president and secretary thereof, shall be audited and allowed by the auditor of the state.

Section 2080. The commission shall organize by electing a president and a secretary who shall be members of the commission. The commissioners may make such rules and regulations as they deem proper. A majority of the members shall constitute a quorum for the transaction of business.

Section 2081. When the buildings and structures under the provisions of this chapter are so far completed that in the opinion of the commission they properly may be used for the purpose of such institution, with the advice and consent of the senate, the governor shall appoint a board of trustees therefor to consist of six members, not more than three of whom shall be of the same political party, for one, two, three, four, five, and six years, respectively, from the date of their appointment. Thereafter, one member shall be appointed each year for a term of six years. Vacancies occurring in the board shall be filled in like manner.

Section 2082. The control and management of the institution shall be vested in the board of trustees in accordance with the general provisions of law relating to state benevolent institutions, which provisions, so far as applicable, shall apply to such board.

OREGON

AN ACT to provide medical and surgical treatment for sick and deformed indigent children, under the supervision of the medical department of the University of Oregon; and providing the manner and method of defraying the necessary expenses thereof.

Be it enacted by the People of the State of Oregon:

Section 1. That any county judge of the State of Oregon may on his own motion, or on complaint filed by any probation officer, school teacher, or school officer, relief officer, or physician authorized to practise his profession in the State of Oregon, alleging that the child named therein is under sixteen years of age and is afflicted with some deformity or suffering from some malady that can probably be remedied, and that the parents or other persons legally chargeable with the support of such child are unable to provide means for the surgical and medical treatment and hospital care of such child, shall appoint some physician who shall personally examine such child with respect to its deformation or malady. Such physician shall make a written report to the county judge giving such history of the case as will be likely to aid the surgical or medical treatment of such deformity or malady and describing the same, all in detail, and stating whether or not in his opinion the same can probably be remedied. Such report shall be made within such time as may be fixed by the county judge and upon blanks to be furnished as hereinafter provided. The county judge may also appoint some suitable person to investigate on the other matters charged in said complaint.

Section 2. Upon the filing of such report or reports, the county judge shall fix a day for said hearing upon the complaint and shall cause the parent or parents, guardian, other person or institution having the legal custody of said child to be served with a notice of hearing, and shall notify the district attorney, who shall appear and conduct the proceedings, and upon the hearing of such complaint, evidence may be introduced; and if the county judge finds that said child is suffering from a deformity or malady which can probably be remedied by surgical or medical treatment, and hospital care, and that the parent or parents, guardian, other person, or institution legally chargeable with his support is unable to pay the expenses thereof, the county judge, with the consent of the parent or parents, guardian, or other person or institution having the legal charge of the child, may enter an order directing that the child shall be taken or sent to the cot, bed, ward, or hospital under the direction of the medical college of the University of Oregon for free surgical and medical treatment and hospital care, and said child shall be provided with proper and sufficient clothing.

Section 3. It shall be the duty of the dean of the medical college of the state university, or other person designated by the authorities in direction of said medical college, upon said child being received, to provide for such child, if available, a cot, bed, or ward in the hospital, and such person shall also designate the clinic of the medical college to which the patient shall be assigned for treatment of the deformity or malady in each particular case.

The said medical college shall not be required to receive any child unless the physician or surgeon in charge of the department of said medical college in which such surgical or medical treatment is to be furnished shall be of the opinion that there is a reasonable probability that the child will be benefitted by the proposed medical or surgical treatment.

If the physician or surgeon of the clinic to which such child has been assigned for treatment declines to treat such child, he shall make a report, in duplicate, of his examination of such child, and state therein his reason or reasons for declining such treatment, and one of said duplicates shall be preserved in the records of said medical college and the other transmitted to the clerk of the court of said county where said order committing said child was entered.

When any patient has been admitted to the clinic for treatment the physician or surgeon in charge thereof shall proceed with all proper diligence to perform such operation and bestow such treatment upon such patient as in his judgment shall be proper, and such patient shall receive proper hospital care while therein.

Section 4. No compensation shall be charged by or allowed to the physician or surgeon who shall treat such patient.

Section 5. The superintendent of the hospital or other person designated by the authorities of the medical college of the university shall keep a correct account of the medicine, treatment, nursing, and maintenance furnished to said patient, and shall set forth therein the actual, reasonable, and necessary cost thereof, and shall make and file monthly with the county judge of the county from which the patient was committed, an itemized, sworn statement, as far as possible, of the expense so incurred at said hospital other than the free surgical and medical treatment, as hereinbefore provided, and the said statement shall be forwarded to the county judge of the county from which the patient was committed.

Section 6. The county judge shall present the said statement to the board of county commissioners which, upon being satisfied that the same is correct and reasonable, shall approve the same, and shall direct that warrants be drawn by the county clerk upon the county treasurer for the amount of such bills as are allowed from time to time, and the said warrants as drawn by the county clerk [shall be transmitted] to the treasurer of the State University of Oregon and the same shall be placed by him to the credit of the university funds which are set aside for the support of the cot or bed, or ward in the hospital under the direction of the medical college of the University of Oregon, and the county treasurer shall pay said warrants out of the funds collected for the relief of the poor of the county.

Section 7. The county judge may, in his discretion, appoint some person to accompany the child from the place where he may be to the medical college of the State University of Oregon, or to accompany the said child from the said medical college to such place as may be designated by the county judge, the parent or

parents, guardians or persons having legal custody of said child consenting.

Any person appointed by the county judge to accompany said child to or from the medical college, or to make an investigation and report of any of the questions involved in the complaint other than the physician making examination, shall receive the sum of Three Dollars per day for the time actually spent in making such investigation (except in cases where the person appointed by the county judge is a parent or a relative or where the officer appointed therefor receives a fixed salary or compensation, in which case there shall be no compensation) and his actual necessary expenses incurred in making such investigation or trip. The physician appointed by the court to make the examination and report shall, if he so demand, be paid not exceeding the sum of Five Dollars for each and every examination and report so made, and his actual necessary expenses incurred in making such investigation, in conformity to the requirements of this Act. The person making claim to such compensation shall present to the county judge an itemized sworn statement thereof, and when such claim for compensation has been approved by the county judge, the same shall be filed and shall be allowed by the board of county commissioners and paid out of the funds of the county collected for the relief of the poor.

Section 8. The medical college of the university may in the discretion of the superintendent or other person designated by the authorities in control thereof, pay the actual, reasonable necessary expenses of returning the said patient to his home, and pay the attendant not to exceed Three Dollars per day for the time thus necessarily employed, unless said attendant be a parent or other relative or be an officer or employee receiving other compensation, and his actual, reasonable, and necessary expenses incurred in accompanying such patient to his home, and such per diem and expenses shall be itemized and verified, and presented to and allowed by the board of county commissioners of the county from which the patient was committed, in connection with the bills for hospital maintenance, as hereinbefore provided.

Section 9. The faculty of the medical college of the university shall immediately on the taking effect of this Act prepare blank or blanks containing such questions and requiring such information as may in its judgment be necessary and proper to be obtained by the physician who examines the patient under order of court; and a supply of such blanks shall be sent to the county judge of each county of the State of Oregon; and the physician making such examination shall make his report to the county judge in duplicate on said blanks, answering the questions contained therein, and setting forth the information required thereby, and one of said duplicate reports shall be sent to the medical college of the University of Oregon with the patient together with a certified copy of the order of the county judge.

The dean of the college of medicine of the University of Oregon shall determine the number of such blanks to be printed and distributed to the county judges of the State of Oregon and the bills for the printing of the same shall be audited, allowed, and paid in the same manner as the printing bills of the medical college of the University of Oregon.

Section 10. The Board of Control of the state institutions of Oregon may in its discretion send any inmate of any of said institutions, or any person committed or applying for admission thereto, to the medical college of the State University of Oregon for treatment and care as provided in this Act without securing an order of court as provided in other cases, and the said patient so sent to the medical college of the state university shall be accompanied by a report and history of the case made by the physician in charge of the institution to which said patient has been committed, or to which application has been made for his admission, containing a history of the case and information required by said blanks, and the Board of Control shall pay the hospital expenses of such patient and the expenses of transporting such patient to and from the hospital out of any funds appropriated for the use of the institution from which such patient has been sent, and may, when necessary, send an attendant with such patient, and pay his traveling expenses in like manner. The institution is to be reimbursed for such expenses as provided by law.

Section 11. It is expressly provided that no child under the terms of this Act shall be treated for any ailment except such as is described by the order of the court, unless permission for such treatment is granted by the parents or guardians; and it is also expressly forbidden that any child shall be used for the purpose of experimentation.

Section 12. Upon the written request, made by the parent or parents, guardian, or other person or institution having the legal custody of any such child, and filed with the county judge at the time of the hearing mentioned in Section 2 of this Act, to the effect that such parent or parents, guardian, or other person or institution having the legal custody of any such child, desires such child taken or sent to a designated hospital or medical college of recognized standing or character or to any cot, bed or ward connected therewith, not under the direction or supervision of the medical college of the University of Oregon, said judge may make and enter an order directing that such child be taken or sent to such designated institution for free surgical and medical treatment and hospital care, and to be provided by it with proper and sufficient clothing. The reception by such institution of such child as a patient, pursuant to such order, shall be taken and considered to be an acceptance on its part of all the provisions of this Act, except as hereinafter provided, which relate or in any wise apply to the medical college of the University of Oregon, in cases where any child is taken or sent pursuant thereto; and such institution shall then be held and bound to furnish such child with all proper and requisite medical or surgical care and attention without compensation, and to keep and observe in every manner and respect all such requirements and provisions of this Act, as long as such child remains in such institution as such patient.

Section 13. When any child, pursuant to the provisions of Section 12 of this Act, may become a patient at any institution not affiliated with the medical department of the University of Oregon, the superintendent or other person in charge thereof shall perform all duties and requirements set forth in Section 5 of this Act; and all warrants in payment of any bills or accounts therein mentioned shall be made payable to such institution.

[*General Laws of Oregon, 1917; Chapter 145.* Approved by the Governor, February 15, 1917. Filed in the office of the Secretary of State, February 16, 1917.]

WISCONSIN

Section 573-aa. Competent Cripples or Deformed. In addition to the classes of children now received at the state public school for neglected or dependent children at Sparta, pursuant to existing laws, there shall also be received as pupils in the said school, any children under fourteen years of age, residents of this state, who are crippled or deformed in body, or who are suffering from disease through which they are likely to become crippled or deformed, provided their bodily ailments or diseases are curable by surgical operation or hospital treatment at the school with facilities, appliances, material, equipment and professional skill and assistants provided therefor, subject only to the limitations contained in the next section.

2. The board of control shall engage and fix the salaries of additional physicians, surgeons, nurses, teachers, and other employees necessary to carry out the provisions of this section, and shall equip such

school with the necessary appliances, material, equipment and facilities therefor.

3. The expense of treating, educating and maintaining any child in said school under the provisions of this section shall be borne by the parent, parents, or guardian of such child, if not indigent, and the amount thereof shall be determined by the board, but no child shall be denied admission to such school under the provisions of this section for the reason that such child or its parents or guardian are unable to pay for treatment, education and maintenance therein.

Section 573-ab. Existing Laws Applied to Crippled Children. All existing provisions of law for the commitment, care, disposition, control, and discharge of the inmates of said school, and all restrictions upon their admission, except the three years' age limitation, and except as herein provided, shall apply to such crippled or deformed children.

GENEVA SUPPLEMENT:
THE FIRST INTERNATIONAL CONFERENCE
PROCEEDINGS AND RESULTS

THE FIRST INTERNATIONAL CONFERENCE.

PROCEEDINGS AND RESULTS.

A T the end of July a body of more than fifty experts, drawn from a dozen countries, assembled at Geneva and spent four days in exploring a new avenue of work. We live in a world of national States. Every one of us finds himself born into membership of some political aggregate, in contact with other units of like kind, but cut off from them by barriers of geography and history and often of language. Each of these States regards it as part of its duty to concern itself with its children, to watch over their health, educate their minds and equip them for life. The child, therefore, is set in its nationalist environment practically from birth. The question posed at Geneva was whether a child not physically normal was, by the very fact of his disability, so far removed from his local setting as to become an international figure, or whether, on the contrary, he remained so rooted in his local conditions that international co-operation must be limited to the exchange of ideas in matters of therapeutic technique. To this question the Conference gave a decisive answer. It was a gathering of orthopædic surgeons and of social workers, and it speedily satisfied itself that the workers could exchange ideas as profitably as the surgeons. All were engaged in the same task of instructing and stimulating public opinion. All were confronted by the same difficulties, for the forces of inertia and prejudice operate identically everywhere, and mutual encouragement was evidently worth a great deal to them. As Dr. Hans Würtz of the German delegation put it, the figure of the cripple is the same object of aversion and mockery and contempt in the whole literary tradition of Europe from Thersites to Rigoletto; and, what is even more important, the exceptions who successfully defied adverse circumstances, all the long line of noble figures from Tyrtaeus to Michael Dowling, present a line of figures equally international. Moreover, in modern times a third force which has never taken the least account of national boundaries has become potently operative. The cripple need no longer look for inspiration only to the examples of men and women who have risen superior to their disabilities. A new hope has come to him from the advances of medical science which can reduce his deformity and even abolish it altogether. But if modern medicine is to reveal its full capa-

24

cities it must be given its fair chance, thanks to the action of vigorous and enlightened opinion. By this track, too, then, the Conference was led to realize the need for united effort; for if, on the one hand, opinion is hard to move and is even hostile to progress—one American speaker had come across parents who objected to the treatment of spine disease in children because a hunchback brought good luck—it is, on the other hand, extremely sensitive for its reputation. No nation cares to be despised as retrograde. Every nation aspires to the honour of setting a good example. It is significant that a most brilliant paper, distinguished even at a conference of experts, by its sympathetic insight into the essence of the problem, was contributed by Dr. Bartos, of Prague—the representative of a young country eager to make itself a name among the nations. It is equally significant that the Czecho-Slovak delegation referred to the example set by Italy, a state whose absence from this meeting is alone sufficient reason for the assembly of a future conference. There is, in fact, abundant evidence that as the Conference proceeded its members found their energies quickened and their horizons broadened. Naturally, therefore, it set itself to make its new co-operation permanent. The international committee appointed to draw up the resolutions has been kept in being and strengthened by the addition of representative men—Sir Robert Jones and Professor Biesalski conspicuous among them—who could not be present at Geneva, and arrangements are already in train for a second conference to be held in 1931.

NEGATIVE LESSONS.

The Conference was equally instructive in its revelation of the limits of internationalism. Time after time it happened that a speaker would describe some form of organization, point to its successful working and conclude that it satisfied the requirements of sound orthopædic theory, only to find that equally good results were chronicled and the opposite conclusion drawn from an account of some quite different principle by a speaker from some other country. Few of those present can have noticed beforehand how far the conditions under which they worked were determined not by the actual evils to be remedied, but by the general social conditions of their respective communities. It became clear, for example, that it was exceedingly difficult to lay down any precise definition of the functions to be discharged by public authorities, central and local, on the one hand, and by voluntary agencies on the other. The differing political structure of the two countries made it inevitable that the part played by the central government should be preponderant in Germany and negligible in the United States. The question thus presented itself how far the systems of which social workers availed themselves were really suitable to their special requirements, and how far they had been adopted out of mere force of habit. A careful paper by Miss Shelley Barker approached from this standpoint the distinction observed in England between the functions of official and voluntary agencies, and separated the requirements of orthopædic theory from those of English administrative custom. A discussion upon this paper would have been of exceptional value.

And here another negative lesson of the Conference requires to be noted. The problem of international co-operation arose in connection not only with its subject but with its proceedings. Now that international conferences have become a part of the world's routine, it would be no bad thing if their technique were more thoroughly worked out and a manual of procedure made available for the organizers of conferences on special subjects. The matter is worth the attention of the Paris Committee on Intellectual Co-operation. Profitable though the Geneva Conference was, its success would have been greater had more effective steps been taken in advance to overcome the barrier of language. In the first place, it was not realized that every paper would have to be given in three languages—English, French and German. As a result the Conference, in spite of its long hours— it opened daily at 9 a.m., and had not always finished at midnight— could barely get through its agenda and had no time whatever for discussion. In the second place, the work of interpretation requires something more than mere knowledge of tongues for its adequate performance. A grip of the subject in hand is essential if the thought of a speaker is to be properly conveyed. The Conference was fortunate in its French interpreter, who swiftly developed an enthusiasm for a subject of which he had hitherto known nothing, but the difficulties of translation into and out of German proved greater and were not overcome until the Conference was nearing its end.

The Question of Emphasis.

This barrier of language was reinforced by a barrier of thought. It became apparent as the Conference developed that its members were approaching the problem of the crippled child from varying standpoints. Four points of view may be distinguished. The Anglo-American papers, while differing markedly in matters of detail, agreed in directly attacking the question of arousing public opinion. Their common attitude is sufficiently indicated by

Mr. Allen's presidential address, which we are privileged to print elsewhere in this number, with its clear emphasis on social considerations. The Swiss contributions represent an opposite point of view. Save for one reference to the society "Pro Juventute," public opinion was not noticed. It seemed to be taken as a matter of course that Switzerland was a country whose peculiar climate gave unique facilities for healing disease. But since these facilities had not yet been thoroughly explored, the problem for Switzerland was a problem of method. Accordingly, the Swiss papers were concerned with technical matters. It would appear that Swiss institutions attach great value to freedom in questions of method, and that the co-ordinated orthopædic policy which, in England, has been the foundation of the attack on crippling disease is not congenial to Swiss thought.

A third line of approach is presented by the German contributions. In them the Government takes the place which in Britain and America is occupied by the public. The standpoint is well brought out by the different tone adopted by German and by Austrian speakers. The Germans are proud and rightly proud of their Cripples Law. No State, as they are well aware, has so definitely recognized the cripple's right to full civic status. The law, they feel, provides the whole framework within which practical policy is shaped, and the individual is concerned to work out details according to his special aptitudes. It would appear that every German institution is not only very conscious of its own specific contribution to the working out of the national scheme, but is concerned to make that contribution as specific as may be. It is not an accident that the most highly specialized paper at the Conference, a discussion of the methods to be employed in the education not merely of cripples but of cripples who were bedridden, came from a member of the German delegation, Dr. Stärke, of Cologne.

In striking contrast with his German colleague, Dr. Siegfried Braun, of Vienna, dwelt on the absence in his country of a legislative framework. The Austrian law, such as it is, dates, he explained, from 1863 and is itself only a revision of an ordinance of Maria Theresa. Dr. Braun evidently felt his own work hampered by the lack of an authoritative national policy, and again it is not an accident that he is the delegate who proposes to continue the work of the Conference by organizing an international intelligence service. Such a service will, of course, prove of value to all workers. But in Austria it will do more; it will be a means of rousing the Government to a sense of its shortcomings.

Yet a further point of view was put forward by the representatives of Czecho-Slovakia. Their tendency was to throw all possible emphasis on their institutions. Magnificent work was done in them but was insufficiently appreciated. If only the medical and educational authorities were properly acquainted with them, they would send their cases along. So strong was this feeling that Dr. Frejka wished to incorporate in the Conference resolutions a recommendation that orthopædics should form part of the normal medical course. The contrast with America, where this work of propaganda is so largely undertaken by social workers, is very instructive.

It will be apparent that the significance of these various attitudes and the precise international value of each could only be brought out by discussion, and discussion, in the time available, was impossible. It is imperative that this difficulty should be overcome at future conferences, and an examination of the papers delivered suggests a means of handling it. Broadly speaking, they fall into two main groups—papers of method and papers of policy. The papers of method were all of a technical character. Thus, Dr. Leroy Lowman, of California, described, with the aid of a cinematograph, a therapeutic pool in which orthopædic exercises were performed under water; Dr. Nicod, of Switzerland, supplied details of a treatment of tuberculous children; and Herr Fritz Koehler, of Leipzig, gave an account of some very ingenious little machines which combined muscular exercise with the solution of some small problem. All these papers were much appreciated both by orthopædists interested in one another's work and by social workers anxious to be acquainted with the latest achievements of curative medicine. But none of them were of a character to provoke discussion. A question or two might be put, but could be put just as well privately at a social gathering as publicly in full conference. There is, indeed, no reason for papers of this group to be read at all. It is, of course, desirable for the Conference to be acquainted with recent original work, but the accounts could quite well be printed beforehand and distributed to delegates for their information. The facts would be better digested and valuable time saved.

The position in the case of papers on policy is very different. Such issues as centralized and decentralized treatment or the relation of the doctor to the teacher require to be argued. There are two methods of argument. The first is to arrange a series of short papers, all on the same subject but presenting different points of view, to be read consecutively at the same session. The second is for one paper to be prepared which should definitely raise controversial issues and should be followed by a discussion. The Conference actually adopted the first method, though this was not the intention of its promoters. The second deserves, and will doubtless obtain, a thorough trial in 1931.

THE PROGRAMME.

The agenda of the Conference grouped itself under the four main heads of discovery, treatment, education and prevention. It was found that these issues tended to run into one another, that treatment depended on the quickness or slowness of discovery, that education was inseparable from treatment, that prevention completed the circle by its dependence on effective discovery, and that the whole problem of the crippled child was linked up with his ultimate status in society and therefore with the attitude of society towards him. To experts, each engaged in dealing with some specific branch of work, this revelation of the ultimate unity of the whole problem and of its connection with general concepts of social policy was particularly illuminating. This was, they felt, the international outlook, and nothing but an international conference could have enabled them to achieve it, and it was under this impulse that they passed the fifth resolution which commends the crippled child to the particular notice of the League of Nations. In detail the contributions resolved themselves into arguments for or against opposite policies—in discovery, the use of public or private agencies; in treatment, the adoption of centralized or decentralized methods; in education, the alternative of special classes or special schools. About prevention there was no parallel diversity of thought. It was agreed on all hands that much crippling disease could be prevented altogether if only public opinion were sufficiently zealous.

DISCOVERY.

Discovery is the keystone of the orthopædic arch, not merely in the obvious sense that if a child is not discovered he cannot be treated at all—though even this is not as obvious as it sounds in regions where parental superstition keeps the "lucky hunchback" hidden—but in the sense that the whole course of the disease turns on the promptitude with which it is discovered. Everywhere the orthopædists agree that they do not get their cases early enough. "The number of children attending hospital," observes a British delegate, Miss Shelley Barker, "who on their first visit are suffering from some already established deformity, is an index of the incompleteness of our preventive methods." Dr. Frejka, of Czecho-Slovakia, gives an admirable illustration of this general statement. After pointing out that lateral curvature of the spine is in 90 per cent. of cases due to rickets, he observes that if we wish to prevent curvature

"We must not only treat rickets as a general malady, but must also face the orthopædic part of the problem and must carry out such treatment as we know will prevent lateral curvature. And here you see the problem. As long as physicians who generally treat rickets are not instructed in orthopædics we cannot prevent spinal deformity."

But on whom does the onus of discovery rest? Dr. Frejka places the chief responsibility on the general practitioner; Miss Barker, as the context of the passage quoted shows, is thinking of the effective combination of public and private agencies. The practice of different States varies with the national temperament. In some countries reliance is principally placed on the authority of a Government official, in others on the zeal of a social worker. England, as is her habit, has sought a middle way. Effective discovery, explained Dr. Norman Carver, in one of the first papers read to the Conference, depends on the willing co-operation of no fewer than seven agencies—the midwife, the mother, the health visitor or infant welfare worker, the general practitioner, the general hospital, the school medical officer and the tuberculosis officer. It may seem surprising that any patient should escape this net, but the parental agency in particular is by no means trustworthy. The American system resembles the British in theory rather than in practice. It is worth noting that the birth registration officer tends to replace the midwife; several States of the Union have enacted that physical deformities must be reported along with the birth. But what particularly distinguishes the American system is the extraordinary prominence given to private enterprise. Here again we observe the adjustment of orthopædic methods to the general habit of the national life.

Since the war and as a consequence of the country's exuberant prosperity, a wave of social good-feeling has swept over the United States. The American people are grouping themselves into clubs, some of them with names surprising even to English ears familiar with Buffaloes and Rechabites, all aiming at the alleviation or removal of material misery. It is interesting to observe how even a social problem is presented in economic terms: "Our one big job to start with," observes Mr. Williamson, of Kentucky, "was, as we say in America, to sell the problem of the crippled child to

the public," and Dr. Clark, of California, congratulates himself that
" experience has shown that the crippled child is probably the
most appealing of all the charities for which public subscriptions
are taken." Orthopædics, indubitably a paying proposition, has
known how to avail itself of this social zeal. There is ample room
for its exercise. Though Europeans are well aware that American
civilization, the result of successive waves of recent immigration,
is naturally much less uniform than their own, which has incorporated no fresh racial elements since the tenth century, they
must needs be surprised by such a declaration as this from Miss
Marian Williamson, of Kentucky, at the second session of this
Conference :—

> " The official files carry literally hundreds of records of unfortunate
> cripples whose parents refuse outright to allow the helpless little creatures
> to be even examined at the clinic. This is particularly true of congenital
> deformities. The usual answer to the worker's plea that the child be
> taken to a clinic is, ' The Lord sent him into the world like he is, and we
> ain't gonna have nothing done to him.' Moreover, there exists in the
> minds of a large part of the populace a mental terror of hospitals or any-
> thing in the nature of a surgical operation. Frequently it has been my
> experience to spend hours trying to convince a parent of the necessity of
> committing a child to the hospital, only to have him appear the next day
> and take the child home with the dogged statement, ' I ain't gonna have
> no cuttin' done on him.' "

We quote this remarkable passage in no pharisaical spirit, but
rather as an example of work which requires to be done on this
side of the Atlantic as well as on the other. There is ignorance,
though doubtless less of it, in Western Europe as in America, the
difference being that in the United States it is visible and even
blatant, whereas with us it tends to lurk in the deepest recesses
of slumdom, so that even social workers may overlook it. In
America the very magnitude of the problem makes the workers
resolute to overlook nothing, and has spurred them to undertake
comprehensive social surveys of a type which in the Old World
would be regarded as emphatically the Government's job. The
results are certainly remarkable. Dr. W. A. Clark reports a survey
undertaken in his own town of Pasadena by the local Rotarians
six years ago. Pasadena is a place of some 90,000 inhabitants,
that is to say, an organized social centre with its proper equipment
of public and private medical agencies. Yet the survey revealed
thirty-three little cripples previously unrecorded. It would be
interesting if we could compare the result of a similar undertaking
in an English town of the same population.

The papers contributed by the American delegation contain

example after example of the really amazing results accomplished by this organized social zeal. Space permits us only a single quotation, from a paper by Miss Margaret Lison, of Madison, Wisconsin :—

"One of the most successful clinics we have ever had was held in a county when much of the rural section was settled by fugitives from justice. . . . . Heretofore these people had always been very non-co-operative with any public health movement, it being considered almost dangerous for a stranger to enter some of that territory. Fortunately, in visiting their houses I was accompanied by the County Superintendent of Schools, a young woman who had managed to win the confidence and respect of these people. They received us kindly and listened to our story. We promised that if they came to the clinic, no one would force them later to send their child away to a hospital unless they themselves wished the child to have treatment. Sixty cases were invited to come. They were to furnish their own transportation. On the day of the clinic only one case failed to appear."

Even in the most highly organized Old-World community there are elements in the population which somehow elude Government control. Only private zeal can trace them out and enlist their sympathy, and American experience is eloquent of what it can accomplish.

Prejudice must, of course, be met halfway, and Miss Lison gives one tip, the value of which has already been appreciated by English workers. The name hospital has extraordinary terrors for the ignorant, whereas the name clinic is alarming only in so far as it is unfamiliar. It should therefore be stressed. Moreover, if arrangements can be made for holding the clinic in the school building, an expedient often adopted in America, it tends to get accepted as a part of the normal educational routine.

Miss Lison goes on to examine a question of the liveliest interest to all unofficial workers—the enlistment of public sympathy. She recommends close relationship with the local Press, and states that a good "story" is welcomed.

In Europe the problem is more difficult. It is more closely settled and its internal communications are good, with the result that local papers tend to disappear and to be replaced by papers published in the capital and a few large towns, whose columns have no room for matter which their news editors regard as of merely parochial interest. Publicity, itself a very important instrument of discovery, is greatly needed by the orthopædic movement in the Old World. In this connection a valuable hint was dropped by a Dutch delegate, Dr. Fagel, of Utrecht. Until quite recently voluntary agencies in Holland operated for the most part locally and independently. Within their range and according to their means they did admirable work, but there was no one to call attention to the gaps in their operations or to co-ordinate their activities with a view to framing an orthopædic policy covering the whole country and backed by the authority of the State. Recently, however, a Central Union has been formed to focus opinion and consolidate effort. It has been fortunate enough to win the patronage and active help of the Queen Mother, and has so far influenced opinion that it is hopeful of stirring the Government to effective legislation. In Holland, then, the progress of orthopædics has received more publicity than it has gained in most countries of Western Europe. But even in Holland the problem of arousing and maintaining public interest has not been solved, and as its international interest is obvious it might very profitably be discussed at the next conference.

TREATMENT.

The papers on treatment present an interesting parallel with those on discovery. In the latter group the issue lay between official and voluntary agencies, in the former between centralized and decentralized institutions. It is really one and the same issue viewed from different aspects. A centralized institution is generally controlled or supported by public authority, central or local, whereas decentralized methods involve appeal to voluntary workers. There is really no golden rule governing the choice of one system or the other.

"The best method in any one country (writes Dr. Carver) is the method which is most in harmony with the practical or social genius of that country. States with a highly centralized system of government will, if they deal with crippled children at all, do so naturally by means of their State machinery. States in which much public work is left to private enterprise will leave the care of the unfit largely to voluntary bodies."

Much of the material laid before the Conference amounted to a detailed commentary on this wise doctrine, which was endorsed, almost in so many words, by Dr. Rugh, of Philadelphia, with reference to the very various conditions of the States of the American Union. But the further point was brought out that the method adopted results from the physical as well as from the social characteristics of the country concerned.

The English genius has asserted itself characteristically enough in the system operated in the main by voluntary agencies with the co-operation of the public authorities. The sun of the system is

the central orthopædic hospital. Dependent upon it and sur-
rounding it at varying distances are the clinics. They are true
planets, for the staffs are mobile and travel from clinic to clinic,
opening it weekly or fortnightly on days suited to the convenience
of each locality. The clinics, Dr. Carver explains in his descriptive
account of the scheme,

> " are held in market towns in the area, as a rule on market day, so that
> patients from outlying villages can come into the town in the market
> 'buses and carriers' carts. These out-patient departments may be 30 or
> 40 miles from the central hospital, and children could not possibly be
> brought regularly from their homes to the hospital for treatment; so the
> surgeon and his assistant travel to the local centres close to the patients'
> homes. For instance, when the surgeon visits the out-patient depart-
> ment at a market town, he may see forty or fifty patients from that town
> or from the many small villages around. It is easy to realize how much
> more difficult it would have been—indeed utterly impossible—to get all
> those patients to come to the central orthopædic hospital at least
> 30 miles from their homes, involving a tedious railway journey with
> possibly one or more changes, the train service being very limited."

Dr. Carver points out one great advantage of this system if
properly worked. It overcomes one of the most heartrending
defects of orthopædic treatment—the presence in central hospitals,
often for long periods, of children who, had their cases been com-
petently dealt with earlier, would never have been there at all.
Miss Barker points out that the converse aspect of the system is
equally beneficial.

> " The work of the clinic shortens very considerably the stay in residence
> of hospital patients. The surgeon who feels that, after leaving hospital,
> his patient is going back to an unorganized area out of touch with appro-
> priate facilities is bound to keep that patient under his care in hospital for
> many weeks in order to minimize the risk of possible relapse. If, on the
> other hand, the patient through good local organization can still remain
> under direct medical supervision, he may safely return home."

It would be superfluous to point out that the existence of a
clinic accelerates the date of a patient's transfer from a central
hospital to a convalescent home, were it not that the abundance
of such homes in Europe, and particularly in England, is specially
noted by one of the American experts, Mrs. Solenberger. Their
rarity in the United States is due to the reluctance of American
sentiment to interrupt family life, a feature of social thought which
markedly affects the American attitude towards the problem of the
cripple's education. In other respects the American system is
fairly parallel to that of England, but a difficulty has arisen in
regard to the central hospital. Miss Marian Williamson, of
Kentucky, states the ideal requirement in good round terms:—

"The State, primarily, is responsible for the child's treatment. This involves his examination by a competent orthopædic surgeon, such surgical treatment as may be necessary, and hospitalization, both acute and convalescent. All this, we believe, should be in the hands of trained experts with the expense met by the State. Any attempt by volunteer agencies to invade this strictly professional field probably would result only in confusion and in the unnecessary duplication of effort and increase in expense. This is the State's specific and distinct field of operation."

This sweeping doctrine, against which the whole magnificent English tradition of voluntary hospitals rises up in emphatic protest, is challenged in America itself on very remarkable grounds. Dr. Rugh, of Pennsylvania, alludes to "the contaminating and deleterious effects of politics and politicians, it being almost impossible to carry on without some interference on the part of unscrupulous individuals." Dr. Clark, of California, notes that in his State orthopædic legislation was actually opposed by some orthopædic surgeons for fear that it might lead to the increase of State institutions; and Dr. Campbell, of Tennessee, reports that "in America the political situation may entirely change the staff of an institution." The moral of these facts is all-important. They are conclusive evidence of the need for a public opinion truly well informed. If opinion across the Atlantic had been entirely ignorant it would not have insisted upon the State establishment of hospitals; if it were properly instructed it would not allow them to become the playthings of party.

These political suspicions inclined the American members of the Conference to favour the maximum of decentralization, and consequently to lay stress upon the incidental advantages it is found to possess.

"The entire effort" observes Dr. Rugh, "is a wonderfully potent factor in educating the public towards civic responsibility and improvement."

And again :—

"The knowledge on the part of the local public that a large proportion of its special work can be done in its own institutions develops a feeling of pride which adds greatly to the building-up of that community of interest so essential to the full and highest development of every locality."

The British tradition of voluntarily supported hospitals makes this doctrine something of a truism to English readers. But it is worth careful attention in Teutonic countries where the tendency is to develop to their maximum a limited number of central institutions admirably equipped and staffed by the ablest experts in the country.

This general Anglo-American scheme of central institutions,

each surrounded by its network of itinerant clinics, depends for its functioning on certain material conditions. England is a small and closely-populated country. It can thus easily accommodate a number of orthopædic hospitals at no great distance from one another which, when properly equipped with their attendant clinics, bring effective treatment within the reach of almost the whole population. In America the distances are immensely greater and the distribution of the people far less compact. But America is the land of the universal motor, and the army of Rotarian and other social workers, with their abundant zeal and their fleets of fast cars, makes it possible for the English system to work in the ampler transatlantic setting. Its successful operation demands, however, a very considerable number of specialized hospitals, for there are limits to the distance to which even an American car with its willing driver can transport a patient in a day. This need has been effectively met, the general anxiety to anticipate the politicians having led the social organization known as the Shrine to devote its ample resources to the endowment and equipment of institutions. Orthopædically speaking, therefore, America is an enlarged and somewhat modified England. Clearly, however, these arrangements are inapplicable to a country with greater distances, a small population, relatively undeveloped communications and limited funds. Sweden is such a country, and the quiet efficiency of Swedish life was illustrated by the paper—one of the three or four outstanding contributions to the Conference—presented by the Swedish delegate, Dr. Patrik Haglund. Sweden owes her organization to a national catastrophe, which the courage of her people effectually surmounted. In 1911 there broke out

" the severest epidemic of acute infantile paralysis which has ever befallen a small country. In the course of a few years 14,000 cases were reported, and the large invalidity which the disease far too frequently left behind became, especially in certain parts of the country, so very conspicuous that it was obvious to everybody, both private individuals and the authorities, that something would have to be done in order to provide special care and nursing for the victims of the disease. . . . Large provisional institutions for patients suffering from infantile paralysis were accordingly opened."

At this stage another set of considerations came into play. As a result of the general revision and modernization of Swedish invalidity and poor law legislation which dates back to the general Strike of 1909, it was discovered that economic incapacity was often the result of disabilities which orthopædics could remedy. Thus, while necessity was forcing the erection of institutions for the treatment of children, the public conscience was demanding the treatment of adults. Accordingly, when the force of the infantile epidemic began to abate, Sweden equipped herself with orthopædic hospitals for the treatment of cripples of all ages. This policy developed naturally out of Swedish conditions, but Dr. Haglund is at pains to insist that it is socially sound in that it acquaints the crippled child with the problems which he will have to face and keep him in touch with the general life of the community. As worked out it has equipped Sweden with three specialized orthopædic hospitals in the relatively populous south, and is now constructing a fourth to serve the needs of the sparsely-people Northland. Associated with these institutions, but not dependent upon them, are orthopædic wards in general hospitals throughout the country. The whole system is thus centralized and the question thus presents itself, What of the out-patients? Even though, as a consequence of the infantile epidemic, Sweden finds herself in possession of an exceptionally large number of orthopædic beds, there must needs be a large number of cripples who should not be completely hospitalized but who cannot be given the treatment they require unless they are accommodated within reach of the appropriate centres. Sweden has solved this problem by availing herself of the voluntary agencies which she found established. Under official guidance they have abandoned in part the specialized work on which they had previously been engaged, and turned themselves into something approaching convalescent homes of the English type.

> "The institutions are owned by private associations and run by the boards of these associations. But the running is financed almost entirely by contributions from the State, the country and the parishes, and the magnitude of these contributions is estimated according to the actual cost which has been found to be approximately equally large at all State-aided cripples' institutions. By this arrangement private initiative for improvement, amelioration and reform gets a freer hand than in State institutions, and other means collected by private associations can be employed in a freer manner for the improvement and development of the institutions."

Dr. Haglund is at pains to point out that the development of the system is by no means complete, and a good part of his paper is taken up with plans for the future, more especially in connection with the establishment of orthopædic centres in university towns, but it is clear that Sweden has found a thoroughly effective means of associating private enthusiasm with the system of official centralization imposed upon her by her circumstances.

On the whole it would appear that the general tendency in continental Europe is towards centralization. It is certainly remarkable to find a centralizing policy at work in Belgium. Here is a country even more compact and even more closely populated than England herself. On the face of it the conditions are peculiarly favourable to the adoption of the English system of mobile clinics. But it would appear from Dr. M. A. Dourlet's paper that in Belgium the wheel has come full circle. When distances are small, communications good and travel cheap, it is more convenient for the patient to come to the hospital than for the hospital to be brought to the patient. The examples of Sweden and Belgium are a clear warning against any assumption that the decentralized Anglo-American system is essential to sound orthopædic practice. We are back again at Dr. Carver's dictum, and must realize that experience prescribes no particular method, but that on the contrary the choice of method is inspired by the habits and circumstances of each particular State, and that that method will serve best which the national genius is most likely to operate with intelligence and zeal.

EDUCATION.

The diversity of views which manifested itself in regard to educational policy may be summed up in a phrase. Is the ideal a special school or a special class in an ordinary school? Of course there is common ground between the parties. Clearly a child whose disability is slight enough to permit his participation in a great many of the ordinary activities of life requires but little special consideration, and can be taught with other children provided that arrangements are made for his treatment. Clearly, too, the child terribly crippled is necessarily cut off from his fellows and cannot really be taught at all unless he is an inmate of an institution which combines education with treatment. Even in regard to the mass of cases between these two extremes there is a certain measure of agreement, for the advocates of segregation aim at effecting such a cure as will enable the patient to return to the society of his fellows before the expiry of the school period. Nevertheless, there is a real problem. Where is education to throw the emphasis of the crippled child's thought? Is his mind to be induced, by the circumstances of his educational environment, to dwell on the qualities which he has in common with normal children or on the disabilities which set him apart? The answer differs according to the social ideal aimed at, and in this matter America and Germany stand at opposite extremes. American life is standardized to a degree unknown in Europe. There is an

American type, transcending all occupational differences, a type whose outstanding qualities are energy and independence, and to this type the American cripple endeavours to conform. An American delegate, Dr. Burt Chollett, told the Conference an illuminating story of a cripple with whom he once shared a room in a crowded hotel, and to whom he naturally offered some slight assistance :—

> " He resented these courtesies. It was then I discovered that he had his own way of doing things and did not want my help. What was the reason for this? First . . . he had evolved his own system for getting things done, and my help was really a hindrance. Second, and perhaps more important, he was independent and he wanted me to know it. After that we succeeded splendidly."

German life, on the contrary, is organized hierarchically according to occupation. In no other country is a man's profession used as his title, and such typical German music-hall humour as two bedraggled women addressing one another as " Mrs. Charlady " and " Mrs. Senior-gutterwasher " is hardly intelligible to Anglo-Saxons. But in this stratified society the cripple takes his own rank by virtue of his disability. Characteristically enough, Herr Hans Würtz expressed his hope that the general status of cripples would be raised by the " Cripples' Self-Help League." To an American the very title of this body must almost amount to a contradiction in terms.

These diverse social conceptions do not merely go far to determine the original attitude of mind towards segregation, but even colour the arguments by which it is advocated. Thus, Dr. Chollett declares that the educational aim is to eliminate " the attitude of inferiority so apparent in competition with normals," and contends that this aim can best be realized " in an institution where, by segregation, a group of individuals similarly handicapped are in competition with one another." Here, then, segregation is advocated as tending to produce a good average man. On the other hand, Pastor Klütz lays it down that segregation is the only way to enable the cripple to stand up to the labour exchange manager.

> " We are only too familiar with the official who, out of his almost complete ignorance of orthopædic methods, lays it down as a matter of course that a one-armed man must be given office work, without bothering to ask whether his aptitudes and character fit him for such an occupation or not."

Here, then, segregation is advocated, as tending to produce a good specialized man, and though the contradiction between the two arguments need not be pressed too far, it would be idle to deny that they reflect a real difference in standpoint.

It is notable that the American argument for segregation is put forward almost apologetically and is justified by the presentation of individual cases. An extract from Dr. Chollett's paper will illustrate its tone :—

> "A 15-year-old girl was presented for treatment. Her condition required operative procedures. . . . She proved to be a difficult child to manage and there was no co-operation from the family. . . . Both hips, both knees and both feet were straightened, and after several months she returned home in braces, able to walk a few steps on crutches. During the next year the welfare worker, on her numerous calls, always found her with the braces off, nor had any effort been made to teach her to walk. Later she . . . returned to the hospital, where all the surgical procedures were repeated. . . . Instead of returning home she was placed in a supervised boarding home in the city. . . . During the last year she has taken part in gymnastic exhibitions ; she has learned to sew and cook, and now walks long distances. Nor is she any longer the unmanageable child we first knew."

It will be observed that this is the argument of a man conscious that he is running contrary to the tide of current opinion. A European orthopædist addressing a gathering of experts would not feel it incumbent upon him to elaborate the point that a patient who required operations to both hips, both knees and both feet, stood in need of institutional supervision during convalescence. But the attitude which Dr. Chollett is combating is very much the attitude of the average Old-World working-class parent, and for this reason the American policy, adopted as it has been in deference to democratic opinion, deserves rather more consideration than it has yet received in European countries, England excepted. The American principle is clearly set forth by Mrs. Solenberger. After explaining that the number of special classes provided for crippled children in the public elementary schools of America has increased nearly tenfold in ten years, and that the system has now been extended to quite small communities, she continues :—

> "The provision for such classes—including even a good deal of physical supervision—is really a part of the general belief in America that family home life, in the concluding words of a conference called at the White House by President Roosevelt, is 'the highest and finest product of civilisation.' I am sure we all believe that. . . . This view was re-stated in 1919 at another Washington conference on child welfare standards as follows : Unless unusual conditions exist, the child's welfare is best promoted by keeping him in his own home. No child should be permanently removed from his home unless it is impossible so to reconstruct family conditions . . . as to make the home safe for the child."

25

In strict conformity with this point of view, Miss Constance Leigh, herself the superintendent of a residential institution in Connecticut, dwells at some length on the pains taken to maintain the relationship between the child-patients and their parents :—

> "This is a phase of our work about which we are very vigilant indeed, and every effort is made to establish a real understanding in the attitude of the parents towards their children's handicaps, remedies, and the possibilities for usefulness."

The English contributions, though not altogether hostile to special classes, showed a distinct preference for the special school on practical as well as theoretical grounds :—

> "In 'special classes' (comments Dr. Carver), that is, classes attached to and accommodated on the same site as the ordinary school, we have a minimum of the advantages arising from specialization. If there is one class only, it will contain pupils ranging in age from 7 to 16 years, a manifest disadvantage from the educational point of view."

The paper develops the whole argument for segregation, laying stress on the fact that the invalid child usually finds himself at the bottom of a class of his contemporaries, or, if placed among younger children, loses the stimulus of competition. It calls attention to the difficulty which the crippled child at an ordinary school experiences in taking part in school treats and excursions, or in profiting by the normal vocational instruction for which he requires special apparatus. On the more psychological aspect of the question Dr. Carver writes with some emphasis :—

> "Segregation in special classes as opposed to special schools may also lead to a loss of instruction in such 'mass' work as class singing, physical exercise in the form of rhythmic exercises and quiet dances, and dramatic work. The joy and interest aroused by such combined lessons cannot be replaced by individual work.
>
> In ordinary school festivals, such as concerts, plays and drill displays, it is seldom possible to allow a physically defective child to take a prominent part when there are normal children who could take the part with more convenience to the other performers. In a special school the character of the performance may be such as to enable all the children to have an equal chance of participating, and in such a case the removal of the child to a special school is the only way to secure for it an advantage which it would lose among normal children."

This extract really gives the clue to the difference between the European and the American standpoints. The Europeans have their eyes on the temperament of the crippled child, the Americans on the society which he will enter.

It would be unfair to suggest that the American writers are

blind to the psychological aspect of the problem. Miss Grace Wolfenden, of Detroit, for example, enters into the whole question of temperament and advises segregation for the child whom the mockery of his companions has made sullen, as for the child whom the excessive devotion of parents has made soft. But it is not an accident that the crippled child's psychology is studied most fully by an ardent segregationist, Dr. A. Bartos, Director of the Jedlicka Institute at Prague, whose charmingly delicate and sympathetic insight into child-nature infuses itself into the exceptionally difficult German in which his paper is written. Just as Sir Arthur Pearson used to teach the men at St. Dunstan's how to be blind, so Dr. Bartos teaches his little pupils how to be crippled. These children are not petted. There are only two nurses among fifty of them. They get up and dress themselves. But if they are to achieve this degree of independence they must have the necessary apparatus, and all the Director's sympathy and insight is put into their provision. The standardized appliances are not enough. Each child has some special need which study will discover and will satisfy by a special mechanism. One morning the child wakes up and finds that the very thing he has wanted has been placed by his bedside during the night. It is for him to discover how to use it. The whole organization of the institution is directed to socializing the sense of independence thus fostered. The children form a community functioning through what Dr. Bartos, borrowing the word from Soviet terminology, calls the collective. The collective operates through a kind of parliament which has elaborated its own rules of procedure. It maintains discipline and controls the economics of the little community, not merely deciding what is to be bought, but placing orders with the tradespeople. This parliament is encouraged first to contrive an economic surplus and then to spend it. It has already provided the institution with a cinema and is now setting up a printing press, after having first equipped some of its members with the technical knowledge to use it.

But it is not enough for this community to be as nearly as possible self-sufficing. Dr. Bartos is at great pains to bring it into contact with the world. All knowledge comes from experience, and the crippled child's experience is of a very specialized kind. He may never have seen wild flowers growing in a wood, but he has a very precise knowledge of the technical terms of orthopædics. The extent to which the crippled child's acquaintance with external phenomena is a matter not of knowledge but of hearsay, and the bearing of this fact upon orthopædic pedagogics were worked out in some detail in a paper by Dr. Winkler, of Berlin. Dr. Bartos was content to state the situation and to pass on to an account of his means of dealing with it. He brings his children into touch with the outside world by means of excursions. They are undertaken in a motor caravan which accommodates sixteen children in addition to a nurse and a chauffeur, and last for from two to ten days, according to the age of those taking part in them. They are very carefully planned beforehand. The children decide on their main objectives and then work out the route. One of their number is put in charge of the maps and sits beside the chauffeur, who is dependent upon him for direction. The various aspects of the excursion are then examined by little committees, each with its supporters. One of these bodies examines the character of the landscapes to be traversed, another deals with the history of the towns passed through, a third reports on the architecture of the buildings to be visited, and a fourth explores the industrial significance of factories on the line of route and describes the processes which they employ. Library books are freely consulted for this work and all the possibilities of the tour are mastered. The children are keen enough to waste no time; there is even an astronomical committee which gathers material for use after dark. The whole scheme is rounded off by the compilation of a proper record after the tour has taken place. It is an amazing conception amazingly carried out, and any millionaire among our readers might do worse than provide the funds for a troupe of English crippled Boy Scouts to visit the Jedlicka institution. Its children will doubtless work out an effective means of breaking down the language barrier. No wonder that Dr. Frejka deplores the inability of ordinary Czecho-slovakian medical opinion to recognize the full value of such work as this! But let him be patient. As the Jedlicka pupils go out into the world the significance of their training will not long remain hid.

RESULTS.

In a paper on preventive methods Dr. Helmuth Eckhardt produces some exceedingly instructive statistics. Rickets is, of course, an urban disease, but other cases of serious crippling disability originated in the countryside rather than in the towns. The reason is, of course, that the town-bred cripple stands a better chance of being discovered before his injury has developed. The production of such statistics is thus a measure of present achievement and a stimulus to further effort, but their compilation is only possible if a number of separate institutions co-operate to pool their information. They thus illustrate the advantage of a national outlook. It will be for future conferences to define more precisely the significance of an international outlook, but this Conference was sufficiently aware of it to define that its own proceedings should be duly summed up. To this end it appointed a small international committee to draw up resolutions for sub-mission to its final session. The Committee did not mistake the importance of its own work, and in the fifth and last of its resol-utions[1] recommended that it should be made the nucleus of a permanent body. Action has aready been taken on this resolution. Another form of international co-operation was advocated in the fourth resolution, as follows :—

Whereas the solution of the problems incident to the locating or finding, treatment, care, education, vocational training and placement of crippled persons is a task confronting every nation in the world to-day ;

And whereas much progress has been made in many countries in this important field of endeavour which involves not only humanitarian and philanthropic considerations, but economic welfare ;

And whereas the International Society for Crippled Children is making a forceful effort to bring about a unity of thought and action in this con-nection, and is receiving the cordial co-operation of many agencies in many countries ;

And whereas the Child Welfare Committee and the Health Organization of the League of Nations are in a position to further this activity to the very great advantage of its member nations, and thus to render a tremendous service to the whole world :

Therefore be it resolved by the delegates to the World Conference of Workers for Crippled Children now in session in the City of Geneva, Switzerland, and composed of representatives of twelve countries—Great Britain, Sweden, Belgium, the Netherlands, Germany, Czecho-slovakia, Austria, Hungary, Spain, Switzerland, Canada and the United States— that we join in an earnest appeal to the League of Nations that the enumeration, treatment, care, educational and vocational training, and placement of the crippled, also the prevention of the causes of crippling conditions among children, be made subjects of investigation, study, report and recommendation at the earliest time consistent with pending activi-ties ; and that the League of Nations be requested to establish a department in the Secretariat of the League for the accomplishment of these purposes.

The main conclusions of the Conference are set out in the public statement of policy which forms the third of its resolutions :—

---

[1] Of the other resolutions, the first dealt with the finances of the Conference, and the second extended its thanks to the organizations and persons assisting its labours. The third and fourth are printed below.

Whereas in the discussions of this Conference certain clear and well-defined propositions have been evolved and appear to have been received with general approval;

And whereas we believe it to be our duty as students of the problems incident to the relation of society to the crippled, finding him and securing for him medical examination and diagnosis, treatment, care, education or vocational training and placement, as well as preventing crippling conditions, and as workers for the solution of these problems, to place before the public the results of our deliberations;

Now therefore be it resolved by the World Conference of Workers for Crippled Children that we declare:—

(1) That every cripple has the right to expect of his State or country physical, mental and social equality.

(2) That assistance to crippled persons is not only a humanitarian but an economic social responsibility.

(3) That there is a regrettable lack of accurate information as to the number of cripples in many of the countries; that in these adequate surveys should be made without delay, that their results may guide intelligent, comprehensive action; and that in all countries where such legislation does not now exist, laws be enacted making it compulsory upon the part of physicians, surgeons, midwives, nurses and teachers to report crippling conditions to the proper authorities.

(4) That a great need exists for an adequate number of competent professional workers, both surgical and pedagogical, and that universities throughout the world be urged to create courses, where they do not now exist, for the training of a large number of orthopædic surgeons, nurses and teachers, to provide for compulsory examinations therein, and to establish, where not at present existing, Chairs in Orthopædics.

(5) That all efforts in the furtherance of the education and vocational training of the crippled should be encouraged and assisted in every possible way; for without education, training and equipment to fit the cripple to take his place in the world and putting him where he can have an equal opportunity, much of the remedial effort is wasted.

(6) That responsibility does not end with remedying existing conditions, but must extend to preventive work and the practical eradication ultimately of crippledom.

Be it further resolved that copies of these resolutions be sent to all known societies engaged in work for the crippled, to the various universities throughout the world, to the Health Departments of the several Governments, to all medical and surgical societies and journals, also the leading newspapers and general publications.

This resolution gives the starting-point for the Conference of 1931.

NOTES ON PHYSICAL MEDICINE
IN EUROPE IN 1951

Sidney Licht

NOTES ON PHYSICAL MEDICINE IN EUROPE IN 1951

SIDNEY LICHT, M.D.

During the summer of 1951 we visited several countries in Europe to see at first hand how physical medicine was practiced there. Most of our visits to hospitals and centers were very brief and the impressions formed sketchy but we believe that a recitation of our observations may improve somewhat the hazy picture entertained by American physiatrists concerning the specialty in other countries.

We tried to visit those countries and cities not recently visited or described by American physical medicine specialists, although some repetition was inevitable. In each country we were greeted by physicians or therapists with whom we had engaged in correspondence and were escorted by them or their friends. We were received with overwhelming kindness wherever we went and when we mentioned this fact we were told that Americans were the most hospitable people in the world. Many people told us that they were repaying us for the courtesies shown them by Americans on their visits to the United States. Thus, we are indebted not only to our European hosts but to our fellow Americans who have established a bank of international good will on which we were privileged to overdraw. It is not possible to express adequately with the printed word the degree to which people inconvenienced themselves to make our trip informative and pleasant. We saw physicians and therapists treat patients with the same kindness extended to us and satisfied ourselves that good will is universal and not the property of any one nation or class.

The physical medicine we saw was very variable. For the most part, we visited only the best physical medicine departments in the community (based on a long study of medical literature). Because of severe time limitations, we were unable to visit all of the best institutions and this was especially true of the very large cities where the number of clinics is great.

Our remarks will be limited largely to what we saw or heard. Occasional statements will be based on letters we received while traveling, or items passed on to us by interested persons with valued information. We shall include much statistical data because, whether we like it or not, the magnitude of our task and the acceptance of the specialty are intimately associated in the minds of many with the number of patients treated and the size of departmental staffs. We shall describe the things we saw according to locality, and to some extent, according to the amount of time spent at each place. We spent most time in the United Kingdom.

GREAT BRITAIN

A few observations about medicine and especially physical medicine in the United Kingdom may be of interest. The educational system is not too different from the American but the nomenclature is. At the age of five, the British child enters a "prep" school where he remains until he is eleven. He then enters a secondary (free) school or a public (boarding) school or a grammar (small fee) school. At the age of 15 to 16 he takes the General School Examination to determine eligibility for university entrance but he may not enter the university for another year. The intervening time is spent in the "sixth form" (senior high school) in one of three types of school: science, arts, or, for the student who will not take university training, the modern school. During his higher school edu cation, the student who wants to become a physician must pass a special examination for admission to medical college. If he succeeds, he enters the medical school where after five and a half years he may receive the degree of M.B. which is the equivalent of the American M.D. It is possible to earn an M.D. in Britain but this means further graduate work and relatively few try it. The British medical school, with few exceptions, is an integral part of a hospital. At Oxford and Cambridge Universities, pre-clinical subjects are taught locally, but the last years are spent by the student in a London hospital (that is, medical school). There are a dozen teaching hospitals in London and although they are quite separate, graduates of all receive a diploma from the University of London. As a result of the close connection between hospitals and schools, British medical education is more clinical and individual than in the United States. Students are divided into small groups for instruction during several years. Upon graduation, each student spends six months as a house physician and six months as a house surgeon. These positions add up to the American one year rotating interneship. The next two years must be spent in the military service at the end of which time the young physician is given a "government grant" for six months of specialized training in the discipline of his choice. At this point the physician may enter private practice, full or part-time, or proceed to take further training. If he chooses the latter, he will become a junior registrar* in some hospital or clinic for a year. During that year he may study for Part I of his specialty Diploma (Board examination), which in the case of Physical Medicine would include the subjects of anatomy, physiology and physics; all this while engaged in the routine hospital work of physical medicine. At the conclusion of the year as junior registrar, he will take a second year as registrar with an increase in salary from £1,000 to £1,100. The third year is spent as senior registrar, and during this period he may take Part II of his specialty examination. If he passes both parts he is *qualified* and may place after his name the letters *D. Phys. Med.* At this time he may continue to be employed as a senior registrar in the hospital of training or elsewhere. When the specialist reaches the age of 35, he is eligible for the highest medical title which is consultant. A consultant may be full or part-time, and there may be more than one to a hospital department, but only one of these is designated *physician-in-charge.*

Physical medicine in the United Kingdom consists of three branches: 1. rheumatology (physical medicine men give cortisone), 2. rehabilitation (which is considered an integral part of physical medicine and defined as fitting the disabled for work in open or sheltered situations), and 3. medical electricity. There

* The closest American equivalent to the British word registrar is resident. A junior registrar usually has the duties and responsibilities of a senior house officer. The senior registrar may perform the duties of a senior resident, fellow, or even attending physician.

is little hydrotherapy in hospitals other than those for poliomyelitis, although exceptions to this statement will be noted below.

Approximately 32 physicians had qualified for the Diploma in Physical Medicine (first offered in 1944) at the time of our visit and we were told that about 20 *sit* for it each year. There is a British Association of Physical Medicine with almost 130 members, and there is a Section of Physical Medicine in the Royal Society of Medicine. The British Association of Physical Medicine planned to bring out a new journal in December 1951 with Dr. Hugh Burt as editor.

There are now more than 12,000 chartered (registered) physiotherapists in the United Kingdom, which also boasts over two dozen schools of physiotherapy. No school is affiliated with a university but each is part of a hospital. Students are accepted at the age of 19 if they have the equivalent of a high school diploma. The first six months are spent in didactic study, the remaining 33 months are largely clinical. Students are used far more in treatment of patients than is common in the United States. To a certain extent, they are regarded as working members of the staff. Because most of their training is at the hospital, which is their school, their supervision by teaching therapists is very close. There is a distinct category of *teaching therapist* and even one of *teacher-in-training*. In order to qualify as a physiotherapist, the student must pass three examinations given by the Chartered Society of Physiotherapy. Successful candidates may place after their names the letters M.C.S.P. (member). After the candidate has been a member for at least five years he may submit a thesis for the higher qualification of fellow (F.C.S.P.).

The training of occupational therapists is also heavily weighted on the clinical side but is of shorter duration. There are nine schools in the United Kingdom. The qualifying examination is given by the Association of Occupational Therapists and successful candidates may place after their names the letters M.A.O.T.

Since one of the first questions raised by Americans on my return was about "socialized medicine," a few words will be devoted to it. The National Health Service Act of 1946 imposed on the Minister of Health the duty of promoting a comprehensive health service for the nation. The service is financed by the national treasury partially out of payments which every person must make weekly in the form of tax stamps (purchased at the Post Office and affixed to a wallet-sized folded sheet of heavy paper). In actual practice the employer usually does this for his workers. The tax (National Insurance Acts) varies from two to nine shillings a week.*

* The direct translation of foreign currency to that of the United States does not give an accurate picture of finances. In general, rentals in most of Europe are about one-third of those in the United States or less. The cost of living except for clothing is about two-thirds of that in the United States; salaries are from one-half to two-thirds that of America. Luxury items and goods manufactured in America are about the same price as in this country; eggs are about sixty cents a dozen in most countries. In Britain the devalued pound still buys more than its $2.80 American equivalent. In Denmark, many people told us that the crown (14 cents) buys the equivalent of the American half-dollar. The following official exchange values of 1951 are listed for those who wish to convert currencies quoted in this paper. British shilling, Danish crown, Norwegian crown, each about 14 cents; the Swiss franc, about 23 cents.

When the Act went into effect all but 200 religious hospitals and a few others became nationalized, that is, could bill no one for services except private patients. In most hospitals private blocks (pavillions) were preserved for private patients in variable degrees. Even these beds are subject to nationalization on emergency. Those hospitals which had endowment funds were permitted to retain such funds and use them in any manner desired by their own Boards of Governors (trustees). The Act specifies the salaries of physicians and auxilliaries attached to hospital staffs by age, specialization and qualification, allowing for certain annual step increases. Any practitioner not serving at a full-time position may engage in private practice during his unassigned hours. Every person is entitled to choose his family doctor from the list of those physicians who have accepted the Act, if that physician is able and willing to accept him. Both the patient and physician have a relatively free choice in the matter of selection. If the patient wishes to change his family doctor he notifies the local council and at the end of 14 days his name is removed from the list and he becomes free to select another physician. A patient cannot see a specialist unless referred by a general practitioner, except in genuine emergencies. Theoretically a physician is free to practice where he wishes but if the Medical Practices Committee decides that a community has a surplus of physicians, the applicant may be denied placement on the local council list of approved practitioners under the Act. A general practitioner is not permitted to have more than 4,000 persons on his list, unless he has a partner, in which case the combined list may reach 5,000. Physicians are paid about one. pound a year for each person carried for a year regardless of the amount of medical care administered during the period. Very few physicians are able to carry the maximum load; 4,000 pounds is considered a very good income in Britain where the beginning wage for a London bus driver is about 350 pounds a year.

For purposes of administration, England and Wales are divided into 14 regions, each with its own Regional Hospital Board on which the chairman and secretary are usually prominent lay citizens and the third member or Senior Administrative Medical Officer is a prominent physician. Scotland, which has a separate similar Act, has five regions. In each region hospitals are formed into groups for reasons of economy of medical personnel and facilities. Thus in each region all thoracic surgery might be sent to one hospital designated as the center for that specialty.

There is still private practice in England; Harley Street still has its row of private offices. Patients with emergent conditions receive the same speedy attention as previously but patients with chronic or minor complaints may find themselves on "waiting lists", and this is of course especially true in the majority of patients seen in physical medicine clinics. There are still long waiting lists for appliances and spectacles and recently patients have been asked to pay something towards their purchase. Impatient patients keep private practice alive. Most of the physical medicine specialists to whom we spoke were full-time employees of hospitals. To them, nationalization meant little change from their previous status and they have accepted it. The complaints we heard were from private practitioners who find too few beds available for their private patients and are annoyed by government regulations and paper work. Opinion was divided among the physicians we asked about nationalization but several were hurt at the slurs cast by laymen in the American lay press which inferred that the quality of medicine had suffered. Such statements are an indictment against the integrity of British physicians whom we consider the intellectual and ethical equal of American physicians. We do not see how it would be possible for any reliable survey to be made on this question in less than six months by a team of trained impartial investigators. Since we were in Britain for only three weeks we were unable to form a defensible opinion about socialized medicine. Medical practice is an integral part of a nation's culture and temper. The British are a people with great patience and relatively low income. They cue for one thing or another every day of their lives, without complaint and with great consideration for their fellow citizen. Even if a survey found nationalization the best medical plan for Britain, life there is so different from ours, that any conclusion concerning socialized medicine would have no validity for this country.

ENGLAND

We visited many institutions in England and found the same diversity of practice and acceptance of physical medicine as exists in the United States. Thus, the oldest hospital in the country, the Royal Hospital of St. Bartholomew (Bart's), where William Harvey did his monumental research in physiology, has no physician in the department of physical medicine. St. Thomas' Hospital, second in age in the Kingdom, is unsurpassed in size and strength to any we saw.

LONDON

Our time in London permitted only a few hospital visits. We were unable, for instance, to visit the Royal Free Hospital where Dr. Ernest T. D. Fletcher heads a large Rheumatism Department with three physical medicine diplomates and others in training. There are eight other hospitals in London in addition to those mentioned below, which have departments of physical medicine headed by specialists.

St. Thomas' Hospital. This great 600 bed general hospital has been known as St. Thomas' since the canonization of Thomas a Becket in 1173. It is situated on the bank of the Thames River directly across from the Houses of Parliament, which accounted for considerable bombing destruction of it during World War II; the aim of the German aviators was poor. The destroyed buildings here as in most places in London still await repair or reconstruction. There was far more destruction in London than we had thought. At St. Thomas' we had long talks with Dr. Philippe Bauwens, director of the physical medicine department, and his senior registrars, particularly Dr. A. T. Richardson who visited many departments in the United States during 1950. Dr. Richardson was our host in London and gave us much valuable time and information. Another senior registrar, Dr. Curwen, told us of his excellent results with the Bisgaard method of treating varicose ulcers. The method, which has had little acceptance in the United States, includes contact ultraviolet radiation, massage of the entire limb and deep massage about the ulcerous area, followed by tight bandaging. The patient is encouraged to carry out his daily routine during the treatment period which lasts about three months. Of 200 patients followed for three years 80 per cent have remained well. At this hospital we saw the excellent electronics laboratory personally supervised by Dr. Bauwens. We were shown a recently designed diathermy device which automatically keeps the patient circuit in resonance. We also visited a very well equipped laboratory for electromyography.

The physical therapy section is large and well equipped. A striking feature was the brilliant red woolen blankets on the plinths and screen covers. One room with three plinths is devoted to septic cases (infection) for in spite of the use of antibiotics, many skin infections and superficial cellulitides are still treated during some phase with contact or radiant ultraviolet light. We found considerable emphasis on the use of electrotherapy, other than diathermy.

About 250 new patients are seen each week in the department which is staffed by 43 qualified therapists. One reason for the large staff is the presence of a physiotherapy school, the first hospital school to be established (1911). Mrs. Ursula Vidler, the school principal took us through the class rooms. Classes enter twice each year. The tuition for three years is £210; the examinations and final registration cost another £31.

We also interviewed the lady almoner (social worker) who spends her entire time in connection with physical medicine patients. Miss Nora Bell is one of 22 almoners attached to this hospital. She is responsible for seeing every patient admitted to the department. If necessary, at the end of treatment she arranges for the transfer of the patient to a capacity or job-assessment center or sees to it that the D. R. O. (Disablement Resettlement Officer) obtains further training or employment for the patient in need. Among her many duties is that of lining up a baby sitter for the mother who must come to the hospital clinic, of solving the food problems for the bedfast home patient. The social worker in Britain does not investigate financial ability of patients. This is done by the health visitor (public health nurse).

There is much use of home physical therapy about London. A private organization known as the Mobile Physiotherapy Service supplies therapists and equipment for home care at a fee to the patient. On request of the hospital physician the almoner may sometimes arrange to find funds for needy patients for home service.

King's College Hospital also has a very large department of physical medicine able to treat 600 patients daily. The director of this department, Dr. F. S. Cooksey is also in charge of physical medicine for the Ministry of Health. The department is staffed by two registrars, 18 qualified physiotherapists, 5 physiotherapy teachers, 2 remedial gymnasts and 4 occupational therapists. It is usual to have 120 students in physiotherapy at any one time. Here as in several other hospitals we found great emphasis on class gymnastics and we saw private patients taking their exercises along with the others. The following schedule for the two hospital gymnasia will indicate the importance attached to this aspect of treatment.

PHYSICAL TREATMENT DEPARTMENT

GYMNASIUM TIME TABLE

	Section One		Section Two
9.30	Spastic Group		Individuals
10.00	Women's Posture		Plaster Class
10.30		Head Class	
11.00	Mild Arm Class		Colles Class
11.30	Knee Class	Off Weight Leg Class	Mild Weight Leg Class
12.00	Children (small groups)		Women's Posture Class
1.30	Chest (children)		Chest (adult)
2.00	Off Weight Leg Class		Mild Weight Leg Class
2.30	Mild Arm Class		Colles Class
3.00	Mild General Activity		Prophylactic Movements
3.30	Children's Activity		Children's Feet and Knees
4.00	Children's Posture		Children's Posture
4.30	Boy's Posture		Boy's Posture

Ante-Natal Classes: Tuesday and Thursday at 4.30.

* Children's Posture Classes held on Mondays, Wednesdays and Fridays; younger children at 4 and older children at 4.30.

Dr. Cooksey does not believe in distributing equipment in uniform groups since this tends to over-specialization among therapists. Since his is a training center for the therapist who may one day staff smaller hospitals in the provinces, and in fact, be the only one on duty there, he prefers that each therapist carry out the entire physical prescription on the patient.

Our most impressive experience at this hospital was that gained from attending a resettlement clinic (rehabilitation conference). At this meeting (held weekly) were two registrars, the department almoner, the D.R.O. (similar to the American D.V.R.) and Dr. Cooksey. Two patients were brought to the conference room for evaluation during the half hour we were there. Each case was thoroughly worked up and thoughtfully presented. Each person in the room seemed to be familiar with some aspect of the problem and had some constructive suggestion to make regarding specific employment objectives. All disabled persons who have difficulty in finding employment are urged to register with the Ministry of Labour. All factories or businesses over a certain size must reserve three per cent of their positions for those on the Disabled Registry. While awaiting employment or while receiving treatment, the disabled receive benefits. If a patient cannot work because of illness (certified by a physician) he may, if married, receive 42 shillings a week plus other monies depending upon his rental or associated hardship. A like amount of money is paid him if he is unemployed through no fault or unwillingness of his own. In addition it is possible to obtain the same amount of money under National Assistance, a sort of relief administration. Ordinarily, only two of these benefits are possible at one time.

At this and other hospitals, infirm patients may be transported to and from the hospital by a city (London County Council) operated vehicle when needed. This saves hospital beds since many of the patients so treated would receive nothing in the hospital in the way of treatment except physical medicine. At this hospital we were told of the liberal provision which grants a motorized vehicle to certain severely disabled persons. We saw several of such vehicles on the highways. They reminded us of a cross between a motorcycle and a jeep. For the most part they are one-seaters, to discourage owners from using them for any but the prime purpose of transportation for the disabled individual. Recently the law has permitted drivers one passenger.

Middlesex Hospital has 600 beds. The director of its physical medicine department, Dr. Frank Howitt saw us at his Harley Street consulting rooms (office). It was through his efforts that in 1931 the balneologists and electrotherapists within the Royal Society of Medicine merged to form the Section of Physical Medicine. The assistant director at this hospital is Dr. A. C. Boyle. There is one S.H.M.O. (senior hospital medical officer, the grade between senior registrar and consultant at some hospitals), a senior registrar and three other registrars. There are 22 qualified therapists, 7 teachers and 120 students. In this department about 700 patients are treated daily.

A large new occupational therapy section is headed by Miss Daphne Birkbeck who is assisted by two graduate therapists, a technician (craft teacher), a joiner (carpenter) and a store keeper (stock clerk). About 20 to 30 patients are treated in the shop each day and a similar number is visited on the wards. In addition, the staff workers visit 20 to 30 homebound patients on a regular schedule. In between home visits materials are mailed to these patients. On the basis of work production, patients who attend the clinic may earn up to one pound sterling a week. Here as at almost all hospitals in Europe, articles made by patients are offered for sale.

St. Mary's Hospital is famed among physiotherapists as the institution at which Mrs. Olive Guthrie-Smith, now retired, first introduced suspension therapy. Here we were greeted by Dr. Michael Woodhouse, physician-in-charge, who directs three part-time registrars, 12 qualified therapists, 10 teachers and 120 students. This 400 bed general hospital treats about 400 patients daily in physical medicine. At this hospital, physical medicine is a *reference* department which means that the referring physician writes the physical prescription. It is common for reference departments to be under the control of the Orthopedic division as was for a time ordered by the surgeon general of the United States Army during World War II. The reaction of British physical medicine men is about the same as seen among American physiatrists under such circumstances. Most of the teaching hospitals in London are *open* departments where the physician-in-charge of physical medicine and his staff prescribe.

Guy's Hospital first saw static electricity applied for local conditions in 1837 when Dr. Golding Bird established one of the first electrotherapy departments. This hospital has 600 beds in London and an additional 200 at Orpington. Dr. Eric J. Crisp, the physician-in-charge of physical medicine supervises 18 therapists, 7 teachers and 120 students who administer treatment to about 600 patients each day. Occupational therapy is available only to those patients in the psychiatric pavillion (the York Clinic). Dr. Crisp has two registrars and regularly receives seven clinical clerks for training. He prefers individual to group therapeutic exercises.

MANSFIELD

The *Harlow Wood Orthopaedic Hospital* is situated on the outskirts of the town. It is of more recent construction than the hospitals visited in London. Of its 300 beds, about 200 are occupied by adults. We were escorted by Mr. Peter Jackson, the assistant surgeon. (All surgeons in the United Kingdom are called Mister). The large physical therapy section takes care of about 150 patients daily. At the time of our visit many people were "on holiday" and in this case the supervisor was Miss Mary Moore, assistant head physiotherapist, who told us that the hospital had twelve establishments (position allocations) but only eight qualified therapists on duty. We witnessed all modalities and were especially impressed by the high quality of functional reeducation. There is no physician in charge of physical medicine; prescriptions are written by ward surgeons.

At this hospital we saw a modern therapeutic pool about 30 by 80 feet graded from two to five feet in depth and used by patients of all ages for underwater exercise. The temperature of the water is maintained at 90 to 94 degrees. A new overhead electrically operated crane for lowering patients into the pool was demonstrated to us. Of the many ingenious devices shown us throughout Europe to achieve this end, the Harlow Wood device seemed the most secure and rapid. It is an overhead concealed half horse power motor which drives four gears (4 to 1 ratio) that allow vertical bars in each of four corners to telescope up or down and carry a wooden platform litter with them.

YORK

Just outside the walled beautiful city of York, on Heslington Road, where it was established at the end of the eighteenth century is the *Retreat* with its original buildings in a wonderful state of preservation, outside and in. We were greeted in the room that has served as the staff dining room since the inception of the hospital, by acting director Dr. Gwendolyn Knight. We were taken on a very complete tour of the buildings and grounds and saw a sufficient number of patients to marvel at the serenity of the institution and its patients. Most of the bedrooms and sitting rooms resemble those seen in better homes or hotels. As has been customary at this hospital since its foundation by William Tuke, activity plays an important role in the care of patients. About 160 of the 260 patients are engaged in some activity each day. There are two qualified occupational therapists. We spoke to the head therapist, Mr. Oliver. He is in charge of arts, crafts, recreation, sports and the library. There is also a part time librarian. The occupational therapy building is a converted cricket house and most crafts are available within it. There is also a large hall for dances, plays, motion pictures, and during inclement weather, for morning exercises.

The grounds are very spacious and beautiful. Lovely gardens flank two great lawns on which bowls, cricket and other games are played. Although there is some patient participation, games are frequently played for the passive entertainment of patients. The British weather, never as hot or cold as that of the United States, permits more outdoor sports than do most sections of the United States and patients spend more time out of doors. An outdoor swimming pool is available for the patients.

This is one of the 200 hospitals which has not been nationalized. It is a Friend's (Quaker) institution. In addition to the medical director there are five staff physicians.

OXFORD

The *Radcliffe Infirmary* is a 500 bed general hospital which services the University and townspeople. During World War II a medical school was established here. The department of physical medicine established by Dr. Walter Turrell is now headed by Dr. E. F. Mason. Sister Morag Hutcheson is the superintendent of physiotherapists. (A sister is a nurse with supervisory qualifications; not all graduate nurses may be called sister). Her first assistant, Mr. William Jarman, is called the senior physiotherapist. The number of men in this profession in England in relation to the number of women is about the same as in the United States. Mr. Jarman showed us several exercise devices developed by him including a simplified resistance exercise table. He believes in applying the maximum resistance "straight off" and progressively reducing the load during a session so that the patient receives the impression of non-increasing load throughout, which is said to delay the onset of fatigue. In this department we saw a large floor bath about four feet square and sixteen inches deep. This is filled with warm water and patients with below-knee fractures sit on the bath rim while doing exercises under water.

The physical medicine department has two large treatment rooms and a "temporary gymnasium," twenty by forty feet. The short wave diathermy machines seen at this hospital were typical of those seen throughout England. They are of English or German manufacture; most electrodes are glass covered. There are very few American machines, almost no drum or "moulded" electrodes. There are still many long wave diathermy machines in operation in England and most people to whom we spoke wanted to continue using them and did not seem too concerned about the international agreement which outlaws them in 1952, unless properly shielded.

In this department about 1,000 patients are treated each week by 11 qualified physiotherapists and 2 occupational therapists. Among the devices we were shown here was the vibrator developed by Dr. Ritchie Russell for treating phantom limb pain.

BUXTON

There are three important spas in England: Harrowgate, Bath and Buxton. Each spa is operated by a lay manager; at Buxton the manager is also a qualified physiotherapist, Mr. Rupert A. Lockwood. Buxton is a thousand feet above sea-level. Its waters were used by Roman soldiers in olden times and on at least two occasions, Mary, Queen of Scots took the cure here. The treatment buildings on the high side of town are well run and well equipped. There is no physician attached to the spa (as is common in France) but there are several practitioners in the town to whom patients frequently go for a regimen (much as in Saratoga Springs). The spa is open all year as are most of the local hotels and boarding houses. During the height of the summer season as many as 600 patients are treated daily at the spa. In the winter the number falls, but not below 100 a day. During the season 35 qualified therapists work at the spa.

The main building is set up for the administration of most forms of physical therapy. There are quite a few rooms with individual sunken baths in which the water is heated to 90 degrees. Here therapists can administer individual underwater exercises. There are many rooms equipped with electrotherapeutic machines.

In another pavillion (Natural Baths) the waters seep through holes in the bottom of two tiled pools from springs on which the pool is built. The pressure of the springs permits a complete change in water every four hours. The water issues at a temperature of 82 degrees, and since it is only slightly mineralized, it has almost no taste or odor. The chemical analysis shows some concentration of magnesium and calcium bicarbonate. The spa brochure lists the waters as diuretic and sedative.

There is a drinking house (St. Anne's) where patients may drink the waters direct from the spring or mix them with orange squash sold at the same place. A fourth building is a partially converted hotel for patients who are not ambulatory. The center is devoted almost exclusively to the treatment of rheumatic disorders. Among the treatments we saw given and which we were told about in other British hospitals was contact ultraviolet light over involved arthritic joints. On successive treatment days second or third degree burns are given to the skin over joints until most of the local skin area is irradiated.

The use of mud and peat so common on the continent is used in very few places in England but finds great favor at Buxton. The town of Buxton is surrounded by moors. There, from six feet under the top soil, peat is collected and brought to the spa. The peat is injected with steam and maintained at an elevated temperature in special cabinets. The warmed peat is applied directly to the skin; the treatment may be local or include much of the body. For the latter purpose there are specially constructed rooms with openings in the floor through which the patient is lowered into a tub shaped carriage full of heated peat, wheeled on rails to the opening from the heating station.

In some of the rooms with sunken bath we saw overhead cranes for lowering the invalid patient on a wooden chair. In one room there was a home-made Hubbard tank of excellent design and construction.

All patients with foot ailments are seen by the center's chiropodist before further physical treatment. No patient is admitted without a prescription from a physician but Mr. Lockwood admitted that some of the prescriptions were as vague as they are in other parts of the world. A few costs are listed: diathermy—

10 shillings; massage—10 shillings; six exposures to ultraviolet light—25 shillings. This spa is municipally operated and a fee is charged all patients. Under the National Health Service Act, patients may be referred here by their own physician and receive treatment for which the government is billed.

About 100 yards above the spa is the imposing structure of the *Devonshire Royal Hospital,* the largest rheumatology hospital in Britain. Buxton has long been famous as a resort but also as a place where the weather is quite variable. As a source of amusement for visitors an arena for riding horses was built here early in the nineteenth century. The roof of the arena was, and according to local claims still is, the largest spherical dome in the world. About a century ago, the sixth Duke of Devonshire dedicated the structure to the care of the infirm and wards and rooms were placed about the huge hemisphere to house 200 patients. Since all the patients have joint disabilities, physical medicine plays an important role here. The physiotherapy department is large; it consists of two well equipped gymnasia and four other treatment rooms. Miss Ida Hough, the superintendent, is in charge of 15 qualified therapists. In the basement there is an extensive hydrotherapy section under Miss Florette R. Hills. There are ten immersion baths, two vapor baths and two "Buxton" (Vichy type) massage-douche tables. The patient lies in a shallow copper trough and is continuously sprayed by a hose hung over the shoulder of the masseuse during massage. This department has one of the few whirlpool baths we saw in Europe. It is a huge wooden tub of such depth that a patient must mount three steps to reach its rim. On the floor of the tub is a ship's propellor which agitates the water. The feet of the patient are protected from the propellor by a metal grid. A therapeutic pool was nearing completion.

The occupational therapy department occupies two large areas and is staffed by three qualified therapists. Miss Francina Sarabji showed us many patients at work on specific kinetic therapy; in fact we visited no hospital where better use was made of occupational therapy.

CAMBRIDGE

Addenbrooke's Hospital (named after an eighteenth century physician) is a 420 bed general hospital. At Cambridge University medical students receive instruction on preclinical medicine at the hospital. While here, we saw a group of eight students making rounds in the physical medicine department with its physician-in-charge, Dr. William A. Fell. Dr. Fell, a one-time anatomist was placed in charge of the department only a year ago. Previous to that time there was no physiatrist assigned here. In line with the National Health scheme, Dr. Fell visits several other hospitals in the neighboring country once a week or less often depending on the demand for his services.

At this hospital there are 14 establishments in physiotherapy but three of them must be shared mornings with nearby Chesterton Hospital (for the chronic sick). There is a good gymnasium and two fair sized general treatment rooms. The occupational therapy section is located in another building and occupies about 600 square feet of floor space. Miss Annette Bourdillon, acting head therapist showed us several ingenious adaptations of craft equipment. Unlike so many devices which photograph well but are seldom used, we saw patients use them properly. About 40 patients are seen daily in the wards and about 14 come to the clinic each day.

The Medical Interviewing Committee (rehabilitation conference) for the Ministry of Labour meets at this hospital for patients in this area. Dr. Fell is chairman and meets with representatives of local industry who advise on employment possibilities for the disabled.

PAPWORTH EVERARD

In the small village of Papworth Everard, about 12 miles west of Cambridge, Dr. Pendril Varrier-Jones introduced a scheme for the rehabilitation of the tuberculous over thirty years ago which has continued to grow and remain the best of its kind anywhere. All but one of the more than 200 buildings in the town belong to the scheme called *Papworth Village Settlement*. Almost all the buildings in the town were built and continue to be built by ex-patients. Papworth accepts two types of patients: 1. those who have good prospects of recovery but require hospitalization; 2. those who have had successful treatment and will soon be able to work under sheltered conditions. For the sick there are three modern beautiful hospitals with a total of 200 beds. For the convalescent there are hostels to house over 200 men and 100 women. Elsewhere in the village for working ex-patients and their families are 200 houses with from four to six rooms.

The medical aspects are managed by Dr. R. R. Trail who directs the enterprise from its London office and visits the Settlement regularly each week. The chief medical officer Dr. L. B. Stott is assisted by two other physicians and there are establishments for another two. Mr. Kent Harrison, a thoracic surgeon attends four times weekly to do the chest surgery not only for Papworth patients but for all patients in the large area known as East Anglia. The latter are transferred to this center for surgery and returned to their original hospital for convalescence.

At Papworth little differentiation is made between treatment and rehabilitation since the latter is considered a part of the former. All convalescents are eligible for rehabilitation in one of the many large modern industrial plants. The shortest working period acceptable is three hours a day. At this time the patient will receive room and board and an allowance of 34 shillings a week. During his vocational training the working time is increased on medical prescription to seven hours daily. When convalescents reach that level they are paid prevailing union wages and must pay a rental for the quarters they occupy. There are more than a thousand inhabitants in the town who have had tuberculosis or are in the immediate family of a former patient.

The local industries carry the trade name of *Pendragon*. Many of the employees are the children and relatives of ex-patients who have colonized at Papworth. Children may begin work at the age of fifteen.

We were permitted to tour the entire village but because it was vacation time most of the plants were closed. We visited the Pendragon Press, the largest publishing enterprise in East Anglia. This consisted of a glass-roofed building with about 20,000 square feet of floor space and dozens of modern presses and binding machines. The Pendragon Press prints and binds, among other things, the four volume telephone directory of the world's largest city.

Among the other industries are cabinet making, automobile-body making and leather goods. When the Royal Family visited South Africa, all the luggage of the Queen and Princesses bore the Pendragon label.

LEICESTER

At Leicester we visited one of Great Britain's thirteen *Government Training Centres*. These Centres are an outgrowth of vocational training centers begun thirty years ago to supply the building trades with needed workers. At present they have Industrial Rehabilitation Units where disabled or convalescent workers are sent by their physician or D. R. O. for assessment and hardening. At the Leicester Centre the assistant manager, Mr. T. W. Clark introduced us to the rehabilitation team captain Mr. Humphrey Martyn, the Rehabilitation Officer. The team consists of a vocational guidance officer, six occupational supervisors (teachers) under the direction of a chief supervisor, a social welfare worker, and a remedial gymnast. For medical guidance the team looks to the rehabilitation physician, Dr. Grayling.

We visited a very large well equipped workshop which was one of several devoted to mechanics, typewriter repair, garment making and drafting. Barbering is another of the subjects taught. In the machine shop the convalescents do simple work such as filing and assembling with more emphasis on production than education since the goal is to determine physical capacity or to increase it. About half of the convalescents live on the premises and the other half commute from nearby towns. The Ministry of Labour under its training scheme allows single men three and a half pounds sterling a week for living expenses.

The entire rehabilitation program is rather complete and well integrated with time for sports and recreation. We visited the large excellent gymnasium and saw patients hard at play.

The average trainee remains for about eight weeks at the end of which time an assessment report is sent to the referring agency.

Upon discharge from such a center a man is assisted in finding regular employment or if he is not fit to compete in the open labor market, he is eligible for admission to one of Britain's 86 *Remploy* factories. To learn more about these we spoke to Mr. W. S. Coburn, an officer of the Disabled Persons Branch at the Ministry of Labour head office in London.

Remploy Limited is a privately run enterprise. When Remploy factories were first begun there was rapid expansion with resultant weaknesses in the economic structure. By the end of 1949 it became evident that the gap between expenses and returns had to be narrowed. By consolidation, improved salesmanship and higher rate of production per worker the books are approaching a state of balance. By the end of 1950 more than 6000 workers were employed with an average weekly value of orders of over £27,000. Each factory specializes in one or a few trades not in competition with local industry. At Bolton, the cotton-spinning center, the Remploy factory makes leather products and appliances; at Stoke-on-Trent, the pottery center, the Remploy factory does light engineering. Remploy has its own sales force; its best customer is the Government which orders such items as orthopedic appliances and printed forms. Workers may continue at Remploy indefinitely and eventually reach full union-scale wages.

SCOTLAND

Scotland has its own National Health Service Act and its own medical education system but the differences between the Scottish and English systems are too slight to warrant explanation here.

EDINBURGH

The *Edinburgh Royal Infirmary* is a 1500 bed teaching hospital established in 1729. We were greeted by its medical superintendent, Major General E. A. Sutton. Its large physiotherapy department serves as the training unit for Scotland's only physiotherapy school. In the absence of its principal Miss M. I. V. Mann, we were escorted by Miss E. D. Thomson who is in charge of the treatment section. There is at present no qualified physiatrist in Scotland as far as we could determine. In this department 350 patients receive treatment daily at the hands of 10 qualified therapists, 4 teachers and 50 students. There is no occupational therapy department but in one small gymnasium we saw weaving equipment for hand and elbow cases. Miss Thomson supervises the small amount of occupational therapy performed. We had a brief talk with Miss H. Y. Watt, the head almoner. She and her five assistants are interested in rehabilitation. Patients who require further rehabilitation are sent to the Industrial Rehabilitation Unit at Granton, the north end of the city. Here too is a Remploy factory which specializes in furniture fabrication. Miss Watt is anxious for her patients to work at Remploy because workers receive a greater income and become better known to the D.R.O.

The *Princess Margaret Rose Hospital* was built at the southern edge of the city shortly after the Princess was born. It houses 170 children up to the age of 16, with orthopedic disabilities. It is primarily a surgical center. We were shown about by the senior surgeon, Mr. Robert Sterling, who told us of the Sir Robert Jones plan of preventive orthopedics. In the relatively small Southeastern Region of Scotland there are 96 clinics, largely in small villages, to each of which is assigned a physiotherapist or a nurse with special orthopedic training. These nurse-therapists come to Edinburgh periodically for a revisory (refresher course). The surgeons of the Princess Margaret Rose Hospital visit the 96 clinics and by conservative early treatment of scoliosis, flat feet and other functional conditions believe they lessen considerably the quantity of orthopedic operations.

This hospital has a very progressive physiotherapy department with a large gymnasium and excellent therapeutic pool under a glazed roof. Miss Ena Catto, the head therapist is assisted by 8 qualified therapists. The occupational therapy building which had been excellently equipped was burned out earlier in the year and at the time of our visit its activities were transferred to a small but adequate room under the guidance of the head therapist, Miss Betty Gardner.

The Astley Ainslie Hospital is one of the oldest of its kind. David Ainslie of

Costerton willed his money to his nephew John Astley Ainslie but because the nephew pre-deceased him the estate was left in 1900 for "the purpose of erecting, endowing and maintaining a hospital for the relief and behoof of the convalescents in the Royal Infirmary at Edinburgh." Since the hospital was opened in 1930 it has stressed physical treatment. The original building was equipped with "a gymnasium for remedial exercises." We were greeted by the director, Lt. Col. John Fraser and shown about by his assistant Dr. James Somerville, who headed the R. A. F. rehabilitation program at Devon during the war. There are three other physicians on the staff of this 240 bed hospital.

The very spacious and well landscaped grounds consist of several merged private estates, one of which had been occupied by the amputation-famed surgeon Symes. Each of the major patient pavillions has its own physiotherapy section under the supervision of Miss M. Lambert. In addition, there is a Scientific Department or building which has several treatment rooms and gymnasia.

On this site is Scotland's only school of occupational therapy, which accounts in part for the establishment of six occupational therapy positions at a hospital of this size. At this hospital we saw the largest and most modern occupational therapy building of our trip. In it men, women and children of all ages work side by side at a great many crafts. Miss I. D. B. Bramwell who is in charge of the school and the department took us through the school buildings and the shops. Twenty students are enrolled each year for a course which lasts two and a half years.

All patients are seen on the day of admission by a physician who consults the complete records which accompany every patient on transfer. Rounds are held daily on the wards and rehabilitation conferences are held at the bedside by those making rounds: a physician, charge nurse, physiotherapist, occupational therapist, social worker and remedial gymnast. (The gymnast is responsible for the recreation program which has the use of playing fields for cricket and football, and a recreation hall where motion pictures are shown two nights each week).

The education program for the 60 children in the hospital is conducted by three regularly assigned teachers.

WALES

The *Cardiff Royal Infirmary* is a 350 bed general hospital in Wales' largest city. Dr. Kenneth Lloyd, physician-in-charge of physical medicine attends part-time. He is assisted by a registrar and house officer. We were shown about by Miss Barbara Pegler, Principal of the only physiotherapy school in Wales, and by her deputy Miss Joan Vaughan-Lewis. There are 15 establishments in physiotherapy, 4 teachers and 70 students. A large gymnasium is used for treatment in the mornings and for student instruction in the afternoons. In addition there are two large general treatment rooms and a room devoted to diathermy. In the hydrotherapy section we saw two whirlpool baths—one for upper and one for lower extremities. It was the only hospital visited where we found two. The source of agitation as in the one at Buxton was a guarded propellor and these baths were supplied in addition with air under pressure for further agitation. In this section we saw an Aix-les-Bains type of massage table. There are plans for a therapeutic pool to complete the hydrotherapy section.

One of the newest additions to this hospital is a building of about 25 by 35 feet near the physiotherapy department entirely devoted to occupational therapy. Miss Hazel Owen, the qualified therapist in charge is also secretary of the Welsh Occupational Therapy Association. She told us that there are at present about 25 qualified therapists at work in Wales.

We would encourage anyone who intends to visit hospitals in the United Kingdom to write in advance seeking permission or at least giving fair warning of the intention. At several hospitals we "popped" in without advance warning and were treated as we deserved but always with great politeness and consideration. At the Cardiff Royal Infirmary we found an almost American attitude toward our informal visit. We found great interest in America and within twenty minutes of our unexpected arrival were asked to address a class of physiotherapy students, on America, and physical therapy.

While in the United Kingdom we were in communication with Brigadier Gelston Atkins of Eire. He more than any one in that country has been working for the recognition of physical medicine in Ireland. He wrote us that at long last a rehabilitation unit for convalescent tuberculous women was opened this year in Dublin. In all of Eire there are only three qualified occupational therapists.

DENMARK

In Denmark there exists a form of socialism in which the individual is guaranteed security without wealth. There are exceedingly few very rich or very poor people. All workers contribute regularly to sickness and welfare benefits. When they become ill, their entire hospitalization bill comes to less than two crowns a day. Physical medicine is much further advanced in Denmark than in the other Scandinavian countries. The Danish Society of Physical Medicine has more than forty members; there are more than 70 qualified occupational therapists in 40 hospitals, and the number of physical therapists in clinics throughout the land is much greater proportionately than in the United States. Our chief host in Denmark was Dr. Svend Clemmesen; he interrupted his vacation to act as our guide.

COPENHAGEN

The *Kommunehospitalet* (Community Hospital) is a 1000 bed general city hospital. Dr. Clemmesen is director of physical medicine and has two assistant physicians. There are 60 qualified remedial gymnasts (physical therapists) on duty, not all of them full time. In spite of their title, they handle all phases of work including electrotherapy. The physical facilities here are good but crowded. We were shown the foundation and partial construction of a large new building which will be devoted entirely to physical medicine. The building will require about two years for completion; materials are still hard to come by in Denmark.

As is the case in most continental European departments, mud packs play an important role in treatment. In Scandinavia the mud is heated and wrapped in towels and macintosh and applied more as a heating measure than a peloid application. Steam or heated water vapor is also commonly used in Scandinavia and at this hospital we saw steam cabinets resembling large beer barrels into which the patient slides the lower extremities while seated on an elevated chair at the open end of the barrel.

As a result of much research done at this hospital on electrodiagnosis and electrical muscle stimulation, Dr. Clemmesen has developed an apparatus called the *Myotensor* which we saw in use here and at other Scandinavian hospitals. It is an electronic device which delivers rectangular shaped impulses that permit stimulation at minimum amperage and hence minimum pain. The frequency and amplitude of impulses are readily regulated. Dr. Clemmesen believes that voltage measurements are superfluous because they are influenced by tissue resistance which is not constant. With his device he can measure the milliamperage as it enters the stimulated area.

There are two well-equipped occupational therapy shops under the supervision of qualified therapists. One large shop is for neuropsychiatric patients and the other for kinetic work. There is excellent correlation between functional exercise of physical and occupational therapy. Here we also saw utilization of scrap material so common in supply-short Europe, so uncommon in the United States. Instead of throwing beef bones in the hospital garbage can they are thrown into a boiling caustic solution and then dried. The cleaned dried long bones (usually the femora) of the ox are cut and used by patients for carving and the fabrication of small objects, for instance, of napkin rings. When the bone is thoroughly buffed it is hard to distinguish it from ivory. Needless to add, all operations are performed with non-motorized tools.

In this hospital we were also taken through the research laboratory which has excellent equipment and boasts a full-time biophysicist.

There are seven clinics for out-patients in Copenhagen devoted exclusively to Fysiurgi (physical medicine). We visited the largest of these, located on the Valdemarsgade (these clinics are known by the name of the street on which they are located). Our guide in this clinic was Dr. Egill Snorrason, another of our very genial hosts in Denmark. In this modern building, 600 out-patients are treated daily by 50 qualified therapists supervised by five physicians.

In Denmark, systematic rehabilitation of cripples was begun by a minister, Reverend Hans Knudsen in 1872 when he founded the Society for the Care of Crippled and Disabled Children. From this beginning, aided by the social welfare legislation passed in 1933, the Society developed into an unusually complete rehabilitation scheme called the *Samfundet Og Hjemmet For Vanføre* (Society and Home for Cripples) with headquarters in Copenhagen. Here we met Mr. Egil Nygaard-Jensen, the inspector (manager) and visited the many buildings. The headquarters receives convalescent patients from orthopedic hospitals in Copenhagen (225 beds) and Aarhus (115 beds). There are rooms for 70 children from the ages of 7 to 15 who receive in addition to treatment, schooling from 10 assigned teachers. There are 100 young men, of whom 70 live on the premises. They may enroll in such training courses as carpentry, tailoring and watch repair. The trades available for the 60 young women (16 to 22) include millinery and dress-making. Meals, quarters, clothing and pocket money are provided by this state supported institution. Many of the adults attend technical schools elsewhere in the city. All spend 43 to 46 hours in workshops and 9 hours in didactic training each week. On admission to the center the adults are given psychologic and aptitude tests and placed in an exploratory workshop for 6 months. Vocational training usually takes another 4 to 5 years at the end of which time the center places its graduates in industry within the community. In a recent ten year follow up, it was found that at least half of these severely disabled trained persons were employed, 10 per cent as independents and the other 40 per cent working for others.

Fig. 1. From left to right, Dr. Egill Snorrason, Dr. Lilli Bernstein, Dr. Vagn Porsman, Dr. Svend Clemmesen and Dr. Børge Sury.

We saw no beggars on the streets of Copenhagen. Although there is no poverty there are idlers. These are picked up by the police and sent to the *Kofoeds Skole* (school) on the Island of Amager. This beautifully situated former farm is a shelter where the idler may receive further elementary general education and a chance to learn the habit of working. He spends 4 hours a day at school and 4 hours in the workshops or on the farm. There are dormitories for 50 men under the age of 26. They remain for 9 months after which a job is found for them. Their disability is not physical but sometimes associated with early mental disease. While at the school they receive points for work accomplished and these are credited to their account. They may earn up to 20 crowns a week of which 10 are placed in a bank for them so that at the time of discharge they have increased their skill or work capacity and have about 300 crowns in their pocket for a fresh start in life. About half of those trained are rehabilitated as proven by their continued occupation.

We visited the *Arbejdsskolen* (Work School) and met its director Mr. Jens N. Ubbesen. This center was established in 1933 for the vocational assessment of disabled persons. There are quarters for 20 residents and places for another 15 in the workshops. Most of the disabled here are men from 14 to 60 years of age. The average stay is about 2 to 3 months but some may remain as long as 6 months. The occupations on the premises include book-binding, carpentry, bicycle repair (almost everyone in Scandinavia rides a bicycle), blacksmithy, shoe repair and gardening. Products from the garden are sold directly to the public at a roadside stand in front of the buildings. The disabled are referred by a physician or social agency and at the end of the test of work capacity the individual and his record are returned to the reference source. The director told us that his organization was based on the work of the *Institute for Crippled and Disabled* in New York City.

The Danish people are so proud of their care for the aged that they insisted on our visit to the *Boliger For Aldersrentemodtagere* (Tenements for Aged Pensioners). After the inspection we were glad they had insisted. There are seven large housing developments for old people in Copenhagen. The center we visited had 534 apartments of very modern construction with all conveniences. A married couple is charged 34 crowns a month for rent, a single person 28. Each day residents may purchase two courses of a hot meal for 1.5 crowns. We visited the serving kitchen and were impressed with the quality of preparation and the courtesy of the server. The aged receive a monthly pension from the government of 200 crowns. Applicants do not have to be destitute to be eligible but their holdings must be under 10,000 crowns.

We were taken to another center for the aged by Dr. Vagn Porsman, a pnysiatrist who teaches at Denmark's school of occupational therapy (a two year course, 20 students accepted twice each year). At *De Gamles By* (The Old People's Town) which accomodates 800 well and 800 sick people, we visited the medical division which is under the direction of Dr. Torben Geill. Here we saw excellent medical care and some occupational therapy.

Artificial ultraviolet light was first introduced into medical treatment by Dr. Niels Finsen in 1895 (lupus). We visited the *Finsen Institute* which is now a general clinic although still largely attended by persons requiring ultraviolet or x-radiation. The original equipment first used by Finsen and many items of interest associated with his life and work are housed in a fine museum on the grounds. Here, as in most clinics in Europe, the carbon arc lamp is more popular than mercury arc lamps. Dozens of carbon arc lamps are used daily for treatment; several rooms are furnished with no other apparatus except arc lamps.

The treatment center of the Danish poliomyelitis society, *Landsforeingen Til Bekaempelse Af Børnelammelse Og Dens Folger* is a recently converted private estate on the Tuborgvei. We were shown through the building by Dr. Elsa Arnsø who supervises the physical treatment there (out-patient). We saw an excellent Hubbard tank with a four point suspension pulley lift and watched workmen laying the tiles in a new large indoor swimming pool (only one other in Copenhagen). The building has a gymnasium and general treatment rooms with a capacity for treating 100 patients a day.

DIANALUND

About 60 miles west of Copenhagen is the small town of Dianalund where in 1897 the *Kolonien Filadelfia* (Colony of Brotherly Love) was established for the care of epileptics and other nervous disorders. We were escorted by the chief of the epileptic service, Dr. Stubbe Teglbjrberg. Here 700 epileptic patients receive medical treatment and rehabilitation. There are 13 physicians and two qualified occupational therapists on the staff as well as 10 technical teachers. We were shown through the many excellent shops and occupational facilities which include weaving, dressmaking, shoe repair, farming and gardening, the last of which is currently most popular. There is a turnover of more than half the patients each year and it is estimated that about 60 per cent of the patients are rehabilitated.

NORWAY

In Norway health insurance is even more inclusive than in Denmark for in Norway insured patients, and that means almost all patients, may receive medical attention and hospital care at no cost. Recently physicians have won the right to charge five crowns for the first visit and a smaller amount for subsequent visits. All employed persons must carry national health insurance. People of means may have insurance at a slightly higher rate and receive the same medical benefits. Many Norwegian physicians supplement their income by working for certain hospitals or insurance companies. In addition, they may see private patients for a few hours a day. Our hostess in Norway was Dr. Lilli Bernstein who spent the greater part of a year in the United States recently studying physical medicine.

OSLO

Ulleval Sykehus is a 2000 bed general municipal hospital. We visited the psychiatric service (130 beds) of Dr. Trygve Braatøy. To this department are attached two occupational therapy shops for open ward patients; one for men, the other for women. Each shop is supervised by a graduate nurse who devotes her full day to such activities. Still another nurse spends her day in this fashion on a locked ward for criminal patients. Miss Gunvor Basberg in charge of occupational therapy for men, told us that there were then three British-trained therapists in Norway and that a school would be started in Oslo early in 1952. It is further planned to introduce occupational therapy to the geriatric patients soon. The geriatric problem has long been receiving attention in all of Scandinavia. The main road leading to this hospital is flanked by rows of small well kept houses for the aged infirm. The occupants are under the medical care program of the hospital. At this hospital we also spoke to Miss Aadel Bülow-

Hansen, a physical therapist attached full time to the psychiatric service for instruction in relaxation. Tense patients are given individual attention by her for one hour sessions which begin with general massage followed by breathing exercises, postural exercises and finally instructions in relaxed standing. Because of the individual nature of the work she can treat only six patients a day. This program is concurrent with psychotherapy. Miss Bülow-Hansen told us that at the physiotherapy school in Oslo there is a two year course and that each year there are two classes of 35 each.

The *Sanitetsforenings Sykehus* (Health Association Hospital) is a private hospital of 150 beds for orthopedic patients under Dr. Vilhelm Forbech. In the physical therapy department we saw many deep wooden tubs for medicated baths and many cubicles for mud packs, given as a form of heat for about a half hour per session.

The *Rikshospitalet* (State Hospital) is the university hospital. We visited the new beautifully decorated Children's Pavillion which has 110 beds. There is a modern out-patient department where a cerebral palsy rehabilitation clinic has been started. Dr. Lilli Bernstein is in charge of the speech rehabilitation. We were greeted by the director of the service, Professor Leif Salomonsen who showed an excellent interest in progressive physical medicine. On the wards we met one of the two recreational workers who were keeping the children happily occupied.

The *Trygdekasse* (best translated freely as the Health Insurance Administration) occupies a large building near the beautiful new City Hall. Two entire floors of the Trygdekasse are given to the administration of out-patient physical medicine. The general practitioner may send patients in need of physical medicine to this building and when the capacity for patients is reached the physicians at this institution may refer patients to other recognized private clinics. Patients usually come with a referral form indicating diagnosis and recommended treatment. We spoke with Dr. Halvard Hegna, chief of physical medicine and his assistant Dr. Ove Mellbye, president of the newly formed Norwegian Society of Physical Medicine (Fysikalsk Medisin). During the winter 1200 patients are treated daily by 90 graduate therapists who work in two shifts—eight to two and two to eight at night. We saw about 100 cubicles or treatment rooms, each with two dressing rooms attached. While one patient is being treated, the next is undressing. The two floors are divided according to modality into special sections. In one section we saw a traxator in use. Both the patients and physicians spoke highly of this form of localized negative pressure especially for certain soft tissue lesions such as fibrositis. The pressure cup is used statically or as a moving massage instrument. The traxator is also used over the legs of patients with thrombo-angiitis obliterans. At this clinic the gymnastic therapists give radiant heat, massage and exercise but only specially trained graduate nurses may administer electrotherapy. In another section we saw ultrasound equipment; the staff was not impressed with its results.

There are so many referrals that the physicians on duty see only the problem cases or patients specifically referred for consultation by the physician or a doubtful staff therapist. The referring physician authorizes a course or number of treatments at the end of which the patient must return to his physician if further treatment is desired. Certain physical treatments such as packs and baths are given at one of the city hospitals. Electrodiagnosis is referred to a neurologist.

At the western edge of town is Refstad where we visited the *Registreringssentralen For Omskoling* (Central Registry for the Disabled; a misnomer for rehabilitation center). Here in 1946 Dr. Gudmund Harlem began a rehabilitation center which is very complete and progressive. (Papworth Village Settlement remains in our opinion the most complete and meaningful rehabilitation center we have ever seen anywhere). In this center there are dormitories, physical treatment rooms, workshops, instruction halls and recreational facilities. The director, Dr. Harlem, is assisted by two full-time physicians and has the consultive services of specialists in tuberculosis, orthopedics and psychiatry. The dormitories have a capacity of 125 but an additional 25 trainees sleep out and may even work away from the center if desirable. On admission to the center each trainee is psychologically tested and for the first fourteen days is subjected to many diagnostic procedures. At the end of this period a board meets to consider the findings in respect to fitness and vocational aptitudes. At this point some may be sent home with a final assessment but most remain and may remain for a year. About half of all admissions are convalescent tuberculous patients. Second in frequency are patients with residuals of poliomyelitis of one or more years duration. No person is considered rehabilitated until he has been gainfully employed for two years following discharge, as compared with the 30 day period used by some agencies in the United States. We studied the most recent statistics of the Registry. Of 1500 persons discharged from the center, 880 were at work, 290 in training and 160 unemployed—an enviable record considering the high percentage of tuberculous convalescents.

SWEDEN

In Sweden there is much physical medicine but only one physician, Dr. G. Edström of Lund has declared himself a specialist in the field and begun to organize physicians interested in the work.

STOCKHOLM

The *Karolinska Sjukhuset* (Royal Charles Hospital) is the 2100 bed general hospital of the University. On the fourth floor of a very modern and spacious building there are two very large rooms for heat, massage and exercise under the direction of an orthopod, Dr. Nils Silfverskiöld. We spoke to one of his assistants, Dr. S. Alvar Swensson who discussed with us his views on the treatment of low back pain. He is in favor of rest on a not too firm mattress for about a week, followed by abdominal and back exercises, done on the abdomen and back, which he demonstrated to us. In this department there are six qualified therapists and 30 students to administer 80,000 treatments a year. In this department the simple forms of heat are preferred. We saw an excellent device for administering heat and exercise to hand cases. A piece of canvas slung in the form of a crib was filled with heated white sand and the patient was directed to pick up fistfuls of the heated sand which he dropped rhythymically. The chief therapist, Mrs. Nystrom told us that 30 students were taken into each of two classes a year and rotated through several hospitals in the city to learn all aspects of physical therapy. This hospital has no department of neurology or neurosurgery.

That part of *fysikalisk terapi* which we call electrotherapy is run by the radiology department, located in the basement. The director of this department, Dr. Gerts, supervises the therapists who are graduate nurses with a special training in electrotherapy. In this very well equipped department we saw three ultrasound machines, six short wave machines and many tubs for medicated baths as well as rooms for mud packs.

The occupational therapy department is headed by Mrs. Annike Hällström-Nilssen, our hostess in Stockholm. She is assisted by two qualified therapists and three students. There is no physician in charge of the department; prescriptions are sent directly by the referring physician. About half the treatments are administered in a well equipped and well lighted large divided room. The other treatments are given on the wards. The school of occupational therapy in Stockholm is in its second year of operation. At present there are 12 young women and 8 young men in the class for which 200 applied. The course lasts 39 months, the last 9 of which are spent in clinical affiliation.

The *Söder Sjukuset* (South Hospital) is a 1000 bed city hospital of the most modern construction we witnessed. The building was begun in 1943 and is not yet complete. The physical therapy department was planned with unusual skill. When the patients enter the very large attractive waiting room, they draw a numbered check indicating their order of arrival; each is called for examination or treatment according to number. When the patient is called into a small individual treatment room, the therapist flicks a toggle switch which lights a red lamp at the administration desk. When the patient leaves, the therapist flicks another toggle which shows green on the enunciator board. Traffic control has been simplified in this very large department. The physical therapy clinic is a section of the Rheumatology department headed by Dr. Eric Jonsson, who assigns four of his assistants to the department for supervision. In addition there are twelve therapists and seven nurses to treat 400 patients daily (in the summer when heat baths are discontinued). A graduate nurse is in charge of all therapists.

Here as in other European clinics, mud constitutes an important element in physical treatment. Usually a local mud is preferred but at this hospital mud is imported from Czechoslovakia. At least 50 patients receive mud packs daily. The mud is heated to 120° is then rolled between two towels which are placed in a rubber sheet and then into still another towel which is packed around the patient for 30 minutes. We saw eight full sized tubs for medicated baths. For certain skin conditions, bran is placed in the water; for psoriasis a tar oil; for polyarthritis pine oil or the salt extracted from the Mediterranean Sea. We visited the occupational therapy clinic which consisted of two small rooms used mostly as a preparation room since most of the treatment is executed on the ward. The head therapist Miss Astrid Lindquist is assisted by three qualified therapists and students. About 120 patients are seen daily by this staff.

FRANCE

PARIS

In the field of physical medicine, one of the most distinguished hospital names is that of the *Salpetrière*. Here Philippe Pinel introduced occupational therapy, here Jacques-Arsène d'Arsonval in 1887 first used high frequency currents (diathermy), and here Dr. Georges Bourguinon who did the first chronaxy determinations in man still visits several days a week, to do chronaxy determinations. We visited Dr. Bourguinon in his office and hospital laboratory, both in the Latin Quarter (far more respectable than Americans have been lead to believe), and watched him test a patient on the huge original condenser set, which is so large

FIG. 2. Dr. Georges Bourguinon (left) performing a chronaxy test in his laboratory in the Salpetrière. The interested observer is Dr. Meulemans of Brussels.

that an assistant must keep on the move adding and subtracting capacitances, giving the appearance of a man playing a xylophone. This is the same assistant who has been with Dr. Bourguinon since the start of the work more than a quarter of a century ago. We saw a chronaxy determination performed on a patient suspected of CS_2 poisoning. Bourguinon claims that each muscle has three chronaxy values which may be found at three separate points and which have approximate values of 0.1, 1.0, and 10 milliseconds. He demonstrated this to us on the left biceps brachii of the patient the skin over which he proceeded to mark with an indelible pencil. He applied a tetanizing current to the muscle for a few minutes and demonstrated an elevation of chronaxy (slight but definite) which fell gradually during the next thirty minutes. The examination, during which Dr.

Bourguinon was kept very busy testing one motor point after the other, took 80 minutes.

In the physical therapy department of this hospital, now headed by Dr. Gally, we were shown the original high frequency coil used by d'Arsonval (about a foot in diameter and about three feet long). All physical therapy is administered by graduate nurses (two year training) with an additional year of training in electrotherapy. The specialty of the nurse is indicated by the color of the ribbon on her cap; green for physical therapy, red for operating room; a gold star for chief.

In this clinic dielectrolysis, first introduced by Dr. Bourguinon, is obviously very popular. In this procedure the direct current is supposed to pass through the brain by way of the eyes and carry therapeutic ions along the course of current. Each patient has his own container in which his solution and pads are kept. We saw one cabinet with about 200 bowls marked with the names of current patients. We saw a similar array at another French hospital. The method seems to have taken root in France.

In this hospital we visited Dr. Gabriel Bidou's department of functional re-education. This consists largely of mechanotherapy although we saw paraffin baths and electrotherapy devices in use. There were two relatively small gymnasia with parallel bars made of heavy rope, bicycles and other equipment. Another room was used for energometry,* a contribution of Dr. Bidou for determining muscle strength and joint measurement. In still another room there were some machines resembling Zander equipment for active and passive exercise of the large muscles of the body.

In front of the hospital is a life size statue of Philippe Pinel. Since the days of Pinel much about the Salpetrière has changed. The concept of occupational therapy is neither practiced nor known here; it is no longer a psychiatric hospital.

NEUILLY SUR MARNE

About five miles east of Paris is a psychiatric center consisting of two hospitals: the Maison Blanche for 1000 women and the *Hôpital de Ville Evrard* for 1300 men and women. We visited the Ville Evrard, one of the most progressive mental hospitals in France. Except for the Charenton Hospital in Paris which is run by the national government, all mental hospitals in France are departmental (state hospitals) and are generally located in or near the large cities. A few years ago Dr. Paul Sivadon in his desire to establish a modern rehabilitation center for psychiatric patients won the support of private contributions and began at this hospital to return to the "belle tradition" of France begun by Pinel. Six pavillions were placed under his supervision and called "The Treatment and Social Rehabilitation Center." In these pavillions 250 patients receive a full psychotherapeutic and activity program.

* Further information about the automatic recorder of muscle strength may be obtained from the Association Française pour le Développement de l'Energamétrie, 17, rue Gerbert, Paris 15⁰, France.

We visited one large building with two workshops and another with seven workshops. The major crafts at which we saw patients working were ceramics, carpentry, basketry and metal work. There is almost no mechanization and the printing press is manually operated. In the print shop we saw six patients at work assembling type and operating the press. The hospital authorities are very proud of their patient magazine now in its fourth year. It is called *Le Tremplin* (the spring board) and is entirely designed, written and printed by patients. Dr. Follin, who escorted us is most anxious to exchange his patients' journal with other hospitals having similar projects. (Address: Dr. Follin, Ville Evrard, Neuilly Sur Marne, France). We saw patients engaged in outdoor sports and were shown a large recreation hall used in inclement weather. We inspected the mess on a wine day. Patients are served wine twice a week and beer on some other days. (In France every adult drinks wine daily and the patients are French adults; it would not be good treatment to deny them normal living conditions).

The occupational therapy projects are supervised by all members of the staff, nurses and physicians included. In addition, there are craft "monitors" in each shop who work a 46 hour week. The farm (12 cows) and laundry are worked by patients. On the rehabilitation team are also a gymnast, a psychologist and a vocational and placement counselor. The counselor told us of the Association L'Elan, a club for discharged mental patients at 77 rue de Château des Rentiers in Paris.

Occupational therapy as treatment rather than hospital convenience is also practiced at the mental hospitals in Rouen and Orleans.

PLATEAU D'ASSY

In the French Alps there is a town which you will not find on any but the most detailed maps, yet people from all over the world come to this almost inaccessible spot to get an excellent view of Mont Blanc (highest in Europe) or the most modern Catholic church (decorated by Picasso and many other famous artists of the *avant garde*) or the large progressive tuberculosis center.

The town of Plateau D'Assy is almost vertical. At the top of the hill is a large sanatorium for children up to the age of 14. About 100 feet below is *Martel de Janville*, a 175 bed hospital for officers of the French Army. Lower down are several other institutions for the tuberculous, so that in all, about 2000 tuberculous patients and convalescents reside on the hill. Near the foot of the hill, but still at a considerable elevation is the *Passerane*, a tuberculosis rehabilitation center conceived and directed by Dr. Edouard Sivrière, our host in this region. The Passerane is a residential school with a capacity of 48 men all of whom receive training in watch repair and watch making. The center has become so popular that there is usually a waiting list of about 40 applicants. This craft was selected because the French watch center is at near-by Annemasse, a source of teachers and parts and a likely place for employment of graduates. Since the center was established 200 graduates have been placed and are still working at factories in Annemasse and Cluses.

At Passerane Dr. Sivrière is in daily attendance. There is a fluoroscope in the

building (a converted hotel) for the periodic examination of all trainees. We also
visited a newly purchased building about 300 yards distant which is being re-
modeled to house 40 graduates who will work in a sheltered watch-repair shop.
All convalescents have frequent sputum examinations and only negative cases
are permitted to continue.

Dr. Sivrière told us of a colony for "good chronics" at Tour De Pin in Isère
which adjoins the *Sanatorium du Vion* under the direction of Dr. Boissel. Here
sputum-positive patients may live and work and are paid in a special currency
issued by the Sanatorium. At Valence there is a tuberculosis rehabilitation center
for women where dressmaking and secretarial courses are taught. We asked about
Rollier and were told that he is still actively engaged in practice at Leysin,

FIG. 3. The Physical Therapy Building of Ospedale Maggiore in Milan.

Switzerland where the heliotherapy center has expanded to a capacity of 3000
patients and where bone tuberculosis is still the chief interest.

ITALY

MILAN

We visited one of Italy's most modern hospitals, *Ospedale Maggiore*. This is
a vast group of snow-white buildings housing 2000 patients. One of the largest
and most centrally located buildings is the four story building of physical medicine. In the absence of the department director Prof. Felice Casari we were
guided by his assistant Dr. Silvano Boccardi. All treatment rooms are very large,
well lighted and impressively furnished. In the basement we saw 6 rooms for

Fango (mud) therapy, several rooms for inhalation treatments with sprays of saline, sulfur and other chemicals. Two large hydrotherapy rooms were equipped with just about every type of water device of which we had heard, and then some. On the ground floor were separate large rooms for diathermy, ion transfer, ultra-violet light, Bier's hyperemia, local and general heat baths. A rather large room had several ultrasound machines and another room was completely air conditioned for the treatment of upper respiratory diseases of children. Several rooms were specially designated for physical procedures against poliomyelitis in young children. For older patients requiring mechanotherapy there is a very large gymnasium containing more active and assistive exercise devices than we saw anywhere else. Still another large gymnasium was equipped with exercise devices for scoliosis and other posture work.

The chief therapist, a nun, supervises four qualified therapists and three aides. In Italy therapists are qualified nurses who spend one year after graduation, studying physical therapy. This clinic treats 200 patients daily. There is no occupational therapy at this hospital.

Although Chiarugi of Florence prescribed "work for cure, for relief, or for purposes of diagnosis" in 1788, occupational therapy (ergoterapia or terapia occupazionale) is found only in a few mental and tuberculosis hospitals (such as the University of Genoa Hospital) in Italy. With the exception of a few institutions for the rehabilitation of the war-mutilated, Miss Anne Nicholson Turchi,* an American trained therapist found no kinetic occupational therapy in all of Italy. As a Fulbright Scholarship teacher, she established the first such clinic at the pediatric department of the University of Florence Medical School in 1950.

SWITZERLAND

Switzerland is divided into 22 Cantons (states) each of which has its own Kantonsspital (public hospital). In the four largest cities, the Canton hospital is also the University hospital. Switzerland has a form of health insurance. A typical hospital bill for an insured family man earning 6500 francs a year would be 1.5 francs a day. If he does not carry insurance he will pay 7.3 francs a day which will pay for everything but surgery. For a major operation the cost will vary from 12 to 60 francs. This is the rate for third class (ward) patients. There are also second class (semi-private) and first class (private) accomodations, in the last of which categories the daily hospital bill without drugs or treatment may be as high as 24 francs a day. Physical medicine in Switzerland as a specialty closely resembles the practice as seen in England. There are physical therapy schools in the four largest cities in Switzerland. Students attend the university and hospital for a period of three years. At Geneva, at the time of our visit there were only seven students in the three classes.

The first *Kurs fur Beschäftigungstherapie* (course in occupational therapy) was offered at the School for Social Work in Zurich for four months beginning in June 1951, to 17 full-time and 3 part-time students. Credit for starting this movement must be shared by Dr. K. Oppikofer, medical director of the tuber-

* Occupational Therapy In Italy. Scottish J. O. T., June 1951, 1: 5.

culosis rehabilitation center at Appisberg, and Mrs. E. Christoffel-Hubacher, a therapist who for several years had headed the occupational therapy program at Montana, one of Switzerland's four military tuberculosis hospitals. At Montana in Valais, there are workshops for weaving and leather work and a poultry farm where patients work on a doctor's prescription. Mrs. Christoffel-Hubacher is now in charge of occupational therapy for all the hospitals of the Canton of Zurich.

The *Canton Hospital* has about 700 beds. The physical medicine department consists of general treatment rooms and a gymnasium. The approach to physical medicine at this hospital was more like that seen in the United States than is true of the neighboring countries. The department director, Prof. Kurt Walthard has spent a considerable amount of time in the United States. He is assisted by Dr. Gerard Kohler and Dr. Roddolo-Reh. The staff includes two electrotherapists and six therapists for massage and exercise. The approximate daily load here was 40 in electrotherapy and 56 in the rest of the department.

Fango therapy is popular here as is simple radiant (luminous) heat. Prof. Walthard has had the use of ultrasound generators for some time and is not too impressed with the results obtained. We watched him do a chronaxy determination on a machine of his own design. He has plans for enlarging his department and these include a therapeutic pool for young polio patients of which he sees about six a year. In Switzerland physical medicine is completely divorced from radiology as is the case with its neighbors to the north but not those to the south and west.

SPAIN

BARCELONA

The *Hospital De Santa Cruz Y San Pablo* (Holy Cross and Saint Paul) is a 1250 bed general hospital. The splendor of its interior decorations is surpassed only by the exotic treatment of the many facades. The brilliantly colored tiles and gold trimmings give it the appearance of an oriental palace. We saw other beautiful hospitals in Spain and on discussing this subject with Prof. Sigerist later in Switzerland learned that Spanish hospitals are indeed among the world's most beautiful but not, in his opinion, as beautiful as those of Russia. We were taken on a complete tour of the hospital by Dr. José Cornudella, chief of the Tuberculosis Service. The 400 beds for the tuberculous were divided into sections according to age, sex and stage of the disease. All phases of hospital care and treatment seemed to be the same as that in the United States except for occupational therapy of which there is none. We visited many wards of apparently contented patients at complete bed rest.

The *Hospital Clinico* is part of the University of Barcelona Medical School. We were shown about by Dr. Mariano Badell Suriol, Adjunct Professor of Radiology, which in Spain includes physical medicine. Dr. Suriol is a fully trained physicist as well as a physician. We were shown a department of mechanotherapy which had fallen into disuse following the death of its last director. Exercise is considered a specialty apart from radiology. The electrotherapy equipment included the usual variety of devices, largely of German manufacture, although we were told that Spanish manufacturers have begun to produce such equipment. The department of *terapeutica fisica* has three divisions: 1. radiology, 2. electrotherapy, and 3. hydrotherapy and ultraviolet light. In the last named division we saw several ultraviolet lights in use but the water equipment had fallen into disuse. Physical therapy is administered by qualified nurses who take additional training in the specialty after graduation. Some of the nurses were nuns and others lay persons.

Fig. 4. The Director of the Instituto Pedro Mata, Dr. Salvador Vilaseca Anguera, center; Dr. J. Solé Sagarra, at right. Others are Dr. Antonio Cavallé Maresma, Dr. José Colom Martorell, Dr. Emílio Sagimón Rabassa and Dr. José Maria Jaén Teixidó.

We were impressed by the kind manner in which the Spanish physicians dealt with their patients and the admiration and respect which the patients showed in return.

REUS

About 60 miles south of Barcelona is the town of Reus, on the outskirts of which is the 600 bed private mental hospital called *Pedro Mata*. We were taken there by Dr. José Solé Sagarra, our host in Spain and consultant to this very progressive hospital, the most beautiful we have ever seen anywhere. We were taken on a complete tour of inspection by the medical director, Dr. Salvador Vilaseca Anguera and his staff of five full-time psychiatrists. Here, almost every able-bodied patient is engaged in some worth-while activity. Acres of flower and vegetable gardens are cultivated by the patients during the ten month growing season. We were taken through a new four story chicken house the cleanliness of which was enhanced by the fact that all the chickens were white Leghorns. The animal farm was well stocked with cows, pigs and goats, all cared for by patients. We saw large playing fields flanked by beds of brilliantly colored flowers. A black spot on the lawn was pointed out as the place where fire works were set off for the amusement of patients the week before on Midsummer's Eve

In each pavillion the rooms were tastefully and comfortably furnished. In almost every pavillion there are small to medium sized workshops. In one building we visited a very large carpentry shop. Most of the housekeeping chores are done by patients. We visited the laundry—still done almost entirely by hand, and the kitchens where patients were performing some of the culinary tasks. We went through a large auditorium where dances and plays are given and an occasional motion picture shown. Throughout there was an atmosphere of great serenity in exotic surroundings of bougainvillea vines and camelia trees in flower.

We also visited a small museum in one of the hospital buildings where there is a permanent display of the arts and crafts executed by the patients as well as samples of the mimeographed patient newspaper.

The Mediterranean Sea is only eight miles away and on hot summer days patients are taken there on swimming parties. Occupational therapy and recreation are supervised by physicians, nurses, teachers and other patients.

Very little restraint or hydrotherapy is used at this hospital. Electroshock, insulin and psychosurgery are used to the same degree as seen in most hospitals in the United States. The physicians, as congenial as any we met anywhere, all seemed well informed about psychiatry in Europe and the United States.

We set out to learn something about physical medicine in Europe and did, but that was the least important information we gained. What impressed us most was the universal kindness and generosity of the people we met. We were so graciously received everywhere we went that we were embarassed at our inability to express our gratitude adequately.

THE PHYSICALLY HANDICAPPED IN SOCIETY

An Arno Press Collection

Anderson, Roy Nels. **The Disabled Man and His Vocational Adjustment.** 1932

Axford, Wendy Anne, ed. **Handicapped Children in Britain** *and* McMurtrie, Douglas C., ed. **Index Catalogue of a Library on Rehabiliation of the Disabled.** 2 vols. in one. 1959/1919

Barton, George. **Teaching the Sick.** 1919

Berkowitz, Edward David. **Rehabilitation.** (Doctoral Dissertation, Northwestern University, 1976) 1980

Carling, Finn. **And Yet We Are Human** *and* Haecker, Theodor. **Kierkegaard.** 2 vols. in one. 1962/1948

Charity Organisation Society. **The Epileptic and Crippled Child and Adult.** 1893

Cleveland Symposium on Behavioral Research in Rehabilitation. 1959

Education and Occupations of Cripples. 1918

Girdlestone, G.R. **The Care and Cure of Cripple Children.** 1924

Graham, Earl C., and Marjorie Mullen, eds. **Rehabilitation Literature.** 1956

Hathaway, Katharine Butler. **The Little Locksmith.** 1942

Hinshaw, David. **Take Up Thy Bed and Walk.** 1948

Hoyer, Louis P. **Services to the Orthopedically Handicapped.** 1942

Hunt, Agnes. **This Is My Life.** 1942

Kelsey, Carl, ed. **Rehabilitation of the Wounded.** 1918

Kenny, Elizabeth, and Martha Ostenso. **And They Shall Walk.** 1943

Kessler, Henry H. **The Crippled and the Disabled.** 1935

Kessler, Henry H. **The Principles and Practices of Rehabilitation.** 1950

Landis, C., and M.M. Bolles. **Personality and Sexuality in the Physically Handicapped Woman.** 1942

Leavitt, Moses A. **Handicapped Wage Earners as Studied by a Family Welfare Agency,** 1928

MacDonald, Mary E. **Federal Grants for Vocational Rehabilitation.** 1944

Mallinson, Vernon. **None Can Be Called Deformed.** 1965

Mawson, Thomas. **An Imperial Obligation.** 1917

McMurtrie, Douglas C. **The Disabled Soldier.** 1919

McMurtrie, Douglas C. **The Evolution of National Systems of Vocational Re-education for Disabled Soldiers and Sailors.** 1918

Obermann, C. Esco. **A History of Vocational Rehabilitation in America.** 1965

Orr, H. Winnett. **On the Contributions of Hugh Owen Thomas of Liverpool, Sir Robert Jones of Liverpool and London and John Ridlon, M.D. of New York and Chicago to Modern Orthopedic Surgery.** 1949

Phillips, William, and Janet Rosenberg, eds. **Changing Patterns of Law.** 1980

Phillips, William, and Janet Rosenberg, eds. **The Origins of Modern Treatment and Education of Handicapped Children.** 1980

Phillips, William, and Janet Rosenberg, eds. **Social Scientists and the Physically Handicapped.** 1980

Pintner, Rudolf, Jon Eisenson, and Mildred Stanton. **The Psychology of the Physically Handicapped.** 1945

Sullivan, Oscar M., and Kenneth O. Snortum. **Disabled Persons.** 1926

Tracy, Susan E. **Studies in Invalid Occupation.** 1912

Watson, Frederick. **Civilization and the Cripple.** 1930

Watson, Frederick. **The Life of Sir Robert Jones.** 1934

Wright, Beatrice, ed. **Psychology and Rehabilitation.** 1959

Wright, Henry C. **Survey of Cripples in New York City.** 1920

Würtz, Hans. **Das Seelenleben des Krüppels.** 1921

Ziegler, Carlos Ray. **The Image of the Physically Handicapped in Children's Literature.** (Doctoral Dissertation, Temple University, 1971) 1980